From Karamzin to Bunin:

AN ANTHOLOGY OF
Russian Short Stories

EDITED,

with a CRITICAL COMMENTARY *and*

ELEVEN NEW TRANSLATIONS *by*

CARL R. PROFFER

Indiana University Press

BLOOMINGTON

Library of Congress catalog card number: 79–85097

cl. ISBN 0-253-32505-6   pa. ISBN 0-253-32506-4

MANUFACTURED IN THE UNITED STATES OF AMERICA

7 8 9 10 92 91 90

FOR *Ellendea*

CONTENTS

PREFACE

THIS NEW ANTHOLOGY DIFFERS FROM MOST OTHERS in three respects. First, it contains what is generally regarded as the *best* work by each of the authors represented—not five or six first-rate stories mixed in with several minor works. Second, the selection of authors is broad, ranging from Karamzin and the beginnings of modern Russian prose to Bunin and the years just before the Revolution. Only by buying several different collections could the selections be duplicated. Third, a strenuous effort has been made to provide reliable translations which are unmarred by omissions, vague paraphrases, inconsistencies, and invented imagery. Eleven of the translations are new; the others—Soviet ones—have been checked and, in all cases but one, subjected to major or minor revisions.

The book is for the general reader, but the "practical criticism" is intended especially for undergraduate and graduate students who are studying Russian literature. Often introductions to anthologies consist of biographical material and a few generalizations which are of little help to students. I have tried to provide, as compendiously as possible, information on style, structure, characterization, and theme. This is not a history of the Russian short story, but rather a commentary intended to isolate important details and typical devices in each work. For this reason, it will probably be more profit-able for the student to read one section *after* reading one story—rather than reading through the whole thing before reading the works. I assume that many readers will have some knowledge of Russian, so some crucial quotations and examples of stylistic features are quoted in transliteration, always with an English translation. Of course, all value judgments and interpretations should be examined critically.

Bloomington
July 27, 1968

From Karamzin to Bunin:

AN ANTHOLOGY OF

Russian Short Stories

CARL R. PROFFER

Practical Criticism
for Students

"Poor Liza"

KARAMZIN'S CONTEMPORARIES rightly considered his prose revolutionary. Before Karamzin the Russian prose language had
undergone only rudimentary development; according to the neoclassical canons of the eighteenth century, poetry was the language
of the gods, prose was plebeian. From the 1760s to the 1790s "original" Russian fiction consisted primarily of picaresque adventure
novels such as Emin's *Inconstant Fortune; or, the Adventures of
Miramond*—lengthy tales of persevering heroes who overcome bandits and typhoons in order to recover trueloving heroines. What success these primitive novels had was based on complicated plots and
rapid action. Stylistically, they were clumsy combinations of spoken
Russian and Russian Church Slavic, laced with lexical borrowings
from Polish, French, German, and English. Labyrinthine syntax
made comprehension difficult, pleasure improbable.

"Poor Liza" (1792) is a good example of Karamzin's simplifica-
tion of prose style. Even beginning students can read the story with
little difficulty. Karamzin insisted that the cultivated spoken language of the aristocratic salon be the basis of the literary language,
saying that one should write "so that ladies can understand." This
meant avoiding both liturgical archaism (high style) and coarse

1

colloquialism (low style), while using calques from French—the only language many Russian women could speak properly. Karamzin clarified syntax by sweeping away the clutter of archaic conjunctions and introducing symmetry into the way clauses were subordinated. He shortened sentence length. When he did use long sentences, he preferred to build them by combining short independent clauses. Anaphora, parallel structure, and a careful balancing of rising and falling intonation were used to make the prose flow smoothly and melodically. Graceful symmetry replaced shaggy sentences, good taste replaced pedantry.

Of course, it is not only in style that Karamzin's prose was innovative. Karamzin was largely responsible for popularizing sentimentalism in Russia. His *Letters of a Russian Traveler* (1791-92) were widely imitated, and the genre of travel notes remained important until the 1830s. Until the 1820s his short stories ("Poor Liza," "My Confession," "A Knight of Our Time," etc.) were copied tirelessly—in such tales as "Unfortunate Liza," "Poor Chloe," and "Lovely Tatyana." Symptomatic of Russian sentimentalism was the return to "small" forms—the letter, the short story, and, in poetry, elegies, album inscriptions, and epitaphs. It was precisely in the short genres that style was of paramount importance. Novels and epics, very few of which were published between 1790 and 1825, may succeed in spite of stylistic deficiencies; but in short genres every imperfection is noticeable.

The imperfections which we now see in "Poor Liza" are the very things which made the story so successful in Karamzin's day; they are less matters of style than of temperament. Lachrymose effusions do not suit our age of irony, but many of Karamzin's readers found them refreshing after the cold coffee of neoclassical odes. The appearance of a gracefully written Russian work permeated with *sensibility* could not fail to please young readers who had already sampled Rousseau's reflections on the "reasons of the heart," *The Sorrows of Young Werther*, or Karamzin's own translation of Young's *Night Thoughts*.

The influence of Rousseau's *Rêveries du promeneur solitaire*— as well as kinship with peripatetic heroes like St. Preux and Werther —can be seen in the opening lines of "Poor Liza" when the narrator discusses his love of lonely promenades. Other favorite preromantic themes are used in the narrator's introduction: gloomy Gothic towers, ruins, religious musings, death-knells, grieving autumn, and tombstone meditations. This section sets the tone for the story proper, and as Gukovsky notes: "In general the plot by itself never interests Karamzin; it is the tonality of the thing which is important for him, not the events of the external world . . ." The pathetic tone of "Poor Liza" is created by several devices—emotionally loaded epithets ("poor" Liza, "dear" Liza), frequent exclamations and interjections ("Oh, I love those things which touch my heart and make me shed tears of tender grief!"), dashes to give the impression of leaping hearts and intense emotion ("Liza sobbed—Erast wept —he left her—she fell—she got up . . ."), emotional repetitions ("And Liza, Liza stood with lowered eyes . . ." "Oh, Liza, Liza!"), apostrophizing the characters ("Foolish young man!"), and rhetorical questions to characters ("Ah, Liza Liza, where is your guardian angel?") and to the narrator himself ("Oh! Why am I not writing a novel instead of a sad, true story?"), and finally, frequent interpunction marking pauses which suggest inexpressible sentiments. Of course, Karamzin's uniformly "pleasant" style itself is important for the tone of the story. He avoids all coarseness—and even plain statement. The story abounds in metaphor and periphrasis. Thus, he says "the luminary of the day" instead of "sun" or "the green coverlet of nature" instead of "grass." To Gallic refinement Karamzin adds Russian sweetness by using diminutives; his frequent use of these affectionate forms (nouns and adjectives) is calculated to make the reader share the narrator's involvement with Liza. The riparian, pastoral setting and certain repeated motifs also contribute to tonal uniformity. The conventional cottage in a birch grove, the green meadow and blue pool are idyllic ornaments. Karamzin uses nature to show the emotional state of his characters; Liza's different attitude toward nature before and after she meets Erast in his rowboat is one example. Nature is also used as a portent —when Liza loses her purity there are no stars in the black sky and a furious storm breaks out. Liza herself is repeatedly associated with the sun: "Her cheeks burned like the sunset on a clear day," "a pure joyous soul shone in your eyes as the sun shines on drops of heavenly dew." There is also the theme of love of nature (or love of love of nature) which is expressed by Liza, Erast, and the narrator. The image of flowers is repeated throughout the story—the lilies Liza sells, the imagined red garland, the flowers which smell so sweet when Liza meets Erast.

The plot of "Poor Liza" was not new. Here the narrator's use of phrases such as "everyone will guess that" or "is it necessary to say" show that he is aware that many situations are familiar. Although Karamzin himself had translated such things as an idyll by Gessner, Erast's naive fascination with the usual shepherdesses of idylls is viewed with mild scepticism. Obviously, Karamzin is aware of the clichés in the story, but plot was not his main concern. So Karamzin has little opportunity to display technical skill in handling complex narration—the short "interior monologue" of Liza (as she images what it would be like if Erast had been born a shepherd), with the subsequent exact repetition of words when Erast appears in reality, is one of the few interesting narrative devices.

Characterization is weak. Liza's mother is a plot device (it is essential that Liza have someone to sacrifice herself for) who, mercifully, expires when her function is fulfilled. Liza herself is only a paternalistic aristocrat's idealized version of a peasant girl. Only when she has vague feelings of guilt does she threaten to come to life. Although his name itself suggests how artificial he is, Erast is somewhat more interesting—one of the first in a long line of Russian cads and superfluous men. His predilection for novels leads to Liza's downfall. The narrator makes it clear that when Erast is no longer satisfied with labial bliss and has taken Liza's virginity, he has ruined his ideal and is left with nothing. Superficial idealism, weak flesh, lack of will, and financial problems all play a role in his motivation. Erast's treatment of Liza (giving her 100 rubles) is hardly tactful, and in the end he expiates his sins, like an ancient mariner, by telling everyone he meets the story of his poor Liza.

"The Station Master"

PUSHKIN's "THE STATION MASTER" was first published as one of the *Tales of the Late Ivan Petrovich Belkin* (1831). This slim collection was introduced by a note from the "publisher" (A. P.) in which he provided a biography of Belkin. The mystification was modeled on Washington Irving's collections (by "Geoffrey Crayon") and Walter Scott's introductions to his novels (the figure of "Jedediah Cleishbotham"). It is usually suggested that the device of the "found manuscript" is used to create the illusion of reality, and that Pushkin used this device only to fool hostile critics. But it could also be argued that the device *underlines* the fictionality of the stories, and we know that Pushkin gave instructions for his friends to spread the word that he was the author. Each of the five Belkin tales contains parodic elements. Pushkin pokes fun at dark romantic heroes ("The Shot"), E. T. A. Hoffman ("The Coffin-maker"), and fashionable romances ("The Storm" and "Mistress into Maid"). "The Station Master" is obviously a parody of sentimental stories like "Poor Liza." In prose and poetry, including such important works as Baratynsky's "Eda" or Pushkin's own "A Prisoner of the Caucasus," a clean, quiet, bloodless suicide was expected at the end; but "poor Dunya" (as the narrator calls her) ends up with children, love, and wealth. The dashing hussar upsets the convention by not abandoning the innocent country girl. Specific motifs suggest that Pushkin had Karamzin's story in mind: the chance meeting of the carriage in the street, the crude attempt (by Erast and Minsky) to use money, and the graveside visit at the end.

But "The Station Master" is also a parody of the story of the Prodigal Son. So naturally did Pushkin work in the description of four pictures on the wall of the station, that not until seventy years later did a critic, M. O. Gershenzon, notice them and see that the main point and irony of the whole story depends on them. Dunya, whom the station master calls a *zabludshaja ovechka* (lost lamb) to match the *bludnyj syn* (prodigal son), does not follow the Biblical pattern. It is because her father *believes* that the moral illustrated by the pictures is universal truth that he sees everything in a false light. He cannot admit that Dunya might be happy with Minsky. Even when he sees her amid luxury and Minsky swears he would never abandon her, Vyrin cannot give up his belief in the parable. One of the ironies is that the station master himself resembles the prodigal son when he takes to drink and ruins himself. In the end the prodigal daughter returns, but she is not ragged or repentant, and there is no forgiving, all-wise father. The real tragedy is in the station master's inability to adjust his view of the situation to fit reality.

The story opens with a seriocomic discourse on station masters which serves two purposes. It characterizes the narrator by taste and, to a certain extent, language. It distracts the reader and delays the actual description of the station. The story would lose little if it began (as I suspect it originally did) with the paragraph, "In 1816, in the month of May . . ." But this would make it more difficult to divert the reader from the true purpose of the pictures. After this introduction, the tale is structured on the three visits of the traveling narrator—I. L. P. The first time he finds two people in a clean, orderly, happy station; the second time (three or four years later) he finds only the old man, surrounded by decay and neglect— and, he notes, the same pictures; the third time he finds no one and the station no longer exists. The last scene is in a gloomy cemetery on a gray cold autumn day which contrasts to the hot May day of the first visit. One feature which complicates the narrative structure is the station master's telling of his story when I. L. P. makes his second visit.

It is primarily in Samson Vyrin that one can see an advance in characterization from Karamzin's time. Without using exaggerated colloquialism (after "setting" the speech level, Pushkin does not indulge in constant sylization), Pushkin deftly individualizes Vyrin's language. We see him in a variety of contrasting situations —both from I. L. P.'s point of view and from his own. Still, it is not in detailed and explicit psychological characterization that Pushkin excels—this was for later writers to develop. Pushkin's strong point is *economy*. Brevity of style is combined with tautness of structure. Digressions are functional. Every detail has a purpose. Hints and hidden ironies are everywhere—the kiss which the fourteen-year-old Dunya gives I. L. P. on his first visit; the fact that she leaves her father on Sunday—supposedly on the way to church; the fact that the man who picks up the money which Vyrin scornfully throws away (foreshadowing various Dostoevskian heroes) is "well-dressed." The subtle repetition of the theme of money is another example: the money Minsky gives to the doctor[1] (so much that it should have aroused Vyrin's suspicions), the banknotes he gives Vyrin in Petersburg, the seven rubles I. L. P. initially regrets spending to see the station master, and the money Dunya gives to the priest and little Vanka.

"*The Queen of Spades*"

IN STYLE "THE STATION MASTER" is somewhat more old-fashioned than "The Queen of Spades." Digressions, comments addressed to the reader, and even a few "sympathetic" epithets ("poor" Dunya) mark this. But Pushkin disapproved of many features of Karamzinian prose. He once noted: "Question—whose prose is the best in our literature? Answer—*Karamzin's*. This is still not much praise . . ." Pushkin objected to the "traces of European finicality and French refinement" which he found in sentimental and romantic prose, saying "coarseness and simplicity" were more appropriate to Russian prose. He condemned the flaccid metaphors and periphrasis so characteristic of many writers after Karamzin: "These people will never say 'friendship' without adding 'this sacred feeling, whose noble flame' etc." Where his friend Vyazemsky wrote "perhaps he would have been totally swallowed up by the abyss of oblivion" Pushkin corrected: "And he was completely forgotten (simpler and better)." Abram Lezhnev's summary of characteristics suggests ways in which Pushkin's prose is different from that of his predecessors:

> Laconism, lack of embellishment, concreteness, business-like character of the metaphors and similes, rapidity of sentence, dynamism, a tendency to the "noun-verb" type, quickness of tempo, evenness and restraint in intonation—these are the basic features of Pushkin's style.[2]

In "The Queen of Spades" (1834) these features appear in extreme form. Forty-four percent of the words are nouns, forty percent verbs. Even frugal Mérimée, Pushkin's first French translator, could not restrain himself from adding adjectives and adverbs.

Plot is more important in "The Queen of Spades" than in most Russian short stories. Indeed, Pushkin's rough drafts usually begin with plot outlines—in contrast to Turgenev's working drafts, where *characters* come first, or Dostoevsky's, where clarification of the "main idea" is often given priority. Furthermore, the popularization of the "society tale" in the 1820s and 1830s saw renewed concentration on action and intrigue; Lermontov's "Fatalist" and "Princess

Mary" are good examples, as are the tales of Odoevsky and Marlinsky.

"The Queen of Spades" is a model society tale, and part of its appeal is in the cold, hard glamour of it all. But it is curious that in spite of the heavy plot interest, the story can be read many times with equal fascination. This indicates that manner is more important than matter. Pushkin has achieved the ultimate in concision; each detail has a purpose. For example, take the character of Lizaveta. She is necessary for the plot of the story—in the way Liza's mother is necessary to Karamzin's story. Also like *that* Liza's mother, Lizaveta Ivanovna is a cliché. But Pushkin's attitude toward her is not pathetic—it is ironic. In the epilogue he has her marry a man whose money would appear to have come from robbing the Countess (he is the steward's son), and Liza has a ward whom, one may surmise, she treats as poorly as she was treated: "She was selfish, keenly aware of her position, and looking for a savior." A similar kind of irony can be seen in Pushkin's description of the funeral. The young priest says the Creator found the Countess "engaged in pious meditations" (which the reader knows is eulogistic nonsense) and "waiting for the Midnight Bridegroom," i.e. death. But *Hermann* was her midnight bridegroom; it was he who came at night and caused her death, it was he who considered becoming her lover (though she is eighty-seven), he who walked along the same corridor by which her real lover in the three-cornered hat had crept into her bedroom sixty years before.

Note that most of the details are "doubled"—if a theme is mentioned once, it will be repeated, however briefly, later in the story. Sometimes these are minor things—as when Pushkin notes that the Countess, returning to her unexpected meeting with Hermann, has powdered hair decorated with roses. The beauty in the picture on her wall also has powdered hair with a rose in it, so we are certain it is her portrait when she had another kind of man visiting. Hermann, appealing to her feeling as a "wife, lover, and mother," promises the Countess that his "children, grandchildren, and great-grandchildren" will revere her. Then at her funeral her own "children, grandchildren, and great-grandchildren" attend in mourning while Hermann is pointed out as her illegitimate son. Another example of doubling is in the throwing of the queen and ace to the left and right. This is paralleled early in the story when the old lady herself sits "swaying back and forth from left to right," and one could think this "swaying resulted not from her own will, but by the action of a hidden galvanism." This hidden galvanism is the same Fate which calls the cards—or which makes Hermann go to the right instead of the left (as instructed by Lizaveta) when he enters the Countess's home. Here he goes to the right—which leads to the Countess's death; in the last card game the queen ("lady") lies on the right and he is beaten.

It is often assumed that the plot of "The Queen of Spades" is based on fantastic events: a winking corpse, a ghostly visit, an ace which becomes a queen, a card that winks. But close reading reveals that none of these are really presented as fantastic events. On the contrary, the pivotal points in the plot are based on the realistic development of Hermann's monomania. Pushkin notes that "it seemed to Hermann" that the corpse winked. "It seemed to him" that the card winked. The queen which appears at the end is easily explained by the rules of the game and Hermann's growing disorientation. Stuss is played with *two* decks of cards. The "punter" (who plays against the banker) can look through his deck, choose any card he wishes, and then put it face down on the table. So in the end Hermann beats himself. He pulls the *queen* out of the deck instead of the ace. He does this because unconsciously he is obsessed with the idea that he is responsible for the Countess's death. His guilt feelings leak through and overwhelm his other *idée fixe*—the three cards. Pushkin hints at this development with the aphorism which opens the last chapter: "Two fixed ideas cannot exist together in moral nature, just as two bodies cannot occupy one and the same place in the physical world."

The fourth "fantastic" event is the Countess's posthumous visit to Hermann's quarters. But this is a *dream*. Pushkin does not have to say so explicitly, because he leaves a number of clues for the careful reader. The dream begins with the misleading sentence, "It was still night when he awoke" (*On prosnulsja eshche noch'ju*). This exactly parallels the opening (also unannounced) of Proxorov's dream in "The Coffinmaker" (1831): "It was still dark outside when Adrian was awakened." It is partly because Pushkin had already used the device of a dream which is explained only at the end of the story (this is what he does in "The Coffinmaker") that his only explicit indication in "The Queen of Spades" is the sentence which *ends* Hermann's dream: "For a long while Hermann could not come to his senses" (*Germann dolgo ne mog opomnit'sja*). This is considerably more subtle. But Pushkin gives other indications that this incident is a dream: Hermann has been drinking very heavily (contrary to his custom) in an attempt to calm himself, "But the wine inflamed his imagination even more." At first Hermann takes the ghost *for his wet-nurse* (*kormilica* here is symbolic of feeder or lover—Hermann would take sustenance and love from the Countess). This is an example of the regressive character of dreams—otherwise why should his wet-nurse be mentioned at all? The ghost "slides" (*skvozit*) across the room and turns up in front of him; this is the kind of cinematographic trick that we all know from dreams. Finally, the whole incident is a wish-fulfillment: Hermann gets the secret cards (including a three and a seven—two numbers *he himself* thought of earlier—"increase my capital three-fold, increase it sevenfold"), he is forgiven (he fears she will punish him), and he is to marry Liza. Obviously, a wish-fulfillment like this ending with the ambiguous words *Germann dolgo ne mog optomnit'sja* is a dream. Moreover, it is a logical extension of Hermann's *first* dream at the end of chapter two. With all of these clues, Pushkin no more had to say it was a dream than to say the Cherkeshenka drowns herself at the end of "The Prisoner of the Caucasus."

Pushkin's characterization of Hermann shows the progress he had made since the *Belkin Tales*. In fact, Hermann is one of the first characters in Russian literature who really comes to life. The dualism of his character is one of the features which Dostoevsky found so congenial when he used Hermann as a model for Raskolnikov. Hermann's German side—caution, calculation, and thrift—is summed up in the aphorism: "I am not in a position to sacrifice the essential in hope of acquiring the superfluous." But the feverish trepidation with which he watches the gambling points to his Russian side—to the "fiery imagination" or "unbridled imagination" which will make him decide that confronting the Countess is "essential." His first, German, reaction to the anecdote is to say "fairy tale," but his fancy immediately toys with the idea of tripling or increasing sevenfold his capital, and he has a revealing dream. His first messages to Liza are copied from a German novel, but soon he writes his own passionate letters. We also learn he is secretive and proud, and that one of his most important traits is superstitiousness. The development of his obsession is handled swiftly and subtly—from the opening game through the various steps, to the time when he sees everything as threes, sevens, and aces, until finally he goes totally insane. Pushkin characterizes primarily from the outside—Hermann's actions are described, what he says is reported, and a few epithets ("secretive" and "proud") are given. Pyschological states are suggested by description of physical reactions. For example, the cold does not bother him, he trembles like a tiger—so intense is he about entering the Countess's house. The tiger simile is an example of Pushkin's occasional lapses into clichés of the type he was to a certain extent parodying.

Pushkin makes fun of romantic steretoypes several times. Lizaveta's view of Hermann as Napoleon or Mephistopheles (prompted by Tomsky's teasing) is gently ridiculed. One of the reasons why Hermann becomes unhinged is his belief in Faustian stories about demonic pacts and soul-selling. (Note that after his second dream, he writes it all down—suggesting he is conditioned by literary conventions.) The superstitious part of his character becomes progressively more obvious as the story rushes ahead; his expiatory visit to the funeral is a good example.

Cards, the Countess, Hermann, and Fate go together. Card games have traditionally been seen as metaphors for life; the cards are people, and Fate decides the outcome. In Pushkin's story the symbolic and realistic levels are intertwined, and in the end Hermann's losing of the game is losing at life too. According to the fortune-telling books of Pushkin's day, the queen of spades signified an old, evil or vengeful woman—hence Pushkin's epigraph and Hermann's fear of the Countess. Hermann and she are joined—by means of cards and the theme of incomprehensibility—in the opening of the story: "Hermann is a German . . . But if there is someone I cannot understand, it's my grandmother, Countess Anna Fedotovna." At the end of the story the symbolic and realistic levels of meaning merge in Chekalinsky's relieved remark to Hermann: V*asha dama ubita*—which means both "your queen is beaten" and "your lady has been murdered." The narrator's comment that "the game went on in its normal course" may be applied either to the card playing or to life itself—life in its usual fashion marries off Tomsky to Pauline and Lizaveta to a wealthy young man.

The brevity of the final chapter is structured on repetition with alteration. Narumov takes Hermann to Chekalinsky's. As they go in the first time, Pushkin notes: generals and privy councillors playing whist, young men on divans eating ice cream and smoking (compendious details), Chekalinsky's smile is totally self-confident. Hermann has to reach clumsily around a fat general to place his bet. The second time certain details are changed: a place is made for him once he arrives, Chekalinsky shows some fleeting discomfort. The third time the details change completely: everyone is *waiting* for him, the generals and privy councillors leave their whist, the young officers get up from the divans and ice cream, and Hermann plays alone against Chekalinsky—whose smile is belied by his paleness. One might compare Pushkin's exquisite use of fine details here (the ice cream, reaching around the general) to the frenetic cataloguing and microscopic analysis in Dostoevsky's gambling scenes.

Pushkin's tonal consistency is different from that of Karamzin. Irony is Pushkin's mode. The "lowering epigraphs (i.e. all except the master epigraph) are good examples. They create a dissonance as one reads each brief chapter. Pushkin forces the reader to have a kind of double vision—he makes us both see the humor in these situations and take them seriously. The irony is pervasive, but not destructive. Indeed, while the urbane coolness of Pushkin's humor is that of an eighteenth-century writer, in his tone one also senses the temperament of a man who prefers Shakespeare to Racine. Irony is a protective device. It is a sign of restraint—it enables Pushkin to parody certain situations and literary types while still communicating the feeling that the story is much more than a clever game of words.

"The Overcoat"

AFTER THE TONAL AND STYLISTIC CONSISTENCY of Karamzin or Pushkin, Gogol comes as a shock. He is rightly regarded as Russia's foremost verbal gymnast. Tongue-twisting names, rhymes, and puns spring up like clowns. Using metaphor and metonymy to turn people into toe-nails or noses, he works more transformations than

a drunken Roman mythologist. His prose is poetic and onomato-
poetic—rhetorical figures abound, rhythmic and phonetic considerations help determine each phrase. Pushkin's favorite punctuation is
the period. Gogol's is the semicolon; and at first glance, the profusion of dependent clauses and qualifications may bring to mind
a fishing reel's backlash.[3] Many of Gogol's old-fashioned contemporaries considered him a vulgarian, both because of his in-
elegant subject matter and the "non-literary" vocabulary which he
introduced (colloquialisms, bureaucratese, dialectisms, jargon, and
neologisms); but with time his lexical salmagundi, syntactical
intricacies, and sometimes shaky grammar became "estheticized,"
and his style was imitated by writers as different as Dostoevsky,
Saltykov-Shchedrin, Remizov, Bely, and Abram Tertz.

"The Overcoat" (1842) was Gogol's last story. Partly because
it was published in a four-volume collection of his works—and in
the same year as *Dead Souls*—his contemporaries paid little attention to it. I say this because one of the folklore items among teachers
of Russian literature is the belief that Belinsky's interpretation of
the story has been followed by all socially-oriented critics, but in
fact Belinsky wrote no critique or analysis of "The Overcoat." He
did not "interpret" Gogol's best story.[4] Most Russians take it as a
philanthropic tale. Indeed, the entire philanthropic trend of
Russian literature, with "little men" as heroes, has been traced back
to Pushkin's "The Station Master" and Gogol's Petersburg stories.
Dostoevsky's remark, which he did not make (and which is not
true), that "We all came from under Gogol's 'Overcoat' " is reprinted in almost every literary history written in the last seventy
years. The first axiom of this theory, variations on which are used
by every Soviet critic, is that Gogol was a realist.

Following the lead of V. V. Rozanov,[5] the Russian Symbolists
preferred to emphasize the non-realistic aspects of Gogol's work,
his hyperbole and fantasy. They suggest it is impossible to sympathize with such grotesque humanoids as Akaky. The second assault
on the philanthropic interpretation came from the Formalists. Boris
Eichenbaum interpreted the story simply as an excuse for unfolding
the verbal material.[6] According to him, Gogol's switching from the
comic to the pathetic to the ironic is all a game—acoustical play on
the part of a narrator who mugs and mimes, changing his voice
unexpectedly to entertain the listener. Akaky Akakievich's remark,

"Leave me alone, why do you insult me" and the passage about the clerk who was so touched by these words are not meant to arouse pity—they are there simply to shatter the comic play and create a grotesque contrast in intonation. The sterility of this part of Eichenbaum's analysis results from the theoretical straight-jacket which the Formalists sometimes mistook for armor in their revolt against the sociological critics. In reaction to Soviet criticism, most Western scholars have expanded on the Symbolist or Formalist views of "The Overcoat." For example, Čiževskij[7] claims that the story does not attack social evils or defend underdogs; its theme is the development of a passion for a nothing (an idea first suggested by Apollon Grigoriev). Since Akaky sees the coat as a wife, Čiževskij interprets it as a parody of romantic love stories. Critics of Formalist inclination like to see parodies in everything because it emphasizes the *literariness* of a work as opposed to its bases in real life. While Čiževskij's article contains several ridiculous assertions (e.g. that Petrovich is the devil), he does offer some sophisticated stylistic analysis. For example, the adverb *dazhe* (even) is used dozens of times, often illogically. It intensifies where there is no need of intensification. Čiževskij hypothesizes that the use of "even" projects Akaky's "view from below" through the narrator. Akaky is such a limited, insignificant creature that he sees ordinary things as strange, grand, and beyond his sphere.[8]

One man's heresy is another man's cliché, as is seen by the different attitudes (in communist countries and in western ones) toward the assertion that Gogol is not a realist. It seems clear to us that Tolstoy and Flaubert are poles away from Gogol, that his "realism" is the literary analogue of Potemkin's villages. His sometimes microscopic description is designed to trick the reader; when you step back a little you see that things are much vaguer than they seemed. The student should note some of the features of style which help create this impression. For example, the narrator staggers from omniscience to senility in the same paragraph—although usually the things which he cannot remember (the date the coat is finished) are not important anyway. Digressiveness is not a characteristic of realistic style, and the Sternian divagations of the narrative begin after only two words. Compare the final version of the opening to this early (1839) draft:

In the department of taxes and collections [*podatej i sborov*] which, incidentally, is sometimes called the department of frauds and nonsense [*podlostej i vzdorov*], not because there were in fact frauds there, but because Mssrs. the civil servants like to joke just as much as military officers do—thus, in the department . . .

The fungi-like growth of "irrelevant" details is characteristic of Gogol's work on the successive versions. Often the reader is so hypnotized by the details that he forgets to question absurdities "such as the bland assumption that 'full-grown young pigs' commonly occur in private houses," says Vladimir Nabokov, referring to the last paragraph of the story.

Following hints by Bely, James Woodward[9] has carefully catalogued a number of specific devices which Gogol uses to blur reality, to make things indefinite: affirmative statements which are immediately made dubious by qualifications, a plethora of adversative conjunctions (but, however, nevertheless, etc.) used to introduce comments which cast doubt on the veracity of statements in previous clauses, negative statement ("not without pity," "not without terror"), direct and indirect questions, a profusion of indefinite pronominal adjectives (*kakoj-to, kakoj-nibud', kak-to*, etc. which are often untranslatable), the frequent use of *kazat'sja* (to seem), *kak budto, kak budto-by, pochti* (as if, almost). These combine to create the vagueness which is typical of Gogol's unreal world of phantoms and fantasy. To this catalogue one might add Gogol's constant use of euphemism and humorous periphrasis. For example, the important person does not have a mistress, he has a "lady for friendly relations."

But there is fact in fantasy, and we can feel sympathy even for caricatures. Even an unrealistic story full of comedy can be philanthropic. While Gogol shows us the ways in which Akaky Akakievich is ridiculous, he never scorns him; while he shows his ignorance, he puts him in positions so universal that the reader can feel pity. The plot itself is archetypically tragic: the painful quest for the desired object, acquisition, and then unjust loss and defeat. Defeat follows on the heels (or shoulders) of victory—for kings or Akakys. The plainly philanthropic comments (such as "I am your brother"), the episode with the young clerk, and perhaps most important, the character change in the significant personage—to whom, incidentally, several significant pages of the story are devoted—cannot be explained away simply as "contrast." Gogol wrote "The Overcoat" as he was finishing the first part of *Dead Souls*, and there are several parallels between the two works. For example, Akaky dies:

> Gone and disappeared was a being who was protected by no one, interesting to no one, who had not even attracted the attention of a naturalist who does not fail to impale an ordinary fly [earlier Akaky is compared to a fly] on a pin and examine it in his microscope.

In *Dead Souls* Gogol uses the same metaphor when declaring that his artistic principles include the portrayal of just such characters:

> For the judgment of the writer's own times does not recognize that equally marvelous are the lenses that are used for contemplating suns and those for revealing to us the motions of insects imperceptible to the naked eye; for the judgment of his times does not recognize that a great deal of spiritual depth is required to throw light upon a picture taken from a despised stratum of life, and to exalt it into a pearl of creative art. (Chapter Seven)

Akaky Akakievich is one of Gogol's dead souls, perhaps the most dehumanized of all; but it is clear from his works and correspondence that he felt deep sadness for his creatures. The lessons he hoped to teach by making the world look through his microscope were not those of art for art's sake.

We can also learn a lesson from the Freudian view of "The Overcoat."[10] There is an abundance of coprological detail in the story: Akaky Akakievich's name itself suggests the child's word for excrement, the other names he was almost given suggest sucking and urination, his complexion is hemorrhoidal, and in one variant he even has a coat the color of a cow pie. Akaky's retarded sexual development is indicated by this imagery connected to other overt sexual imagery—the coat itself as a wife with a good thick lining, the woman that he inexplicably trots after, the picture of the Frenchwoman with her leg bared, the jokes about his landlady, the policeman's suggestion that he has been to a bordello, and the significant personage's inexplicable visits to Karolina Ivanovna. Freudian commentators have a tendency to fantasize about the implications of these remarks for *Gogol's* psychology. This, I think, is dangerous and mostly irrelevant; but their theory does focus our attention on facts (i. e. details) of the story which otherwise might be overlooked.[11] One level of the story's humor remains closed to the reader if he does not notice the persistence of these scatological and sexual allusions.

Finally, I would warn that it is possible to exaggerate the importance of digressions in "The Overcoat." The fact that digressions occur at the very beginning and at the very end tends to make us remember the story as more digressive than it really is. Actually, in the main body of the story, Gogol is quite business-like. For example, the central block of material is a single gigantic paragraph (unique in Gogol's fiction) almost nine pages long. This digressionless unit covers the entire period from Akaky Akakievich's decision to get a new coat until the moment when he steps onto the square where it will be stolen. Twelve pages precede this middle section and twelve pages come after it. There are two major dialogue scenes (one with Petrovich, one with the significant personage); the first begins seven and one-half pages from the beginning of the story, the second seven and one half pages from the end. Thus, these sections give the story an underlying symmetrical structure from which one is distracted by letter-writing captains, weak policemen, and ordinary full-grown young pigs.

"Bezhin Meadow"

"Bezhin Meadow" was published in *The Contemporary* in 1851, and the next year Turgenev included it in the first edition of *Notes of a Hunter*. Although reading rustic tales such as George Sand's *La Mare du diable* and *La Petite Fadette* helped suggest some of his themes, Turgenev apparently intended the collection primarily as an exposure of serfdom. The censor who passed *Notes* was dismissed by Tsar Nikolai himself, but the book was extremely popular in liberal circles and had influence analogous to that of *Uncle Tom's Cabin* in this country. Russian literature had few realistic descriptions of peasant life to offer when Turgenev went abroad (where he wrote most of the twenty-two stories) in 1847, but in the mid-1840's the writers of the Natural School[12] did publish a few works—by Herzen, Grigorovich (*The Village*), and Dal—which presented more than the cardboard muzhiks of historical novels or Gogol's human vegetables.

Of course, "Bezhin Meadow" is only very indirectly didactic. It is famed for its lyrical qualities, for Turgenev's pastel descriptions of nature, and for his portrayal of the poetic imagination of the boys. Melting sunlight, the shimmer of linden leaves, traces of dew on the meadow—these are Turgenev's specialties. His *paysage* is done in fond detail—words for colors are used heavily, outlines of trees and clouds are drawn in full, visual details are "crossed" with details appealing to sound, smell, or touch. Nature comes alive as Turgenev applies psychological epithets to animals or inanimate objects—although the personification is usually not obtrusive. On the other hand, he regularly shows similarities between man and nature; in many metaphors and similes human behavior or physiognomy is compared to the birds and animals of which Turgenev the hunter was so acute an observer. As in "Bezhin Meadow," the way a human perceives nature is often determined by his external circumstances. The narrator begins by exulting in the beautiful day, when he gets lost he begins to see things as gloomy and hostile, at the fire he cheers up somewhat, and the next morning everything is glorious again.

Turgenev's prose style is richer than Pushkin's, steadier and more sedate than Gogol's. For the speech of the boys Turgenev uses some dialect words, as well as repetitions and syntax characteristic of peasant speech, but beyond this it is not individualized. The educated narrator's language underlies everything.

Quite apart from the fact that "poetic" nature description may not be one's cup of tea, there are several apparent weaknesses in the story. For example, is it a story? It seems to be a cross between a short story (with a plot) and a "sketch" (*ocherk*), i. e. a descriptive piece devoted primarily to local color and ethnographic detail. "Bezhin Meadow" gives the impression of being fragmentary— and that is the way it was written. It grew out of a marginal note to "The Singers": "Describe how the boys drive horses." The first draft dealt only with the boys and their storytelling. The long nature description which opens the story is a "piece" of material sewn on later—the last nature description was added still later, and the three-line epilogue about Pavlusha came last. The "block" characterization of the five boys is extremely clumsy: first there was A, description of face, clothes; second there was B, description of face, clothes; third there was C, etc.—all in one lumpy paragraph. Furthermore, as Turgenev agreed, the children talk like adults. Turgenev himself had a rather low opinion of the stories in *Notes of a Hunter*. He said they were written in "the old manner," and he preferred his later stories. Nevertheless, the story has come to be regarded as a classic, and it is typical of Turgenev's early short fiction.

"*Lady Macbeth of the Mtsensk District*"

"A LADY MACBETH OF OUR DISTRICT" was the title of this early story by Leskov when it appeared in Dostoevsky's journal *Epoch* in 1865. It was the first of twelve sketches of feminine types which Leskov planned to write. Turgenev had already written "A Hamlet of the Shchigri District," but his Shakespearian parallel is closer than Leskov's—Katerina gets her nickname from a local wit, and the similarities between her and Lady Macbeth are fairly superficial. Though she has an "ardent character," Katerina is repressed by the unwanted marriage and six years of boredom with Izmailov. In the beginning Sergei is much cleverer than she, but from the time when she "involuntarily presses against his mighty body" (chapter three), her "dormant character" develops rapidly. It is Katerina who poisons the father-in-law, she who first grabs her husband by the throat, she who eventually plays the dominant role in the murder of Fyodor. All of this—and her later sacrifices—result from her attempts to please Sergei, the only man she has ever loved. Leskov is careful to make the reader have mixed feelings about Katerina. She is a chillingly indifferent murderess, but her first two victims engage little sympathy. The husband accuses her of being barren when, as we discover, it is he who is sterile through two marriages. One feels a certain amount of sympathy for anyone who does give all for love, but on the other hand the object of Katerina's love is a cheat and coward. After his betrayals and cruelty, the reader is likely to feel a certain satisfaction when she finally spits in his face and takes Sonya beneath the waves.

Leskov is reported to have said his hair stood on end when writing the story, but he does not seek to inspire horror by indulging in hysterics or hyperbole, as did Marlinsky before him and Andreev after. There is more blood during the second murder than the first, but even in this scene Leskov uses great restraint. The narrator generally refrains from direct emotional appeals and moralizing—until the last three chapters, where one finds: (1) an irrelevant satirical remark on social-democratic communes, (2) an attempt to affect the reader with a gloomy present-tense "picture" of the prisoners—ending with a Biblical quotation, (3) a few exclamatory remarks such as, "They are equals! Fiona, submissive to the first suggestion, and Katerina Lvovna, ending a drama of love!" Until this point (except for the use of "our" in the opening paragraph), the narrator had worn his guise of omniscience with greater consistency, so these lapses in the narrative tone may be counted among the story's weaknesses. Fortunately, the powerfully terse ending makes one forget Leskov's momentary breakdown.

"Lady Macbeth" is not characteristic of Leskov's works. It is better unified than most of his stories, and potentially melodramatic subject matter seldom attracted him. He is known as one of the foremost practioners of *skaz* narration, i. e. first-person narration which is individualized and intended to create the illusion of orality.[13] Typically, the master narrator—a somewhat old-fashioned stylist such as the narrator of this story—introduces some peculiar character who, in turn, tells the main story. Colorful individualized speech itself was one of Leskov's prime concerns—he took endless pains to reproduce the intonation, puns and malapropisms characteristic of a wide variety of Russian types. The style of "Lady Macbeth" is definitely a *written*, literary style. He uses many participles and inversions (predicate—subject), and generally the Russian is somewhat old-fashioned and ponderous. But it also has a strong folk coloration. Many of the devices suggest the language of folk songs and tales. The tautologies, repetitions, and formulas which characters use (Katerina's *prenepostojannyj-nepostojannyj*—"very-inconstant-inconstant") are also used by the narrator (*pretolstjush-chij-tolstyj*—"veryfatted-fat"). The polysyndeton and epizeuxis typical of folk poetry are used repeatedly: *celovalo, celovalo* (kissed, kissed), *i poshel i poshel* (and walked and walked). Noun-epithet inversions are common and often have the dactylic ending of folk poetry: *sxoronili po zakonu xristianskomu.* ("They buried him with

Christian rites.") The first paragraphs of chapter four are good examples of Leskov's use of folk intonation and rhythm.

Leskov's merits are a subject of wide disagreement, varying from those who acclaim his verbal inventiveness to those who say even writers do not live by words alone. Among the virtues of "Lady Macbeth" one might note the clever use of details such as the husband's watch ticking when Katerina first makes love to Sergei, or the way Katerina uses her "firm breast" (*uprugaja grud'*)—on which Sergei has slept—to suffocate Fyodor. The story moves briskly through short chapters, the sensual scenes are all the more effective for being muted, and there are several good psychological touches, such as the way Katerina reacts wordlessly to her public execution. Finally, Leskov's distinctive prose style offers a pleasant change of pace.

"*The Dream of a Ridiculous Man*"

THIS STORY was published in the April, 1877 issue of Dostoevsky's *Diary of a Writer*. Philosophical themes and stylistic devices found in all of Dostoevsky's major works appear here in condensed form: the urban setting; a fifth-floor underground type with his touchy sensibility, insomnia, paradoxes, and first-person confession-monologue; metaphysical buffoonery; a "crisis dream"; utopian visions; innocent children; scandalous neighbors; the offended girl; cruel sensuality; suicide; pride; love through suffering; escape from responsibility to the moon; sticky green leaves and communication with celestial animals; kissing of the feet; a Christ figure; the heart versus the head; and mutual responsibility.

Baxtin sees this dream with its combination of philosophical universalism and naturalistic detail as an archetypical example of the "carnivalized Menippean satire."[14] He notes that in terms of genre it is also related to various "fantastic journeys" and utopian works. To the rather esoteric list Baxtin gives (Voltaire's "Micromegas" is the only well-known story he mentions), one might add items Dostoevsky was more likely to have read, such as Swift's *Voyage to the Country of the Houyhnhnms* (particularly chapters eight and nine), or Osip Senkovsky's clumsy *Fantastic Journe*

of Baron Brambeus (1833), the fourth part of which describes an upside-down double of earth discovered inside Mt. Etna.

Dreams play an exceptionally large role in all of Dostoevsky's major novels, but they are an important device in all of Russian literature. They occur in most of the stories in this anthology. There are many other famous ones beginning with Svyatoslav's dream in *The Igor Tale* down to the works of Abram Tertz.[15] Partly because the literary dream frees the "realistic" writer from normal time and space considerations, it is an extremely flexible device. Most often literary dreams are premonitory, but they may be used for symbolic characterization, to suggest hidden fears or hostilities in a character, to vary the technique of digression, to introduce otherwise unprintable material[16] or, as in the case of Dostoevsky's story, to present complex philosophical ideas by means of *ostranenie* ("estrangement," "making strange").

In the ordinary sense "The Dream of a Ridiculous Man," subtitled "a fantastic story," is not so much a story as a philosophical monopolylogue. Dostoevsky purposely creates ambiguity about whether the dream itself is really a dream, and ultimately the "dream" is not so much a nighttime hallucination as a vision of an attainable ideal. For Dostoevsky, the ideal of universal love and mutual responsibility lies outside the framework of rational theory. This is the main theme of the story. As the underground man, that most rational of Dostoevsky's anti-Darwinians, says:

> Reason satisfies only the rational side of man's nature, while will is a manifestation of that whole life, that is, of the whole life including reason and all the impulses . . . Reason only knows what it has succeeded in learning . . . and human nature acts as a whole, with everything that is in it consciously or unconsciously, and, even if it goes wrong, it lives.

Let "living life" teach you about life, not theories, said Dostoevsky's conservative friends Straxov and Grigoriev in answer to the materialist doctrines of the 1860's. Then Dostoevsky presented their tautological formula more convincingly in *Crime and Punishment* and the other great novels. In all of these Dostoevsky juxtaposes reasoned lives to natural lives—Raskolnikov versus Sonia, Ivan Karamazov versus Alyosha. He shows how often men's attempts to be rational go askew.[17]

Symbolically, the ridiculous man shoots himself in the heart rather than in the head (a change in plan he emphasizes by repetition), but even that does not destroy him: "the essence of my heart remained with me." When he arrives on the little star, a power there "echoed in my heart and resurrected it, and I experienced life." Of course, as he notes, dreams are ruled by the heart, not the intellect. The meaning of the songs sung by the people in the utopia "remained inaccessible to my intellect, but instinctively my heart was as if pierced through by it more and more." The narrator hero repeatedly uses the words *oshchushchenie* (sensation, experience) and *chuvstvo* (feeling): "Let it be nothing but a dream. But the sensation of being loved by those innocent and beautiful people will remain with me forever, and even now I can feel their love pouring down on me." The "sensation" that this dream contains the truth is more important than rational evidence that it was only a dream. Thematically this parallels the incident with the girl earlier: he has decided nothing matters, but when he drives her off, he has "a momentary sensation, and this sensation continued even at home." He feels *sorry* for the girl; in spite of his logical conviction that nothing matters, he feels pity. These sensations and feelings that men have come from their whole being, not the brain. So for the ridiculous man, even if it was a dream (and he makes this ambiguous—he does not recall falling asleep), he saw the "living image" of that world and that is the certain truth discovered on November 3. He knows it is rationality that perverted the people on the star. Once they have a *concept* of brotherhood, once they have a *word* for love—they can no longer experience brotherhood and love, they cannot *live* it. This is why the ridiculous man attacks the doctrine that "knowledge is higher than feeling, consciousness of life higher than life."

The ridiculous man's monologue contains many stylistic devices characteristic of Dostoevsky's works in general. Chapters ending on points of intense interest (I, V) are typically suspenseful. While the monologue has little true oral flavor, it does contain an unusually large number of mono- and bi-syllabic words. Many of these are the little fillers and helpers, adverbs and conjunctions, characteristic of Russian style (especially Dostoevsky's) when the author is trying to be very logical and take into consideration all of the possible objections of his readers: *i vot, posle togo uzh . . .* ; *a tak*;

takie-to; tak, kak; kak-to, kak by, tak-chto; pochemu-to (and then, already after, and so, such-like, since, somehow, as if, so that, for some reason). Dostoevsky, even more than Gogol, is given to interrogatives and to adversative conjunctions: *no, no ved' a, odnako* (but, but, however). These result from the continual process of questioning every idea, every proposition. Dostoevsky could also be called the writer of the "conditional" in Russian—"if . . . then" (*esli by . . . to*) clauses abound—these arise from the speculative nature of his characters. The heavy use of intensifiers is also characteristic of Dostoevsky's style: *sovsem, sovershenno, dazhe* (completely, totally, even). Intensification can also be seen in his repetitions and gradatio: "it was a dark, the very darkest evening that could ever be," "but soon, very soon," "but I knew, infinitely and indestructibly I knew and believed that without fail all would soon change." Again, this may result from the nature of his characters, their desire to take every concept or description and convey it as precisely as possible—this means they have to consider all qualifications to find just the right modifier, and once it is found, emphasize it as strongly as possible, as if saying, "Yes, this is it." Dostoevsky's desire to intensify sometimes leads to tautology" *nemnogo i slegka* (a little and slightly), *vsex i vsjakogo* (everyone and everybody), *ukory i upreki* (reproaches and rebukes), *rasxodit'sja i ras' edinjat'sja* (disperse and break up). If one looks favorably upon this he calls it synonymy; if he considers it prolix, he calls it redundancy. The young Dostoevsky consciously imitated Gogol's style (in *Poor Folk* and *The Double*), and certain traces of Gogolian phraseology[18] stayed with Dostoevsky all through his career. But the poetry of Gogol's style is alien to Dostoevsky. Dostoevsky is an argumentative writer, so the lyric flow of Gogolian syntax gives way to the fragmented, stop-and-go syntax of a dialectician for whom "therefore," "but," and "if" are key words.

"God Sees the Truth, but Waits"

DURING THE 1870's Tolstoy devoted much of his energy to the education of the peasants. He re-opened his school for peasant children at Yasnaya Polyana, and he wrote a long series of moralistic stories which were to be read to and by the peasants. These were published as four *Russian Books for Reading*. Most of them were retellings of Aesop's fables and fairy tales of many nations. Tolstoy said he wanted the tales to be "pure, elegant, without anything superfluous, like all of ancient Greek literature." He reported that he reworked each story ten times and that these collections cost him more effort than any of his previous works, including *War and Peace*. "God Sees the Truth, but Waits," written in 1872, was published in the third *Russian Book for Reading*. Presumably, peasants could understand the story without scholarly exegesis.

"*The Death of Ivan Ilych*"

STUDENTS TEND TO REACT to Tolstoy's most famous story in one of two ways: some are affected by it ("infected," if we use Tolstoy's term) and get sick and depressed; but the majority roundly abuse it, accusing Tolstoy of being didactic, unrealistic, arbitrary, and heavy-handed. All of these charges are in some measure true. For us Tolstoy *is* old-fashioned. The modern reader who values ambiguity, uncertainty, and impartiality above all things will consider Tolstoy alien. Nevertheless, we should realize that these are not absolutes, but current values which will someday fall out of fashion. And actually, there is a more basic cause of hostility to Tolstoy's story: young people, especially in our age, are unsympathetic to many aspects of Tolstoyan morality. His ideas on the "place" of women in marriage and society enrage feminists; his proposals for sexual abstinence generate little enthusiasm; his ideal peasants seem painfully unreal; and his attacks on science smack of obscurantism. ("Nowadays Ivan Ilych's cancer would show up in his annual x-ray, it would be removed, and there would be no problem," says the cynic.) The mere fact that "The Death of Ivan Ilych" is a compendium of Tolstoyan themes, motifs, and devices can be a liability. Students who have just read other works by Tolstoy are likely to moan "here we go again": officials are selfish and bad, women are bad, doctors are stupid and bad, peasants are clean and good, children are good—until they learn to masturbate.

The question remains: why did Tolstoy use such direct meth-

ods? Obviously, had he wanted to, Tolstoy could have made everything more ambiguous. He did not *have* to use omniscient narration
—the form most suitable for *ex cathedra* pronouncements on character motivation and social evils. In fact, Tolstoy used a completely
different—and somewhat more "modern"—narrative technique in
the original drafts of the story. There it is told in first person by
Tvorogov, an acquaintance of Ivan Ilych. The story opens: "I found
out about Ivan Ilych's death at court." The narrator (in most, but
not all respects, he is the Peter Ivanovich of the final version) goes
to Praskovia Fedorovna's. She gives him a diary which Ivan Ilych
kept during his last two months. A sample from the diary is quoted.
Then Tvorogov makes numerous visits to the widow, Gerasim, and
others connected with Ivan Ilych's life. He amalgamates all of this
information and gives the biography. Presumably, when Tolstoy
reached the last two months, he would end the story with Ivan
Ilych's diary. These complications would perhaps appeal to more
sophisticated readers—there would be more ambiguity, the conflict-
ing evidence given by the wife and others would be bounced off a
"reflector" with a definite character of his own, Ivan Ilych's diary
would add a new view—with its peculiar unreliability—and, most
important, there would be no God-like omniscient narrator evaluating and clarifying everything.

But perhaps that was just the trouble. Tolstoy was not interested
in puzzling his readers. He had a lesson to teach. The age of ethical
relativity had not yet dawned, and the theories of James, Ford
Madox Ford, and Robbe-Grillet had not yet been invented and
propagated among the intellectual elite. So Tolstoy did not consider
it his task to tell the story in such a way that it would seem a special
case with dozens of purely personal features—or, still less, to tell it
using witnesses who might be unreliable. The life of Ivan Ilych was
not unique—it was the life of everyone in his class. His death was
not unique—it was universal. And for a universal parable, it is suitable to have a narrator who sees, understands, and tells all.

Life is repetition, and Tolstoy uses repetition as one of the main
devices in "The Death of Ivan Ilych." He wishes to convince us
that Ivan Ilych's life and death are ordinary and monotonous. Instead of an emotionally involved first-person narrator, we have an
"epic" narrator who is far removed and, at times, almost bored with
Ivan Ilych's life. The narrative tone seems to say, this is an old

story, we all know it perfectly well. Everything is "the same," "the usual," "the ordinary," "familiar," "just as always," "continually," "over and over." In Russian all is *to samoe, chto byvaet u vsex, tot zhe, ta zhe, te zhe.* The impression of monotony, inevitability, and tiresome ordinariness is also created by the extremely large number of sentences beginning with the conjunction "and." "And Ivan Ilych got married." "And Ivan Ilych became this new person." "And Ivan Ilych worked out such an attitude toward conjugal life." "And the service, and the worries about money, and so it went for a year, and two, and ten, and twenty—and always the same thing. And the further he went, the more deadly it got." A number of these sentences begin paragraphs or chapters. The same is true of numerous summary sentences beginning *tak* or *itak* (thus, and thus): "Thus he lived seven more years." "Thus went Ivan Ilych's life during the course of seventeen years." "Thus they lived." And so life goes on, always the same until death as usual begins, and then: *vse bol', vse bol', vse toska i vse odno i to zhe* (always pain, always pain, always anguish, always the very same thing); *vse chernee i chernee, i vse bystree i bystree* (it kept getting blacker and blacker, faster and faster); *tak i vsja zhizn' shla vse xuzhe i xuzhe* (thus all life kept getting worse and worse). The heavy accumulation of repetitions is intended to give the feeling that the opening sentence of chapter two is true: "The past history of Ivan Ilych's life was most simple and ordinary and most terrible."

Repetition is perhaps the most characteristic feature of Tolstoy's style. As R. F. Christian has shown, the translators of *War and Peace* have always "corrected" Tolstoy, using synonyms instead of reproducing his repetitions.[19] The same is true of all previous translations of this story. In "The Death of Ivan Ilych" there are several key words which are used over and over. These repetitions create *ostranenie.* The meaning of the word can either be destroyed (as when we rapidly repeat a single word until it becomes nonsense) or it can be reversed. For example, the way Tolstoy pounds on the word "joys" (*radosti*) drains the joy from it: "His official joys were the joys of egotism, his social joys were the joys of vanity, but Ivan Ilych's real joys were the joys of playing bridge." More important are the words which symbolize the kind of life Ivan Ilych dreams of; he wants everything to be "easy" (*legkoe* also means light, without strain), "pleasant," and "decorous" (*prijatnoe i prilichnoe—*

"pleasant and proper" would be a better translation phonetically). All through chapter two Tolstoy hammers away at these words, using their adjectival, adverbial, and nominal forms. Their repetition, combined with the empty things Ivan Ilych thinks are pleasant and proper, soon turns the words inside out and empties them of real meaning. By the end of chapter three when Tolstoy says, "And everything went along thus, without changing, and everything was good," we know that everything was *not* good. When Ivan Ilych gets married, the first unpleasantness and indecorum (*neprijatnost' i neprilichie*) enter his life, and when he falls ill everything becomes the opposite of what he wanted; it is unclean, hard, and unpleasant:

> He saw that everyone around him had reduced the terrible, horrible act of his dying to the level of an accidental unpleasantness, partly a lack of decorum (something like what happens to a person who walks into a drawing-room and breaks wind), and they did this using the same "decorum" which he had served all his life.

Other key ideas which are repeated are "torture," "falsehood," "loneliness," "sadness," and finally "death" itself—the personified "It" (which, appropriately for Tolstoy, is feminine in Russian) that comes and stands in the corner.

Juxtaposition is another of Tolstoy's favorite devices. In the opening scene we learn about the tastes and thoughts of the other court officials—and later we discover that they are exactly like Ivan Ilych. Tolstoy carefully doubles specific details. Thus in the opening chapter, the funeral inconveniences Peter Ivanovich—he comes late and has to play bridge with five people. At the end of chapter three, we learn that Ivan Ilych dislikes odd numbers: "With five it is very annoying to sit out, although one pretends that one likes it very much." In passing, we learn that Petrishchev, the fiancé, is a court examiner—the same post Ivan Ilych held when he got engaged to Praskovia Fedorovna. Praskovia Fedorovna's reaction to Ivan Ilych's sickness is juxtaposed to that of Gerasim. Gerasim's health, strength, and cleanliness are juxtaposed to Ivan Ilych's rotting flesh and dirtiness.[20] The daughter's naked, healthy body is compared to Ivan Ilych's when she comes to his room before leaving for the theater.

Other typical features of Tolstoy's art that students should watch for include psychological generalization, the use of parenthetical comments on hidden motives, and especially, the "speaking" eyes, smiles, or gestures (i. e. "Just his look said: 'the incident of Ivan Ilych's funeral can in no way serve as sufficient cause' ..."). Tolstoy believed that although people may lie when they speak, their true thoughts can often be read in their facial or bodily expressions. (Favored characters, such as Natasha in *War and Peace*, are quick to perceive these signs.) There are many examples of Tolstoy's use of *ostranenie*, notably the destruction of funereal solemnity by the battle with the springy pouffe and Ivan Ilych's meditations on himself as a child. Tolstoy's fondness for similes and metaphors taken from physics and mechanics is also apparent; he likes to use "scientific" analogies to explain philosophical concepts. Examples are Ivan Ilych's image (chapter ten) of the rock falling faster and faster (which, incidentally, is not quite accurate), the image of the railroad car in chapter twelve, and the Caius syllogism.

Tolstoy adds variety to his narrative technique by occasionally shifting into the historical present (as at the end of chapter seven). In a few cases this is accompanied by an unmarked shift into a kind of interior monologue. Ivan Ilych's point of view penetrates the narration itself. In chapter eight, for example: "An hour, two pass like this. But there's a ring in the anteroom. Maybe the doctor. Precisely, it's the doctor ..." etc. The third paragraph of chapter six provides another good example of this "hidden" interior monologue. It is a very sophisticated device which enables Tolstoy to have his narrative cake and eat it too. He has both the flexibility of omniscient, third-person narration, and the immediacy of impression of first-person narration (the diary which he decided not to use). The fact that the shift to Ivan Ilych's point of view is not marked makes the device all the more effective. We enter Ivan Ilych's mind *directly*, without the usual artificial warning signals (such as quotation marks or "he thought").

In the process of changing the story from a "first-person minor" narrative to an omniscient one, Tolstoy overlooked several points. The internal chronology of Ivan Ilych's life is inconsistent. In the last chapter Tolstoy makes the daughter around twenty, while the dates given earlier show she can be no older than fifteen. If she is really twenty she would have been born in 1862, before Ivan Ilych met his wife. Similarly, internal data show his son is only eight or nine, while in the end Tolstoy makes him a sympathetic boy of thirteen or fourteen. There are other chronological inconsistencies as well. But more important is the structural function of the first chapter. Critics unaware that the story was originally planned as a first-person narrative have confidently asserted that the funeral comes first so that Tolstoy can show that the other people are just like Ivan Ilych.[21] There is some truth to this, but the original reason for having the death and funeral first was a much simpler technical one: Tolstoy had to introduce the narrator and have him explain how he got the diary. Sending him to the funeral where Praskovia Fedorovna has some specific business with him was the logical way. All of this was a structural and plot necessity. In the final version Praskovia Fedorovna's "business" with Peter Ivanovich is the discussion of the pension—which is hardly essential for the development of the story, or even for characterization.

It is somewhat embarrassing to discuss the "ideas" in the story, since Tolstoy usually took great pains to make everything clear. However, here as in other works by Tolstoy the critical moment—death in this case—is a little ambiguous. To explain the moment of conversion, the moment when one "sees the light," Tolstoy often had recourse to delirium or dreams—such as Andrei's dream in *War and Peace* or the dreams in *The Confession*, "Father Sergius," or "Master and Man." Andrei's dream—where he dies at the moment he wakes up—is closest to Ivan Ilych's case. As Ivan Ilych dies he says, "Death is over." This reversal in meaning, this paradox, is the most important one in the story: joys are not joys, pleasantness and decorum are unpleasantness and indecorum, and finally, life is death. If we consider the hero's own words, the title of the story has two meanings. It refers to his physical death, but Ivan Ilych's *life* itself is the real death. (The story could as well be entitled "The Life of Ivan Ilych"—*Zhitie Ivana Il'icha*, to match the hagiography it in some ways echoes.) When his life of falsehood ends, death is over.

It is clear to the reader what is wrong (*ne to*) with Ivan Ilych's life. But what is the right thing? Judging by the last chapter, the most important thing is *pity*. Here as in the rest of the story, love is not mentioned. Ivan Ilych feels sorry (*zhalko*) for his family; he wants to stop tormenting them. Like Dostoevsky's ridiculous man, pity leads Ivan Ilych out of the horrible black bag to philosophical light. The darkness that Ivan Ilych sees in death when he is sick (see especially the incident with the candle, and the remarks that he no longer has light in his eyes) is reversed in the end. Up until this point religion has hardly been mentioned in the story (except for the fact that Ivan Ilych had prosecuted Old Believers), but now there is a reference to the "one who will understand." If we recall Ivan Ilych's cry to God (chapter nine), "Why hast Thou done all this?"—and combine it with the paradox of the last two paragraphs, the implication may be that there is life after physical death, but at this point Tolstoy left the story ambiguous. This might be compared to "Master and Man" where there is an actual vision of Christ, and the story ends with a direct address to the reader: "Whether he [Nikita] is better or worse off there when he awoke after his death, whether he was disappointed or found there what he expected, we shall all soon learn."

"The Red Flower"

"THE RED FLOWER" is not the worst story in this collection, but Garshin is undoubtedly the least important writer represented here. A series of deaths, conversions, and silent declines ended the Golden Age of fiction at the beginning of the 1880's, and the decade is correctly considered a bleak one in the history of Russian literature. It was Garshin's fortune—and misfortune—to be the best of the second-raters. He wrote little, and most of his work is not very inventive; plots, devices, and character names are repeated rather monotonously. As for Garshin himself, he was an unhappy and unstable man. Pathologically sensitive to evil, his own stays in mental hospitals provided him with most of the material for "The Red Flower." Here as in several other stories, the tragedy of empty sacrifice is a central theme.

Garshin said he invented only the end of the story, and the description of the hero's mania drew praise from professionals for its almost clinical accuracy. There are elements of paranoia and megalomania in the hero's madness. He sees himself as a Christ-figure, partly because of a chain of associations including the color of the flowers, red blood, the red crosses on the hat he wears, and the fact that there are *three* flowers, one of which has special significance. He plans to absorb all of the world's evil in his own body and then die—taking the sins of mankind on himself. He succeeds in his design and dies happily, but this, as the reader knows, will have no effect on mankind or the evil in the world. Garshin leaves his sacrificial madman nameless, suggesting that he stands for many people—that his vain act is repeated in many forms.

The story is written in clear but colorless Russian. Mimicking the feverish pacing of the hero, the style is somewhat "nervous." Tense scenes are usually followed by periods of lucid calm. In general the pace of the story is rapid. Considering the emotion-charged subject matter, and its melodramatic potential, Garshin shows considerable restraint. He even avoids the heavy didacticism characteristic of other Russian stories (such as Chekhov's "Ward No. 6") about insane asylums. The narrator's simulated detachment holds up through most of the story. In the end, however, the dead man's steely grasp on the flower, which then has to be buried with him, is a conventional melodramatic touch the emotional impact of which Garshin seems to have miscalculated.

"Makar's Dream"

KOROLENKO'S BEST WORK is his autobiographical trilogy *The History of My Contemporary*. But the grandfatherly dispassion which makes his autobiography a delight evirates most of his fiction. After translating the story, I am disinclined to make "Makar's Dream" an exception, but for some tastes there may be "mighty poetry" in the story, as D. S. Mirsky suggests. Originally, Makar's dream was a real dream—comparable to "The Dream of a Ridiculous Man" or the original version of Gogol's "The Nose." At the point where it now ends, Makar woke up, went out, and was met by the same series of hardships and torments he had always known. This would have weakened the poetry of the ending in favor of direct social comment. Even as it is, there is no doubt that the story belongs in the philanthropic tradition. Makar is one of the many "little men" of Russian literature. His name itself is symbolic—it is that of an unfortunate peasant in several proverbs. This Makar drives his calves measureless distances; all "acorns" and woes fall upon his head.

The populist literature of the 1880s and 1890s was often burdened with ethnography. The local color of the romantics degenerated into dull *ocherki* (sketches) describing the customs and surroundings of various social types from the lower classes. Korolenko uses his ethnographic detail much more artistically than most of these writers. The presentation of Makar's character governs the use of such material; only that which is essential for understanding Makar is introduced. As Korolenko discovered when he was a political exile to Siberia, the naïve mixture of Christianity and pagan beliefs was one of the amusing aspects of Yakut culture. For example, like a Siberian, Toyon lives in a hut with a fire burning all the time. And we at once laugh at and pity Makar when he tries to use simple Yakut trickery on Toyon—not yet realizing you can't con God. Makar's naïve view of the world at times affects the narration itself, as when Korolneko writes: "Everyone felt sorry for kind Father Ivan; but since all that was left of him were his legs, no doctor in the world could cure him." But in the end Makar's naïveté and meek acceptance of hardship fall away. Korolenko has not presented a Christian moral. Makar is not saved by humility; it is only when he gets angry that injustice is adverted. God is not an altogether sympathetic character, and even his son (recall it is a "Christmas story") is somewhat ineffectual.

Korolenko's style is in the tradition of Turgenev. The descriptions of the taiga are written in lyrical prose marked by "poetic" inversions and frequent use of personification. For example: "Bright, kind stars peeped through the thick branches and seemed to be saying: 'There, you see, a poor man has died.' " Nature comes alive, especially when Makar is drunk and delirious. In the old Karamzinian manner, the emotional involvement of the narrator is shown by rhetorical questions or exclamations such as: "Heavy is the work of a man from Chalgan!" At the end of chapter five, the series of exclamatory single-sentence paragraphs, with the incantatory repetition of "and" (polysyndeton), changes the tone from lyric to triumphant. This section and the ending are the most heavily rhetorical passages in the story. Perhaps it is just twentieth-century criticism that makes such writing seem overly sentimental, but even Chekhov said, "The trouble with Korolenko is that he will never write better unless he deceives his wife. He is too noble."

"Heartache"

READING CHEKHOV'S EARLY STORIES is something like reading the young Lermontov's poems—among dozens of bad works one occasionally comes upon an angel or a sail. "Heartache," published in the *Petersburg Newspaper* (January, 1886), is one of these. Chekhov's temperament and editorial mandate led him to discover the virtues of brevity. The two word "non-sentence" which begins "Heartache" is characteristic; often his stories open with one word or phrase which sets the time or day and/or place. His sentences are short. He uses metaphor and simile with restraint—sometimes to add a lyric touch, sometimes to tinge a description with humor (the gingerbread horse). As he revised this story, he removed literary polysyllables and foreign words (e. g. *tradicija, neobxodimost'*— tradition and essentiality), replacing them with simple, colloquial words (*privychka, nuzhda*—habit, need). In some respects Chekhov resembles Pushkin, but his prose does not have the cold, crisp, slightly archaic quality we see in Pushkin. Chekhov is less dynamic, but softer and more supple.

Economy of means can be seen in a structural device which Chekhov uses in "Heartache" and many of his other stories, including "The Darling." The device is to take one "block" of material, one scene or sequence of events, and to repeat it two or three times. Simply by altering a few key details in the repeats of the scene Chekhov can convey or symbolize changes in a character.[22] Or, once the pattern is established and the reader's expectations controlled, he can spring a surprise—introduce an unexpected element in the last part of the series. "Heartache" opens with a description of Iona and the horse motionless in the snow, a fare gets in, Iona is unsuccessful in communicating his grief. Again Iona becomes motionless, snow—a symbol of isolation—covers him and the horse, again fares get in, a variation on his attempt to communicate is played, again he fails. Again he and the horse become motionless—but this time they start up to return to the stable, where Iona makes another attempt and again fails. We are surprised, in the end, by the way the pattern is broken.

The opening paragraph foreshadows the closing one. Iona and his horse are seen together all through the story—in the beginning both are vaguely unreal (Iona like a ghost, the horse like a cookie) and both are sunk in thought. Each time they move, both stretch out their necks—one of the repeated details. Finally, the only character in the story who is as lonely and sad as Iona is his horse. Chekhov's remark in the first paragraph that "in all probability" the horse is thinking about being torn away from the country suggests that Iona is responsible for the unhappiness of the very creature with whom he finds solace. And, as so often in Chekhov, the solace is illusory.

It should be noted that the story is told entirely in the present tense. Present tense narration is popular nowadays, especially in French literature, but it is extremely rare in Russian literature, and this story is probably one of the very first examples. Chekhov also practiced this innovation in "Gusev" and, I imagine, other stories. The obvious advantage is that it gives a feeling of immediate vision. It imitates the camera eye roving around and seeing things at the very moment they happen.[23]

"Anna on the Neck"

THE PARODISTIC ELEMENTS in this story put it in the tradition of "The Station Master." Like Pushkin, Chekhov turns a platitude inside out. When the poor girl marries for money, she does not come to ruin. Adultery, so far as we know, leads to happiness. The story is a parody of *Anna Karenina*. The heroines' names are identical. Both are constrained to marry older men—Modest Alexeich and Alexei Aleksandrovich. Both husbands are wealthy and, for the respective social circles, highly-placed government functionaries. Karenin's escape into religiosity is echoed in Modest Alexich's verbal adherence to "principles" and religion—including the grotesque honeymoon visit to a monastery. Anna Karenina's meeting (early in the novel) with Vronsky at the railroad station is doubled when (early in the story) Chekhov's Anna encounters Artynov in a railroad station scene. The ball scene where electricity first passes between Vronsky and an all-conquering Anna is echoed in Chekhov's ball scene where Anna flirts with Artynov and undergoes a triumphal emancipation. The parody is apparent not only in Chekhov's ironic twist of the ending, but in small details such as those used to undercut the status of Artynov as rakish lover—Chekhov makes him an Armenian, and gives him asthma and a ridiculous red cloak. Modest Alexeich, who claims to put religion and morality first, meekly submits to his young wife's dissolute behavior because she gains influence with his superior.

Of course, the story is more than a parody. The theme of poverty is one of the complications Chekhov introduces. If there were no description of Anna's family, the reader would have much less ambiguous feelings at the end of the story. If Anna were alone in the world, we would be on her side; Modest Alexeich is physically and morally repugnant—Anna is what he deserves. Because her father's misfortunes stem mainly from his own weakness, even his presence would not be enough to complicate our reaction; but the two boys suffer in innocence, and their pitiful cries, repeated three times, force us to have more ambiguous feelings toward Anna's triumph. Their cries serve the moral function of the hammer knocking on the door which Burkin mentions in "Gooseberries." The careful wedding of the theme of poverty with the theme of selfishness and adultery is characteristic of Chekhov's craftsmanship.

Chekhov is the first Russian after Pushkin to write stories which give a sense of everything in its place. At the end of a story by Turgenev and Dostoevsky, one may feel that the different thematic threads were hastily stuck together with bailing wire and scotch tape—but in stories like "Anna on the Neck," Chekhov brings everything together as tightly as a zipper.

Chekhov is often called an "objective" writer. Critics say that he does not preach, that he does not tell the readers what to think, that he merely poses questions without giving answers. This is true only in a limited sense. He does not moralize like a Tolstoyan. He does create ambivalent pictures of *some* characters. For example, we sympathize with Anna for the humiliation and terror she experiences as a young girl; but her petty-bourgeoise imitations of coquetry (the "screwing up of the eyes" so well known to readers of Russian literature, the pronouncing of "r" like "l," etc.) are as unpleasant as Modest's jelly-like jowls. So in spite of some good points, Anna is never an attractive character. In most of Chekhov's stories one has no difficulty telling the negative characters from the positive ones. By the end of the story the position of the author has been made fairly clear. Every writer must make an incredibly complicated series of choices for each sentence he sets down, and constant evaluation is implicit in this process of selection. Modest Alexeich is a good example of Chekhov's "non-objective" character portraits. Every physical detail is chosen to make us loathe him—his puffy face with its small eyes, wet lips and "chin resembling a heel." His stinginess and gluttony are mentioned tersely—but repeatedly. This is typical of Chekhov's kind of indirect comment: "And holding a knife in his hand like a sword, he would say: 'Every person must have his responsibilities!' " The "objective" writer has structured his reader's response with the simile. Chekhov prejudices the case with many of his main characters and virtually all of his minor ones. Thus, for his excellency's wife he uses a grotesque simile: "it seemed as if she were holding a big stone in her mouth." And then, in the Gogolian manner, he realizes the metaphor (by dropping the "as"): "the middle-aged lady with the stone in her mouth." The wives of the civil servants are described simply as "ugly, tastelessly dressed, and as coarse as cooks." In fact, the "even" in the opening sentence of the story shows that the narrator is not objective: "There was not even a light snack after the ceremony . . ." The "even" is unnecessary, except for the narrator to show that he is amazed by Modest Alexeich's stinginess and wishes the reader to react the same way.

There is no excess material in the story. Each detail counts. For example, Anna's wedding makes her think of her mother's funeral; and then, as if the internal chain of associations affects the narrator, Artynov's cloak is described as dragging on the ground "like a bridal train." The shame of poverty is originally related just to Anna's family, but it is repeated, without fanfare, by having her triumph at a charity ball where his excellency says: " 'This luxurious dining room is an appropriate place to drink to the success of those poor dining rooms . . ." Chekhov knows his readers will not be as obt~ as his characters. Economy of means can also be seen in th~ of the leitmotif for characterization—a physical or verbal t~ is repeated each time a character appears. Thus, hi~

chews his lips each time he sees a pretty woman. The suggestions of lust and gluttony are conveyed by a single prejudicial detail.

"Gooseberries"

"GOOSEBERRIES" is the middle story in Chekhov's "little trilogy" which was published in 1898 with consecutive pagination from the beginning of "The Man in a Case" to the end of "About Love." The two epigraphs Chekhov considered using suggest the trilogy's thematic unity: "But how many of those in cases remain" and "Man needs more than six feet—he needs the whole universe." The latter is aimed at Tolstoy's story "How Much Land Does a Man Need," which concludes that the six feet of the grave are all man could or should expect. Death was a philosophical *idée fixe* for Tolstoy, but the gloomy, ascetic penchant for measuring life against death was alien to the unromantic Dr. Chekhov. Regarding the afterlife as dubious as unicorns or elves, he thought we should make the most of the life we have—life should be measured by life. It seems reasonable to consider Ivan Ivanych as Chekhov's puppet; most of what he says corresponds to the Chekhov we know from his letters. Note that Ivan Ivanych is a medical man, and both in stories and plays Chekhov often made physicians unofficial spokesmen. Ivan is more verbose than most of these, and because of this, the story is more openly didactic than is typical for Chekhov. Since he himself was the grandson of a serf and went through the long process of picking out an estate and settling down as a landowner, we may assume there are a few autobiographical demons which Chekhov was exorcising by writing the story.

Characters who are afraid of life or who narrowly circumscribe the limits of their life appear in many of Chekhov's tales, but Belikov, his man in a case, is the archetype. He smiles only when he is in his final case, a coffin. This is the first story of the trilogy; it is narrated by Burkin when he and Ivan Ivanych are out hunting. "Gooseberries" is Ivan Ivanych's reply. Alyokhin tells Burkin and Ivan Ivanych the last story—the story of how, due to over-analysis and timidity, he failed to get together with the woman he loved. Two details in "Gooseberries" foreshadow Alyokhin's story: (1)

the pictures of the generals and ladies (two references to which "frame" Ivan Ivanych's story) look down as if saying it is tedious to hear about a poor clerk who ate gooseberries, so that Burkin and Alyokhin "For some reason wanted to speak and hear about elegant people, about women." (2) the brief but repeated description of "beautiful Pelageya"—the triple repetition of the same adjective is a typically Chekhovian device—who moves softly and efficiently about Alyokhin's house. At the beginning of Alyokhin's story we learn she is not, as we might suspect, his mistress; she is unreservedly in love with an ugly, drunken cook who beats her.

In the drafts, Ivan Ivanych's story about gooseberries ends differently. Originally, his brother comes to realize that what he has achieved is a caricature of his petty dreams. He knows the gooseberries taste bad, and eventually dies with the bitter taste of his life in his mouth. But Chekhov apparently decided that Peter Ivanych's self-revelation and death would not affect readers as much as his smug satisfaction with an illusion. The brick factory, coffee-colored river, servant resembling a pig, dog resembling a pig, etc., make it clear how illusory Peter Ivanych's accomplishment is. The gooseberries perfectly symbolize his trivial aspirations.

The last line of the story is Chekhovianly compendious. It refers back to the opening paragraph and serves as a kind of deflection. The bad smell of Ivan Ivanych's pipe would not be a good final impression for the reader. The rain helps remove the bad air, and at the same time it is a natural symbol for insomnia, pensiveness, and misfortune—perhaps echoing the knocks of the hammer on the door of happy people.

"The Darling"

IN "THE DARLING" Chekhov again uses one of his favorite structural devices: a single situation, repeated three times, is the basic building block. But after the pattern is set, the reader is fooled by an unanticipated change in direction. Olenka, a quiet, goodhearted woman with a loving heart and "naïve smile," meets Kukin, the manager of the Tivoli. He proposes. After the marriage they live well, but have no children. She repeats all of his opinions. But he dies and she laments, "Oh, my dove . . . Why did we ever meet." Three months later she meets the lumber agent Pustovalov. And having married, they "live well," but they are childless. She repeats all of his opinions and jargon. But he dies too, and Olenka repeats the same lament. When she begins repeating the veterinarian's opinions (Chekhov carefully introduces him in section number two), it appears the pattern will soon be repeated. The reversal comes when Smirnin goes away, then unexpectedly returns after several years, and Olenka falls in love not with him but with his son Sasha. Her naïve smile reappears, her long dormant motherly feelings flourish, and in the end she is happily suffocating Sasha. His threats, in the last paragraph, end the story on a strange discordant note which is apparently a comment on her mindless bliss.

While the repetitions are obvious enough to be unmistakable (indeed perhaps they are too obvious),[24] even in the second sequence Chekhov introduces variations partly designed to keep the story from seeming schematized. For example, the darling's dream is a new device; Pustovalov's world dominates even her nocturnal fantasies.

As usual, Chekhov characterizes both by physical description (which in the case of minor characters is limited to a few caricaturistic details) and by psychological description. The latter is given in the traditional manner by a faceless omniscient narrator:[25] "She was constantly in love with someone, and could not live otherwise." The language of the characters is individualized, Olenka adjusts her speech to her environment; she is like an empty glass that becomes the color of whatever is poured into it. Chekhov is a master at choosing a small phrase or gesture which conveys the whole personality of a character. Thus Kukin is happy to get married, "but since it rained on the day of the wedding, and on that night too, the expression of despair did not leave his face." The leitmotif is used again—Olenka's "naïve smile" and repeated phrases. Names are also important. In Russian Kukin suggests "fig" or "cuckoo"; Pustovalov means "empty wave."

"The Darling" was one of Tolstoy's favorite short stories; he delighted in reading it aloud, and reprinted it in A Circle of Reading, a collection of moralistic items which he edited. Tolstoy's interpretation of the story was characteristic. He said that in Olenka Chekhov wanted to show what a woman should not be—because

Chekhov had newfangled notions about feminine intellect, equality, and emancipation. But "the god of poetry prevented him and ordered him to bless her." Olya, said Tolstoy, comes out not ridiculous, but "holy," a model of what a woman can be for her own happiness and the happiness of others. However, it appears that the god of poetry was insufficiently stern, because in order to make his interpretation fit more comfortably, Tolstoy excised various details which throw negative light on Olya and her husbands.

"Chelkash"

GORKY BEGAN HIS CAREER in 1892 when Chekhov was already fairly well known. "Chelkash" (1894) was the first of Gorky's stories to be published in a "thick journal." The contrast between Chekhov and Gorky somewhat resembles that between Pushkin and Gogol, but there are quantitative and qualitative differences. We again have the phenomenon of two important writers working simultaneously in widely divergent styles. If Chekhov can safely be oversimplified as the short-winded singer of "twilight Russia" whose favorite theme is the inability to communicate, and whose favorite characters are weak, ineffectual, vaguely unhappy members of the intelligentsia—Gorky might be called the singer of dawning Russia, whose favorite theme is the struggle between pride and pity, and whose favorite characters are strong, energetic, independent representatives of the lower classes. While Chekhov's heroes mope around their cherry orchards and houses with mezzanines, Gorky's tramp from the mountains of Tiflis to the flophouses of Petersburg.

Chelkash is archetypically Gorkian. His character is revealed primarily through the time-honored device of contrast. Gavrila is an almost unnecessary accessory to the crime, but he is essential for purposes of characterization. The peasant background of Chelkash and Gavrila is identical, and they both speak of the value of freedom; but there the similarities end. It is Gavrila's lack of self-respect which most enrages Chelkash. Gavrila's greed for money is a function of this deficiency. Greed might conceivably be forgiven, but a man who begs for pity can only be scorned.

Gavrila's repeated remarks on religion are also an important negative feature of his character. When he is frightened or insecure, he immediately falls back on religion. He asks Chelkash "in the name of Christ" to let him out of the boat, promises to pray for him in return for all the money, and when he returns after throwing the rock, he says "the devil made me do it." Chelkash, who at first likes Gavrila and feels fatherly toward him, is offended by Gavrila's cowardice (especially his fear of the sea), and in the end his grand gesture is an insult. Only at one point does Chelkash himself break down—by indulging in nostalgia for the past. But there is no real freedom when one is tied to the land, so Chelkash quickly reproaches himself. He has to remain the cat, the stylized hawk which Gorky makes him in a repeated simile.[26] The hawk is his symbol, the sea his element.

Although we are all stuck with them, "romanticism" and "realism" are amoebic terms which do little to refine our understanding or appreciation of literature—especially when they mate and generate monsters such as "romantic realism," "realistic romanticism," "reactionary romanticism," or "revolutionary romanticism." Ordinarily, Gorky is seen as partly "romantic," partly "realistic." This is true—if the two can be separated—both in subject matter and in style. The dialogue in "Chelkash" is a realistic imitation of colloquial Russian. Gorky had both the background and the ear to provide this individualized speech of peasants, workmen, or thieves. The narrative passages, however, tend to be romantic—especially the long descriptions of setting and nature. Indeed, the opening scene and the description of the sea are as floridly written as anything published in the 1830s. One might call Gorky a working-class Marlinsky. Gorky's personification of the sea, his heavy use of metaphor, premonitory clouds and waves, sharp contrasts, hyperbolic images, and synathrismus[27] all combine to duplicate the Marlinsky style popular in Pushkin's day.[28] Gorky writes:

> He, a thief, loved the sea. His nervous, restive nature, always thirsting for new impressions, never had enough of contemplating its dark expanses, so free, so powerful, so boundless.

This could easily be mistaken (in Russian) for a passage from *Ammalat Bek* or any of Marlinsky's other stories about Caucasian super-mountaineers. In character, too, Chelkash would feel quite at home with those picturesque, heroic figures. Because subject matter and style are attuned, "Chelkash" succeeds; but many of Gorky's other works fail when the romantic-realistic ambitendency results in the kind of literary schizophrenia which later developed into socialist realism.

"*The Garnet Bracelet*"

KUPRIN, like Garshin, may be classified among the competent second-rate writers of Russian literature. But quantitatively he is more important than Garshin. His two "exposé" novels *The Duel* and *The Pit* are well known. His numerous stories cover a wide range of social backgrounds and character types, and it is difficult to say what is "typical." While he has many stories marked by complex plots and sensationalism, he also has a lyrical, sentimental strain exemplified by stories such as "Olesya" (made into a fine French movie) and "The Garnet Bracelet" (1911).

"The Garnet Bracelet" seems a very old-fashioned story now, especially when we consider that the innovations of modernists like Andreev and symbolists like Bely antedate its writing. Straight-forward chronology and unity of setting help make the story a neatly-constructed one, but the only real example of technical aplomb is the way the *Vorgeschichte* of Vera's relation to Zheltkov is introduced—as a joking story by Vasily Lvovich. His version (" 'At last he died, but before his death he willed Vera two telegraph-office buttons and a perfume bottle filled with his tears.' ") ends chapter six and foreshadows, parodistically, the true death and Vera's visit at the end of chapter twelve.

In general the characters are convincingly drawn, particularly Anosov, the conventional, faithful army officer who has many literary forebears, beginning with Pushkin's Captain Mironov. The juxtaposition of Vera and Anna is successful in bringing out their differences in character. Like all of Kuprin's tools for characterization, this one was a standard device of Russian realism.

At its best Kuprin's style is commonplace. His nature descriptions are ponderous, and even where they are supposed to be portentous they seem irrelevant. The physical portraits he gives of the main characters also seem clumsy—weighted down by strings of adjectives wrapped around strings of participles. As for Kuprin's metaphor, an example will suffice: "The other flowers, whose season of luxurious love and overfruitful maternity was over, were quietly dropping innumerable seeds of future life." One of the main faults of the story is this kind of verbosity. One can imagine what Chekhov would have done with it.

It takes some talent to adapt an inherently tragic story from real life and make it seem so falsely sentimental. Kuprin succeeds in this. His clumsy lyricism and the pitiful way he presents Zheltkov result only in what might be called a "pathegedy." Nevertheless, the story stands as a fair example of Kuprin's work and the doldrums of conventional Russian prose fiction during the first years of this century.

"The Gentleman from San Francisco"

THE FACT THAT WE NEVER LEARN the name of the gentleman from San Francisco—nor his wife's name, nor his daughter's—suggests the basic difference in orientation between Bunin's story and "The Death of Ivan Ilych." While the two works share the themes of vanity, spiritual isolation, and death, Tolstoy focuses on the *change* which his hero undergoes. Enlightenment comes to Ivan Ilych and he breaks through the black bag, but for the gentleman from San Francisco there is no revelation—he remains in his black box in the bowels of the "Atlantic." Tolstoy makes us feel Ivan Ilych's growing pain, and by the time he learns to feel pity for others, we have come to pity him. Bunin is more pessimistic.[29] He wrote:

> "Woe unto thee, Babylon!" These terrible words of the Apocalypse kept persistently ringing in my soul when I was writing "The Brothers" and conceived "The Gentleman from San Francisco," only a few months before the war, when I had a presentiment of . . . the abysses which have since been revealed in our present-day civilization.

World War One and the Russian Revolution showed that the Biblical warning was still relevant; the new Babylon was falling.

The surface themes in Bunin's story present no difficulty for the reader. At this level it seems we have a simple attack on the vanity of wealth and power by another Russian didact. But the careful reader may also be haunted by a feeling that the story has hidden depth and density. There is a wealth of detail, allusion, and symbol which gives the work this disturbing resonance. Critics have failed to provide an explanation of the, as it were, *inner* structure of the story—the allusions and imagery.[30]

I think the key to the inner sanctum of the story is in the allusion to Tiberius. Let us ask a simple question: Why did Bunin choose to set the story on Capri? There are any number of fashionable tourist spots that would have served the same purpose. Only one thing distinguishes Capri from all the rest—it was the residence of Tiberius Claudius Nero. Recall how Bunin introduces the allusion:

> On that island, two thousand years ago, there lived a man who got hopelessly entangled in his foul and cruel deeds, who for some reason rose to power over millions of people and who, losing his head from the senselessness of this power and from his fear that someone might thrust a knife into his back, committed atrocities beyond all measure. And mankind remembered him forever, and those who with combined effort are now ruling the world with as little reason and, on the whole, with as much cruelty as he did, come here from all over the world to take a look at the remains of the stone house on one of the sheerest sides of the island, where he used to live.

Why did Bunin choose Tiberius? Tiberius retired to Capri, neglected affairs of state (including incursions by the barbarians), and devoted himself to relaxed debauchery. He drank so much he was nicknamed Biberius, and he kept a house of adepts in perverse sexual practices. He was miserly and often refused to pay his staff. Above all, he was cruel—there were executions every day, and as Suetonius writes: "In Capri they still show the place at the cliff top where Tiberius used to watch his victims being thrown into the sea after prolonged and exquisite tortures." Finally, it should be remembered that Pontius Pilate was the officer of Tiberius when Christ was crucified.

The gentleman from San Francisco is a cruel representative of power too, but he is a smaller, shabbier version. He too retires from affairs to indulge himself, he has plans for debauchery with

Neopolitan prostitutes, he rules an empire of coolies, he gives beggars nothing, and he too indulges in gluttony. Most important, his world is a *pagan* world just as Tiberius's was. And this leads to some of the other images in the story that have never been explained: the pagan idol, the "Atlantis," the pagan gong, the "Descent from the Cross," and the statue of Mary. These make little sense unless connected to the allusion to Tiberius. The gentleman's paganism is suggested by his itinerary; he plans to put Easter in Rome in between roulette at Monte Carlo and bull-fights in Spain. He is bored with all the paintings entitled "Descent from the Cross" (Remember who was Caesar when Christ was crucified.) His daughter dreams of marrying the ugly oriental (pagan) prince. The gentleman himself is described as having somewhat Mongolian features. The "Atlantis" is a symbol for the pagan world of all the gentlemen from San Francisco.[31] It protects the man from the fierce black waves, its siren blows "hellishly," and its captain looks like "a huge idol," "like a merciful pagan god," "like a pagan idol." The ship was made by the New Man (i. e. from the New World) with the old heart (the heart of a pagan ruler, a Tiberius). It takes the gentleman past the "Devil" (at Gibraltar) into the Old World— to the hotel on Tiberius's mountain where the gong, which calls the gentlemen and gentlewomen to eat, rings "sonorously as in a pagan temple." This whole symbolic system is contrasted to Christian symbols. In his article, Gross notes only the second passage on the Abruzzians:

> There . . . stood the Mother of God, bathed in sunlight, warmth and brilliance, clad in snow-white plaster robes, wearing the crown of a queen . . . with eyes raised heavenward to the eternal and blissful abode of Her thrice blessed Son. They bared their heads and raised their flutes to their lips—and praises poured forth, naïve and humbly joyous, to the sun, to the morning, and to Her, the Immaculate Intercessor for all the suffering in this wicked and beautiful world, and to the One who had been born of Her womb in a cave at Bethlehem, in the poor shepherds' shelter, in the far land of Judea.

But the *first* reference to the pipers is crucial, because it sets the time when the story takes place. The gentleman and his wife planned to leave Capri only after they:

. . . had trod the stones where once the palaces of Tiberius stood, visited the fabulous caves of the Azure Grotto, and listened to the Abruzzian pipers who, during the month before Christmas, roamed the island singing praises to the Virgin Mary.

In other words, the gentleman dies near the anniversary of the birth of Christ—whom Tiberius put to death. The point is that under Tiberius, Rome—the second Babylon—was already falling. This suggests that the Babylon of the gentleman from San Francisco will soon fall too.[32] The allusions to the birth and death of Christ are intended to combine with the epigraph ("Alas, alas, Babylon, the mighty city!") and make us re-read the *Book of Revelation*. I will quote only a few verses from Christ's revelation to St. John the Divine:

And he cried mightily with a strong voice, saying, Babylon the great is fallen, is fallen, and is become the habitation of devils, and the hold of every foul spirit, and a cage of every unclean and hateful bird. (ii)

For all nations have drunk of the wine of the wrath of her fornication, and the kings of the earth have committed fornication with her, and the merchants of the earth are waxed rich through the abundance of her delicacies. (iii)

And the merchants of the earth shall weep and mourn over her; for no man buyeth their merchandise any more. (xi)

The shipmasters and sailors watch the city burning:

And they cast dust on their heads, and cried, weeping and wailing, saying, Alas, alas, the great city, wherein were made rich all that had ships in the sea by reason of her costliness! for in one hour is she made desolate. (xix)

The resonance of Bunin's story can only be appreciated by reading it in conjunction with Chapter Eighteen of *Revelation*. It appears that the sense of solidity, of "thickness" that one gets from "The Gentleman from San Francisco" is partly the result of Bunin's careful weighing of each allusion and metaphor for complex associative values.

The structure of the story is symmetrical. It is based on the man's journey: across the black storm of the Atlantic (the lights of the ship emphasized), through the Straits of Gibraltar into the sunny Mediterranean (*Sredizemnoe* in Russian, a literal translation), to Italy and Capri, up the mountain to the *royal* suite (another parallel with Tiberius) of the hotel. This sequence is reversed when he dies: he is now in the worst room, goes down the mountain in a soda-water box, and is put in the lowest circle ("ninth circle"— an allusion to Dante's *Inferno*) of the ship, and in this hell, with the ship's sirens wailing and the windows above glowing like fiery eyes, the gentleman is carried through Gibraltar back into the black storm. Within the overall symmetry provided by the journey, there are many parallel scenes and details—from the lovers hired by Lloyd's of London to the two scenes played by Luigi.

Bunin's style gives an impression of being sculptured. It is the prose of a student of Tolstoy who also happens to be—as Bunin was —a good poet. The opening paragraphs provide excellent examples of the way a good writer adjusts style to content. To infect the reader with the boring conventionality of the gentleman's route and shipboard routine, Bunin presents the itinerary and the schedule in slow periodic sentences which stretch out over two hundred words. These are filled with polysyndetons and catalogues—sometimes made up of incongruous elements: *i fason smokingov, i prochnost' tronov, i ob'javlenie vojn, i blagosostojanie otelej* ("the latest cut of dinner jackets, the stability of thrones, the declaration of wars, and the welfare of hotels"). In addition to geographical names, there are dozens of foreign words in these opening paragraphs. This is not just a matter of cosmopolitan coloration—it is meant to make the Russian reader sick of these things. For the Russian intelligentsia *komfortabel'nyj* (comfortable) has connotations of white-handed, leech-like, Western, bourgeois comfort. When Bunin heaps together words such as *otel', ruletka, flirt, bar, flanelevye pizhami, kofe, shokolad, kakao, tualety, appetit, sheffl'-bord, buterbrod, bul'on* and *longshez*, the effect—especially in context—is to make the reader feel revulsion. Nowhere else in the story are these foreign words used nearly so frequently. The device of the "boring" periodic sentence is used once more—the three hundred-word description of tourist routine in Naples.

Like Tolstoy, Bunin stands above everything, explaining and evaluating. The "epic" narrator reveals all hidden motives. Characters themselves have little opportunity to say anything directly; note that there is virtually no dialogue to interrupt the smooth, rich flow of narration. Bunin's descriptive abilities are varied. The story contains heavily symbolic premonitory description (the ship, the ocean), poetic nature description (a wave like a peacock's tail), and realistic physical portraits (the description of the heart attack, with the gold teeth flashing). Bunin seems to handle all of these with equal skill.

NOTES

1. Note that the dishonest doctor is German, and that there are suitable German platitudes under each of the pictures.

2. Abram Lezhnev, *Proza Pushkina* (M. 1966), p. 78.

3. It should be noted that Gogol's first stories appeared a month before Pushkin's first tales, so there is no comforting evolution from simplicity to complexity in the literary language. Pushkin and Gogol are simultaneous occurrences—as unnatural as would be the simultaneous evolution of the serpent and the platypus. The Formalist terms "canonization" and "de-canonization" are inapplicable.

4. All of Belinsky's brief references to "The Overcoat" occur in lists of Gogol's stories. Nevertheless scholars write things such as this: "Belinsky took 'The Overcoat' as a source for the text for his social sermons about the part of humanity deprived of its rights." V. Setchkarev, *Gogol: His Life and Works* (New York, 1965), p. 217.

5. In his "Neskol'ko slov o Gogole" and "Kak proizoshel tip Akakija Akak'evicha," *Legenda o velikom inkvizitore F. M. Dostoevskogo* (St. Petersburg, 1902), pp. 127–46.

6. B. Eichenbaum, "The Structure of Gogol's 'The Overcoat'," *Russian Review*, XXII, pp. 377–99. The essay was written in the twenties.

7. D. Čiževskij, "Zur komposition von Gogols 'Mantel'," *Zeitschrift für slavische Philologie*, XIV (1937), 63–94.

8. He views the entire world the same way the hick does who goes back to the Ozarks saying, "Why they *even* got indoor privies in Memphis."
Against this interpretation of *dazhe* one can argue that almost all of Gogol's narrators either are naïve or feign naïveté (so they all view the world as a marvel), and that verbal alogism is a constant feature of Gogol's style—this includes the frequent use of "even" in other works, especially *Dead Souls*.

9. J. B. Woodward, "The Threadbare Fabric of Gogol's 'Overcoat'," *Canadian Slavic Studies*, I, 1 (1967), 95–105.

10. See for example: I. Ermakov, *Ocherki po analizu tvorchestva Gogolja* (M. 1924) and Leon Stilman, "Gogol's 'Overcoat', Thematic Pattern and Origins," *American Slavic and East European Review*, XI, 1, (1952), 138–48.

11. As Eichenbaum wrote in another context: "I consider the most

important thing in scholarship not the establishment of schemes but the ability to see facts. Theory is essential for this, because it is precisely in its light that facts become visible, i. e. take on the status of real facts. Theories perish or change, whereas the facts discovered and established with their help remain. Therefore, what does it matter if the material does not wholly fit into a scheme—a scheme can never embrace the total multifariousness of the material; what does matter is that things that have remained outside perception, and, so, have not existed for our awareness, become tangible, enter into the sphere of activity of observation." B. Eichenbaum, *Melodika stixa*, quoted in his "O. Henry and the Theory of the Short Story," (Ann Arbor, 1968), p. 35.

12. The Russian "Natural School" should not be confused with French naturalism, with which it has little in common. Bulgarin and Belinsky called Gogol a naturalist. Chernyshevsky said the tradition of "naturalism" begun by Gogol was continued by Turgenev, Goncharov, Tolstoy, and Dostoevsky. But these writers do not really form a cohesive school. V. V. Vinogradov has devoted several studies to Russian naturalism which, as he more clearly defines it, involves: (1) average or below-average men, often inarticulate petty clerks, as heroes (in contrast to the smooth-talking Zvonsky's and Pronsky's of the romantic society tale), (2) detailed, usually insulting descriptions of "bare nature" with emphasis on shabby clothing and grotesque physiognomies, (3) repulsive details like belching, spitting, and stentorian nose-blowing, (4) dirty grey settings and landscapes, (5) humorous and uncomplimentary comparisons of men to animals, (6) schematic presentation of characters, often as paired opposites, (7) dialogue characterized by curses, coarse colloquialisms, alogisms, and awkwardness, (8) a philanthropic attitude on the part of the author. Works which to varying degrees fit this description include those of Dostoevsky before Siberia, some of the early Turgenev and Pisemsky, Herzen's *Who is Guilty*, the works of Grigorovich and other small-fry like Grebenka, Dal, and Butkov.

13. See Hugh McLean, "On the Style of a Leskovian *Skaz*," *Harvard Slavic Studies*, II (1954), 297–323.

14. M. Baxtin, *Problemy poetiki Dostoevskogo* (M. 1963), pp. 197–206.

15. For example, Tatyana's dream in *Eugene Onegin*, a dream within a dream within a dream in Gogol's "Portrait," Grinev's dream in *The Captain's Daughter*, Oblomov's dream, Vera's dreams in *What Is To Be Done*, Andrei's dream in *War and Peace*—and many other crisis dreams or hallucination sequences in Tolstoy. In the Soviet period orthodox writers have tended to avoid such manifestations of irrationality as dreams, but practitioners of the phantasmagoric from Olesha (*Envy*) to Bulgakov (*Master and Margarita*) still invent dreams for a variety of purposes.

16. In Soviet works literary dreams are sometimes used to get around

the censor—just as our personal dreams are disguises designed to circumvent the censor (superego).

17. For example, Raskolnikov plans a reasoned and controlled crime, but his leaping heart betrays him, and only untidy chance covers his clumsy trail of errors. Kirilov, in *The Devils*, plans a calm and philosophical suicide; but Verkhovensky's plot contaminates Kirilov's motive and leads to a final scene full of blood and hysterics. In *The Brothers Karamazov* the prosecutor makes a brilliantly reasoned speech proving that Dmitri killed his father; the defense attorney makes an equally brilliant and logical speech proving that Dmitri did not kill his father—and the reader discovers that all of their logic is empty, simply because Smerdyakov had foreseen it and placed one false clue.

18. The heavy use of words such as *dazhe, sovershenno, nepremenno, stranno*, and especially, *kakoj-to*—as well as tautologies.

19. R. F. Christian, *Tolstoy's "War and Peace"* (Oxford, 1962), pp. 148–52.

20. This obvious juxtaposition is probably the most painful one for the modern reader—Gerasim seems just *too* good, clean, kind, strong, and neat. As for the description of Ivan Ilych's difficulties with the chamber pot (and the earlier comparison of death to breaking wind), Tolstoy obviously considered these necessary to shock the reader; but one is likely to be more shocked at Tolstoy than horrified by Ivan Ilych's plight.

21. See for example, Edward Wasiolek, "Tolstoy's 'The Death of Ivan Ilyich' and Jamesian Fictional Imperatives," *Modern Fiction Studies*, VI, 4 (1960–61), 314–24. This is the only good article in English on the story.

The chronological inconsistencies and variants are discussed by A. P. Grossman in the commentaries to "The Death of Ivan Ilych" in Tolstoy, *Polnoe sobranie sochinenij*, Volume 26 (M. 1936).

22. Chekhov's "Ionych" and "The Black Monk" are other stories where the triple repetition can be found. The device is related to the structure used in fairy tales and jokes. (Pushkin's use of three cards and three nights of gambling in "The Queen of Spades" is another literary example.)

23. The first of Tolstoy's Sevastopol sketches is written in precisely this way. It too is in present tense as Tolstoy mimics the camera of a reporter.

24. For example, when Olya is married to the rather ascetic Pustovalov: " 'Vasechka and I have no time to go to theaters,' she would answer in a dignified way. 'We are working people; we aren't interested in these trifles. What is good about theaters?' " Only the *first* sentence here was really necessary for Chekhov to make his point.

25. For those who think Chekhov is an objective writer, it is worth noting that even this narrator asks an occasional rhetorical question ("Is that what she needs?") or makes an exclamation ("Oh, how

she loves him!")—lapses into the old emotive manner of Karamzin's narrators.

26. After Gorky has used appropriate cat and bird comparisons for Chelkash all through the story, near the end he applies one of each to Gavrila. These seem inappropriate and suggest a certain lack of invention on the part of a beginning writer.

27. "Heaping up" of words which are the same part of speech. *Nagromozhdenie* in Russian.

28. The comparison of Marlinsky and Gorky is meant neither as a joke nor as abuse.

29. Bunin also parallels specific situations from "The Death of Ivan Ilych": the importance of the wife and daughter, the daughter coming to the death-bed with a half-bare bosom (contrast in flesh again), the reaction of other people to death, etc. Luigi could be Bunin's answer to Gerasim.

30. Only one critic has even tried to make sense of the imagery. S. F. Gross takes the reference to the two peasant pipers as the key to the symbolism and concludes: "The frozen prison of insulation and isolation which modern man has erected about himself is . . . the result of his having become insensitive to the mystery of the universe, of his having lost that religious sense of awe which pervades the life of the pipers, and without which communion with man and nature is impossible," ["Nature, Man and God in Bunin's 'The Gentleman from San Francisco'," *Modern Fiction Studies*, VI (2), p. 161.] There is obviously some truth to this, although I feel it is put a bit too "romantically." More important is the fact that Gross does not manage to make the image of the pipers part of a coherent system; he is forced to quote passages from "The Brothers" and other works when there is no evidence for his own generalizations.

31. In ironic contrast to the pious asceticism of its namesake, Saint Francis, at the turn of the century San Francisco was thought of as a symbol of crude materialism.

32. A common interpretation of John's allegory in Chapter 17 of the Book of Revelation has the seven-headed monster which supports the whore Babylon as a symbol for Rome with its seven hills. The entire Apocalypse was written as a prediction of Rome's fall. Of course, San Francisco too is built on seven hills. Presumably, this is one of the main reasons why Bunin chose that city. If we extend the prediction of the Apocalypse to the New World, then its fate is clear.

NIKOLAI KARAMZIN

Poor Liza

P ERHAPS NO ONE WHO LIVES IN MOSCOW knows the environs of the city as well as I, because no one spends as much time in the fields as I, no one wanders about on foot more than I—without plan, without goal—wherever my nose leads me through meadows and groves, across hill and dale. Each summer I find pleasant new places or new beauties in the old ones.

But the most pleasant place for me is the one where the gloomy Gothic towers of Si . . . nov Monastery rise up. Standing on this hill you can see almost all Moscow to the right—the terrible mass of houses and churches which strikes one's eyes in the form of a majestic *amphitheater*: a marvelous picture, especially when the sun is shining on it, when its evening rays burn on the countless golden cupolas, on the countless crosses rising up to the sky! The fluffy, dark-green, flourishing meadows stretch out below, and beyond them, over yellow sands flows the clear river ruffled by the light oars of fishing dories or gurgling under the rudders of heavily-laden barges which sail from the most bountiful areas of the Russian Empire and supply ravenous Moscow with grain. On the other side

Translated by CARL R. PROFFER.

of the river one can see an oak grove beside which numerous herds graze; there, sitting in the shade of the trees, young shepherds sing simple, doleful songs and thus shorten the summer days which are so monotonous for them. A little farther, in the thick green of ancient elms, glitters the goldcapped Danilov Monastery; even farther away, almost on the edge of the horizon, Sparrow Hills look blue. On the left side one can see spacious, grain-covered fields, small woods, three or four hamlets, and in the distance, the village of Kolomensk with its tall castle.

I often go to this place, and I almost always greet spring there; I go to the same place in the gloomy days of autumn to grieve along with nature. The winds howl frightfully against the walls of the deserted monastery, between the graves overgrown with tall grass and through the dark passageways of the cells. There, leaning on the ruins of the tombstones, I heed the dull moan of times which have been swallowed up in the abyss of the past—a moan at which my heart shudders and trembles. Occasionally I enter the cells and imagine the men who lived in them—and pictures! Here I see a gray elder on his knees before a crucifix and praying for the quick removal of his earthly chains, because all pleasures in life have disappeared for him, all of his feelings have died except the feeling of sickness and weakness. Over there—a young monk with a pale face and languishing gaze is looking at the field through the window-grating; he sees joyous birds freely swimming in the sea of air, he sees them and bitter tears pour from his eyes. He is languishing, withering, drying up; and the doleful tolling of the bell heralds his untimely death for me. Occasionally I examine on the portals of this temple representations of the miracles which took place in the monastery: here fish fall from the sky for the nourishment of the inhabitants of the monastery which has been besieged by numerous enemies, there an ikon of the Virgin Mary is setting the enemy into flight. All of this renews in my memory the history of our fatherland, the sad history of those times when the fierce Tatars and Lithuanians plundered the environs of the Russian capital with fire and sword, and when unhappy Moscow, like a defenseless widow, looked to God alone for help in her ferocious calamities.

But most often I am drawn to the walls of Si . . . nov Monastery by the memory of the lamentable fate of Liza, poor Liza. Oh! I love those things which touch my heart and make me shed tears of tender grief!

About a hundred and fifty yards from the monastery wall, by a small birch grove in the middle of a green meadow stands an empty cottage without doors, without windows, without a floor; the roof has long since rotted and caved in. In this cottage thirty years ago lived beautiful, dear Liza with her old mother.

Liza's father was a rather well-to-do settler because he loved work, tilled the land well, and always led a sober life. But soon after his death the wife and daughters were impoverished. The lazy arm of the hired worker worked the field poorly, and the grain stopped growing well. They were forced to rent their land—and for an extremely low rate. Besides this, the poor widow, almost constantly shedding tears over the death of her husband (for even peasant women know how to love!) got weaker day by day and could not work at all. Only Liza—who was fifteen when her father died—only Liza worked day and night, without any mercy for her tender youth, without mercy for her rare beauty; she wove flax, knitted stockings, picked flowers in the spring, and gathered berries in the summer—and she sold them in Moscow. The kind, sensitive old woman, seeing her daughter's tirelessness, often pressed her to her weakly beating heart, called her God's mercy, her provider, and the joy of her old age; and she prayed God that He reward her for all she was doing for her mother. "God gave me hands to work," Liza said, "you fed me with your breast and took care of me when I was a baby; now it is my turn to take care of you. Only stop grieving, stop weeping; our tears will not bring father back to life." But often tender Liza could not hold back her own tears—oh! She remembered that she had a father and that he was no more, but to comfort her mother she attempted to conceal the sadness of her heart and to seem calm and happy. "In the next world, dear Liza," the grieved old woman would answer, "I will stop weeping in the next world. There, they say, everyone will be happy; I surely will be happy when I see your father. Only I don't want to die now—what will happen to you without me? Whom can I leave you to? No, let God arrange a place for you first! Perhaps we'll soon find a good man. Then, blessing you, my dear children, I will cross myself and calmly lie down in the damp earth."

Two years passed after the death of Liza's father. The meadows were covered with flowers and Liza went to Moscow with lilies of the valley. In the street she met a well-dressed young man of pleasant appearance. She showed him the flowers and blushed. "Are you selling these, Miss?" he asked with a smile. "Yes," she answered. "And how much do you want?" —"Five kopecks." —"That's too cheap. Here's a ruble for you." Liza was surprised; she dared to glance up at the young man—she blushed even more and lowering her eyes to the ground, she told him she would not take the ruble. —"Why not?" —"I don't need extra." —"I think that beautiful lilies of the valley picked by the hands of a beautiful girl are worth a ruble. But since you won't take it, here are five kopecks for you. I would like to buy flowers from you all the time; I would like for you to pick them only for me." Liza gave him the flowers, took five kopecks, bowed, and wanted to leave; but the stranger stopped her by the arm. —"Where are you going, Miss?" —"Home." —"And where is your home?" Liza said where she lived—said it and left. The young man did not want to hold her, perhaps because passers-by had begun to stop, look at them, and smirk treacherously.

When she got home Liza told her mother what had happened to her. "You did well not to take the ruble. Perhaps he was some bad man. . . ." —"Oh, no, mother! I don't think so. He had such a kind face, such a voice. . . ." —"Still, Liza, it's better to feed yourself by your own labors and not to take anything free. You still don't know, my dear, how evil men can offend a poor girl! My heart is always in my throat when you go to the city; I always put a candle before the ikon and pray the Lord God for Him to save you from any misfortune and harm." Tears appeared in Liza's eyes; she kissed her mother.

The next day Liza picked the last lilies of the valley and again went to the city with them. Her eyes were quietly looking for something. Many people wanted to buy her flowers, but she answered that they were not for sale, and she looked from one side to the other. Evening fell; she had to return home, and the flowers were thrown into the Moscow River. "No one will possess you!" said Liza, feeling a kind of grief in her heart. The next evening she was sitting by the window, spinning and singing plaintive songs in a soft voice; but suddenly she jumped up and cried out, "Oh!" The young stranger was standing by the window.

"What's wrong?" asked her frightened mother, who was sitting beside her. "Nothing, mama," Liza answered in a timid voice, "I just saw him." —"Who?" —"The man who bought my flowers." The old woman glanced out the window. The young man bowed to her so courteously, with such a pleasant expression, that she could think nothing but good of him. "How do you do, my good old woman!" he said. "I am very tired; would you have some fresh milk?" Obliging Liza, without waiting for her mother's answer, perhaps because she knew it in advance, ran to the storeroom, brought a clean pot covered with a clean wooden plate—she grabbed a glass, washed it, and dried it with a white towel, filled it and handed it through the window, but she herself kept looking at the ground. The stranger drank up—and nectar from the hands of Hebe could not have seemed more tasty to him. Everyone will guess that after this he thanked Liza and thanked her not so much in words as in looks. Meanwhile the good-hearted old woman managed to tell him about her woe and comfort—about her husband's death and the fine qualities of her daughter, about her love of work and tenderness etc. etc. He listened to her attentively, but his eyes were—is it necessary to say where? And Liza, timid Liza was occasionally glancing at the young man; but lightning does not flash and disappear in a cloud as fast as her blue eyes turned to the earth when they met his glance. "I would like," he said to the mother, "for your daughter not to sell her work to anyone except me. Then there will be no reason for her to walk to the city so often, and you will not be forced to part with her. I can drop by on you myself from time to time." At this point joy flashed in Liza's eyes, joy which she wanted vainly to conceal; her cheeks burned like the sunset on a clear summer evening; she looked at her left sleeve and picked at it with her right hand. The old woman willingly accepted this proposition without suspecting any bad intention in it, and she assured the stranger that the cloth that Liza wove and the stockings she knitted were exceptionally good and wore better than any others. It was getting dark, and the young man wanted to leave. "But what is your name, good and kind sir?" asked the old woman. —"My name is Erast," he answered. —"Erast," said Liza softly, "Erast!" She repeated the name five times as if trying to memorize it. Erast said good-bye to them and left. Liza followed him with her eyes, but her mother was sitting in meditation, and then, taking her daughter by the hand, said to her, "Oh, Liza! How kind and good he is! If only your fiancé is like that!" Liza's heart kept fluttering. "Mama! Mama! How could that happen? He's a gentleman, but among the peasants. . . ." Liza did not finish her sentence.

Now the reader should know that this young man, this Erast, was a rather rich nobleman with a decent mind and a good heart, good by nature—but weak and flighty. He led a carefree life, thought only of his own pleasure, sought this in worldly amusements, but often did not find it: he was bored and complained about his fate. At the first meeting Liza's beauty made an impression on his heart. He often read novels and idylls; he had a rather lively imagination and often he transported himself mentally to those times (real or unreal) when, if we are to believe poets, all people wandered carefree across meadows, went swimming in pure springs, they kissed like turtledoves, rested under the roses and myrtle, and passed all their days in happy idleness. It seemed to him that in Liza he had found what his heart had long been seeking. "Nature is calling me into its embrace, to its pure joys," he thought, and he decided—for a while at least—to abandon high society.

Let us turn to Liza. Night fell—the mother blessed her daughter and wished her sweet dreams, but on this occasion her desire was not fulfilled: Liza slept very badly. She imagined the new guest of her soul—the image of Erast—so vividly that she awoke almost every minute, awoke and sighed. Liza got up before the rising of the sun, went to the bank of the Moscow River, sat down on the grass, and feeling despondent, she looked at the white mists which trembled in the air and, rising upwards, left glittering droplets on the green coverlet of nature. Silence reigned everywhere. But soon the rising luminary of the day awakened all creation: groves, hedges came to life, little birds fluttered and began to sing, flowers raised their little heads in order to drink in the life-giving rays of light. But Liza kept sitting despondently. Oh, Liza, Liza! What has happened to you? Until now, waking up with the birds, you were as merry as they were in the morning; and a pure joyous soul shone in your eyes as the sun shines on drops of heavenly dew; but now you are pensive, and the general joy of nature is alien to your heart. Meanwhile a young shepherd was driving his herd along the bank of the river, playing his pipes. Liza fixed her gaze on him and thought: "If the one who occupies my thoughts now had been born a simple peasant shepherd—and if it were he that was driving his herd past me now: oh! I would bow to him with a smile and say pleasantly: 'How do you do, kind shepherd! Where are you driving your flock? And here grows green grass for your sheep, and here there are red flowers from which you can plait a garland for your hat.' He would glance at me with a caressing look—perhaps he would take my hand. . . . A dream!" The shepherd playing his pipes walked past and disappeared behind a nearby hill with his flock.

Suddenly Liza heard the sound of oars—she glanced at the river and saw a boat, and in the boat was Erast.

All of her veins began to throb, and of course this was not from fear. She got up and wanted to leave, but could not. Erast jumped out onto the bank, approached Liza, and her dream was partially fulfilled: for *he glanced at her with a caressing look and took her by the hand.* . . . And Liza, Liza stood with lowered eyes, with fiery cheeks, with a trembling heart—she could not take her hand away from him, could not turn away when he came close to her with his pink lips. . . . Ah! He kissed her, kissed her with such ardor that the whole universe seemed to her to be blazing in fire! "Dear Liza!" said Erast. "Dear Liza! I love you!" And these words resounded in the depths of her soul like an enchanting heavenly music; she scarcely dared believe her ears and. . . . But I abandon my brush. I will say only that in this moment of rapture Liza's timidity disappeared—Erast discovered that he was loved, loved passionately by a new, pure, open heart.

They sat on the grass in such a way that there was not much space between them—they looked into each other's eyes, and talked to each other: "Love me!" And two hours seemed an instant to them. Finally Liza remembered that her mother might get worried about her. They had to part. "Oh, Erast!" she said, "Will you always love me?" —"Always, dear Liza, always," he answered. —"And can you swear to me that this is true?" —"I can, darling Liza, I can." —"No, I don't need an oath. I believe you, Erast, I believe. Could you deceive poor Liza? That couldn't be." —"It could not, it could not, dear Liza!" —"How happy I am, and how mama will cheer up when she learns that you love me!" —"Oh, no, Liza! There's no need to tell her anything." —"Why not?" —"Old people are suspicious. She will imagine something bad." —"That

couldn't happen." —"Still, please don't say a word to her about it."
—"All right. I must obey you, even though I don't want to hide
anything from her." They said good-bye, kissed for the last time,
and promised to see each other every evening either on the bank
of the river or in the birch grove, or somewhere near Liza's hut—
only they would definitely, unfailingly see each other. Liza walked
away, but her eyes turned back a hundred times to Erast who was
still standing on the bank and watching after her.

Liza returned to her cottage in a completely different mood
than the one in which she had left. Her heartfelt joy revealed itself
on her face and in her movements. "He loves me!" she thought,
and she was enraptured by the thought. "Oh, mama!" said Liza to
her mother, who had just woken up. "Oh, mama! What a beautiful
morning! How joyous everything is in the field! Never have the
skylarks sung so well, never has the sun shone so brightly, never
have the flowers smelled so good!" Leaning on her crutch the old
woman went out into the meadow to enjoy the morning which
Liza had described in such exquisite colors. Indeed, it seemed to
her extremely pleasant; her dear daughter had cheered up all of
nature for her with her own cheer. "Oh, Liza," she said, "How good
everything is with the Lord God! I am in my sixties, and I still
cannot look upon the Lord's works enough, I cannot see too much
of the pure sky which resembles a high tent, or of the earth which
is covered by new grass and new flowers every year. It must be that
the Heavenly King loved man very much when he decorated this
world so well. Oh, Liza! Who would want to die if we did not sometimes have grief? Apparently it has to be like this. Maybe we would
forget our souls if tears never dropped from our eyes." And Liza
thought: "Ah! I will forget my soul, before I forget my dear friend!"

After this, Erast and Liza, fearing not to keep their word, saw
each other every evening (when Liza's mother went to bed) either
on the bank of the river or in the birch grove, but most often under
the shade of hundred year old oaks (about a hundred and seventy
yards from the hut), oaks which shaded a deep, clear pond that
had been dug in ancient times. There, through the green branches,
the rays of the moon often silvered Liza's light hair, with which
zephyrs and the hand of her dear friend often played; often these
rays illuminated a glittering tear of love in the eyes of tender Liza—
which Erast always dried with a kiss. They embraced—but chaste,

shy Cynthia did not hide from them behind a cloud: pure and sin-less were their embraces. "When you," said Liza to Erast, "say to me 'I love you my friend!', when you press me to your heart, and glance at me with your tender eyes, oh! then I feel so good, so good, that I forget myself, I forget everything except—Erast! Wonderful! It is miraculous my friend, that I could live calmly and merrily with-out knowing you! Now that seems incomprehensible to me, now I think that without you life is not life, but sadness and boredom. Without your eyes the bright moon is dark, without your voice the singing nightingale is dull, without your breath the breeze is un-pleasant to me."

Erast was enraptured by his shepherdess—thus he called Liza—and seeing how much she loved him, he seemed more amiable to himself. All of the glittering amusements of high society seemed insignificant to him in comparison to the pleasures with which the passionate *friendship* of an innocent soul nourished his heart. With revulsion he thought about the despicable voluptuousness with which he formerly sated his feelings. "I am going to live with Liza as a brother with his sister," he thought, "I will not use her love for evil and I will always be happy!" Foolish young man! Do you know your own heart? Can you always answer for your impulses? Is reason always the tsar of your feeling?

Liza demanded that Erast often visit her mother. "I love her," she said, "and I wish her good, and it seems to me that seeing you is a great blessing for anyone." Indeed, the old woman always cheered up when she saw him. She liked to talk to him about her late husband and to tell him about the days of her youth, about how she met her dear Ivan for the first time, how he fell in love with her and in what love, what accord he lived with her. "Ah! We could never look at each other enough—right up to the hour when ferocious death cut him down. He died in my arms!" Erast listened to her with unfeigned pleasure. He bought Liza's work from her, and he always wanted to pay ten times more than the price which was set by her, but the old woman never took extra.

Thus passed several weeks. One evening Erast had been waiting for his Liza for a long time. Finally she came, but so unhappy that he was frightened; her eyes had turned red from tears. "Liza, Liza! What has happened to you?" —"Oh, Erast! I've been crying!" —"About what? What has happened?" —"I must tell you everything. A suitor is courting me, the son of a rich peasant from a neighboring village; mother wants me to marry him." —"And you agree?" —"Cruel man! Can you ask about that? Yes, I am sorry for mother; she cries and says that I do not want her peace, that she is going to be tormented at death if she does not marry me off while she's alive. Oh! Mother doesn't know that I have such a dear friend!" Erast kissed Liza, said that her happiness was dearer than anything on earth to him, that after her mother's death he would take her to his house, that he would live with her never to part, in the country, and in the sleepy forest, as if in paradise. "But you cannot be my husband!" said Liza with a quiet sigh. "Why not?" —"I am a peasant." —"You insult me. Most important of all for your friend is the soul, a sensitive innocent soul—and Liza will always be nearest to my heart."

She threw herself into his arms—and this was to be the hour when her purity would perish! Erast felt an unusual agitation in his blood—never had Liza seemed so exquisite to him—never had her caresses touched him so strongly—never had her kisses been so flaming—she did not know anything, did not suspect anything, did not fear anything—the dark of the evening fed desire—not a single little star shone in the heavens—no ray of light could illuminate the error. —Erast feels himself trembling—Liza too, not knowing why—not knowing what is happening to her. . . . Ah, Liza, Liza! Where is your guardian angel, where is your innocence?

The error took only a minute. Liza did not understand her feelings, she was astonished and began asking questions. Erast was silent—he searched for words and did not find them. "Oh, I am afraid," said Liza, "I am afraid of what has happened to us! It seems to me that I am dying, that my soul . . . no, I cannot say it! . . . you're silent Erast? You are sighing? . . . My God! What is this?" Meanwhile, lightning flashed and thunder rolled. Liza began to tremble all over. "Erast, Erast!" she said. "I am terrified! I am afraid that the thunder will kill me like a criminal!" The storm raged threateningly; rain poured from black clouds—it seemed that nature was lamenting Liza's lost innocence. Erast tried to calm Liza, and he walked her to the cottage. Tears were rolling from her eyes when she said good-bye to him. "Oh, Erast! Assure me that we will be happy as before!" —"We will be, Liza, we will be!" he answered.—"God grant it be so! I cannot disbelieve your words;

after all I love you! Still, in my heart. . . . But enough! Farewell! Tomorrow, tomorrow we will see each other."

Their meetings continued, but how everything changed! Erast could no longer be satisfied just by innocent caresses of his Liza, just by her glances full of love, just by the touch of her hand, just by a kiss, just by pure embraces. He desired more, more, and finally, he could desire nothing—and he who knows his heart, he who has meditated on the quality of his tenderest pleasures will of course agree with me that the fulfillment of *all* desires is the most dangerous temptation of love. For Erast Liza was no longer the angel of purity which had formerly flamed in his imagination and enraptured his soul. Platonic love had given way to feelings of which he could not be *proud* and which were not new for him. As for Liza, having given herself to him completely, she lived and breathed only in him; in everything, like a lamb, she submitted to his will and she supposed that her own happiness was in his pleasure. She saw the change in him and often said to him: "You were in better spirits before; we were calmer and happier before, and I wasn't so afraid of losing your love before!" Sometimes parting from her, he said to her: "I cannot come to see you tomorrow Liza, I have important business." And every time Liza sighed at these words.

Finally she did not see him for five days in a row and she was greatly disturbed; on the sixth day he came with a sad face: "Dear Liza, I must say farewell to you for a while. You know that we are at war; I am in the service, my regiment is going on a campaign." Liza turned pale and almost fainted.

Erast caressed her, said that he would always love dear Liza, and that he hoped on his return he would never part from her again. She was silent for a long time, then she burst into bitter tears, grabbed his hand, and glancing at him with all the tenderness of love, she asked: "Can't you stay?" —"I can," he answered, "but only with the greatest ignominy, the greatest stain upon my honor. Everyone will despise me; everyone will shun me as a coward, as an unworthy son of the fatherland." —"Oh, if it's like that," said Liza, "then go, go where God commands! But you could be killed." —"Death for the fatherland is not terrible, dear Liza." —"I will die, as soon as you are no longer on earth." —"But why think that? I hope to return to you, my friend." —"God grant it be so! God grant it be so! Every day, every hour I will pray for it.

Oh, why is it I do not know how to read or write! You would inform me about everything that happens to you, and I would write to you about my tears!" —"No, spare yourself Liza, spare yourself for your friend. I do not want you to weep without me." —"Cruel man! You can think of depriving me of this consolation too! No! When I have parted from you I will stop weeping when my heart dries up." —"Think about the pleasant minute when we will again meet." —"I will, I will think about it! Oh! If only it would come soon! My dear, kind Erast! Remember your poor Liza who loves you more than herself!"

But I cannot describe everything that they said on this occasion. The next day was to be their last meeting.

Erast wanted to say good-bye to Liza's mother who could not hold back her tears when she heard that her *kind handsome gentleman* had to go away to war. He forced her to take some money from him saying: "In my absence I do not want Liza to sell her work, which according to our agreement belongs to me." The old woman showered him with blessings. "God grant that you return to us safely," she said, "and that I see you again in this life! Maybe by then my Liza will find herself a suitor who pleases her. How I would thank God if you came to our wedding! And when Liza has children, you know sir, that you must be their godfather! Oh! I want so much to live until then!" Liza was standing beside her mother and did not dare to glance at her. The reader can easily imagine what she was feeling at this moment.

But what did she feel when, having embraced her for the last time, having pressed her to his heart for the last time, Erast said: "Farewell, Liza! . . ." What a touching scene! Like a scarlet sea the dawn was spreading across the eastern sky. Erast was standing under the branches of a tall oak tree holding in his embrace his pale, languid, bereaved friend who, bidding him farewell, said farewell to her own soul. All nature attended in silence.

Liza sobbed—Erast wept—he left her—she fell—she got up on her knees, raised her hands toward the sky, and watched Erast who was walking away, farther—farther—and, finally, disappeared—the sun rose and poor, abandoned Liza lost her feelings and consciousness. She came to—and the world seemed doleful and sad to her. All of the pleasures of nature had disappeared for her along with the one who was dear to her heart. "Oh!" she thought, "Why have

I been abandoned in this wasteland? What is preventing me from flying after my dear Erast? War does not terrify me; I am terrified only without my friend. I want to live with him, to die with him or to save his precious life with my death. Wait, wait my dear! I will fly to you!" —She already wanted to run after Erast but the thought: "I have a mother!"—stopped her. Liza sighed and, bowing her head, walked toward her cottage with soft steps. —From that hour her days were days of melancholy and grief which she had to hide from her tender mother: and her heart suffered all the more! It found relief only when Liza, isolating herself in the depths of the forest, could freely pour forth her tears and moan over being parted from her dear one. Often the sad turtledove joined its plaintive voice to her moaning. But sometimes—although extremely rarely—a golden ray of hope, a ray of comfort brightened the darkness of her sorrow. "How happy I will be when he returns to me! How everything will change!" —At this thought her eyes brightened, the roses on her cheeks grew fresh, and Liza smiled like a May morning after a stormy night. —About two months passed in this way.

One day Liza had to go to Moscow in order to buy some rosewater with which her mother treated her eyes. On one of the big streets she met a magnificent carriage, and in that carriage she saw—Erast. "Oh!" Liza cried out and she rushed toward him, but the carriage drove past and turned into a courtyard. Erast got out and was going to go up onto the porch of a huge house, when suddenly he found himself in Liza's embrace. He turned pale—then, not answering a word to her exclamations, he took her by the arm, led her into his study, locked the door, and said to her: "Liza! Circumstances have changed; I am engaged to be married; you must leave me in peace and forget me for your own peace of mind. I loved you, and I love you now, that is, I wish all the best to you. Here is a hundred rubles—take it," and he put the money in her pocket. "Allow me to kiss you a last time—and go home." —Before Liza could come to her senses he led her out of his study and said to his servant: "See this girl to the street."

At this minute my heart is surging with blood. I forget the man in Erast—I am ready to curse him—but my tongue does not move— I look at the sky, and a tear rolls across my face. Oh! Why am I not writing a novel instead of a sad, true story?

So Erast deceived Liza telling her that he was going into the army? —No, he was in fact in the army, but instead of fighting with the enemy, he played cards and lost almost all of his estate. Soon peace was concluded, and Erast returned to Moscow burdened with debts. He was left with only one way of correcting his circumstances—marrying a rich, middle-aged widow who had been in love with him for a long time. He decided on this and moved into her house after devoting a sincere sigh to his Liza. But can all of this justify him?

Liza found herself in the street and in a state which no pen can describe. "He, he drove me out? He loves someone else? I am lost!" These are her thoughts, her feelings! A cruel fainting spell interrupted them for a while. One kind woman who was walking along the street stopped over Liza, who was lying on the ground, and tried to bring her to; the unhappy girl opened her eyes, got up with the help of this kind woman, thanked her, and began walking without knowing where. "I cannot live," thought Liza, "I cannot! . . . Oh, if only the sky would fall upon me! If only the earth would swallow up a poor girl! . . . No! The sky will not fall, the earth will not shake! Woe is me!" She left the city and suddenly found herself on the bank of a deep pond in the shade of the ancient oak trees which several weeks before had been the silent witnesses to her raptures. This reminiscence shook her soul; the most terrible, heartfelt torment was depicted on her face. But in a few minutes she was lost in thought—she looked around her, saw the daughter of her neighbor (a fifteen year old girl) walking along the road; she called to her, took the ten imperials out of her pocket and giving them to her said: "Dear Anyuta, dear friend! Take this money to my mother—it is not stolen—tell her that Liza is guilty before her, that I have hidden from her my love for a certain cruel man, for E. . . . Why know his name? Tell her that he betrayed me—ask her to forgive me—God will be her helper—kiss her hand as I am kissing yours now—say that poor Liza told you to kiss her—say that I. . . ." At this point she threw herself into the water. Anyuta screamed, began to cry, but could not save her; she ran to the village—the people gathered and they pulled Liza out, but she was already dead.

In this way one who was beautiful in soul and body ended her life. When we are *there* in the new life, we will see each other; I will recognize you, tender Liza!

She was buried near the pond under a somber oak, and they put a wooden cross on her grave. I often sit here in meditation leaning on the receptacle of Liza's dust; the pond ripples before my eyes; the leaves rustle above me.

Liza's mother heard of the terrible death of her daughter and her blood turned cold from horror—her eyes closed forever. —The hut was deserted, the wind howls in it and superstitious villagers, hearing this noise at night say: "The dead girl's moaning there, poor Liza is moaning there!"

To the end of his life Erast was unhappy. Having learned of Liza's fate, he could not find solace and he considered himself a murderer. I made his acquaintance a year before his death. He himself told me this story and led me to Liza's grave. —Now, perhaps, they have already become reconciled!

ALEXANDER PUSHKIN

The Station Master

*The Collegiate Registrar
Is the poststation's dictator.*
PRINCE VYAZEMSKY

WHO HAS NOT CURSED STATION MASTERS, who has not quarreled with them? Who, in a moment of anger, has not demanded the fatal book from them in order to enter in it a useless complaint about extortion, coarseness, and inefficiency? Who does not consider them renegades from the human race, equals of pettifogging clerks or, at least, of bandits from Murom? Let us, however, be just; let us try to put ourselves in their position, and perhaps we will begin to judge them more indulgently. What is a station master? A veritable martyr of the fourteenth class, shielded by his rank only from beatings, and not always even that (I appeal to my readers' conscience). What is the function of this dictator, as Prince Vyazemsky jokingly calls him? Is it not real penal servitude? No peace day or night. It is on the station master that the journeyer vents all of the vexation accumulated during a hard ride. Unbearable weather, a rotten road, a stubborn coachman, the horses do not pull—and the station master is to blame. Entering his poor dwelling, the traveler sees him as an enemy; it is all right if he manages to rid himself of the uninvited guest quickly, but if

Translated by CARL R. PROFFER.

there happen to be no horses? . . . God! What curses, what threats will pour on his head! He is forced to run about outside in the rain and muck; during a storm, during winter frost he goes out to the entrance-way just to rest a moment from the shouting and shoving of an irritated wayfarer. A general arrives; the trembling station master gives him the last two troikas, including the courier's. The general drives away without saying thanks to him. Within five minutes—there's a bell! . . . And the courier throws his order for a team onto the table! . . . Let us understand all of this clearly, and instead of indignation our heart will be filled with sincere compassion. A few words more: for twenty consecutive years I have traversed Russia in all directions; I know almost all of the post routes, I am acquainted with several generations of coachmen; it is a rare station master whose face I do not know, a rare one with whom I have had no business; in the not-too-distant future I hope to publish my curious collection of travel observations, for the meantime I will say only that the class of station masters has been presented to public opinion in a very false light. These much-calumniated station masters are in general basically peaceful men, by nature obliging, inclined to hospitality, modest in their pretensions to honors, and not too avaricious. From their conversations (which are wrongly disclaimed by traveling gentlemen), one may get much that is curious and instructive. As for me, I confess that I prefer their talk to the speeches of some official of the sixth rank who is traveling on government business.

It may easily be guessed that I have friends among this respectable class of station masters. In fact, the memory of one of them is precious to me. Circumstances once brought us together, and it is of him that I now intend to talk with my amiable readers.

In 1816, in the month of May, I happened to be passing through N*** province on a route which has now been cancelled. I was of low rank, traveling by post-chaise, and paying for two horses. As a consequence of this the station masters made no ceremony with me, and often I would take by battle that which, in my opinion, I should have had by right. Being young and volatile, I was indignant at the baseness and cowardice of the station master when the latter harnessed the troika prepared for me to the carriage of some gentleman of rank. For just as long a time I could not get accustomed to discriminating flunkeys skipping over me when serving a dish at the governor's dinner. Nowadays both of these seem to me in the order of things. Indeed, what would happen to us if instead of the generally convenient rule, "Let rank honor rank," another were put into use, for example. "Let intelligence honor intelligence?" What arguments would arise! And whom would the servants serve first? But I turn to my tale.

The day was hot. Three versts from the station N*** it began to drizzle, and within a minute a pouring rain soaked me to the skin. On arrival at the station my first concern was to change clothes as quickly as possible, the second was to ask for some tea. "Hey, Dunya!" shouted the station master, "set up the samovar and go get some cream." At these words a girl of about fourteen came out from behind the partition and ran out into the entry. Her beauty struck me. "Is that your daughter?" I asked the station master. "My daughter, sir," he replied with a look of satisfied pride, "and such a bright, such a clever one she is, just like her late mother." Here he began to copy my orders, and I occupied myself by examining the pictures which decorated his humble but tidy abode. They depicted the story of the prodigal son. In the first a respectable old man in a night-cap and dressing-gown is taking leave of a restless youth who hastily accepts his blessing and bag of money. In the next the dissolute behavior of the young man is depicted in vivid colors: he is sitting at a table surrounded by false friends and shameless women. Further on, the ruined youth, in rags and a three-cornered hat, is tending swine and sharing their meal with them; deep sadness and repentance are depicted on his face. Finally his return to his father is presented; the kind old man in the same night-cap and dressing-gown runs out to meet him: the prodigal son is on his knees; in the background the cook is killing the fatted calf, and the older brother is asking the servants the reason for such joy. Under each little picture I read appropriate German verses. All of this has been preserved in my memory to this day—as have the little pots of balsamine, the bed with its variegated curtain, and the other objects which surrounded me at the time. I see, as if now, the host himself, a man of about fifty, fresh and vigorous, and his long green coat with three medallions on faded ribbons.

I had not managed to pay off my old driver when Dunya returned with the samovar. With her second glance the little coquette noticed the impression she had produced on me; she lowered her large blue eyes; I started to chat with her and she answered me without any timidity, like a girl who has been in high society. I offered her father a glass of punch; to Dunya I gave a cup of tea, and the three of us began to chat as if we had known each other all our lives.

The horses had long been ready, and I still did not want to part with the station master and his daughter. Finally I said good-bye to them; the father wished me a good trip, and the daughter accompanied me to the wagon. In the entry I stopped and asked her permission to kiss her; Dunya agreed . . . I can count many kisses:

"Since first I started this."

But not one left such a long, such a pleasant recollection in me.

A few years passed, and circumstances led me to that same route, to the same locales. I recalled the daughter of the old station master and rejoiced in the thought that I would see her again. But, thought I, perhaps the old station master has already been replaced; Dunya is probably married already. The thought of the death of one or the other also flashed through my mind, and I approached station N*** with sad foreboding.

The horses stopped at the little station house. Entering the room I immediately recognized the little pictures depicting the story of the prodigal son; the table and bed stood in their former places; but there were no longer any flowers on the window-sills, and everything around indicated decay and neglect. The station master had been sleeping under his sheepskin coat; my arrival woke him and he stood up . . . It really was Samson Vyrin, but how he had aged! While he was getting ready to copy my orders, I looked at his gray hair, the deep wrinkles in a long unshaven face, his bent back— and could not but be amazed how three or four years could transform a vigorous person into a feeble old man. "Do you recognize me," I asked him, "we are old acquaintances." — "Could be," he replied gloomily, "it's a big road here, many travelers have spent time with me." — "How is your Dunya," I continued. The old man frowned. "God knows," he replied. "She's evidently married," I said. The old man pretended he had not heard my question and continued reading my orders in a mumble. I curtailed my questions and ordered the teapot set up. Curiosity was beginning to bother me, and I hoped that punch would loosen the tongue of my old acquaintance.

I was not mistaken: the old man did not refuse the proffered glass. I noticed that the rum cleared up his gloominess. On the second glass he became talkative; he remembered, or pretended to remember me, and from him I learned the story which at the time interested and touched me so much.

"So you knew my Dunya," he began. "And who didn't know her? Ah, Dunya, Dunya! What a girl she was! It used to be everyone that passed by praised her, no one criticized. The ladies would give her handkerchiefs or earrings. Traveling gentlemen used to stop on purpose, as if to have dinner or supper, but really only to look at her a little bit longer. A gentleman, no matter how angry he was, would quiet down in her presence, and talk to me graciously. Would you believe it, sir? — couriers and messengers would talk to her for half an hour at a time. It was she who held the house together: put something in order, get something ready, she managed everything. And I, old fool that I am, could not look at her enough, could not dote enough; didn't I love my Dunya, didn't I pamper my baby, didn't she have a good life? But no, you can't escape misfortune; what has been ordained cannot be avoided." Here he began to tell me about his grief in detail. One winter evening three years before when the station master was putting lines in a new register and his daughter was behind the partition sewing herself a dress, a troika drove up and a traveler in a Circassian cap, military overcoat, and wrapped in a shawl, entered the room demanding horses. The horses were all out. At this news the journeyer raised his voice and whip; but Dunya, who was accustomed to such scenes, ran out from behind the partition and soothingly spoke to the traveler asking him if he wouldn't like something to eat. Dunya's appearance produced its usual effect. The traveler's anger passed; he agreed to wait for horses and ordered his supper. When he took off the wet, shaggy cap, unwrapped the shawl and removed his overcoat, the traveler turned out to be a tall young hussar with a small black moustache. He made his arrangements with the station master and began to talk gaily with him and his daughter. Supper was served. Meanwhile the horses arrived and the station master ordered that they be harnessed to the traveler's chaise immediately, without being fed; but returning to the house he found the young man lying almost unconscious on the bench: he had gotten ill, his head began to ache, it was impossible to drive on . . . What could be done? The station master gave up his bed for him, and it was agreed that if the sick man was not better the next day they should send for the doctor in S***.

The next day the hussar got worse. His servant rode to town on horseback for the doctor. Dunya wrapped his head in a cloth soaked in vinegar and sat beside his bed with her sewing. In the presence of the station master the sick man groaned and hardly said a word, but he drank two cups of coffee and, groaning, ordered his dinner. Dunya did not leave him. He kept asking to drink, and Dunya brought him a jug of lemonade which she had made. The sick man moistened his lips and each time he returned the jug, as a sign of gratitude, he pressed Dunyushka's hand with his weak hand. Toward dinner time the doctor arrived. He felt the sick man's pulse, spoke briefly with him in German, and in Russian announced that all he needed was peace and quiet, and that in a day or two he could set out on the road. The hussar handed him twenty-five rubles for the visit and invited him to have dinner, the doctor agreed; both ate with hearty appetites, drank a bottle of wine, and parted very satisfied with each other.

Another day passed, and the hussar completely recovered. He was extremely good-humored, joked constantly now with Dunya, now with the station master; he whistled songs, talked to travelers, entered their orders in the travel register, and he so pleased the kind station master that on the third morning he was sorry to part with his amiable guest. The day was Sunday; Dunya was getting ready to go to mass. The hussar's chaise was ready. He said good-bye to the station master, generously rewarding him for his lodging and board; he said good-bye to Dunya too, and he offered to take her to the church which was located at the edge of the village. Dunya stood there in perplexity. "What are you afraid of?" her father said, "Why his excellency isn't a wolf, he won't eat you: ride to the church with him." Dunya got in the chaise beside the hussar, his servant hopped up onto the box, the driver whistled, and the horses started off at a gallop.

The poor station master did not understand how he himself could have allowed Dunya to go with the hussar, how he could have been so blind and what was wrong with his mind then. Not half an hour had passed when his heart began to ache and ache, and uneasiness overcame him to such a degree that he could no longer stand it and set off to mass himself on foot. Walking up to the church he saw that the people were already leaving, but Dunya was not in the churchyard nor on the porch. He entered the church hurriedly; the priest was coming down from the altar, the sexton was extinguishing the candles, two old women were still praying in a corner; but Dunya was not in the church. The poor father forced himself to ask the sexton if she had been at mass. The sexton replied that she had not. The station master went home neither dead nor alive. One hope remained for him: perhaps Dunya, in the frivolousness of youth, might have taken it into her head to ride to the next station where her godmother lived. In tormenting agitation he awaited the return of the troika with which he had let her leave. Time passed, but the driver did not return. Finally, toward evening, he arrived intoxicated and alone, with the crushing news: "Dunya went on from that station with the hussar."

The old man could not bear his misfortune; he immediately lay down on the very bed where the young deceiver had lain the evening before. Now, considering all the circumstances, the station master guessed that the illness had been feigned. The poor fellow fell ill with a high fever; he was taken to S*** and another person was temporarily appointed in his place. The same doctor who had come to the hussar treated him. He assured the station master that the young man had been quite healthy and that even then he had guessed his evil intention, but fearing his whip, he was silent. Whether the German was telling the truth or only wanted to boast of his foresight, he did not even slightly console his poor patient that way. Hardly had the station master recovered from his illness when he requested a two months leave from the S*** postmaster, and without saying a word to anyone about his intention, he set off after his daughter on foot. From the register he knew that Captain Minsky was going from Smolensk to Petersburg. The driver who took him said that Dunya cried the whole way, although, it seemed, she was going of her own accord. "Maybe," thought the station master, "I will lead my lost lamb home." With that thought he arrived in Petersburg, and staying at the Izmailov

Regiment in the home of a retired corporal, an old comrade of his, he began his search. He soon learned that Captain Minsky was in Petersburg and lived at Demoute's Inn. The station master resolved to call on him.

Early in the morning he went to his anteroom and asked that his excellency be informed that an old soldier was asking to see him. The orderly, who was cleaning boots on a boot-tree, announced that his master was asleep and that he received no one before eleven o'clock. The station master left and returned at the appointed time. Minsky himself came out to him in a dressing-gown and red skullcap. "What do you need, brother?" he asked him. The old man's blood began to boil, tears rushed to his eyes, and in a trembling voice he said only: "Your excellency! For God's sake, do me a favor! . . ." Minsky glanced at him quickly, flared up, took him by the arm, led him into a private office, and locked the door behind him. "Your excellency!" continued the old man, "there's no use crying over spilled milk; at least give me back my poor Dunya. You've had your fun with her; don't ruin her for nothing." — "What is done cannot be changed," said the young man, in the utmost confusion, "I am guilty before you and glad to ask your pardon; but do not think that I could abandon Dunya—she will be happy, I give you my word of honor. Why do you need her? She loves me; she is no longer accustomed to her former status. Neither you nor she will forget what has happened." Then, having shoved something into his sleeve, he opened the door, and the station master, without recalling how, found himself on the street.

For a long time he stood motionless. Finally he saw a packet of money behind the cuff of his sleeve; he took it out and unrolled several crumpled five and ten ruble notes. Tears again rushed to his eyes, tears of indignation! He crushed the bills into a ball, threw them to the ground, stamped them with his heel, and walked on . . . When he had walked a few steps away he stopped, thought a bit . . . and returned . . . but the notes were already gone. A well-dressed young man, seeing him, ran up to a cabbie, got in hastily, and shouted, "Drive on!" The station master did not pursue him. He resolved to go home to his station, but he wanted to see his poor Dunya at least once. So in a day or two he returned to Minsky's, but the orderly told him sternly that his master was receiving no one, pushed him out of the anteroom with his chest, and slammed the door in his face. The station master stood there and stood there—and then he went away.

The evening of that same day he was walking along Liteynaya Street, having been to a service at Our Lady of All Grieving. Suddenly a smart *droshki* rushed by in front of him and he recognized Minsky. The *droshki* stopped in front of a three-storied house, right at the entrance, and the hussars ran in across the porch. A happy thought flashed through the station master's mind. He turned, and coming up beside the coachman, he asked, "Whose horse is that, brother? Isn't it Minsky's?" —"Precisely so," replied the coachman, "and what's it to you?" —"This is what: your master ordered me to take a note to his Dunya, and I've up and forgot where this Dunya of his lives." —"Why right here, on the second floor. You're late with your note, brother; now he's already with her himself." —"That doesn't matter," objected the station master with an inexpressible emotion in his heart, "thanks for setting me right, but I'll do my job." And with these words he went up the stairs.

The doors were locked; he rang, a few seconds of painful expectation passed. A key rattled, they opened for him. "Does Avdotya Samsonovna live here?" he asked. —"She does," replied a young maid, "why do you have to see her?" Without answering the station master walked into the hall. "You cannot, you cannot!" the maid shouted after him, "Avdotya Samsonovna has guests." But without listening the station master kept going. The first two rooms were dark, there was a light in the third. He approached the open door and stopped. Minsky was sitting in meditation in a beautifully decorated room. Dunya, dressed in all the luxury of fashion, was sitting on the arm of his chair, like a rider on her English saddle. She was looking at Minsky with tenderness, winding his black curls around her glittering fingers. The poor station master! Never had his daughter seemed so beautiful to him; against his will he admired her. "Who is there?" she asked, not raising her head. He remained silent. Not getting an answer, Dunya raised her head . . . and with a cry she fell onto the carpet. The frightened Minsky rushed to pick her up, but suddenly seeing the old station master in the doorway he left Dunya and went up to him, shaking from anger. "What do you want?" he said to him, clenching his teeth, "Why are you sneaking around behind me everywhere like a thief? Or do you want to cut my throat? Get out!" and grabbing the old man by the collar with a strong hand he shoved him out onto the stairs.

The old man came to himself in his apartment. His friend advised him to lodge a complaint; but the station master thought a bit, gave up, and decided to retreat. Two days later he set off from Petersburg back to his station to again take up his post. "Here it's the third year already," he concluded, "that I have been living without Dunya and there hasn't been a word about her. Whether she's alive or not, God knows. Anything can happen. She's not the first or the last to be deceived by a passing rake, and kept there for a while and then abandoned. There are many of them in Petersburg, young fools, today in satin and velvet, but tomorrow, you'll see, they're sweeping the streets along with riff-raff from pot-houses. When you think, sometimes, that maybe Dunya will be lost there too, against your will you sin and wish her a grave . . ."

Such was the story of my friend, the old station master, a story repeatedly interrupted by tears which he picturesquely wiped away with his hem of his coat like the zealous Terentich in Dmitriev's fine ballad. These tears were partly caused by the punch, of which he had drunk five glasses during the course of his narrative; but, however that may be, they touched my heart strongly. Having parted from him, I could not forget the old station master for a long time, and I thought about poor Dunya for a long while. . . .

Not very long ago now, passing through the little town of N***, I remembered my friend and learned that the station which he commanded had already been abolished. To my question, "Is the old station master alive?" no one could give me a satisfactory answer. I resolved to visit the neighborhood I knew, took free horses, and headed for the village of N***.

This happened during autumn. Gray clouds covered the sky; a cold wind blew from the reaped fields, ripping the red and yellow leaves from the trees it encountered. I arrived in the village at sunset and stopped at the little post house. In the entry (where poor Dunya had once kissed me) a fat woman came out and to my questions replied that the old station master had died about a year ago, that the brewer had settled in his house, and that she was the brewer's wife. I began to regret my useless trip and the seven rubles I had spent for nothing. "What did he die of?" I asked the brewer's wife. —"Drinking, sir," she replied. —"And where was he buried?" —"On the outskirts, alongside his late wife." —"Can't you take me to his grave?" —"Why not. Hey, Vanka! You've played with that cat long enough. Lead the gentleman to the cemetery and show him the station master's grave."

At these words a ragged boy, red-haired and one-eyed, ran out to me and immediately led me to the outskirts.

"Did you know the deceased?" I asked him on the way.

"How could I not know him! He taught me to carve whistles. It used to happen (God rest his soul!) he'd be going from the pot-house, and we'd go behind him: Grandfather, grandfather! Some nuts! And he'd give us some nuts. He always used to play with us."

"And do the travelers remember him?"

"There's few travelers now any more; maybe the assessor will turn in, but he doesn't care about the dead. Last summer a lady drove through, and she asked about the old station master and went to his grave."

"What kind of lady?" I asked with curiosity.

"A beautiful lady," replied the boy, "she was traveling in a carriage with six horses, with three little children, and a nurse and with a black lapdog; and when she was told the old station master was dead, she started crying and said to the children: 'Sit quietly, I am going to the cemetery.' And I was called to lead her. But the lady said, 'I know the way myself.' And she gave me a five-kopeck silver piece—such a good lady!"

We arrived at the cemetery, a bare place, with no fence around it, with scattered wooden crosses, not shaded by a single tree. Never in my life had I seen such a sad cemetery.

"There's the old station master's grave," the boy said to me, hopping up on a heap of sand into which a black cross with a brass ikon was stuck.

"And the lady came here?" I asked.

"She came," replied Vanka, "I watched her from a distance. She lay down here and remained lying for a long time. And then the lady went into the village and called the priest, gave him some money and left, and she gave me a five-kopeck silver piece—a fine lady!"

And I gave the boy a five-kopeck piece and no longer regretted the trip or the seven rubles I had spent.

ALEXANDER PUSHKIN

The Queen of Spades

> *The queen of spades signifies secret ill-will.*
>
> THE NEWEST FORTUNE-
> TELLING BOOK

I

And on rainy days
They gathered
often;
They doubled—God forgive them—
From fifty
To one hundred,
And they would win
And they would note the score
With chalk.
Thus on rainy days
They got down to
Work.

ONCE THEY WERE PLAYING CARDS at cavalry officer Narumov's. The long winter night passed unnoticed; they sat down to supper at five in the morning. Those who had won ate with big appetites; the others sat absently in front of their empty plates. But champagne appeared, the conversation livened up, and everyone took part in it.

Translated by CARL R. PROFFER.

"How did you do, Surin?" asked the host.

"Lost, as usual. It must be admitted that I'm unlucky: I play without raising the stake, never get excited; there is no way you can confound me, but I keep losing!"

"And you've never been tempted? You've never raised the bet and played the same card? Your firmness amazes me."

"What about Hermann!" said one of the guests, pointing to a young engineer. "Never in his life has he taken the cards in his hand, never in his life has he doubled the stake, but he sits with us until five o'clock and watches our play!"

"The play interests me intensely," said Hermann, "but I am not in a position to sacrifice the essential in hope of acquiring the superfluous."

"Hermann is a German; he's economical, that's all!" noted Tomsky. "But if there is someone I cannot understand, it's my grandmother, Countess Anna Fedotovna."

"How so? Why?" exclaimed the guests.

"I cannot comprehend," continued Tomsky, "how it is my grandmother does not punt!"

"What is amazing," said Narumov, "about an eighty year old lady who doesn't punt?"

"So you know nothing about her?"

"No! That's true, nothing!"

"Oh, then listen. You must know that sixty years ago my grandmother went to Paris and was in great fashion there. People ran after her to see *la Vénus moscovite*; Richelieu courted her, and grandmother maintains that he almost shot himself because of her cruelty.

"At that time ladies played faro. Once at Court she lost some very large amount to the Duke of Orleans on her word. When she arrived home, peeling the beauty spots from her face and undoing her farthingale, grandmother informed grandfather of her loss and ordered him to pay.

"My late grandfather, so far as I recall, was a kind of house servant to grandmother. He feared her like fire, but when he heard about this terrible loss he blew his top, brought out accounts, showed her that they had expended half a million in half a year, that they had no Moscow or Saratov estate around Paris, and he flatly refused to pay. Grandmother slapped him and went to bed alone as a sign of her disfavor.

"The next day she ordered her husband called, hoping that the domestic punishment had worked on him, but found him inflexible. For the first time in her life she reached the point of debate and explanations with him; she intended to appeal to his conscience, showing condescendingly that there are different kinds of debts and that there is a difference between a prince and a coach-maker. No use! Grandfather was rebelling. No! That's all there was to it! Grandmother didn't know what to do.

"One very remarkable man was her close acquaintance. You have heard of Count St. Germain, about whom so many marvelous stories are told. You know that he passed himself off as the Eternal Jew, as the inventor of an elixir of life and the philosophers' stone and so forth. He was laughed at as a charlatan, and in his memoirs Casanova says that he was a spy; however, in spite of his mysteriousness St. Germain had a very respectable appearance and in society he was a very genial person. To this day grandmother loves him madly and gets angry if anyone speaks of him with disrespect. Grandmother knew that St. Germain could command large sums of money. She decided to resort to him, wrote him a note, and asked him to come to her immediately.

"The old eccentric soon arrived and found her in terrible grief. She described her husband's barbarity to him in the blackest colors and said, finally, that she was putting all her hope on his friendship and kindness.

"St. Germain thought for a moment.

" 'I can provide you with this sum,' he said, 'but I know you will not be calm until you repay me, and I would not want to cause you new troubles. There is another way: you can win it back.' "

" 'But my dear Count,' said grandmother, 'I am telling you that we have no money at all.' "

" 'Money isn't necessary for this,' objected St. Germain, 'hear me out if you will.' "

"Then he revealed to her a secret for which each of us would pay dearly. . . ."

The young gamblers doubled their attention. Tomsky lit his pipe, took a puff, and continued:

"That same evening grandmother appeared at Versailles *au jeu de la Reine*. The Duke of Orleans was keeping bank; grandmother excused herself slightly for not bringing her debt, spun a little tale in justification, and began to play against him. She chose three cards, and played them one after the other; all three cards won and grandmother won back absolutely everything."

"Chance!" said one of the guests.

"A fairy-tale!" remarked Hermann.

"Perhaps marked cards?" put in a third.

"I don't think so," replied Tomsky gravely.

"How is it," said Narumov, "you have a grandmother who guesses three cards in a row, and you still haven't learned this cabalism from her?"

"Yes, dammit!" replied Tomsky. "She had four sons including my father; all four were desperate gamblers, and she didn't reveal her secret to any of them, even though it wouldn't have been a bad thing for them, or even for me. But here is what my uncle, Count Ivan Ilych, told me, and he assured me of it on his honor. The late Chaplitsky, the same who died in poverty after squandering millions, once in his youth lost to Zorich—as I recall—about three hundred thousand. He was in despair. Grandmother, who was always stern toward the follies of young people, somehow took pity on Chaplitsky. She gave him three cards that he should play one after the other, and she took his word of honor that he would never play again. Chaplitsky appeared to his conqueror. They sat down to play. Chaplitsky put fifty thousand on the first card and won; he doubled, doubled again, and won back all he had lost and more. . . .

"But it's time for bed. It's already quarter to six."

Indeed, it was already getting light: the young men finished their glasses and dispersed.

II

—Il paraît que monsieur est
décidément pour les suivantes.
—Que voulez-vouz, madame? Elles
sont plus fraiches.

A SOCIETY CONVERSATION

Old Countess *** was sitting in her dressing-room in front of a mirror. Three maids surrounded her. One was holding a rouge pot, another—a box of pins, the third—a tall lace cap with ribbons of a fiery color. The old Countess did not have the slightest claim to beauty, which had faded long ago, but she preserved all the habits of her youth, kept strictly to the styles of the seventies, and dressed just as slowly, just as carefully as sixty years before. A young girl, her ward, was sitting at the window behind an embroidery frame.

"Hello, *grand'maman*," said a young officer who entered the room. "*Bonjour, mademoiselle Lise. Grand'maman*, I have a request of you."

"What is it, *Paul?*"

"Let me introduce one of my friends to you and bring him to you at the ball Friday."

"Bring him to me right at the ball, and introduce him to me there. Were you at ***'s yesterday?"

"Of course! It was very gay; they danced until five o'clock. How pretty Eletzkaya was!"

"But my dear! What is pretty about her? Isn't she like her grandmother, princess Darya Petrovna? . . . By the way, has princess Darya Petrovna gotten very old?"

"What do you mean gotten old," replied Tomsky absent-mindedly, "it's been about seven years since she died."

The girl raised her head and made a sign to the young man. He remembered that they concealed from grandmother the deaths of her contemporaries, and he bit his lip. But the Countess received this information, which was new to her, with great indifference.

"Died?" she said, "And I didn't know it. We were appointed maids of honor together, and when we were introduced, the Empress. . . ."

And for the hundredth time the Countess told the grandson her anecdote.

"Well, *Paul*," she said then, "help me get up now. Lizanka, where is my snuff-box?"

And the Countess went behind the screen with her maids to finish her toilet. Tomsky was left with the girl.

"Who is it you want to introduce?" quietly asked Lizaveta Ivanovna.

"Narumov. Do you know him?"

"No. Is he a soldier or a civilian?"

"A soldier."

"An engineer?"

"No, a cavalryman. But why did you think he was an engineer?"

The girl laughed and did not answer a word.

"*Paul!*" exclaimed the Countess from behind the screen, "send me some new novel, only please, not one of the current things."

"What do you mean, *grand'maman?*"

"That is, a novel where the hero does not strangle his father or his mother, and where there are no drowned bodies. I'm terribly afraid of drowned people!"

"There are no such novels nowadays. Wouldn't you like some Russian ones?"

"You mean there are Russian novels? . . . Send me one, dear sir, please send me one!"

"Good-bye, *grand'maman.* I am in a hurry. . . . Good-bye, Lizaveta Ivanovna! Why *did* you think Narumov was an engineer?"

And Tomsky walked out of the dressing-room.

Lizaveta Ivanovna was left alone; she left her work and started looking out the window. Soon, from behind the corner house, a young officer appeared on one side of the street. A blush covered her cheeks; she took up her work again and bent her head right over the canvas. At that moment the Countess entered completely dressed.

"Lizanka," she said, "order the carriage harnessed and we will go for a drive."

Lizanka got up from behind the embroidery frame and started picking up her work.

"What's wrong with you, my child! Are you deaf or what?" exclaimed the Countess. "Order the carriage harnessed immediately."

"Right away," the girl replied quietly and ran into the anteroom.

A servant came in and gave the Countess some books from prince Pavel Alexandrovich.

"Good! Thank him," said the Countess. "Lizanka, Lizanka! Where are you running to?"

"To get dressed."

"Later, my dear. Sit here. Open the first volume, read aloud. . . ."

The girl took the book and read several lines.

"Louder!" said the Countess. "What's wrong with you, my dear? Have you lost your voice or what? . . . Wait. . . . Push that footstool over to me, closer . . . there!"

Lizaveta Ivanovna read two more pages. The Countess yawned.

"Get rid of that book," she said, "what rubbish! Send it back to prince Pavel and have him thanked. . . . Well, what about the carriage?"

"The carriage is ready," said Lizaveta Ivanovna, glancing at the street.

"Why aren't you dressed?" said the Countess, "I always have to wait for you. It is unbearable, my dear!"

Liza ran to her room. Not two minutes had passed when the Countess began to ring with all her strength. The three maids ran in one door, and a footman in the other.

"Why is it I have to ring so long for you?" the Countess said to them. "Tell Lizaveta Ivanovna that I am waiting for her."

Lizaveta Ivanovna came in dressed in a mantle and hat.

"Finally, my dear!" said the Countess. "What kind of get-up is that? Why that? Whom are you captivating? . . . And what is the weather like? It looks like there's a wind."

"Not at all, your Ladyship! It's very calm, madam," answered the footman.

"You always talk without thinking! Open the window. Just as I thought—a wind! And a very cold one! Unharness the carriage! Lizanka, we shall not go, there was no reason to get all dressed up."

"And that is my life!" thought Lizaveta Ivanovna.

Lizaveta Ivanovna was in fact a most unhappy creature. "Bitter is another's bread," says Dante, "and difficult are the steps of another's porch"; and who can know the bitterness of dependency better than the poor ward of an aristocratic old woman? Of course, Countess *** did not have an evil soul, but she was capricious like a woman spoiled by society, miserly, and steeped in cold egotism, like all people who have had their fill of love in their own day and are alien to the present. She participated in all the frivolities of high society; she went off to balls where she sat in a corner all rouged, dressed in the old style, like an ugly and indispensible ornament of the ballroom; arriving guests would go up to her with low bows, as if by an established ceremony, and after that no one paid any attention to her. She received the whole town at her house, observing strict etiquette and recognizing no one's face. Her numerous servants, getting fat and growing grey in her anteroom and maids' room, did what they pleased, vying with each other in stealing things from the dying old lady. Lizaveta Ivanovna was the household martyr. She poured tea and was reproached for excess use of sugar; she read novels aloud and was to blame for all of the author's mistakes; she accompanied the Countess on her outings and answered for the weather and condition of the pavement. An allowance had been set for her, but it was never paid, while it was demanded of her that she dress like everyone else, i.e. like very few. She played a most pitiful role in society. Everyone knew her and no one noticed her; at balls she danced only when they were short vis-à-vis, and the ladies took her by the arm whenever they needed to go into the dressing-room to fix something on their attire. She was self-esteeming, keenly aware of her position, and she was looking around—waiting impatiently for a savior; but the young men, who were calculating in their frivolous vanity, did not consider her worthy of attention, even though Lizaveta Ivanovna was a hundred times more lovely than the cold and arrogant marriageable girls around whom they hovered. How many times, quietly leaving the boring and sumptuous drawing-room, she would go away to cry in her poor room where there was a screen covered with wallpaper, a chest-of-drawers, a small mirror, and painted bed, and where a tallow candle burned darkly in a brass chandelier!

One day—this happened two days after the party described in the beginning of this story and a week before the scene on which we stopped—one day Lizaveta Ivanovna, sitting behind her embroidery frame by the window, accidentally glanced at the street and saw a young engineer standing motionlessly with his eyes fixed on her window. She lowered her head and continued working; after five minutes she glanced up again—the young officer was standing in the same place. Not in the habit of flirting with passing officers, she ceased looking at the street and went on sewing for about two hours without raising her head. Dinner was served. She got up, began to straighten up her work, and glancing at the street accidentally, she saw the officer again. This seemed rather strange to her. After dinner she went to the window with a feeling of some disquiet, but the officer was no longer there—and she forgot about him . . .

Two days later, going out to get in the carriage with the Countess, she saw him again. He was standing right at the entrance, his face covered with a beaver collar; his black eyes glittered from under his hat. Lizaveta Ivanovna was frightened, without knowing why herself, and she got in the carriage with inexpressible trepidation.

When she had returned home she ran up to the window—the officer was standing in the same place as before, his eyes fixed on her; she walked away, tormented by curiosity and agitated by a feeling which was completely new to her.

After that not a day passed that the young man did not appear under the windows of their house at the customary hour. Unconventional relations were established between them. Sitting at her place with her work she would sense his approach, raise her head, and look at him longer and longer every day. The young man, it seemed, was thankful to her for this; with the sharp eye of youth she saw how a quick blush covered his pale cheeks every time their eyes met. In a week she smiled at him . . .

When Tomsky asked permission to introduce his friend to the Countess, the poor girl's heart leaped. But learning that Narumov was a cavalryman, not an engineer, she regretted giving away her secret to the frivolous Tomsky with an indiscreet question.

Hermann was the son of a Russified German who had left him some small capital. Firmly convinced of the necessity of consolidating his independence, Hermann did not touch the interest; he lived just on his salary, did not allow himself the slightest whim. However, he was secretive and proud, and his comrades rarely had a chance to laugh at his excessive parsimoniousness. He had strong passions and a fiery imagination, but firmness saved him from the usual errors of youth. Thus, for example, while he was a gambler in his soul, he never took cards in his hand, for he calculated that his financial position would not permit him (as he would say) "to sacrifice the essential in hope of acquiring the superfluous"—and nevertheless he sat whole nights through at the card tables and followed the various turns of play with feverish trembling.

The anecdote about the three cards had a strong effect on his imagination and did not leave his mind all night. "What if," he thought the next evening as he was wandering around Petersburg, "what if the old Countess would reveal her secret to me? Or name the three sure cards for me? Why not try my luck? . . . Introduce myself to her, get in her good graces, perhaps become her lover; but all that will take time and she is eighty years old, she could die in a week, in two days! . . . And the anecdote itself? . . . Can it be believed? . . . No! Calculation, moderation, and industrious-ness—they are my three sure cards, that's what will increase my capital threefold, increase it sevenfold, and gain me peace and independence."

Reasoning in this way he found himself on one of the main streets of Petersburg in front of a house of antiquated architecture. The street was blocked with equipages; one after another the carriages rolled up to the illuminated porch. At one moment the shapely foot of a young beauty stretched out of a carriage, the next there was a rattling jackboot, and then a striped stocking and diplomatic shoe. Fur coats and cloaks flitted past the stately door-man. Hermann stopped.

"Whose house is that?" he asked the corner policeman.

"Countess ***," replied the policeman.

Hermann trembled. The amazing anecdote again presented itself to his imagination. He started walking around the house, thinking about its owner and her wondrous ability. It was late when he returned to his humble little corner; he could not go to sleep for a long time, and when sleep overcame him he dreamed of cards, a green table, piles of banknotes, and heaps of gold coins. He played card after card, bent the corners decisively, won constantly, raked the gold toward himself, and put the banknotes in his pocket. Waking up rather late, he sighed for the loss of his fantastic wealth, again went out to wander about the city, and again found himself in front of the house of Countess ***. An unknown force seemed to have drawn him to it. He stopped and started looking at the windows. In one he saw a blackhaired little head, apparently bent over a book or some work. The head raised. Hermann saw a bright little face and black eyes. This moment decided his fate.

III

*Vous m'écrivez, mon ange,
des lettres de quatre pages
plus vite que je ne puis les
lire.*

A CORRESPONDENCE

Lizaveta Ivanovna had barely managed to take off her mantle and hat when the Countess sent for her and again ordered the carriage readied. They went to get in. While two lackeys were picking up the old lady and shoving her through the door, Lizaveta Ivanovna saw her engineer right by the wheel; he grabbed her hand, she could not collect herself from the fright; the young man disappeared: there was a letter in her hand. She concealed it behind her glove and during the whole drive she neither saw nor heard anything. The Countess had the custom of asking questions constantly when in the carriage. "Who was that we just passed?" "What is the name of this bridge?" "What is written on that sign?" This time Lizaveta Ivanovna answered randomly and irrelevantly, making the Countess angry.

"What is the matter with you, my dear? Are you in a stupor or what? Can't you hear, or don't you understand me? . . . Thank God I don't stutter and haven't lost my senses yet!"

Lizaveta Ivanovna was not listening to her. Having returned home she ran to her room, took the letter out of her glove: it was not sealed. Lizaveta Ivanovna read it. The letter contained a declaration of love—it was tender, respectful, and taken word for word from a German novel. But Lizaveta Ivanovna did not know German and was very satisfied with it.

However, the letter she had accepted did trouble her exceedingly. It was the first time she had entered close, secret relations with a young man. His audacity terrified her. She reproached herself for imprudent behavior and did not know what to do: cease sitting by the window and cool the young officer's enthusiasm for further pursuit with inattention? Send him a letter? Answer coldly and decisively? There was no one from whom to ask advice, she had neither a friend nor a mentor. Lizaveta Ivanovna decided to answer.

She sat down at the desk, took out a pen, paper, and fell thoughtful. Several times she began her letter and tore it up; first her expressions seemed too condescending to her, then too cruel. Finally she managed to write a few lines with which she was satisfied. "I am sure," she wrote, "that you have honorable intentions, and that you did not want to offend me by a thoughtless act; but our acquaintance should not have begun in such a manner. I am returning your letter to you and hope that in the future I shall not have cause to complain about undeserved disrespect."

The next day when she saw Hermann approaching, Lizaveta Ivanovna got up from her embroidery frame, went out into the hall, opened a window, and threw out the letter, depending on the alertness of the young officer. Hermann ran over, picked it up, and went into a pastry shop. Tearing off the seal he found his letter and Lizaveta Ivanovna's reply. He had expected that and he returned home, quite absorbed in his intrigue.

Three days after this a quick-eyed young girl brought Lizaveta Ivanovna a note from a dress shop. Lizaveta Ivanovna opened it uneasily, foreseeing monetary demands, and suddenly she recognized Hermann's hand.

"You've made a mistake, dear girl," she said, "this note is not for me."

"Yes, specifically for you!" replied the bold girl without hiding a sly smile. "Please read it."

Lizaveta Ivanovna ran through the note. Hermann was demanding a rendezvous.

"It cannot be!" said Lizaveta Ivanovna, frightened both by the rapidity of the demands and the method which he had employed. "This is surely not written to me." And she tore the letter into tiny pieces.

"If the letter is not to you, why did you tear it up?" said the girl, "I would have returned it to the one who sent it."

"Please, dear girl!" said Lizaveta Ivanovna, flaring up at her remark, "in the future do not bring me notes. And tell whomever sent you that he should be ashamed. . . ."

But Hermann did not relent. One way or another Lizaveta Ivanovna received letters from him every day. They were no longer translated from German. Inspired by passion, Hermann wrote them; and he spoke a language characteristic of him: they revealed both the inflexibility of his desires and the disorder of an unrestrained imagination. Lizaveta Ivanovna no longer thought of sending them back; she was infatuated by them; she began to answer them, and from day to day her notes got longer and tenderer. Finally she threw him the following letter from the window:

"There is a ball at the * * * ambassador's today. The Countess will be there. We will stay until around two o'clock. Here is a chance for you to see me alone. As soon as the Countess leaves, her servants will probably disperse; the doorman will stay in the front hall, but he usually goes back into his little room. Come at eleven thirty. Go straight up the stairs. If you find anyone in the anteroom, ask whether the Countess is home. They'll tell you no, and there isn't anything you can do. You will have to go away. But you will probably not meet anyone. The maids all sit in their own room. From the anteroom turn left—keep going straight to the Countess's bedroom. In the bedroom, behind the screen, you will see the two small doors; the one on the right is to the study where the Countess never goes, the one on the left is to the corridor, and a narrow winding staircase is there: it leads to my room."

Waiting for the appointed time, Hermann trembled like a tiger. At ten o'clock he was already standing in front of the Countess's house. The weather was terrible: the wind howled, wet flakes of snow were falling; the streetlights burned dimly, the streets were empty. Occasionally a cabby looking for a late fare pulled by on his scrawny nag. Hermann was standing there in just a frock-coat, feeling neither the wind nor snow. Finally the Countess's carriage was brought around. Hermann saw the lackeys carry out the old woman, hunched over, wrapped in a sable coat, and right behind her flitted her ward in a heavy cloak, hair decorated with fresh flowers. The doors slammed. The carriage rolled heavily over the crunching snow. The doorman locked the door. The windows went dark. Herman started walking around the emptied house; he went up to a streetlight and looked at his watch, it was twenty past eleven. He remained under the streetlight, fixing his eyes on the minute hands and waiting out the remaining minutes. At exactly half past eleven, Hermann stepped on the Countess's porch and entered the brightly illuminated entrance hall. The doorman was not there. Hermann ran up the stairs, opened the door into the anteroom and saw a servant sleeping under a lamp in an ancient soiled armchair. Hermann walked past him with light but firm steps. The hall and drawing-room were dark. A lamp in the anteroom illuminated them weakly. Hermann entered the bedroom. Before a case covered with ancient ikons burned a golden lamp. Faded damask armchairs and couches with down pillows and gold trim which was coming off stood in sad symmetry around walls covered with Chinese wallpaper. On the wall hung two portraits painted in Paris by *Madame Lebrun*. One of these depicted a stout, ruddy-cheeked man of about forty, in a light-green uniform and with a star; the other was a young beauty with an aquiline nose, with her guiches combed back, and a rose in her powdered hair. Everywhere there were porcelain shepherdesses, table clocks made by the famous Leroy, little boxes, roulette toys, fans, and various feminine playthings which were invented at the end of the century along with Montgolfier's balloon and Mesmer's magnetism. Hermann went behind the screen. There was a small iron bed behind it; to the right was the door leading to the study; to the left the other one—into the corridor. Hermann opened it, saw the narrow winding staircase which led to the room of the poor ward. . . . But he turned around and went into the dark study.

Time passed slowly. All was quiet. It struck twelve in the drawing-room; one after the other the clocks in all the rooms struck twelve—and all fell silent again. Hermann stood leaning against the cold stove. He was calm; his heart beat evenly, as in a man who has decided on something dangerous but essential. The clocks struck one and then two in the morning—and he heard the distant sound of a carriage. Involuntary agitation overcame him. The carriage drove up and stopped. He heard the thump of the steps being lowered. There was a bustle in the house. Servants ran about, voices rang out, and the house lit up. The three old maids ran into the bedroom, and the Countess, barely alive, entered and sank into a Voltaire armchair. Hermann looked through a crack: Lizaveta Ivanovna walked past him. Hermann heard her hurrying footsteps on the step of her staircase. Something like a pang of conscience murmured in him and again fell silent. He turned to stone.

The Countess began to undress before the mirror. Her rose-decorated bonnet was unpinned; the powdered wig was taken off her gray and closely shorn hair. Pins scattered around her like rain. Her yellow dress, embroidered with silver, fell to her swollen feet. Hermann was witness to the repulsive secrets of her toilet; finally the Countess was in just her nightgown and nightcap: in this attire, which was more proper to her old age, she seemed less terrible and ugly.

Like all old people in general, the Countess suffered from insomnia. Having undressed, she sat down in the Voltaire armchair by the window and dismissed the maids. They took out the candles; again the room was lit by one lamp. All yellow the Countess sat there, moving her pendulous lips, swaying back and forth from left to right. Her cloudy eyes reflected a complete absence of thought; looking at her one could think that the terrible old woman's swaying resulted not from her own will, but by the action of a hidden galvanism.

Suddenly the dead face changed inexpressibly. The lips stopped moving, the eyes became animated: before the Countess stood an unknown man.

"Don't be afraid, for God's sake, don't be afraid!" he said in a distinct and quiet voice. "I have no intention of harming you; I have come to implore you for one favor."

The old lady looked at him, silently and, it seemed, did not hear him. Hermann imagined that she was deaf, and bending down right to her ear he repeated the same thing to her. The old lady remained silent as before.

"You," continued Hermann, "can make my life happy, and it will cost you nothing; I know that you can guess three cards in a row . . ."

Hermann stopped. The Countess, it seemed, understood what he was demanding of her; it seemed she was searching for words for her answer.

"That was a joke," she said finally, "I swear to you, it was a joke!"

"This is nothing to joke about," Hermann objected angrily. "Remember Chaplitsky whom you helped win?"

The Countess was visibly disturbed. Her features portrayed violent agitation in her soul; but she quickly fell back into her previous senselessness.

"Can you," continued Hermann, "designate the three sure cards for me?"

The Countess remained silent. Hermann continued:

"Whom are you saving your secret for? For your grandsons? They are rich without it; they don't even know the value of money. Your three cards won't help a spendthrift. He who does not know how to take care of his patrimony will still die in poverty—in spite of any demonic efforts. I'm not a spendthrift; I know the value of money. Your three cards won't be wasted on me. Well! . . ."

He stopped and waited, trembling, for her answer. The Countess remained silent. Hermann got on his knees.

"If ever," he said, "your heart knew the feeling of love, if you remember its raptures, if even once you have smiled at the crying of a newborn son, if anything human has ever beat in your breast,

I implore you, by the feelings of a wife, lover, mother, by everything that is holy in life, do not refuse me my request! Reveal your secret to me! What is it to you? . . . Perhaps it is connected to a terrible sin, to a pact with the devil . . . Think: you are old, you do not have long to live—I am ready to take your sin on my soul. Just reveal your secret to me. Think: the happiness of a man is in your hands, not only I, but my children, grandchildren, and great grandchildren will bless your memory and will respect it as a holy thing . . ."

The old lady did not answer a word.

Hermann rose.

"Old witch!" he said, clenching his teeth, "Then I'll force you to answer . . ."

With this word he took a pistol out of his pocket.

At the sight of the pistol the Countess displayed strong feeling for the second time. She threw back her head and raised her arm as if warding off a shot . . . Then she fell backward . . . and remained motionless.

"Stop being childish," said Hermann, taking her arm. "I'm asking for the last time: do you want to designate the three cards for me? Yes or no?"

The Countess did not answer. Hermann saw that she was dead.

IV

7 Mai 18—
Homme sans moeurs et sans religion!
CORRESPONDENCE

Lizaveta Ivanovna was sitting in her room still in her ball attire, sunk in deep reflection. Arriving home she hurried to dismiss the sleepy maid who had unwillingly offered her services—she said that she would get undressed herself, and with trepidation she walked into her room, hoping to find Hermann there and wishing not to find him. With her first look she assured herself of his absence and thanked fate for the obstacle which prevented their rendezvous. She sat down without undressing and started remembering all of the circumstances which had lured her so far in such a short time. Not three weeks had passed since the time she first saw the young man through the window—and already she was corresponding with

him and he had succeeded in demanding a night-time rendezvous!
She knew his name only because some of his letters had been
signed; she had never talked to him, had not heard his voice, had
never heard anything about him . . . until this very evening. Strange
thing! At the ball that same evening Tomsky wanted to get revenge
on young princess Polina * * * (at whom he was mad because contrary to her custom she was flirting with someone other than him)
by showing indifference: he invited Lizaveta Ivanovna and danced
an endless mazurka with her. The whole time he joked about her
proclivity for engineering officers; he assured her that he knew
considerably more than she could suppose, and some of his jokes
were so aptly aimed that a few times Lizaveta Ivanovna thought
that her secret was known to him.

"From whom do you learn all this?" she asked smiling.

"From the friend of a person whom you know well," answered
Tomsky, "a very remarkable man!"

"Who is this remarkable man?"

"His name is Hermann."

Lizaveta Ivanovna answered nothing, but her hands and feet
turned to ice . . .

"This Hermann," continued Tomsky, "is a truly romantic character. He has the profile of Napoleon and the soul of Mephistopheles. I think that he has at least three malefactions on his
conscience. How pale you've gotten! . . ."

"My head aches . . . What did Hermann tell you . . . or whatever
his name was? . . ."

"Hermann is very dissatisfied with his friend; he says that in his
place he would act quite differently . . . I even suspect that Hermann himself has his eyes on you; at least he listens to the amorous
exclamations of his friend in anything but an indifferent way."

"But where did he see me?"

"In church, perhaps; out driving! . . . God knows! Perhaps in
your room, while you were asleep. He's capable of it . . ."

Three ladies who came up to them with the question *"oubli
ou regret?"* interrupted the conversation which was becoming so
tormentingly fascinating for Lizaveta Ivanovna.

The lady Tomsky chose was princess * * * herself. She managed
to smooth things over with him while turning an extra circle and
spinning around before her chair an extra time. When he returned

to his place, Tomsky was no longer thinking either about Hermann or Lizaveta Ivanovna. She wanted to renew the interrupted conversation without fail, but the mazurka ended and soon afterward the old Countess left.

Tomsky's words were nothing but mazurka chatter, but they were deeply implanted in the soul of the young dreamer. The portrait which Tomsky had outlined corresponded to the picture she herself had composed; and thanks to the latest novels this already banal character frightened and captivated her imagination. She sat with her bare arms crossed; her head, still decorated with flowers, was bent over her open bosom . . . Suddenly the door opened and Hermann walked in She began to tremble . . .

"Where have you been?" she asked in a frightened whisper.

"In the old Countess's bedroom," replied Hermann, "I've just come from her. The Countess is dead."

"My God! . . . What are you saying?"

"And it seems," continued Hermann, "that I am the cause of her death."

Lizaveta Ivanovna looked at him and Tomsky's words rang out in her soul: *the man has at least three malefactions on his soul!* Hermann sat down on the window-ledge near her and told her everything.

Lizaveta Ivanovna listened to him with horror. So the passionate letters, the flaming demands, the audacious, stubborn pursuit— none of this was love! Money! That was what his soul thirsted for! It was not she who could slake his desires and make him happy! The poor ward was nothing but the blind helper of a robber, the murderer of her old benefactress! . . . She cried bitterly in her tormenting, belated repentance. Hermann watched her silently; his heart too was torn, but neither the tears of the poor girl nor the amazing charm of her grief troubled his stern soul. He felt no pangs of conscience at the thought of the dead woman. One thing horrified him: the irreparable loss of the secret from which he expected enrichment.

"You are a monster!" said Lizaveta Ivanovna finally.

"I did not want her death," replied Hermann, "my pistol is not loaded."

They fell silent.

Morning was breaking. Lizaveta Ivanovna extinguished the

glittering candle; the pale light illumined her room. She wiped her tear-stained eyes and raised them to Hermann; he was sitting on the window-ledge, arms folded, frowning menacingly. In this position he was amazingly like a portrait of Napoleon. The similarity struck even Lizaveta Ivanovna.

"How are you going to get out of the house?" said Lizaveta Ivanovna finally. "I had planned to take you by a secret staircase, but it is necessary to go past the bedroom, and I'm afraid to."

"Tell me how to find the secret staircase and I'll go out."

Lizaveta Ivanovna got up, took a key out of the chest-of-drawers, handed it to Hermann, and gave him detailed instructions. Hermann pressed her cold, unresponding hand, kissed her bowed head and went out.

He descended the steep staircase and again entered the Countess's bedroom. The dead woman was sitting there, turned to stone; her face expressed profound calm. Hermann stopped before her, looked at her for a long time, as if wishing to confirm the terrible truth; finally he went into the study, felt about for a door behind the tapestry, and started down a dark staircase disturbed by strange sensations. Along this same staircase, he thought, perhaps sixty years ago, toward this same bedroom, at this same hour, wearing an embroidered *kaftan*, hair combed *à l'oiseau royal*, pressing his three-cornered hat to his heart, crept a lucky young man who had long since rotted in the grave, and today the heart of his ancient lover had stopped beating. . . .

At the foot of the staircase Hermann found a door which he unlocked with the same key, and he found himself in a transverse corridor which led him to the street.

v

That night the deceased Baroness
von B*** appeared to me. She was
all in white and said to me: "Hello,
Mr. Councillor!"

SWEDENBORG

Three days after the fateful night at nine o'clock in the morning, Hermann set off for * * * monastery where the service for the body

of the deceased Countess was being held. Though he felt no repentance, he could not completely suppress the voice of his conscience which kept telling him: "You are the old lady's murderer!"
Having little true faith, he had a multitude of superstitions. He
believed that the dead Countess could have a harmful influence on
his life, and he decided to make an appearance at her funeral to
beg her forgiveness.

The church was full. Hermann could hardly make his way
through the crowd of people. The coffin stood on an opulent
catafalque under a velvet canopy. The deceased lay in it, with arms
crossed on her chest, in a lace bonnet and a white satin dress. Her
domestics stood around it—the servants in black *kaftans* with
armorial ribbons on their shoulders, and with candles in their
hands; the relatives were in deep mourning dress—children, grandchildren, and great grandchildren. No one was crying; tears would
have been *une affectation*. The Countess was so old that her death
could not surprise anyone, and her relatives had long viewed her
as having lived past her time. A young bishop gave the funeral
oration. In simple and touching phrases he described the peaceful
passing of the righteous woman whose long years were a quiet,
touching preparation for a Christian demise. "The angel of death
found her," said the orator, "engaged in pious meditations and
waiting for the midnight bridegroom." The service was completed
with sad decorum. The relatives were first to go take leave of the
body. Then followed the numerous guests who had come to pay
their respects to the one who had been a participant in their vain
amusements for so long. After them came all of the servants. Finally
an old housekeeper who was the same age as the deceased went up.
Two young girls were holding her under the arms. She was not
strong enough to bow down to the ground—and she alone shed a
few tears when she had kissed the hand of her mistress. After her
Hermann decided to approach the coffin. He bowed down to the
ground and lay for a few minutes on the cold floor which was
strewn with fir twigs. Finally he got up; pale as the deceased herself
he went up the steps of the catafalque and bowed . . . At that
moment it seemed to him that the dead woman glanced at him
mockingly, winking one eye. Hermann moved back hastily,
stumbled, and crashed backwards to the ground. They picked him

up. At this same time Lizaveta Ivanovna was carried out onto the porch in a faint. This episode disturbed the solemnity of this somber ceremony for a few minutes. A muffled murmur arose among the visitors, and an emaciated chamberlain, a close relative of the deceased, whispered into the ear of an Englishman who was standing next to him that the young officer was her illegitimate son, to which the Englishman replied coldly, "Oh?"

Hermann was extremely upset all day. Having dinner in a lonely inn he drank very much, contrary to his custom, in hope of suppressing the inner agitation. But the wine inflamed his imagination even more. When he returned home he threw himself on the bed without undressing and fell fast asleep.

It was still night when he awoke; the moon illumined his room. He glanced at the clock—it was quarter to three. Sleep had left him; he sat on the bed and thought about the funeral of the old Countess.

At that moment someone looked in his window from the street —and immediately walked away. Hermann paid no attention to this. In a minute he heard the door to the anteroom being opened. Hermann thought that his orderly, drunk as usual, was returning from a nocturnal carousal. But he heard an unfamiliar walk: someone was walking, softly shuffling slippers. The door opened. A woman in a white dress entered. Hermann took her for his old wetnurse and was amazed—what could bring her here at such an hour? But the white woman, gliding, suddenly appeared in front of him —and Hermann recognized the Countess!

"I came to you against my will," she said in a firm voice, "but I have been commanded to fulfill your request. The three, seven, and ace will win for you in sequence, provided that you do not play more than one card in twenty-four hours and that you never play in your life afterwards. I forgive you my death provided you marry my ward, Lizaveta Ivanovna. . . ."

With these words she turned quietly, went to the door, and disappeared, slippers shuffling. Hermann heard the door slam in the hall, and saw someone look in the window at him again.

For a long while Hermann could not come to his senses. He went out into the other room. His orderly was sleeping on the floor; with difficulty Hermann woke him up. As was customary, the orderly was drunk; it was impossible to get any sense out of him. The outside door was locked. Hermann returned to his room, lit a candle, and wrote down his vision.

VI

—Attendez!
—*How do you dare say* attendez
to me?
—*Your Excellency, I said* "Attendez,
sir!"

Two fixed ideas cannot exist together in moral nature, just as two bodies cannot occupy one and the same place in the physical world. In Hermann's imagination the three, seven, and ace quickly overspread the image of the dead woman. The three, seven, and ace did not leave his head; they stirred on his lips. Seeing a young girl he would say, "How shapely she is! A real three of hearts." Asked what time it was, he would answer, "Five minutes before the seven." Every fat-bellied man reminded him of an ace. The three, seven, and ace pursued him in his sleep, assuming all possible shapes: the three bloomed before him in the form of a luxurious plant, the seven presented itself as Gothic gates, the ace as an enormous spider. All his thoughts flowed into one: using the secret which had cost him so dearly. He began to think about resignation and traveling. He wanted to extort a treasure from enchanted fortune in the open gambling houses of Paris. Chance saved him the trouble.

A society of rich gamblers was formed in Moscow under the leadership of the famous Chekalinsky, who had spent his entire life playing cards and had once amassed millions by winning promissory notes and losing cash. Long experience had earned him the trust of his comrades, and his open house, famed chef, kindness, and merriness acquired the respect of the public. He came to Petersburg. The young people rushed to him, forgetting balls for cards and preferring the temptations of faro to the allurements of philandering. Narumov took Hermann to him.

They passed through a series of magnificent rooms filled with polite servants. Several generals and Privy Councillors were playing whist; the young men were sprawled languidly on overstuffed divans, eating ice cream and smoking pipes. In the drawing-room behind a long table around which about twenty gamblers were crowded, sat the host, keeping bank. He was a man of about sixty, of the most respectable appearance; his head was covered with silver grey; his full and fresh face displayed affability, his eyes glittered, animated by a constant smile. Narumov introduced Hermann to him. Chekalinsky shook his hand amiably, asked him not to stand on ceremony, and continued dealing.

The round lasted a long time. There were more than thirty cards on the table.

Chekalinsky stopped after each play in order to give the players time to make their arrangements; he wrote the losses down, politely listened to their demands, even more politely straightened out a card whose corner had been bent more than once by a preoccupied hand. Finally, the round ended. Chekalinsky shuffled the cards and prepared to deal another.

"Allow me to bet on a card," said Hermann, stretching his hand out from behind a fat man, who was playing there. Chekalinsky smiled and bowed silently as a sign of his humble consent. Smiling, Narumov congratulated Hermann on the termination of his lengthy fast and wished him a lucky start.

"Stake!" said Hermann, writing the figure in chalk on his card.

"How much, sir?" asked the banker, squinting. "Excuse me, I cannot make it out."

"Forty seven thousand," replied Hermann.

At these words all heads turned at once, and all eyes were fixed on Hermann. "He's gone out of his mind!" thought Narumov.

"Allow me to point out to you," said Chekalinsky with his unchanging smile, "that your bet is high; no one here has staked more than two hundred seventy-five rubles at once yet."

"Well," objected Hermann, "will you play against my card or not?"

Chekalinsky bowed with an air of the same modest consent.

"I only wished to inform you," he said, "that honored by the trust of my comrades I can only play for cash. For my part, I, of course, am sure that your word is sufficient; but for the orderliness of the game and accounts I request you to put your money on the card."

Hermann took a banknote from his pocket and gave it to

Chekalinsky who, cursorily examining it, put it on Hermann's card.

He began to deal. On the right lay the nine, on the left the three.

"It won!" said Herman, showing his card.

A whisper began among the gamblers. Chekalinsky frowned, but the smile immediately returned to his face.

"Do you wish the money now?" he asked Hermann.

"If you will be so good."

Chekalinsky took several banknotes from his pocket and immediately counted them out. Hermann took his money and walked away from the table. Narumov could not get over it. Hermann drank a glass of lemonade and went home.

The next evening he appeared at Chekalinsky's again. The host was dealing. Hermann walked up to the table; the punters immediately gave him a place. Chekalinsky bowed genially to him.

Hermann waited for a new round, placed his card down with his forty seven thousand and yesterday's winnings on it.

Chekalinsky began to deal. A jack fell on the right, a seven on the left.

Hermann revealed his seven.

Everyone gasped. Chekalinsky was visibly disturbed. He counted out ninety four thousand and handed it to Hermann. Hermann took it coolly and departed that very minute.

The next evening Hermann again appeared at the table. Everyone was waiting for him. The generals and Privy Councillors left their whist to watch such unusual play. The young officers jumped up from the divans; all of the servants gathered in the drawing-room. They surrounded Hermann. The other gamblers did not place their cards, waiting impatiently to see how he would end. Hermann stood at the table preparing to punt alone against the pale but still smiling Chekalinsky. They each opened a deck of cards. Chekalinsky shuffled. Hermann took out his card and placed it down, covering it with a heap of banknotes. It looked like a duel. Profound silence reigned all around.

Chekalinsky began to deal, his hands were shaking. On the right lay a lady, on the left an ace.

"The ace won!" said Hermann and revealed his card.

"Your lady is beaten," said Chekalinsky genially.

Hermann shuddered: in fact, instead of the ace, he had the

queen of spades. He did not believed his eyes, not understanding how he could have mispulled.

At that moment it seemed to him that the queen of spades winked and grinned. The extraordinary similarity struck him. . . .

"The old woman!" he exclaimed in horror.

Chekalinsky pulled the lost banknotes toward himself. Hermann stood motionless. When he walked away from the table, noisy talk arose. "Excellently punted!" the gamblers said. Chekalinsky again shuffled the cards: the game went on in its normal course.

CONCLUSION

Hermann went out of his mind. He is in room 17 of the Obukhov hospital; he does not answer any questions, and he murmurs unusually rapidly: "Three, seven, ace! Three, seven, queen!"

Lizaveta Ivanovna married a very amiable young man; he serves somewhere and has considerable property, he is the son of the old Countess's former steward. A poor relative is being brought up at Lizaveta Ivanovna's.

Tomsky has been promoted to captain and will marry princess Polina.

NIKOLAI GOGOL

The Overcoat

IN THE DEPARTMENT OF—but it is better not to say in which department. There is nothing touchier than any type of department, regiment, governmental office and, in a word, any type of official body. Nowadays any private person considers all society insulted when he is. It is said that not very long ago at all a certain police captain (I don't recall from what town) sent in a petition in which he clearly demonstrates that governmental decrees are perishing and that his own sacred name is being uttered most definitely in vain. And in proof he appended to the petition an enormous volume of some romantic work or other in which, every ten pages or so, a police captain appears, in places even in a completely drunken state. And so, to avoid any unpleasantness, we had better call the department in question *a certain department.* And so, in *a certain department* there served *a certain official*; it cannot be said that the official was very remarkable—he was rather short, somewhat pockmarked, somewhat red-haired, even somewhat short-sighted, with a small bald spot on his head, with wrinkles on both sides of his cheeks, and a face the color which is called hemorrhoidal . . . What

Translated by CARL R. PROFFER.

can be done! The Petersburg climate is guilty. As for rank (for with us rank must be announced before anything else), he was what is called an eternal titular councillor—a rank which, as is well known, has been sneered at and jeered at quite enough by various writers whose praiseworthy custom it is to set upon those who cannot bite back. The surname of this official was Bashmachkin. Just from the name itself, it is obvious that at one time it derived from *bashmak**; but when, at what time, and by what means it was derived from *bashmak*—none of this is known. Both his father and his grand-father, and even his brother-in-law, and absolutely all of the Bash-machkins always walked about in *sapogi,*** just changing the soles a few times a year. His name was Akaky Akakievich. Perhaps it will seem somewhat strange and arcane to the reader; but we can assure him that it was not searched for at all, and that quite by themselves circumstances occurred such that it was quite impossible to give him any other name, and that it happened like this: Akaky Akakie-vich was born, if memory does not betray me, on the night before March 23. His late mother, an official's wife and a very good woman, arranged as necessary to christen the baby. His mother was still lying in the bed opposite the door, and at her right hand stood the god-father, Ivan Ivanovich Eroshkin, a most excellent man, who served as head clerk in the senate, and the godmother, the wife of a police officer, a woman of rare virtues, Arina Semyonovna Belobryushkova. The new mother was presented a choice of any of three names she wanted to choose: Mokkiya, Sossiya, or name the baby in honor of the martyr Xozdazat. "No," thought his late mother, "those names are all so queer." To please her, the calendar of saints was opened in another place; three more names came up: Trifily, Dula, and Varakhasy. "What a punishment," murmured the old woman, "such names they all are; I've never heard such things. If it had even been Varadat or Varukh, but Trifily and Varakhasy?" They turned over another page—Pavsikakhy and Vakhtisy came up. "Well, I can see already," said the old lady, "that obviously such is his fate. If that's the case, it'll be better to give him his father's name. The father was Akaky, so let the son be Akaky." And it was in this way that Akaky Akakievich came about. The baby was

---

* The Russian for "shoe."
** The Russian for "boots."

christened, at which he began to cry and made a face—as if he had a premonition that he would be a titular councillor. And so that is how all this came about. We have cited it so that the reader could see for himself that it happened absolutely from necessity and that it was quite impossible to give him any other name. When and at what time he entered the department, and who appointed him, no one could recall. No matter how many directors and chiefs changed, he was seen in exactly the same place, in the same position, in the same job, the same copy clerk—so that after a while they became certain that he, evidently, had been born into the world just like that, already completely ready, in a uniform and with a bald spot on his head. In the department no respect was shown him. Not only did the doormen not get up from their seats when he walked by, they did not even glance at him—as if a simple fly had flown through the waiting-room. The chiefs treated him somehow coldly-despotically. Some assistant of the head clerk would poke papers straight under his nose without saying even, "Copy it" or "Here's a nice interesting little case," or something pleasant as is the custom in cultured offices. And glancing only at the paper he would take it, without looking up to see who had put it in front of him and whether he had a right to do it. He would take it and immediately settle down to copy it. The young clerks snickered and cracked jokes about him with all the wit office clerks can muster; right in front of him they told various stories which they made up about him, about his landlady, a seventy year old woman—they said that she beat him, asked when their wedding would be, and scattered bits of paper on his head calling it snow. But Akaky Akakievich did not answer a word to this, as if there were not even anyone in front of him; it did not even affect his work: amid all of these cracks he did not make a single mistake in copying. Only if the joke was too unbearable, when they shoved his arm and prevented him from doing his work, he would say, "Leave me alone, why do you insult me?" And there was something strange in these words and the voice with which they were pronounced. In it there was a note of something which inclined one to pity so much that one recently appointed young man who, following the others' example, had allowed himself to make fun of him, suddenly stopped as if thunderstruck; and after that everything seemed to change and

appear in a different light to him. Some supernatural power alien-
ated him from the colleagues with whom he had become acquainted,
taking them for decent, well-bred men. And for a long time afterwards, in the midst of his gayest moments, he imagined the short
official with the bald spot on his head and his penetrating words:
"Leave me alone, why do you insult me?" And in these penetrating
words rang other words: "I am your brother." And the poor young
man covered his face with his hands and many times in his life after
this he shuddered to see how much inhumanity there is in man,
how much hidden savage brutality there is in refined, cultured manners, and, Lord, even in a man society regards as noble and
honorable.

It is unlikely that one could find a man who lived more for his
job. It would be too little to say he served zealously; no, he served
with love. There, in the copying, he saw some pleasant and varied
world of his own. Pleasure was expressed on his face; some letters
were his favorites, and when he got to them he was beside himself:
he chuckled, and he winked, and he helped with his lips so that in
his face, so it seemed, one could read every letter which his pen
traced. If he had been given rewards commensurate with his zeal, to
his own amazement he might perhaps have even been promoted to
State Councillor; but as his colleagues the jokesters phrased it, he
had earned only a badge for his buttonhole and a hemorrhoid for
his butt. However, one cannot say that no attention was paid to
him. One director who was a kind person and wanted to reward
him for his long service ordered that he be given something a little
more important than the usual copying; to be precise, out of an
already prepared form he was ordered to make a report for another
official bureau; the matter consisted only of changing the title heading and here and there changing verbs from the first person to the
third. This caused him so much labor that he began to sweat all
over, wiped his forehead, and finally said, "No, better let me copy
something." After that they always let him copy. Outside this copying, it seemed, nothing existed for him. He did not think about his
clothing at all; his uniform was not green, but some mealy-reddish
color. His collar was narrow and short, so that although it was not
long, his neck, protruding from the collar, seemed extraordinarily
long, like on those plaster kittens with bobbing heads whole dozens

of which are carried on the heads of Russian foreigners.* And something was always sticking to his uniform, either a piece of straw or some thread; besides that, he had a special knack, when walking along the street, for happening under a window just at the time when all sorts of rubbish was being thrown out of it; and because of that he was eternally carrying watermelon or muskmelon rinds and such like nonsense around on his hat. Not once in his life had he paid any attention to what was going on in the street daily, to the things which, as is well known, are looked at by his colleagues—young men who extend the penetration of their brisk glances so far that they will even notice that the trouser strap of someone on the other side of the pavement has come loose, which always results in a sly grin on their face.

But if Akaky Akakievich glanced at anything, he saw only his own neat lines written out in an even hand; and only if a horse's muzzle, appearing from no one knows where, came to rest on his shoulder and set loose a whole windstorm on his cheek with its nostrils, only then did he notice that he was not in the middle of a line, but rather in the middle of a street. Arriving home he would immediately sit down at the same table, hastily gulp his cabbage soup and eat a chunk of beef with onion, not noticing their taste in the least; he ate it all with flies and with anything that God might send at that time. Noting that his stomach was starting to puff up, he would get up from the table, take out a jar with ink, and he would copy papers which he had brought home. If there didn't happen to be any of these, he would purposely make a copy of something for himself, for his personal pleasure, especially if the paper was notable not for its beauty of style but for being addressed to some new or important person.

Even at those hours when all the light has gone from the grey Petersburg sky and all the civil service folks have eaten their fill and dined, each as he could, according to his received salary and personal whim—when everything has rested after departmental scratching of pens, the bustle of their and other people's urgent chores, and all of that which, even more than necessary, a restless man voluntarily imposes on himself—when the clerks are rushing to devote the remaining time to enjoyment: those who are livelier go off to

* Foreign hawkers in Russia carried plaster dolls on trays on their heads.—*Translator*.

the theater; others go on the street, setting aside the time for the examination of some kind of hats or other; some go to evening parties to spend it on compliments to some comely girl, the star of a small civil service circle; some, and this happens most often, simply go to their colleague's place on the fourth and fifth floor, two small rooms with a hallway entrance or kitchen and pretensions to fashion, a lamp or some other knick-knack which cost many sacrifices, doing without dinners or outings—in a word, even at the time when all of the clerks have dispersed among the small apartments of their friends to play a stormy game of whist while slurping tea from glasses, nibbling penny-biscuits, drawing smoke from long chibouks and, during the deal, telling about some scandal which had filtered down from high society, something which no Russian of any class can ever refrain from, or even, when there is nothing to talk about, retelling the eternal anecdote about the Commandant who was informed that someone had cut the tail off the Falconet monument —in a word, even when everyone is trying to amuse himself, Akaky Akakievich did not give himself to any amusement. No one could say that he had ever seen him at any evening party. When he had copied to his heart's content he went to bed, smiling in advance about the next day: God would send him something to copy tomorrow. . . . Thus flowed the peaceful life of a man who knew how to be satisfied with his lot on a salary of four hundred, and it would perhaps have flowed on to an advanced age if there were not various calamities strewn on life's road not only for titular but even for state, actual, court, and all kinds of councillors, even for those who do not give counsel to anyone and do not take it from anyone themselves.

There is in Petersburg a powerful enemy of all those who received a salary of four hundred rubles a year or thereabouts. This enemy is none other than our northern frost, although, incidentally, they say it is very healthy. At nine o'clock in the morning, precisely at the hour when the streets are covered by people going to their departments, it begins to deal out such powerful and stinging fillips to all noses without exception, that the poor clerks simply do not know where to stick them. At the time when the foreheads of even those who occupy higher offices hurt from the frost and tears appear in their eyes, the poor titular councillors are sometimes defenseless. Their only salvation consists in running across five or six streets as fast as possible in their threadbare little overcoats, and then vigorously stamping their feet in the vestibule until, in this way, they thaw out all of the abilities and gifts for carrying out official responsibilities. For some time Akaky Akakievich had begun to feel that somehow it had started to penetrate his back and shoulders with special ferocity, in spite of the fact that he tried to run the necessary space as fast as possible. Finally he wondered if there weren't some faults in his overcoat. Examining it carefully at his home, he discovered that in two or three places, precisely in the back and shoulders, it had become just like cheesecloth; so much of the cloth had been rubbed away that it let in the wind, and the lining was falling to pieces. It should be noted that Akaky Akakievich's overcoat also served as a subject for the clerks' jokes; they had even stripped it of the noble name overcoat and called it a bathrobe. It did in fact have a strange cut: with each year its collar got smaller and smaller, because it was used for the patching of its other parts. The patching did not reveal the art of a tailor, and it came out really baggy and ugly. Seeing what the trouble was, Akaky Akakievich decided he would have to take the overcoat to Petrovich, the tailor who lived somewhere on the fourth floor off the fourth flight of stairs; in spite of the fact that he had only one eye and had pockmarks all over his face, he worked rather successfully at repairing the pants and frockcoats of clerks and all kinds of other people— when, it goes without saying, he was in a sober state and was pondering no other project in his head. Little, of course, should have to be said about this tailor, but since it has already become customary for the personality of every character in a story to be delineated fully, there's nothing to be done—give us Petrovich too. At first he was called simply Grigory and was the serf of some landlord; he started calling himself Petrovich when he received his freedom and began to booze it up quite a little on every holiday—the major ones at first, and then, indiscriminantly, on all church holidays, whenever there was a cross on the calendar. In this respect he was true to the customs of his forefathers, and when he quarreled with his wife he called her a worldly woman and a German. Since we have already mentioned his wife, it will be necessary to say a couple of words about her too; but, unfortunately, not very much was known about her, except that she was Petrovich's wife, she even wore a bonnet rather than a kerchief; but she could not, it would seem, boast of her beauty—at any rate when meeting her on the street only guardsmen peeped under her bonnet and they would twitch their moustaches and emit some queer noise.

While climbing the stairway leading to Petrovich's—a stairway which (we must render it justice) was all anointed with water and slops and saturated through and through with that odor of spirits which eats at the eyes and, as is well known, is permanently present on all back stairways in Petersburg houses—while climbing this staircase Akaky Akakievich was already thinking about how much Petrovich would ask, and mentally he determined not to give more than two rubles. The door was open because the mistress, preparing some kind of fish, had set loose so much smoke in the kitchen that you couldn't even see the cockroaches. Akaky Akakievich passed through the kitchen unnoticed even by the mistress herself, and, at last, entered a room where he saw Petrovich sitting on a broad, unpainted wooden table with his legs folded under him like a Turkish pasha. His feet, as is customary with tailors sitting at work, were bare. And the first thing to strike the eye was his big toe, very well known to Akaky Akakievich, with a kind of mangled nail, thick and strong like the shell of a tortoise. Around Petrovich's neck hung a skein of silk and thread, and across his knees there were some sort of rags. He had already been poking the thread at the eye of a needle for about three minutes—without hitting it and therefore he got very angry at the darkness and even at the thread itself, grumbling in an undertone, "Won't crawl in, barbarian: you irk me, you slut!" It was unpleasant for Akaky Akakievich that he had come just at this moment when Petrovich was angry: he liked to order something from Petrovich when the latter was already a little loose, or, as his wife phrased it, "he's bombed on brandy, the one-eyed devil." In that condition Petrovich usually gave way on the price and agreed very willingly, even bowing and thanking him every time. Afterwards, it is true, his wife would come, crying, and say her husband was drunk and therefore had taken the work cheaply; he would add a ten-kopeck piece and it was in the bag. Now, however, Petrovich was, it seemed, in a sober state, and therefore stern, intractable, and anxious to stack on the devil knows what fees. Akaky Akakievich realized this and was all set, as they say, to beat a hasty retreat, but the matter had already been started. Petrovich screwed up his single eye very steadily on him, and Akaky Akakievich involuntarily blurted:

"How are you, Petrovich!"

"I wish you health, sir," said Petrovich, and he squinted his eye at Akaky Akalievich's hands wanting to spy out what sort of booty he was carrying.

"And I here have brought to you, Petrovich, er, see. . . ."

It must be explained that Akaky Akakievich expressed himself for the most part in prepositions, adverbs, and, finally, particles such as have absolutely no meaning. If the matter was very difficult, he even had the custom of not finishing his sentences at all, so that extremely often he started a speech with the words, "This, really is completely er—you know. . . ." and then there was nothing more, and he himself forgot, thinking he had already said everything.

"What's this?" said Petrovich, at the same time scanning his whole uniform with his one eye, beginning with the collar down to the sleeves, back, tails, and buttonholes—all of which was very familiar because it was his own work.

Such is the habit of tailors; it's the first thing they do when meeting someone.

"Well, I here, er . . . Petrovich . . . my overcoat, the fabric . . . here you see, everywhere in other places it's quite strong, it's a little dusty and seems as if it's old, but it's new, except just in one place a little er . . . on the back, and also here on one shoulder it's a tiny little bit rubbed away, and here on this shoulder a little—you see, that's all. And it's not much work. . . ."

Petrovich took the bathrobe, spread it first on the table, examined it for a long time, shook his head, and reached his hand over to the window for a round snuffbox with a picture of some general on it, specifically which one is unknown because the place where his face was had been punched through by a finger and then had a square scrap of paper pasted over it. Sniffing some tobacco Petrovich spread the bathrobe wide over his arms and examined it against the light and again shook his head. Then he turned its lining up and once more shook his head, once more removed the lid with the general pasted over with paper, and having transported some tobacco to his nose, put the snuffbox away and, finally, said:

"No, it cannot be fixed: a bad wardrobe!"

At these words Akaky Akakievich's heart skipped a beat.

"Why can't you, Petrovich?" he said almost in the pleading voice of a child. "Why all there is is it's a bit rubbed down on the shoulders, why you have some pieces of cloth. . . ."

"Yes, pieces can be found, pieces will be found," said Petrovich, "but it's impossible to sew them on. The whole thing's rotten, touch it with a needle and it'll fall apart."

"Let it fall apart, then you'll patch it right away."

"Why there's nothing to put a patch on, there's nothing to anchor it on. It's worn to bits. It's hyperbole to call it cloth—if the wind blows it'll fly apart."

"Well, then reinforce. How to er . . . , really, er! . . ."

"No," said Petrovich decisively, "nothing can be done. It's completely rotten. You'll be better off if when the cold time of winter comes you make yourself leg wrappings out of it, because stockings don't keep you warm. The Germans invented them so they could pick up a little more money for themselves (Petrovich liked to poke at the Germans on occasion), but it's obvious you'll have to have a new overcoat made."

At the word "new" Akaky Akakievich's eyes fogged over and everything in the room started swinging confusedly. The only thing he saw clearly was the general, with the paper pasted over his face, that was on the lid of Petrovich's snuffbox.

"What do you mean new?" he said, still as if in a dream. "Why I don't have money for that."

"Yes, a new one," said Petrovich with barbaric calm.

"Well, and if a new one had to be, how would it er. . . ."

"That is, what will it cost?"

"Yes."

"Why you'll have to put out more than three fifty-ruble notes," said Petrovich, pursing his lips significantly as he did so.

He liked strong effects very much, liked somehow to suddenly nonplus you completely and then look out the corner of his eye to see what sort of face the nonplussed person would make after his words.

"One hundred and fifty rubles for an overcoat?" exclaimed poor Akaky Akakievich—exclaimed for perhaps the first time in his life, for he was always distinguished by the softness of his voice.

"Yes, sir," said Petrovich, "and it still depends on the kind of overcoat. If you put on a marten collar and silk lining for the hood, it'll go to two hundred."

"Petrovich, please," said Akaky Akakievich in a pleading voice, not heeding and not trying to heed the words Petrovich had said, or any of his effects, "fix it somehow so that it'll do for a while yet."

"But no, it's a waste—it would waste my work and spend your money pointlessly," said Petrovich, and after those words Akaky Akakievich went out totally destroyed.

And after his exit Petrovich stood for a long time, his lips pursed significantly, without taking up his work—satisfied that he had not discredited himself nor betrayed the tailor's art. Walking out in the street Akaky Akakievich was as if in a dream. "So that's the kind of thing that is," he was saying to himself. "Really, I didn't think it would come out like er . . ." and then, after a short silence, he added, "So there's how! Finally, that's what came out, but I, really, could not in the least have supposed that it would be such like." After this a long silence followed again, after which he uttered, "So that's it! There's what already, precisely, nothing more unexpected than . . . this would at all . . . such a circumstance!" Having said this, instead of going home he set off in exactly the opposite direction, without suspecting this himself. On the way a chimney-sweep brushed him with his whole dirty side and blackened his whole shoulder; an entire hatful of lime poured on him from the top of a house which was being built. He did not notice any of this, and then only when he bumped into a policeman who had placed his halberd beside him and was shaking some tobacco into his calloused fist, only then did Akaky Akakievich come to his senses a little—and that because the policeman said: "Why are you climbing right in my mug, ain't there enough sidewalk for you?" This made him look around and turn homeward. Only then did he begin to gather his thoughts; he saw his position the way it really was, he started conversing with himself no longer incoherently, but soberly and frankly, as with a sensible friend with whom one may speak about the closest and most intimate matter. "Well no," said Akakievich, "it's impossible to bargain with Petrovich now; now he's er . . . his wife, evidently, beat him somehow. Better I'll go to him Sunday morning; after the previous Saturday night his eye will be squinting and he'll be sleepy; so he'll have to have a hair of the dog that bit him, but his wife won't give him any money, and then I'll put a nice ten-kopeck piece in his hand, and he will be more agreeable, and then the overcoat . . . er. . . ." Thus Akaky Akakievich reasoned with himself, encouraged himself, and waited for the first Sunday; and when, from afar, he saw Petrovich's wife go out of the house, he went straight to Petrovich. Petrovich really was squinting his eye after Saturday, his head hung toward the floor, and he was quite sleepy; but for all that when he found out what the business was, it was exactly as if the devil had prompted him. "Impossible," he said, "be so good as to order a new one." At this point Akaky Akakievich slipped him a ten-kopeck piece. "I thank you, sir, I will fortify myself a bit toasting to your health," said Petrovich. "And please don't worry about your overcoat, it's not good for nothing. I'll sew you a fine new one. I stand firm on that."

Akaky Akakievich was still going to ask about repair, but Petrovich would not listen and said: "I will certainly sew you a new one, please rely on it; I will exert all effort. It could even be like the current style—the collar will be buttoned with silver-plated clasps."

At this point Akaky Akakievich realized that he could not manage without a new overcoat, and his spirits fell completely. Really, how could he? What would he use? Where would he get the money to do it? Of course he could rely partly on the holiday bonus that was coming, but that money had long since been apportioned and disposed of in advance. He needed to inaugurate new pants, pay an old debt to the shoemaker for sticking new top-plates on his old boot-straps, and he had to order three shirts from the seamstress, as well as two pairs of that underwear which it is indecent to mention in print; in a word, absolutely all of the money had to go elsewhere, and even if the director was so generous that instead of a forty-ruble bonus he set it at forty-five or fifty, nevertheless only some silly trifle would be left over, which in terms of overcoat capital would be a drop in the sea. Though, of course, he knew that Petrovich often had the whim of suddenly stacking on the devil knows what price, so bad that, it would happen, his wife herself could not resist exclaiming: "What's wrong with you, are you going crazy, you fool! Other times he'll take work for nothing, and now the devil's goaded him into asking a price that he isn't even worth." Though, of course, he knew that Petrovich would undertake doing it for eighty rubles, still where would he get those eighty rubles? He could come up with half of it, half would be found—maybe even a little more; but where would he get the other half? ... But first the reader must be informed where the first half came from. It was Akaky Akakievich's habit to put a little of each ruble he spent into a small box which was locked with a key, and had a small hole cut in the top for throwing the money into it. On the passage of each half-year, he inventoried the accumulated copper sum and replaced it with small silver. He had gone on like this for a long time, and thus after several years the accumulated sum turned out to be more than forty rubles. And so half was in his hands, but where would he get the other half? Akaky Akakievich thought and thought and decided that it would be necessary to reduce ordinary expenditures for at least one year; to forego the use of tea in the evening; not to light a candle in the evening, and if there was something he had to do, to go into his landlady's room and work by her candle; when walking in the streets to step as lightly and cautiously as possible along the cobbles and paving stones, almost on tiptoe, so as thus not to wear down his soles rapidly; to give his linen to the laundress as rarely as possible and, so that it would not get dirty, to cast it off as soon as he got home every day and remain in just his ancient bathrobe which had been spared even by time itself. The truth must be told—at first it was rather difficult for him to get accustomed to such privations, but then somehow he got accustomed and things went well; he even got competely used to going hungry evenings, but to make up for that he was nourished spiritually by carrying the eternal idea of the future overcoat in his thoughts. From that time it was as if his entire existence became somehow more complete, as if he had got married, as if some other person were present with him, as if he were not alone, but some pleasant companion of life had agreed to travel the road of life with him—and this companion was none other than that selfsame overcoat with thick quilting, with a strong lining which would not wear out. He became somehow livelier, firmer in character even, like a man who has already defined and set himself a goal. Doubt and indecision—in a word, all vacillating and inde-terminate characteristics—disappeared from his face and actions of themselves. At times fire would appear in his eyes; the boldest and most audacious thoughts flashed through his mind: should he really put marten on the collar? His reflections on this nearly made him

absent-minded. Once when copying some papers he nearly even
made a mistake, so that he almost exclaimed "Ookh" aloud and he
crossed himself. At least once during the course of each month he
got himself up to Petrovich's to chat about the overcoat, where it
would be best to buy the material and what color and at what price;
and though a little worried, he was always satisfied when he returned home reflecting that finally the time was coming when all
these things would be purchased and the overcoat made. The
project went even faster than he expected. Contrary to all expectation the director alloted Akaky Akakievich not forty or forty-
five, but a whole sixty rubles—whether he had a feeling that Akaky
Akakievich needed an overcoat or whether it happened like that of
itself, no matter—because of this he turned up with twenty extra
rubles. This circumstance sped up the course of the project. Some
two or three months of slight hunger and Akaky Akakievich would
have saved up precisely around eighty rubles. His heart, generally
quite calm, began to pound. The very next day he set off to the
stores with Petrovich. They bought some very good material—and
that is no surprise because they had been thinking about it for half
a year before and it was a rare month that they did not drop in to
the stores to compare prices, and besides, Petrovich himself said
there was no better material than this. They chose calico for the
lining, but it was so thick and of such good quality that, in Petrovich's words, it was even better than silk and even looked showier
and glossier. They did not buy marten because it really was expensive; instead they bought cat fur, the best that could be found in
the store, which from a distance could always be taken for marten.
Petrovich fussed over the overcoat for all of two weeks because
there was a lot of quilting—otherwise it would have been ready
sooner. Petrovich took twelve rubles for the work, less was absolutely impossible: it was all firmly sewn with silk thread, with fine
double seams, and afterwards Petrovich had gone along each seam
with his own teeth, using them to impress various patterns. It was
. . . it is difficult to say on precisely what day, but, probably, it was
the most triumphant day in Akaky Akakievich's life when Petrovich finally brought the overcoat. He brought it in the morning,
just before the very time when Akaky Akakievich had to go to the
department. At no other time would the overcoat have been so
welcome, because rather heavy frosts had already begun and they

threatened to get worse. Petrovich appeared with the overcoat in the way a good tailor should. On his face he showed an expression more significant than any Akaky Akakievich had even seen before. It seemed that he felt in full measure that what he had done was no small thing and that he had suddenly revealed to himself the chasm which separated tailors who just tack on linings and do repairs from those who sew new items. He took the overcoat out of the handkerchief in which he had brought it; the handkerchief had just come back from the laundry, and now he folded it and put it into his pocket for use. He watched extremely proudly as he took it out, and holding it in both hands, he threw it over Akaky Akakievich's shoulders extremely adroitly; then he pulled it and smoothed it down behind with his hand; then he draped it around Akaky Akakievich like a cape. Akaky Akakievich, as a man of some years, wanted to try it using the sleeves; Petrovich helped him put it on using the sleeves—it came out well using the sleeves too. In a word, it turned out that the overcoat was an absolutely perfect fit. At this point Petrovich did not neglect saying that he only took the work so cheaply because he lived without a sign on a small street and besides had known Akaky Akakievich for a long time, but on Nevsky Prospect he would have been charged seventy-five rubles just for the work. Akaky Akakievich did not want to discuss this with Petrovich, and he feared all of the whopping sums that Petrovich liked to throw around. He paid him off, thanked him, and immediately left for the department in his new overcoat. Petrovich left right after him, and standing in the street he looked at the overcoat from a distance for a long time, and then he purposely went out of his way so that by overtaking him by a shortcut through an alley he could again run out on the street and again look at his overcoat, from the other direction this time, that is, head-on. Meanwhile Akaky Akakievich was walking along with all his feelings in the brightest holiday mood. Every second of each minute he felt his new overcoat on his shoulders, and several times he even laughed from inner pleasure. Really, there were two advantages: one was the fact that it was warm, the other that it was good. He did not notice the road at all and suddenly found himself at the department; in the cloak-room he slipped off the overcoat, examined it all over, and entrusted it to the special care of the door-man. It is not known how everyone in the department all of a sudden found out that

Akaky Akakievich had a new overcoat and that the bathrobe no longer existed. Everyone ran out into the cloak-room at the same moment to look at Akaky Akakievich's new overcoat. They began to greet and congratulate him so much that at first he just smiled, but then he even got embarrassed. But when everyone crowded around him and started saying they would have to drink to the new overcoat, and that he should at least give them all a party, Akaky Akakievich was completely lost; he didn't know how to act, what to answer, or how to beg off. After a few minutes, blushing all over, he had even begun to assure them rather simple-heartedly that this was not a new overcoat at all, really, that it was an old overcoat. Finally one of the clerks, some assistant of the head clerk even, probably to show that he was not an arrogant person at all because he associated even with those lower than himself, said: "So be it, I'll give a party instead of Akaky Akakievich; I invite you all to my place for tea today: as if on purpose today is my name-day." Naturally the clerks immediately congratulated the head clerk's assistant and gladly accepted the invitation. Akaky Akakievich was beginning to make excuses, but everyone started saying it was impolite, that it was simply a shame and disgrace, and there was no longer any way he could refuse. However, he cheered up later when he recalled that because of this he would have an opportunity to stroll about in his new overcoat even in the evening. For Akaky Akakievich the whole day was exactly like the biggest, most triumphant holiday. He returned home in the happiest of moods, slipped off the overcoat and hung it carefully on the wall, once more admiring the material and lining and then, for comparison, he purposely dragged out his former bathrobe which had completely fallen apart. He looked at it and even smiled to himself—so vast was the difference between them. And for a long time after dinner he kept grinning whenever the condition of his bathrobe came to mind. He ate dinner gaily and after dinner he did not copy anything, no papers at all, but luxuriated sybaritically on his bed until it got dark. Then without dawdling he got dressed, put the overcoat on his shoulders and went out in the street. Precisely where the clerk who invited him lived, unfortunately, we cannot say—memory is beginning to fail us terribly, and everything in Petersburg, all the streets and houses have gotten so mixed and muddled in my mind that it is extremely difficult to get anything out of there in proper order. However that may be, it is at least certain that the clerk lived in the better part of the city, therefore not very close to Akaky Akakievich at all. First Akaky Akakievich had to walk through some deserted streets with meagre lighting, but as he drew closer to the clerk's apartment the streets became livelier, more populous, and more brightly lighted. Pedestrians started flitting by more often; he started to come across beautifully dressed ladies and some of the men were wearing beaver collars; he met fewer Vankas with their latticed wooden sledges studded with brass nails—on the contrary he kept coming across smart racers wearing crimson velvet caps with their lacquered sledges and bearskin laprugs, and carriages with ornamental coachman's boxes flew through the streets, their wheels whistling across the snow. Akaky Akakievich looked at all of this as a novelty. It had already been several years since he had gone out on the street at night. From curiosity he stopped to look in an illuminated window at a painting which depicted a beautiful woman who was taking off her shoe, thus revealing her whole foot, not a bad one at all; and behind her back some man with side-whiskers and a handsome goatee under his lips had stuck his head through the door of the next room. Akaky Akakievich shook his head and grinned, and then continued on his way. Why he grinned, whether it was because he had met something totally unfamiliar but about which, however, every person nevertheless has some sort of instinctual feeling, or whether he thought, like many other clerks, the following: "Well, why those French! What can you say if they decide they want something . . . er . . . so, precisely, er. . . ." But perhaps he didn't think even this—naturally, you cannot creep into a man's soul and find out everything he is thinking. Finally he reached the house in which he head clerk's assistant had his quarters. The head clerk's assistant lived in a swanky place: there was a light on the stairs, the apartment was on the second floor. Entering the anteroom Akaky Akakievich saw whole rows of galoshes on the floor. Among them, in the middle of the room, stood a samovar burbling and emitting clouds of steam. On the walls hung all the overcoats and cloaks, several of which even had beaver collars or velvet lapels. Beyond the partition he could hear noise and talking which suddenly became clear and sonorous when the door opened and a lackey with a tray piled with drained glasses, a cream-pot, and basket of biscuits. It is evident that the clerks had gathered some time ago and had already drunk their first glass of tea. Hanging his overcoat up himself, Akaky Akakievich entered the room: candles, clerks, pipes, card tables flashed before him simultaneously, and the fleeting conversation rising all around and the noise of chairs being moved back and forth struck his ears chaotically. He stopped extremely awkwardly in the middle of the room, looking around and trying to think of what he should do. But they had already noticed him, greeted him with a shout, and everyone immediately went into the anteroom and examined his overcoat anew. Although he was somewhat confused, Akaky Akakievich, being an open-hearted person, could not but be made happy to see how everyone was praising the overcoat. Then, of course, they all abandoned both him and the overcoat and turned, as usually happens, to the tables set aside for whist. All of this—the noise, the talk, and the crowd of people —all of this was somehow bewildering to Akaky Akakievich. He simply did not know how to act, where to put his hands, feet, or his whole body; finally he sat down beside the players, looked at the cards, peeped into the face of first one, then another, and after some time he began to yawn, to feel bored, all the more so that the time had long since arrived when he, following his custom, went to bed. He wanted to say good-bye to the host, but they would not let him go, saying that they absolutely had to drink a glass of champagne in honor of the new garment. In about an hour dinner was served—it consisted of vinaigret, cold veal, meat pastries, cream pastries, and champagne. They made Akaky Akakievich drink two glasses, after which he felt that it had become merrier in the room; however, he just could not forget that it was already twelve o'clock and long past the time to go home. So that the host would not think of a way to detain him, he left the room stealthily; in the anteroom he searched out his overcoat which not without regret he saw lying on the floor; he shook it, removed every speck of dust from it, and descended the stairs to the street. It was still light in the street. A few wretched little shops, those round-the-clock clubs for all sorts of servants, were open; some others which were closed nevertheless showed a long stream of light all along the crack under the door, signifying that they were still not devoid of society and, probably, the house maids or men servants were still finishing their gossip and conversations, leaving their masters at a total loss as to their whereabouts. Akaky Akakievich walked along in a merry mood; suddenly, it is unknown why, he even ran after some lady who passed by like lightning, every part of her body full of extraordinary movement. But, however, he immediately stopped and again walked along very quietly as before, even a little amazed himself at this trot which had come out of nowhere. Soon those deserted streets which are not so merry even during the day, let alone at night, stretched out before him. Now they had become even more desolate and lonely: the street lamps began to flicker more weakly, apparently less oil was being released; the wooden houses and fences began; there was not a soul anywhere; only the snow along the streets glittered, the low sleeping hovels with closed shutters were sadly black. He approached a place where the street is interrupted by an endless square with houses barely visible on the other side; it looked like a terrible desert.

In the distance, God knows where, a light flickered in some sentry-box which seemed to be standing on the edge of the world. Somehow Akaky Akakievich's merriness was significantly lessened here. He stepped into the square not without a kind of involuntary fear, exactly as if his heart had a premonition of something bad. He looked from side to side too: it was just like a sea around him. "No, better not look," he thought and walked on closing his eyes, and when he opened them to find out if he was close to the end of the square, he suddenly saw some men with moustaches standing right in front of his nose, but he could not even make out just what kind of men they were. His eyes glazed over and his heart began to pound. "Why that's my overcoat," said one of them in a thunderous voice, grabbing him by the collar. Akaky Akakievich was ready to shout "police," when the other man stuck his fist, which was as big as a clerk's head, right up to his mouth, muttering, "You just screech and. . . ." Akaky Akakievich only felt them take off his overcoat and give him a kick with a knee, and he fell back into the snow—and then he felt nothing more. In a few minutes he came to his senses and got up on his knees, but there was no longer anyone there. He felt that it was cold in this field and that his overcoat was gone; he began to shout, but his voice, it seemed, could not even dream of reaching the end of the square. Desperate, not ceasing to shout, he set off running across the square straight for the sentry-box, beside which a policeman was standing, and leaning on his halberd he was watching, it would seem, with curiosity, wanting to know what devil of a man was running toward him from the distance and shouting. Akaky Akakievich ran up to him and gasping for breath he began to shout that he was sleeping and not watching after anything, not seeing people robbed. The policeman replied that he had not seen anything, that he had seen two men stop him in the middle of the square, but thought they were his friends; and instead of abusing him pointlessly, he should go to the inspector tomorrow and the inspector would find out who took his overcoat. Akaky Akakievich ran home in complete disorder: his hair, a small quantity of which he still had on his temples and the back of his head, was completely disheveled; his side and chest and his trousers were all covered with snow. Hearing the terrible pounding on the door the old woman, his landlady, hastily jumped out of bed and with only one shoe on ran to open the door, modestly holding her chemise against her breast with one hand; but when she opened it she fell back seeing Akaky Akakievich in such condition. When he told her what had happened, she clasped her hands and said he would have to go to the district officer because the local officer would trick him, make promises and not do anything, that it would be best to go straight to the district officer because she was even acquainted with him, because Anna, the Finnish woman who used to be her cook, had now been made a nurse in the district officer's house, that she often saw him personally when he drove past their house, and that he also went to church every Sunday, prayed, and at the same time he would look merrily at everyone, and that from everything it was apparent that he must be a good man. Having listened to this decision, Akaky Akakievich sadly dragged himself to his room; we will leave it to the person who can to some extent imagine the position of another man to judge how he spent the night there. Early in the morning he set off to see the district officer, but they said he was sleeping; he came at ten—they again said he was sleeping; he came at eleven o'clock— they said the district officer was not at home; he came at lunch time—but the copyists in the reception room did not want to admit him at all and insisted on knowing what matter and what necessity had brought him and what had happened. So that for once in his life Akaky Akakievich finally wanted to show some character, and he said point-blank that he had to see the district officer himself personally, that they did not dare not admit him, that he had come from his department on official business, and that if he lodged a complaint against them, then they would see. The copyists did not dare say anything against this, and one of them went to call the district officer. The district officer took the story about the theft of the overcoat somehow in an extremely strange way. Instead of turning his attention to the main point of the matter, he began to interrogate Akaky Akakievich: and why was he returning so late, and hadn't he dropped by and been in some disreputable house, so that Akaky Akakievich was totally confused and left him without knowing whether he had set in motion the proper action about the overcoat or not. He did not go to work all day—for the first time in his life. The next day he appeared all pale and in his old bathrobe which had gotten even more pitiful. The tale of the overcoat's theft, although there were some clerks who did not even neglect this opportunity to joke at Akaky Akakievich, nevertheless touched many of them. They immediately decided to take up a collection for him, but they collected the smallest trifle because even without that the clerks had spent a lot, subscribing for the director's portrait and, at the suggestion of the division-head, who was a friend of the writer, for some book or other—therefore the sum turned out to be insignificant. One of them, moved by compassion, decided at least to help Akaky Akakievich with good advice, telling him not to go to the local police officer because even if it happened that he somehow located the overcoat (because he wanted to earn the approval of his chiefs), the overcoat would still stay at the police-station if he did not present legal proof that it belonged to him, and it would be best if he turned to a certain *significant personage*, that this *significant personage*, corresponding and consulting with the right people, could make the whole matter work out more successfully. There was nothing to be done, Akaky Akakievich decided to go to the *significant personage*. Precisely what the significant personage's job was and what it consisted of has remained unknown to this day. It should be noted that this *certain significant personage* had only recently become a significant personage, and until that time he was an insignificant personage. Incidentally, even now his position was not considered significant in comparison with others still more significant. But one can always find a circle of people for whom what is insignificant in the eyes of others is significant. Incidentally, he tried to increase his significance by many other measures, to be specific: he arranged that the subordinate officials should meet him on the stairs when he was arriving at the office, that no one should dare to appear before him directly, but should strictly follow all of the official procedures: the collegiate registrar should report to the area secretary, the area secretary to the titular councillor or someone else, and that in this way the matter would reach him. Thus it is in holy Russia that everyone is infected with imitation, everyone copies and apes his superior. It is even said that a certain titular councillor, when he was made the head of some small separate office, immediately partitioned himself off a special room, named it "the presence chamber," and stationed at the doors two commissionaries with red collars and galoons who grabbed the door handles and opened them to everyone who came to see him, even though it was hardly possible to place an ordinary writing desk in "the presence chamber." The manners and customs of the *significant personage* were solemn and majestic, but not particularly subtle. The main basis of his system was strictness. "Strictness, strictness and—strictness," he would usually say, and at the last word would usually look very significantly into the face of the person to whom he was talking. Although, incidentally, there was no reason for that, because the ten clerks who made up the entire coordinating mechanism of the office were properly terrified even without that: seeing him in the distance they would leave their work and wait, standing at attention, for their chief to pass through the room. His usual conversation with subordinates reeked of strictness and consisted of three phrases: "How dare you? Do you know whom you are talking to? Do you understand who is standing before you?" Incidentally, he was a kind person at heart, pleasant with his comrades, obliging; but a general's rank nonplussed him completely. When he received the general's rank he somehow got mixed up, lost the road, and did not know how to act at all. If he happened to be with equals he was still an ordinary person, a very decent person, in many respects not even a stupid person; but as soon as he happened to be in a company where there were people even one rank lower than him, he simply got out of hand: he would be silent, and his position aroused pity, all the more that he himself even felt that he could be having a far better time. Sometimes one could see in his eyes a strong desire to join in some intelligent conversation and circle, but he was stopped by the thought: wouldn't this be too much on his part, wouldn't it be familiar and wouldn't his significance be diminished by it? And as a consequence of such considerations he remained eternally in one and the same silent state, just uttering some monosyllabic sounds from time to time; and thus he received the title of a most boring person. It was to this *significant personage* that our Akaky Akakievich presented himself—and he presented himself at a most inauspicious time, extremely inopportunely for himself, though it was, however, opportune for the significant personage. The significant personage was in his private office chatting very, very merrily with an old friend and comrade of his childhood who had recently arrived and whom he had not seen for several years. At that time he was informed that some Bashmachkin had arrived. He asked abruptly, "Who?" He was answered, "Some clerk." "Oh, he can wait, there's no time now," said the significant personage. Here it is necessary to say that the significant personage absolutely fibbed—he did have time, they had long since talked over everything and for some time they had been punctuating their conversation with extremely long pauses, just slapping each other on the knee and saying: "So that's how it is, Ivan Abramovich!" "That's the way she is, Stepan Varlamovich!" But in spite of all this, he nevertheless ordered the clerk to wait in order to show his friend, a man who had settled down firmly in his house in the country and had not worked in the service for a long time, how much time clerks had to wait for him in the anteroom. Finally, when he had had his fill of talking, and even more of being silent, and smoked a cigar in his extremely comfortable armchair with a reclining back, he finally remembered, as if all of a sudden, and told the secretary who was standing by the doors with papers for a report: "Oh, yes, I believe there's a clerk waiting out there; tell him he may enter." Seeing Akaky Akakievich's humble look and his ancient uniform, he turned to him suddenly and said, "What do you want?" in a firm and abrupt voice which he had purposely practiced in his room, alone and in front of the mirror, a week in advance of receiving his present position and general's rank. Akaky Akakievich already felt the proper timidity well ahead of this; it somewhat confused him, and he explained, as best he could insofar as the fluency of his speech would allow him, adding even more often than usual the particle "er," that there was, he said, a completely new overcoat, and now it had been stolen in an inhuman manner, and that he was turning to him so that he would intercede somehow "er" and correspond with the City Commissioner of Police or someone else and find the overcoat. It is unknown why, but this manner of address seemed too familiar to the general. "My dear sir, what are you saying," he continued abruptly, "don't you know procedure? Where have you come? Don't you know how matters are processed? On this you should have submitted a petition to my office first; it would go to the head clerk, to the chief of the division, then it would be transmitted to the secretary, and the secretary would bring it to me . . ." "But, your excellency," said Akaky Akakievich trying to collect all the miniature supply of presence of mind that was in him, and simultaneously feeling that he was beginning to sweat in a terrible way, "I, your excellency, dared to trouble you because the secretaries er . . . unreliable people. . . ."

"What, what, what?" said the significant personage. "Where did you get such impudence? Where did you get such ideas? What rebelliousness against chiefs and superiors has spread among your people!" The significant personage, it would seem, did not notice that Akaky Akakievich had already passed fifty. Therefore, if he could be called a young man, then only relatively so, i.e. in relation to someone who was already seventy years old. "Do you know to whom you are speaking? Do you understand who is standing in front of you? Do you understand this, do you understand this, I am asking you." At this point he stamped his foot, raising his voice to such a loud note that even someone other than Akaky Akakievich would have been terrified. Akaky Akakievich felt faint, staggered, trembled all over, and was quite unable to stand up; if the porters had not run up to support him, he would have flopped onto the floor; they carried him out almost motionless. But the significant personage, satisfied that the effect had even surpassed his expectation, and totally enraptured by the thought that his words could even deprive a man of his senses, glanced at his friend out of the corner of his eye to learn how he was viewing this, and not without pleasure he saw that his friend was in the most uneasy state and for his part was even beginning to feel frightened himself.

Akaky Akakievich remembered nothing of how he got down the stairs, how he got out on the street. He did not feel his arms or legs. Never in his life had he ever been so thoroughly roasted by a general, and not his own at that. He walked through the storm that was whistling through the streets, his mouth agape, stumbling off the sidewalks; the wind, following its Petersburg custom, blew at him from all four sides from all the sidestreets. In an instant a fever was blown into his throat, and he made his way home not strong enough to say a single word, he was all swollen and he took to bed. Sometimes a proper verbal roasting is that powerful. On the next day a high fever manifested itself. Thanks to the magnanimous assistance of the Petersburg climate his illness progressed more rapidly than could have been anticipated, and when the doctor appeared and felt his pulse he found there was nothing to do except prescribe a poultice, solely so that the patient would not be left without the beneficial help of medicine; however at the same time he announced that within a day and a half he would certainly be *kaput*. After which he turned to the landlady and said: "And you, dear woman, don't waste time, order him a pine coffin right away, because oak will be too expensive for him." Whether Akaky Akakievich heard these fateful words uttered about him, and if he heard them whether they produced a shocking effect in him, whether he regretted leaving his woeful life—none of this is known, because he was feverish and delirious the whole time. Scenes, one stronger than the next, presented themselves to his imagination constantly: now he was seeing Petrovich and ordering him to make an overcoat with some kind of traps for thieves which he constantly imagined under his bed, and every minute he was even calling the landlady to drag out one thief from under his blanket; now he was asking why his old bathrobe was hanging before him when he had a new overcoat; now he imagined that he was standing before a general listening to a proper roasting and saying, "Sorry, your excellency;" now, finally, he was even obscenely blaspheming, uttering the most terrible words, so that his landlady was even crossing herself, never having heard anything like it from him, all the more that these words followed immediately after the words "your excellency." After that he uttered absolute nonsense, so it was impossible to understand anything; one could see only that these disorderly words and thoughts revolved around that same overcoat. Finally poor Akaky Akakievich gave up the ghost. Neither his room nor his things were put under seal, because, first, there were no heirs, and second, very little inheritance was left—to be specific: a bundle of goose quills, a quire of official white paper, three pairs of socks, two or three buttons torn off his pants, and the bathrobe which is already known to the reader. Who got all this, God knows; I confess, even the narrator of this story was not interested in this. Akaky Akakievich was taken out and buried. And Petersburg was left without Akaky Akakievich, as if he had never been there. Gone and disappeared was a being who was protected by no one, dear to no one, interesting to no one, who had not even attracted the attention of a naturalist who does not fail to impale an ordinary fly on a pin and examine it in his microscope; a being who had submissively born office jokes and descended into the grave with no excessive fuss, but for whom, nevertheless, even though it was just before the very end of his life, there flashed a radiant guest in the form of an overcoat which enlivened a poor life for an instant, and on whom misfortune had then crashed down irresistably, just as it has crashed down on the tsars and rulers of the world. . . . A few days after his death the porter was sent from the department to his apartment with an order for him to appear immediately: the chief demands it, he said. But the porter had to return alone, giving a report that he could not come anymore; and to the query "why" he replied in these words: "Well, he just can't, he's died, was buried three days ago." In this way they learned of Akaky Akakievich's death at the department, and the next day there was already a new clerk sitting in his place, a much taller one who did not write his letters in such a straight hand, but more slantingly and slopingly.

But who could have imagined that here this is not yet all about Akaky Akakievich, that he was destined to live clamorously for a few days after his death—as if in reward for a life unnoticed by anyone. But it happened thus, and our poor story unexpectedly acquires a fantastic ending. Suddenly rumors flew around Petersburg that at Kalinkin Bridge and far beyond a corpse had begun to appear at night in the guise of a clerk looking for some sort of stolen overcoat, and on the pretext of this stolen overcoat he was dragging from all shoulders, regardless of rank and calling, all kinds of overcoats—trimmed with cat fur, beaver fur, or quilted, racoon, fox, and bear fur coats—in a word, every type of fur and skin that man has thought of covering his own with. One of the department clerks saw the corpse with his own eyes and immediately recognized it as Akaky Akakievich; but this, however, pierced him through with such terror that he took off running as fast as his legs would carry him and therefore could not examine him carefully, but just saw how he threatened him with his finger from a distance. From all sides complaints were constantly coming in that the backs and shoulders not only of titular, but even of secret councillors themselves, had been subjected to absolute cold as a result of this nocturnal pulling off of overcoats. At the police-station a disposition was made to capture the corpse, no matter what, dead or alive, and to punish it, as an example to others, in the cruelest way; and they very nearly even succeeded in this. To be precise, a policeman from some quarter near Kiryushkin Alley had already snatched an absolute corpse by the collar at the scene of his malefaction—an attempt to pull a frieze overcoat off some retired musician who, in his day, used to blow a flute. Having grabbed him by the collar, he called two of his comrades with a shout and he had them hold him; he himself reached into his boot just for a minute to pull out a birch-bark snuff-box with tobacco to revive his nose for a while—it had been frostbitten six times during his life—but the tobacco, probably, was the kind which even a corpse cannot stand. Covering his right nostril with his finger, the policeman had hardly managed to draw half a handful of tobacco up his left when the corpse sneezed so strongly that he completely splattered the eyes of all three. While they were putting up their fists to wipe them, the corpse vanished without a trace, so that they did not even know whether he had been in their hands. Since then the policemen were so terrified of corpses that they were even wary of grabbing the living, and they would just shout from afar: "Hey, you, on your way!" and the corpse-clerk began to appear even on the other side of Kalinkin Bridge, causing not a little terror to all timid people. But we, however, have abandoned the *certain significant personage* who in reality was virtually the cause of this fantastic turn in this, incidentally, absolutely true story. First of all, the duty of being just demands saying that the *certain significant personage* felt something like regret soon after the exit of poor Akaky Akakievich whom he had roasted to a crisp. Compassion was not alien to him; his heart was open to many good impulses in spite of the fact that rank extremely often prevented them from manifesting themselves. As soon as his visiting friend left his private office, he even fell to thinking about Akaky Akakievich. And almost every day from that time on he

imagined pale Akaky Akakievich, who had been unable to with-
stand a proper roasting. The thought of Akaky Akakievich disturbed him to such an extent that a week later he even decided
to send a clerk to him to find out whether he could in fact help
him and how; and when it was reported that Akaky Akakievich
died suddenly of a fever, he was even left thunderstruck; he heard
rebukes from his conscience and was out of sorts all day. Desiring
to amuse himself and forget the unpleasant impression, he set off
for an evening with one of his friends—at whose place he found a
good-sized company, and what was best of all, everyone there was
almost the same rank, so that there was absolutely nothing which
could inhibit him. This had an amazing effect on his mood. He
loosened up, became a pleasant, genial conversationalist—in a word,
he had a very pleasant evening. He had a glass or two of champagne for supper—a device, as is well known, that does not have a
bad effect as regards merriness. The champagne imparted to him
a disposition for various special things, or, to be precise: he decided
not to go home yet, but to drop in on a certain lady he knew, Karolina Ivanovna, a lady, apparently of German extraction, for whom
he felt absolutely friendly relations. It should be said that the significant personage was no longer a young man, he was a good husband, the respectable father of a family. Two sons, one of whom
was already serving in the office, and a nice-looking sixteen-year-old
daughter with a somewhat crooked but pretty little nose, came to
kiss his hand every day, saying *"Bonjour papa."* His wife, who was
still a fresh woman and not even a bad-looking one at all, would
first give him her hand to kiss, and then, turning it over, would kiss
his hand. But the significant personage, completely, by the way,
satisfied with his domestic, familial endearments, found it proper
to have, for friendly relations, a female friend in another part of
the city. This female friend was not a bit prettier or younger than
his wife, but such puzzles do exist in the world, and it is not our
business to judge them. And so the significant personage went down
the stairs, got in his sledge, and said to his coachman, "To Karolina
Ivanovna's," and wrapping himself very luxuriously in his warm
overcoat, he remained in that position better than which you can
think of nothing for a Russian, i.e. when you do not think about
anything yourself but still the thoughts themselves creep into your
mind, one more pleasant than the next, not even giving one the

trouble of chasing after them and searching for them. Full of contentment, he slightly recalled all of the gay points of the evening he had spent, all of the words which made the small circle laugh; he even repeated many of them in an undertone and found that they were still just as funny as before, and therefore it is no wonder that he laughed heartily. From time to time, however, he was disturbed by the gusty wind, which suddenly whipped up from God knows where and for no known reason fairly cut into his face, flinging hunks of snow at him, pushing up his overcoat collar like a sail—or suddenly tossing it up onto his head with unnatural force and thus giving him the eternal bother of scrambling out of it. Suddenly the significant personage felt someone grab him extremely firmly by the collar. Turning around, he noted a man of small stature in an old worn-out undress uniform, and not without horror recognized him as Akaky Akakievich. The face of the clerk was as pale as snow and looked like an absolute corpse. But the significant personage's horror exceeded all bounds when he saw the corpse's mouth twist and, breathing on him terribly of the grave, utter these phrases: "Ah, so here you are at last! At last I've . . . er . . . caught you by the collar. It is *your* overcoat that I need! You didn't bother about mine, and roasted me besides, so give me yours now!" The poor *significant personage* almost dropped dead. No matter how resolute of character he was at the office and in general with subordinates, and although seeing just his manly look and figure everyone would say "Wow, what character," here he, like a great many other people who have the physiognomy of fairy-tale warriors, felt such terror that not without reason he even began to worry about some sort of morbid fit. He even removed the overcoat from his shoulders himself as fast as he could, and he shouted to the coachman in a voice which was not his own: "Home at top speed!" The coachman, on hearing the voice which was usually uttered at decisive moments and was accompanied by something even much more effective, drew his head between his shoulders just in case, waved his whip, and shot off like an arrow. In slightly more than six minutes the significant personage was already at the entrance to his house. Pale, frightened, and without his overcoat, instead of going to Karolina Ivanovna's he went home, somehow made it up to his room, and spent the night in extremely great distress so that at tea the next morning his daughter told him outright, "You are quite pale today, Papa." But papa was silent, and said not a word to anyone about what had happened to him, or where he had been, or where he had wanted to go. This event made a strong impression on him. He even began to say "How dare you, do you understand who is standing before you" much more rarely; and if he did say it, then not before first hearing out what the point of the business was. But even more remarkable is the fact that after that time the appearance of the clerk-corpse ceased entirely: evidently the general's overcoat fit his shoulders perfectly—at least there were no longer any reports of incidents where overcoats were pulled off anyone. However, many active and solicitous people simply did not want to calm down and they kept saying that in remote parts of the city the clerk-corpse was still appearing. And to be sure, with his own eyes one Kolomna policeman saw a ghost appear from behind a house; but being by his nature somewhat of a weakling—so that once an ordinary full-grown young pig which had rushed out of some private house bumped him off his feet, to the very great amusement of the coachmen who were standing around, from each of whom he demanded and got, as a penalty for such derision, a penny for tobacco—and so, being a weakling, he did not dare to stop him, but just kept on walking behind him in the darkness until, finally, the ghost suddenly looked around, and stopping asked, "Whaddaya want?" and held up a fist such as you won't find even among the living. The policeman said "Nothing" and immediately turned back. The ghost, however, was already a much bigger one, wore enormous moustachios, and directing its steps, as it seemed, toward the Obukhov bridge, it disappeared completely in the darkness of the night.

IVAN TURGENEV

Bezhin Meadow

I T WAS A GLORIOUS JULY DAY, one of those days which only come after many days of fine weather. From earliest morning the sky is clear; the sunrise does not glow with fire; it is suffused with a soft roseate flush. The sun, not fiery, not red-hot as in time of stifling drought, not dull purple as before a storm, but with a bright and genial radiance, rises peacefully behind a long and narrow cloud, shines out freshly, and plunges again into its lilac mist. The delicate edge of the strip of cloud flashes in little gleaming snakes; their brilliance is like beaten silver. But, lo! the dancing rays flash forth again, and in solemn joy, as though flying upward, rises the mighty orb. About midday there is wont to be, high up in the sky, a multitude of rounded clouds, golden-grey, with soft white edges. Like islands scattered over an overflowing river, that bathes them in its unbroken reaches of deep transparent blue, they scarcely stir; farther down the heavens they are in movement, packing closer; now there is no blue to be seen between them, but they are themselves almost as blue as the sky, filled full with light and heat. The color

Translated by THOMAS MOORE. *Reprinted from* A Hunter's Sketches. *Moscow*, [n.d.].

of the horizon, a faint pale lilac, does not change all day, and is the same all round; nowhere is there storm gathering and darkening; only somewhere rays of bluish color stretch down from the sky; it is a sprinkling of scarce perceptible rain. In the evening these clouds disappear; the last of them, blackish and undefined as smoke, lie streaked with pink, facing the setting sun; in the place where it has gone down, as calmly as it rose, a crimson glow lingers briefly over the darkening earth, and, softly flashing like a candle carried carelessly, the evening star flickers in the sky. On such days all the colors are softened, bright but not glaring; everything is suffused with a kind of touching tenderness. On such days the heat is sometimes very great; often it is even "steaming" on the slopes of the fields, but a wind dispels this growing sultriness, and whirling eddies of dust—sure sign of settled, fine weather—move along the roads and across the fields in high white columns. In the pure dry air there is a scent of wormwood, rye in blossom, and buckwheat; even an hour before nightfall there is no moisture in the air. It is for such weather that the farmer longs, for harvesting his wheat. . . .

On just such a day I was once out grouse-shooting in the Chern District of the province of Tula. I started and shot a fair amount of game; my full game-bag cut my shoulder mercilessly; but already the evening glow had faded, and the cool shades of twilight were beginning to grow thicker and to spread across the sky, which was still bright, though no longer lighted up by the rays of the setting sun, when I at last decided to turn back homewards. With swift steps I passed through the long "square" of underwoods, clambered up a hill, and instead of the familiar plain I expected to see, with the oak wood on the right and the little white church in the distance, I saw before me a scene completely different, and quite new to me. A narrow valley lay at my feet, and directly facing me a dense wood of aspen-trees rose up like a thick wall. I stood still in perplexity, looked round me. . . . "Aha!" I thought, "I have somehow come wrong; I kept too much to the right," and surprised at my own mistake, I rapidly descended the hill. I was at once plunged into a disagreeable clinging mist, exactly as though I had gone down into a cellar; the thick high grass at the bottom of the valley, all drenched with dew, was white like a smooth table-cloth; one felt afraid somehow to walk on it. I made haste to get on the other side and walked along beside the aspen wood, bearing to the left.

Bats were already hovering over its slumbering tree-tops, mysteriously flitting and quivering across the clear obscure of the sky; a young belated hawk flew in swift, straight course upwards, hastening to its nest. "Here, directly I get to this corner," I thought to myself, "I shall find the road at once; but I have come a verst out of my way!"

I did at last reach the end of the wood, but there was no road of any sort there; some kind of low bushes overgrown with long grass extended far and wide before me; behind them in the far, far distance could be discerned a tract of wasteland. I stopped again. "Well? Where am I?" I began ransacking my brain to recall how and where I had been walking during the day. . . . "Ah! but these are the bushes at Parakhin," I cried at last; "of course! then this must be Sindeyev wood. But how did I get here? So far? . . . Strange! Now I must bear to the right again."

I went to the right through the bushes. Meantime the night had crept close and grown up like a storm-cloud; it seemed as though, with the mists of evening, darkness was rising up on all sides and flowing down from overhead. I had come upon some sort of little, untrodden, overgrown path; I walked along it, gazing intently before me. Soon all was blackness and silence around—only the quail's cry was heard from time to time. Some small night-bird, flitting noiselessly near the ground on its soft wings, almost flapped against me and scurried away in alarm. I came out on the further side of the bushes and made my way along a field by the hedge. By now I could hardly make out distant objects; the field showed dimly-white around; beyond it rose up a sullen darkness, which seemed moving up closer in huge masses every instant. My steps gave a muffled sound in the air that grew colder and colder. The pale sky began again to grow blue—but it was the blue of night. The tiny stars glimmered and twinkled in it.

What I had been taking for a wood turned out to be a dark round hillock. "But where am I, then?" I repeated again aloud, standing still for the third time and looking inquiringly at my spot and tan English dog, Dianka by name, certainly the most intelligent of four-footed creatures. But the most intelligent of four-footed creatures only wagged her tail, blinked her weary eyes dejectedly, and gave me no sensible advice. I felt myself disgraced in her eyes and pushed desperately forward, as though I had suddenly guessed which way I ought to go; I scaled the hill and found myself in a hollow of no great depth, ploughed round.

A strange sensation came over me at once. This hollow had the form of an almost perfect cauldron, with sloping sides; at the bottom of it were some great white stones standing upright—it seemed as though they had crept there for some secret council—and it was so still and dark in it, so flat and mute, so dreary and weird seemed the sky, overhanging it, that my heart sank. Some little animal was whining feebly and piteously among the stones. I made haste to get out again on to the hillock. Till then I had not quite given up all hope of finding the way home; but at this point I finally decided that I was utterly lost, and without any further attempt to make out the surrounding objects, which were almost completely plunged in darkness, I walked straight forward, by the aid of the stars, at random. . . . For about half an hour I walked on in this way, though I could hardly move one leg before the other. It seemed as if I had never been in such a deserted country in my life; nowhere was there the glimmer of a fire, nowhere a sound to be heard. One sloping hillside followed another; fields stretched endlessly upon fields; bushes seemed to spring up out of the earth under my very nose. I kept walking and was just making up my mind to lie down somewhere till morning, when suddenly I found myself on the edge of a horrible precipice.

I quickly drew back my lifted foot, and through the almost opaque darkness I saw far below me a vast plain. A long river skirted it in a semicircle, turned away from me; its course was marked by the steely reflection of the water still faintly glimmering here and there. The hill on which I found myself terminated abruptly in an almost overhanging precipice, whose gigantic profile stood out black against the dark-blue waste of sky, and directly below me, in the corner formed by this precipice and the plain near the river, which was there a dark, motionless mirror, under the lee of the hill, two fires side by side were smoking and throwing up red flames. People were stirring round them, shadows hovered, and sometimes the front of a small curly head was lighted up by the glow.

I found out at last where I had got to. This plain was well known in our parts under the name of Bezhin Meadow. But there was no possibility of returning home, especially at night; my legs were sinking under me from weariness. I decided to get down to the fires and to wait for the dawn in the company of these men, whom I took for drovers. I got down successfully, but I had hardly let go of the last branch I had grasped, when suddenly two large shaggy white dogs rushed angrily barking upon me. The sound of ringing boyish voices came from round the fires; two or three boys quickly got up from the ground. I called back in response to their shouts of inquiry. They ran up to me and at once called off the dogs, who were specially struck by the appearance of my Dianka. I came down to them.

I had been mistaken in taking the figures sitting round the fires for drovers. They were simply peasant boys from a neighboring village, who were in charge of a drove of horses. In hot summer weather they drive the horses out at night to graze in the open country: the flies and gnats would give them no peace in the day-time; they drive out the herd towards evening, and drive them back in the early morning: it's a great treat for the peasant boys. Bare-headed, in old sheepskin coats, they bestride the most spirited nags, and scurry along with merry cries and hooting and ringing laughter, swinging their arms and legs and leaping into the air. The fine dust is stirred up in yellow clouds and moves along the road; the tramp of hoofs in unison resounds afar; the horses race along, pricking up their ears; in front of all, with his tail in the air and thistles in his tangled mane, prances some shaggy chestnut, constantly shifting his gait as he goes.

I told the boys I had lost my way. They made way for me and I sat down with them. They asked me where I came from, and then were silent for a little. Then we talked a little again. I lay down under a bush, whose shoots had been nibbled off, and began to look round. It was a marvellous picture; about the fire a red ring of light quivered and seemed to swoon away in the embrace of a background of darkness; the flame flaring up from time to time cast swift flashes of light beyond the boundary of this circle; a fine tongue of light licked the dry twigs and died away at once; long thin shadows, in their turn breaking in for an instant, danced right up to the very fires; darkness was struggling with light. Sometimes, when the fire burnt low and the circle of light shrank together, suddenly out of the encroaching darkness a horse's head was thrust in, bay, with striped markings, or all white, stared with intent blank eyes upon us, nipped hastily the long grass, and drawing back again, vanished instantly. One could only hear it still munching and snorting. From the circle of light it was hard to make out what was going on in the darkness; everything close at hand seemed shut off by an almost black curtain; but farther away hills and forests were dimly visible in long blurs upon the horizon.

The dark unclouded sky stood, inconceivably immense, triumphant, above us in all its mysterious majesty. One felt a sweet oppression at one's heart, breathing in that peculiar, overpowering, yet fresh fragrance—the fragrance of a summer night in Russia. Scarcely a sound was to be heard around. Only at times, in the river near, the sudden splash of a big fish leaping, and the faint rustle of a reed on the bank, swaying lightly as the ripples reached it. The fires alone kept up a subdued crackling.

The boys sat round them: there, too, sat the two dogs who had been so eager to devour me. They could not for long after reconcile themselves to my presence, and, drowsily blinking and looking askance at the fire, they growled now and then with an unwonted sense of their own dignity; first they growled, and then whined a little, as though deploring the impossibility of carrying out their desires. There were altogether five boys: Fedya, Pavlusha, Ilyusha, Kostya and Vanya. (From their talk I learnt their names, and I intend now to introduce them to the reader.)

The first and eldest of all, Fedya, one would take to be about fourteen. He was a well-made boy, with good-looking, delicate, rather small features, curly fair hair, bright eyes, and a perpetual half-merry, half-careless smile. He belonged, by all appearances, to a well-to-do family, and had ridden out to the meadow not through necessity, but for amusement. He wore a gay print shirt, with a yellow border; a short new overcoat slung round his neck was almost slipping off his narrow shoulders; a comb hung from his blue belt. His boots, coming a little way up the leg, were certainly his own— not his father's. The second boy, Pavlusha, had tangled black hair, grey eyes, broad cheek-bones, a pale face pitted with small-pox, a large but well-cut mouth; his head altogether was large—"a beer-barrel head," as they say—and his figure was square and clumsy. He was not a good-looking boy—there's no denying it!—and yet I liked him; he looked very sensible and straightforward, and there was a vigorous ring in his voice. He had nothing to boast of in his attire; it consisted simply of a homespun shirt and patched trousers. The face of the third, Ilyusha, was rather uninteresting; it was a long face, with short-sighted eyes and a hooknose: it expressed a kind of dull, fretful uneasiness; his tightly-drawn lips seemed rigid; his contracted brow never relaxed; he seemed continually blinking from the firelight. His flaxen—almost white—hair hung out in thin wisps under his low felt hat, which he kept pulling down with both hands over his ears. He had on new bast shoes and leggings; a thick string, wound three times round his figure, carefully held together his neat black smock. Neither he nor Pavulsha looked more than twelve years old. The fourth, Kostya, a boy of ten, aroused my curiosity by his thoughtful and sorrowful look. His whole face was small, thin, freckled, pointed at the chin like a squirrel's; his lips were barely perceptible; but his great black eyes, that shone with liquid brilliance, produced a strange impression: they seemed trying to express something for which the tongue—his tongue, at least—had no words. He was undersized and weakly, and dressed rather poorly. The remaining boy, Vanya, I had not noticed at first; he was lying on the ground, peacefully curled up under a square mat, and only occasionally thrust his curly brown head out from under it; this boy was seven years old at the most.

So I lay under the bush at one side and looked at the boys. A small pot was hanging over one of the fires; in it potatoes were cooking. Pavlusha was looking after them, and on his knees he was trying them by poking a splinter of wood into the boiling water. Fedya was lying leaning on his elbow and smoothing out the skirts of his coat. Ilyusha was sitting beside Kostya, and still kept blinking constrainedly. Kostya's head drooped despondently, and he looked away into the distance. Vanya did not stir under his mat. I pretended to be asleep. Little by little, the boys began talking again.

At first they gossiped of one thing and another, the work of tomorrow, the horses; but suddenly Fedya turned to Ilyusha, and, as though taking up again an interrupted conversation, asked him:

"Come then, so you've seen the goblin?"

"No, I didn't see him, and no one ever can see him," answered Ilyusha in a weak hoarse voice, the sound of which was wonderfully in keeping with the expression of his face; "I heard him. Yes, and not I alone."

"Where does he live—in your place?" asked Pavlusha.

"In the old paper mill."

"Why, do you go to the factory?"

"Of course we do. My brother Avdyushka and I, we are paper-glazers."

"Well!—factory-hands!"

"Well, how did you hear him, then?" asked Fedya.

"It was like this. It happened that I and my brother Avdyushka, with Fyodor Mikheyevsky, and Ivashka the Squint-Eyed, and the other Ivashka who comes from the Red Hills, and Ivashka Sukhoru-kov, too—and there were some other boys there as well—there were ten of us boys there altogether—the whole shift, that is—it happened that he spent the night at the paper mill; that's to say, it didn't happen, but Nazarov, the overseer, kept us. 'Why,' said he, 'should you waste time going home, boys; there's a lot of work tomorrow, so don't go home, boys.' So we stopped, and were all lying down together, and Avdyushka had just begun to say, 'I say, boys, suppose the goblin were to come?' And before he'd finished saying so, someone suddenly began walking over our heads; we were lying down below, and he began walking upstairs overhead, where the wheel is. We listened: he walked; the boards seemed to be bending under him, they creaked so; then he crossed over, above our heads; all of a sudden the water began to drip and drip over the wheel; the wheel rattled and rattled and again began to turn, though the sluices of the conduit above had been let down. We wondered who could have lifted them up so that the water could run; anyway, the wheel turned and turned a little, and then stopped. Then he went to the door overhead and began coming downstairs, and came down, not hurrying himself; the stairs seemed to groan under him, too. . . . Well, he came right down to our door, and waited and waited . . . and all of a sudden the door simply flew open. We were in a fright; we looked—there was nothing. Suddenly what if the net on one of the vats didn't begin moving; it got up and went rising and ducking and moving in the air as though someone were stirring with it, and then it was in its place again. Then, at another vat, a hook came off its nail, and then was on its nail again; and then it seemed as if someone came to the door

and suddenly coughed and choked like a sheep, but so loudly! . . .
We all fell down in a heap and huddled against one another. Just
weren't we in a fright that night!"

"I say!" murmured Pavlusha, "what did he cough for?"

"I don't know; perhaps it was the damp."

All were silent for a little.

"Well," inquired Fedya, "are the potatoes done?"

Pavlusha tried them.

"No, they are raw. . . . My, what a splash!" he added, turning
his face in the direction of the river; "that must be a pike. . . . And
there's a star falling."

"I say, I can tell you something, brothers," began Kostya in a
shrill little voice; "listen what my Dad told us the other day."

"Well, we are listening," said Fedya with a patronizing air.

"You know Gavrila, I suppose, the carpenter up in the big
village?"

"Yes, we know him."

"And do you know why he is so sorrowful always, never speaks?
do you know? I'll tell you why he's so sorrowful; he went one day,
Daddy said, he went, brothers, into the forest nutting. So he went
nutting into the forest and lost his way; he went on—God only can
tell where he got to. So he went on and on, brothers—but 'twas no
good!—he could not find the way; and so night came on out of
doors. So he sat down under a tree. 'I'll wait till morning,' thought
he. He sat down and began to drop asleep. So, as he was falling
asleep, suddenly he heard someone call him. He looked up; there
was no one. He fell asleep again; again he was called. He looked
and looked again; and in front of him there sat a mermaid on a
branch, swinging herself, and calling him to her, and simply dying
with laughing; she laughed so. . . . And the moon was shining bright,
so bright, the moon shone so clear—everything could be seen plain,
brothers. So she called him, and she herself was as bright and as
white sitting on the branch as some dace or a roach, or like some
little carp, so white and silvery. . . . Gavrila the carpenter almost
fainted, brothers, but she laughed without stopping, and kept beckoning him to her like this. Then Gavrila was just getting up; he
was just wanting to go up to the mermaid, brothers, but—the Lord
put it into his heart, doubtless—he crossed himself. . . . And it was
so hard for him to make that cross, brothers; he said, 'My hand was

simply like a stone; it would not move.' Ugh! the horrid witch! . . .
So when he made the cross, brothers, the mermaid, she left off
laughing, and all at once how she did cry. . . . She cried, brothers,
and wiped her eyes with her hair, and her hair was green as any
hemp. So Gavrila looked and looked at her, and at last he fell to
questioning her. 'Why are you weeping, wild thing of the woods?'
And the mermaid began to speak to him like this: 'If you had not
crossed yourself, man,' she says, 'you should have lived with me in
gladness of heart to the end of your days; and I weep, I am grieved
at heart because you crossed yourself; but I will not grieve alone;
you, too, shall grieve at heart to the end of your days.' Then she
vanished, brothers, and at once it was plain to Gavrila how to get
out of the forest. . . . Only since then he goes always sorrowful, as
you see."

"Ugh!" said Fedya after a brief silence; "but how can such an
evil thing of the woods ruin a Christian soul—he did not listen
to her?"

"Strange, isn't it?" said Kostya. "Gavrila said that her voice was
as shrill and plaintive as a toad's."

"Did your father tell you that himself?" Fedya went on.

"Yes. I was lying in the loft; I heard it all."

"It's a strange thing. Why should he be sorrowful? . . . But I
suppose she liked him, since she called him."

"Ay, she liked him!" put in Ilyusha. "Yes, indeed! she wanted
to tickle him to death, that's what she wanted. That's what they
do, those mermaids."

"There ought to be mermaids here, too, I suppose," observed
Fedya.

"No," answered Kostya, "this is a clear, open place. There's
one thing, though: the river's near."

All were silent. Suddenly from out of the distance came a prolonged, resonant, almost wailing sound, one of those inexplicable
sounds of the night, which break upon a profound stillness, rise
upon the air, linger, and slowly die away at last. You listen: it is as
though there were nothing, yet it echoes still. It is as though someone had uttered a long, long cry upon the very horizon, as though
some other had answered him with shrill harsh laughter in the
forest, and a faint, hoarse hissing hovers over the river. The boys
looked roundabout shivering. . . .

"Christ's aid be with us!" whispered Ilyusha.

"Ah, you craven crows!" cried Pavlusha; "what are you frightened of? Look, the potatoes are done." (They all came up to the pot and began to eat the smoking potatoes; only Vanya did not stir.) "Well, aren't you coming?" said Pavlusha.

But he did not creep out from under his mat. The pot was soon completely emptied.

"Have you heard, boys," began Ilyusha, "what happened with us at Varnavitsi?"

"Near the dam?" asked Fedya.

"Yes, yes, near the dam, the broken-down dam. That is a haunted place, such a haunted place, and so lonely. All round there are pits and quarries, and there are always snakes in pits."

"Well, what did happen? Tell us."

"Well, this is what happened. You don't know, perhaps, Fedya, but there a drowned man was buried; he was drowned long, long ago, when the water was still deep; only his grave can still be seen, though it can only just be seen . . . just a little mound. . . . So one day the bailiff called the huntsman Yermil, and says to him, 'Go to the post, Yermil.' Yermil always goes to the post for us; he has let all his dogs die; they never will live with him, for some reason, and they have never lived with him, though he's a good huntsman, and everyone likes him. So Yermil went to the post, and he stayed a bit in the town, and when he rode back, he was a little tipsy. It was night, a fine night; the moon was shining. . . . So Yermil rode across the dam; his way lay there. So, as he rode along, he saw, on the drowned man's grave, a little lamb, so white and curly and pretty, running about. So Yermil thought, 'I will take him,' and he got down and took him in his arms. But the little lamb didn't take any notice. So Yermil goes back to his horse, and the horse stares at him, and snorts and shakes his head; however, he said 'whoa' to him and sat on him with the lamb, and rode on again; he held the lamb in front of him. He looks at him, and the lamb looks him straight in the face, like this. Yermil the huntsmen felt upset. 'I don't remember,' he said, 'that lambs ever look at any one like that'; however, he began to stroke it like this on its wool and to say, 'Chucky! chucky!' And the lamb suddenly showed its teeth and said too, "Chucky! chucky!'"

The boy who was telling the story had hardly uttered this last word when suddenly both dogs got up at once, and, barking convulsively, rushed away from the fire and disappeared in the darkness. All the boys were alarmed. Vanya jumped up from under his mat. Pavlusha ran shouting after the dogs. Their barking quickly grew fainter in the distance. There was the noise of the uneasy tramp of the frightened drove of horses. Pavlusha shouted aloud, "Hey, Sery! Zhuckka!" In a few minutes the barking ceased; Pavlusha's voice sounded still in the distance. A little more time passed; the boys kept looking about in perplexity, as though expecting something to happen. Suddenly the tramp of a galloping horse was heard; it stopped short at the pile of wood, and, hanging on to the mane, Pavlusha sprang nimbly off it. Both the dogs also leaped into the circle of light and at once sat down, their red tongues hanging out.

"What was it? what was it?" asked the boys.

"Nothing," answered Pavlusha, waving his hand to his horse; "I suppose the dogs scented something. I thought it was a wolf," he added, calmly drawing deep breaths into his chest.

I could not help admiring Pavlusha. He was very fine at that moment. His ugly face, animated by his swift ride, glowed with hardihood and determination. Without even a switch in his hand, he had, without the slightest hesitation, rushed out into the night alone to face a wolf. "What a splendid fellow!" I thought, looking at him.

"Have you seen any wolves, then?" asked the trembling Kostya.

"There are always a good many of them here," answered Pavlusha; "but they are only troublesome in the winter."

He crouched down again before the fire. As he sat down on the ground, he laid his hand on the shaggy head of one of the dogs. For a long while the flattered brute did not turn his head, gazing sidewise with grateful pride at Pavlusha.

Vanya lay down under his mat again.

"What dreadful things you were telling us, Ilyusha!" began Fedya, whose part it was, as the son of a well-to-do peasant, to lead the conversation. (He spoke little himself, apparently afraid of lowering his dignity.) "And then some evil spirit set the dogs barking. . . . Certainly I have heard that place of yours was haunted."

"Varnavitsi? . . . I should think it was haunted! More than once, they say, they have seen the old master there—the late master. He wears, they say, a long skirted coat, and keeps groaning like this, and looking for something on the ground. Once grandfather Trofimich met him. 'What,' says he, 'your honor, Ivan Ivanich, are you pleased to look for on the ground?'"

"He asked him?" put in Fedya in amazement.

"Yes, he asked him."

"Well, I call Trofimich a brave fellow after that. . . . Well, what did he say?"

" 'I am looking for the herb that cleaves all things,' says he. But he speaks so thickly, so thickly. 'And what, your honor, Ivan Ivanich, do you want with the herb that cleaves all things?' 'The tomb weighs on me; it weighs on me, Trofimich; I want to get away —away.' "

"My word!" observed Fedya, "he didn't get enough out of life, I suppose."

"What a marvel!" said Kostya. "I thought one could only see the departed on All Hallows' Day."

"One can see the departed any time," Ilyusha interposed with conviction. From what I could observe, I judged he knew the village superstitions better than the others. "But on All Hallows' Day you can see the living too; that is, whose turn it is to die that year. You need only sit in the church porch and keep looking at the road. They will come by you along the road; those, that is, who will die that year. Last year old Ulyana went to the porch."

"Well, did she see anyone?" asked Kostya inquisitively.

"To be sure she did. At first she sat a long, long while, and saw no one and heard nothing . . . only it semed as if some dog kept whining and whining somewhere. . . . Suddenly she looks up: a boy comes along the road with only a shirt on. She looked at him. It was Ivashka Fedoseyev."

"He who died in the spring?" put in Fedya.

"Yes, he. He came along and never lifted up his head. But Ulyana knew him. And then she looks again: a woman came along. She stared and stared at her. . . . Ah, God Almighty! . . . it was herself coming along the road; Ulyana herself."

"Could it be herself?" asked Fedya.

"Yes, by God, herself."

"Well, but she is not dead yet, you know?"

"But the year is not over yet. And only look at her; her life hangs on a thread."

All were still again. Pavlusha threw a handful of dry twigs on to the fire. They were soon charred by the suddenly leaping flame; they cracked and smoked, and began to contract, curling up their burning ends. Gleams of light in broken flashes glanced in all directions, especially upwards. Suddenly, a white dove flew straight into the bright light, fluttered round and round in terror, bathed in the red glow, and disappeared with a whirr of its wings.

"It's lost its home, I suppose," remarked Pavlusha. "Now it will fly till it gets somewhere, where it can rest till dawn."

"Why, Pavlusha," said Kostya, "might it not be a just soul flying to heaven?"

Pavlusha threw another handfull of twigs on to the fire.

"Perhaps," he said at last.

"But tell us, please, Pavlusha," began Fedya, "did you in Shalamov also see the heavenly portent?"*

"When the sun could not be seen? Yes, indeed."

"Were you frightened, too?"

'Yes; and we weren't the only ones. Our master, though he talked to us beforehand and said there would be a heavenly portent, yet when it got dark, they say he himself was frightened out of his wits. And in the house-serfs' cottage the old woman, directly it grew dark, broke all the dishes in the oven with the poker. "Who will eat now?" she said; "the last day has come." So the soup was running all about the place. And in the village there were such tales about among us: that white wolves would run over the earth and would eat men, that a bird of prey would pounce down on us, and that they would even see Trishka."**

"What is Trishka?" asked Kostya.

"Why, don't you know?" interrupted Ilyusha warmly. "Why, brother, where have you been brought up, not to know Trishka? You're a stay-at-home, one-eyed lot in your village, really! Trishka will be a marvellous man, who will come one day, and he will be such a marvellous man that they will never be able to catch him, and never be able to do anything with him; he will be such a marvellous man. The people will try to take him; for example, they will come after him with sticks, they will surround him, but he will blind their

---

* This is what the peasants call an eclipse.—*Author's Note.*
** The popular belief in Trishka is probably derived from some tradition of Antichrist.—*Author's Note.*

eyes so that they fall upon one another. They will put him in prison, for example; he will ask for a little water to drink in a bowl; they will bring him the bowl, and he will plunge into it and vanish from their sight. They will put chains on him, but he will only clap his hands—they will fall off him. So this Trishka will go through villages and towns; and this Trishka will be a wily man; he will lead astray Christ's people . . . and they will be able to do nothing to him. . . . He will be such a marvellous wily man."

"Well, then," continued Pavlusha in his deliberate voice, "that's what he's like. And so they expected him in our parts. The old men declared that directly the heavenly portent began, Trishka would come. So the heavenly portent began. All the people were scattered over the street, in the fields, waiting to see what would happen. Our place, you know, is open country. They look; and suddenly down the mountain-side from the big village comes a man of some sort; such a strange man, with such a wonderful head that all scream, 'Oy, Trishka is coming! Oy, Trishka is coming!' and all run in all directions! Our elder crawled into a ditch; his wife stumbled on the door-board and screamed with all her might; she terrified her yard dog so that he broke away from his chain and over the hedge and into the forest; and Kuzka's father, Dorofeyich, ran into the oats, lay down there, and began to cry like a quail. 'Perhaps,' says he, 'the Enemy, the Destroyer of Souls, will spare the birds, at least.' So they were all in such a scare! But he that was coming was our cooper Vavila; he had bought himself a new pitcher and had put the empty pitcher over his head."

All the boys laughed; and again there was a silence for a while, as often happens when people are talking in the open air. I looked out into the solemn, majestic stillness of the night; the dewy freshness of late evening had been succeeded by the dry heat of midnight; the darkness still had long to lie in a soft curtain over the slumbering fields; there was still a long while left before the first whisperings, the first dewdrops of dawn. There was no moon in the heavens; it rose late at that time. Countless golden stars, twinkling in rivalry, seemed all running softly towards the Milky Way, and truly, looking at them, you were almost conscious of the whirling, never-resting motion of the earth. . . . A strange, harsh, painful cry sounded twice together over the river, and a few moments later, was repeated farther down. . . .

Kostya shuddered. "What was that?"

"That was a heron's cry," replied Pavlusha tranquilly.

"A heron," repeated Kostya. . . . "And what was it, Pavlusha, I heard yesterday evening?" he added, after a short pause; "maybe you will know."

"What did you hear?"

"I will tell you what I heard. I was going from Stony Ridge to Shashkino; I went first through our walnut wood, and then passed by a little pool—you know where there's a sharp turn down to the ravine—there is a water-pit there, you know; it is quite overgrown with reeds; so I went near this pit, brothers, and suddenly from it came a sound of someone groaning, and piteously, so piteously: oo-oo, oo-oo! I was in such a fright, my brothers; it was late, and the voice was so miserable. I felt as if I should cry myself. . . . What could that have been, eh?"

"It was in that pit the thieves drowned Akim the forester last summer," observed Pavlusha; "so perhaps it was his soul lamenting."

"Oh, dear, really, brothers," replied Kostya, opening wide his eyes, which were round enough before, "I did not know they had drowned Akim in that pit. Shouldn't I have been frightened if I'd known!"

"But they say there are little, tiny frogs," continued Pavlusha, "who cry piteously like that."

"Frogs? Oh, no, it was not frogs, certainly not." (The heron again uttered a cry above the river.) "Ugh, there it is!" Kostya cried involuntarily; "it is just like a wood-spirit shrieking."

"The wood-spirit does not shriek, it is dumb," put in Ilyusha; "it only claps its hands and rattles."

"And have you seen it then, the wood-spirit?" Fedya asked him ironically.

"No, I have not seen it, and God preserve me from seeing it; but others have seen it. Why, one day it misled a peasant in our parts, and led him through the woods and all in a circle in one field. . . . He scarcely got home till daylight."

"Well, and did he see it?"

"Yes. He says it was a big, big creature, dark, shapeless, as if it were standing behind a tree; you could not make it out well; it seemed to hide away from the moon, and kept staring and staring with its great eyes, and winking and winking them. . . ."

"Ugh!" exclaimed Fedya with a slight shiver, and a shrug of the shoulders; "pfoo!"

"And how does such an unclean brood come to exist in the world," said Pavlusha; "it's a wonder."

"Don't speak ill of it; take care, it will hear you," said Ilyusha.

Again there was a silence.

"Look, look, brothers," suddenly came Vanya's childish voice; "look at God's little stars; they are swarming like bees!"

He put his fresh little face out from under his mat, leaned on his little fist, and slowly lifted up his large soft eyes. The eyes of all the boys were raised to the sky, and they were not lowered quickly.

"Well, Vanya," began Fedya caressingly, "is your sister Anyutka well?"

"Yes, she is very well," replied Vanya with a slight lisp.

"You ask her, why doesn't she come to see us?"

"I don't know."

"You tell her to come."

"Very well."

"Tell her I have a present for her."

"And a present for me, too?"

"Yes, you, too."

Vanya sighed.

"No; I don't want one. Better give it to her; she is so kind to us at home."

And Vanya laid his head down again on the ground. Pavlusha got up and took the empty pot in his hand.

"Where are you going?" Fedya asked him.

"To the river, to get water; I want some water to drink."

The dogs got up and followed him.

"Take care you don't fall into the river!" Ilyusha cried after him.

"Why should he fall in?" said Fedya. "He will be careful."

"Yes, he will be careful. But all kinds of things happen; he will stoop over, perhaps, to draw the water, and the water-spirit will clutch him by the hand, and drag him into the depths. Then they will say, 'The boy fell into the water.' Fell in, indeed! . . . There, he has gone in among the reeds," he added, listening.

The reeds certainly "shished," as they call it among us, as they were parted.

"But is it true," asked Kostya, "that Akulina has been mad ever since she fell into the water?"

"Yes, ever since. . . . How dreadful she is now! But they say she was a beauty before then. The water-spirit bewitched her. I suppose he did not expect they would get her out so soon. So down there at the bottom he bewitched her."

(I had met this Akulina more than once. Covered with rags, fearfully thin, with face as black as coal, bleary-eyed and for ever grinning, she would stay whole hours in one place in the road, stamping with her feet, pressing her fleshless hands to her breast, and slowly shifting from one leg to the other, like a wild beast in a cage. She understood nothing that was said to her, and only chuckled spasmodically from time to time.)

"But they say," continued Kostya, "that Akulina threw herself into the river because her lover had deceived her."

"Yes, that was it."

"And do you remember Vasya?" added Kostya, mournfully.

"What Vasya?" asked Fedya.

"Why, the one who was drowned," replied Kostya, "in this very river. Ah, what a boy he was! What a boy he was! His mother, Feklista, how she loved him, her Vasya! And she seemed to have a foreboding, Feklista did, that harm would come to him from the water. Sometimes, when Vasya went with us boys in the summer to bathe in the river, she used to be trembling all over. The other women did not mind; they passed by with the pails, and went on, but Feklista put her pail down on the ground, and set to calling him, 'Come back, come back, my little joy; come back, my darling!' And no one knows how he was drowned. He was playing on the bank, and his mother was there haymaking; suddenly she hears as though someone was blowing bubbles through the water, and behold! there was only Vasya's little cap to be seen swimming on the water. You know since then Feklista has not been right in her mind: she goes and lies down at the place where he was drowned; she lies down, brothers, and sings a song—you remember Vasya was always singing a song like that—so she sings it, too, and weeps and weeps, and bitterly rails against God."

"Here is Pavlusha coming," said Fedya.

Pavlusha came up to the fire with a full pot in his hand.

"Boys," he began after a short silence, "something bad happened."

"Oh, what?" asked Kostya hurriedly.

"I heard Vasya's voice."

They all seemed to shudder.

"What do you mean? what do you mean?" stammered Kostya.

"I don't know. Only I went to stoop down to the water; suddenly I hear my name called in Vasya's voice, as though it came from below water, 'Pavlusha, Pavlusha, come here.' I came away. But I fetched the water, though."

"Ah, God have mercy upon us!" said the boys, crossing themselves.

"It was the water-spirit calling you, Pavlusha," said Fedya: "we were just talking of Vasya."

"Ah, it's a bad omen," said Ilyusha, deliberately.

"Well, never mind, don't bother about it," Pavlusha declared stoutly, and he sat down again; "no one can escape his fate."

The boys were still. It was clear that Pavlusha's words had produced a strong impression on them. They began to lie down before the fire as though preparing to go to sleep.

"What is that?" asked Kostya, suddenly lifting his head.

Pavlusha listened.

"It's the curlews flying and whistling."

"Where are they flying to?"

"To a land where, they say, there is no winter."

"But is there such a land?"

"Yes."

"Is it far away?"

"Far, far away, beyond the warm seas."

Kostya sighed and shut his eyes.

More than three hours had passed since I first came across the boys. The moon at last had risen; I did not notice it at first; it was such a tiny crescent. This moonless night was as solemn and hushed as it had been at first. . . . But already many stars, that not long before had been high up in the heavens, were setting over the earth's dark rim; everything around was perfectly still, as it is only still towards morning; all was sleeping the deep unbroken sleep that comes before daybreak. Already the fragrance in the air was fainter; once more a dew seemed falling. . . . How short summer nights are! . . . The boys' talk died down when the fires did. The dogs even were dozing; the horses, so far as I could make out in the hardly perceptible, faintly shining light of the stars, were asleep with downcast heads. . . . I fell into a state of weary unconsciousness, which passed into sleep.

A fresh breeze passed over my face. I opened my eyes; the morning was beginning. The dawn had not yet flushed the sky, but already it was growing light in the east. Everything had become visible, though dimly visible, around. The pale-grey sky was growing light and cold and bluish; the stars twinkled with a dimmer light, or disappeared; the earth was wet, the leaves covered with dew, and from the distance came sounds of life and voices, and a light morning breeze went fluttering over the earth. My body responded to it with a faint shudder of delight. I got up quickly and went to the boys. They were all sleeping, as though they were tired out, round the smouldering fire, only Pavlusha half rose and gazed intently at me.

I nodded to him, and walked homewards beside the misty river. Before I had walked two miles, already all around me, over the wide dew-drenched prairie, and in front, from forest to forest, where the hills were growing green again, and behind, over the long dusty road and the sparkling bushes, flushed with the red glow, and the river faintly blue now under the lifting mist, flowed fresh streams of burning light, first pink, then red and golden. . . . All things began to stir, to awaken, to sing, to flutter, to speak. On all sides thick drops of dew sparkled in glittering diamonds; to welcome me, pure and clear as though bathed in the freshness of morning, came the notes of a bell, and suddenly there rushed by me, driven by the boys I had parted from, the drove of horses, refreshed and rested. . . .

Sad to say, I must add that in that year Pavlusha met his end. He was not drowned; he was killed by a fall from his horse. Pity! He was a splendid fellow!

NIKOLAI LESKOV

Lady Macbeth
of the Mtsensk District:

A SKETCH

Sing the first song blushingly.

A SAYING

I

IN OUR PART OF THE WORLD one sometimes comes across people of such character that one cannot recall them without a spiritual shudder even when many years have elapsed since the last encounter. To this type belonged Katerina Lvovna Izmailova, a merchant's wife, who at one time played out such a terrible drama that some wit dubbed her *Lady Macbeth of the Mtsensk District,* and it was by that name that she was afterwards known amongst our gentry.

Katerina Lvovna was not born a beauty, although she was a woman of very pleasing appearance. She was in her twenty-fourth

Translated by GEORGE HANNA. *Reprinted from* The Enchanted Wanderer. *Moscow,* [n.d.].

year; although not tall, she was graceful, her neck was like white marble, her shoulders well-rounded, her bosom firm, her nose fine and straight, her eyes black and vivacious, her white forehead high and her hair of that dense blackness that seems almost blue. She was given in marriage to our merchant Izmailov of Tuskar, in Kursk Gubernia, not for love or even infatuation but because he asked for her hand and she, a girl of poor family, could not afford to pick and choose. The house of Izmailov was not the least in our town; they dealt in flour, rented a big mill in the district, owned a big orchard just outside the town and kept a good house in town. In general they were merchants of affluence. Their family, moreover, was quite small: the father-in-law, Boris Timofeyich Izmailov, already close on eighty and long a widower, his son Zinovy Borisich, Katerina Lvovna's husband, a man well over fifty, and, lastly, Katerina Lvovna herself. Although she had been married to Zinovy Borisich nearly five years there were no children. Nor had Zinovy Borisich any children from his first wife with whom he had lived twenty years before he was widowed and married Katerina Lvovna. He thought and hoped that in his second marriage God would grant him an heir to his merchant's name and capital; but he had no better luck with his second wife than with his first.

This childless state was a source of great grief to Zinovy Borisich, and not to him alone, but to old Boris Timofeyich as well; even Katherina Lvovna sorrowed over it. The great boredom of the merchant's cloister-like house with its high wall and savage dogs running loose in the yard was at times so oppressive that the young woman was a prey to a melancholy that dulled her brain; how glad she would have been—God knows how glad she would have been— to have a babe to fondle; she was, moreover, tired to death of the reproaches—"Why did you marry, what did you want to marry for; what did you want to foist yourself on a man for, if you're barren" —just as though she had committed some crime against her husband, against her father-in-law and against the whole of their honest merchant tribe.

For all its sufficiency and comfort, Katerina Lvovna's life in her father-in-law's house was most boring. She rarely went visiting anywhere and even when she went with her husband to visit his fellow merchants there was but little pleasure in it. They were all of them so strict; they would watch to see how she sat down, how she walked and how she got up; and Katerina had such an ardent character and, coming as she did from a poor family, she had been used to simplicity and freedom; she would gladly have run down to the river with her buckets, bathing in her shift under the landing stage, or throw sunflower seed husks at any young fellow who passed her gate; but here everything was different. Her father-in-law and husband were early risers; at six o'clock they would drink tea and then go about their business while she was left to wander idly from room to room. All was clean, all was silent and empty, the lamps burning brightly in front of the icons, but nowhere was there a sound of any living thing or of a human voice.

Katerina Lvovna would wander from one empty room to another, would begin to yawn from boredom and then climb the ladder to their conjugal bedchamber situated in a high but small attic room. Here she would sit and watch the people weighing hemp or pouring flour in the sheds down below—again she would yawn and be glad of it; she would doze for an hour or two, but would awake again to that Russian boredom, the boredom of a merchant's home, to escape which, it is said, even to hang oneself is a pleasure. Katerina Lvovna was no lover of reading and, anyway, there were no books in the house apart from the Kiev *Lives of the Christian Fathers.*

It was a boring life that had been her lot in her father-in-law's house for those five long years of her marriage with an unaffectionate husband; but as usual, nobody paid the slightest attention to this boredom of hers.

II

In the sixth spring of Katerina Lvovna's married life the Izmailov's mill-dam burst and at a time, too, when there was an abundance of work at the mill. The breach was a big one, the lower beams of the dam impounding the mill-pond were torn away and the water escaped at such a rate that it could not be quickly stopped. Zinovy Borisich took people from all over the district and sent them to the mill and he himself spent all his time there; the old man was able to manage their town affairs and for days on end Katerina Lvovna was left all alone in the house. At first she was even more bored without her husband but then it began to seem better without him; she had more liberty when she was alone. She had never been particularly fond of him and without him, at any rate, there was one person less to order her about.

One day Katerina Lvovna was sitting at the little window in her high room, yawning and yawning, and thinking of nothing in particular until at last she grew ashamed of her yawning. The weather was wonderful: warm, bright and jolly and through the wooden green garden fence she could see perky birds flitting from branch to branch on the trees.

"What's the matter with me, yawning so much?" thought Katerina Lvovna. "I might at least get up and talk a walk in the yard or through the garden."

She threw an old brocade coat over her shoulders and went out.

It was light outside and so easy to breathe; roars of merry laughter came from the gallery around the storehouses.

"What are you all so happy about?" Katerina Lvovna asked her father-in-law's warehousemen.

"Oh, Katerina Lvovna, madam, they're weighing a live pig," answered the senior warehouseman.

"What pig?"

"That pig Aksinya, what had a son, Vasily, and didn't ask us to the christening," brashly and gaily answered a young fellow with a bold, handsome face framed in curls as black as pitch and a newly sprouting beard.

At that moment the flushed, fat mug of Aksinya the cook peeped out of a flour tub hanging from the scale beam.

"Devils, imps of Satan," cursed the cook, struggling to get hold of the iron beam and climb out of the swinging tub.

"Eight *poods* she weighs, before dinner. Give her a measure of hay for supper and you won't find weights enough for her," said the handsome young man, and, tipping over the tub, threw the cook on to a heap of sacks lying in the corner.

The woman, swearing jokingly, started putting her dress in order.

"See how much I weigh," joked Katerina Lvovna and, catching hold of the rope, jumped on to the scale board.

"Three poods seven pound," answered that same handsome young man, Sergei, throwing weights into the scale pan. "It's a miracle!"

"What's miraculous about it?"

"That you should weigh three poods, Katerina Lvovna. As I see it, a fellow could carry you in his arms all day. He wouldn't get tired, but would feel it only a pleasure for himself."

"Do you think I'm not human, or what? You'd probably get tired all right," answered Katerina Lvovna, blushing slightly, being unaccustomed to such speeches and feeling a sudden urge to chatter away, to have her fill of jokes and merriment.

"Good Lord, I'd carry you all the way to happy Araby," said Sergei in answer to her comment.

"Your thinking is all wrong, young man," said an elderly peasant who was pouring flour into a bin. "What is it gives you weight? Your body, young man, is nothing on the scale: it is your strength, your strength that counts and not the body!"

"Yes, I was awfully strong when I was a girl," put in Katerina Lvovna again, unable to contain herself. "Not every man, even, could get the better of me."

"Then let me try your grip if it's true, what you say," asked the handsome young man.

This confused Katerina Lvovna but still she held out her hand.

"Oh, let go, the ring hurts!" she cried when Sergei squeezed her hand, and with her free hand she gave him a push in the chest.

The young man let go of the mistress's hand and staggered a couple of paces back from the force of her push.

"Well, there's a woman for you," said the elderly peasant.

"Will you please let me test your strength like this, like we was wrestling," said Sergei, turning to her and tossing his curly head.

"All right, then," answered the now happy Katerina Lvovna and lifted her elbows.

Sergei put his arms round the young mistress and pressed her firm bosom to his red shirt. She only had time to jerk her shoulders before Sergei had lifted her off the floor, held her in his arms, squeezed her, and seated her gently on an upturned flour measure.

She did not have a chance to make use of her boasted strength. Flushing a deep red, she sat on the measure and adjusted the coat on her shoulders, then went quickly out of the storeroom while Sergei coughed pertly and shouted:

"Come on, you sainted blockheads! Pour it in an' tip the measure. All you scrape off you keep."

He pretended to be paying no heed to what had just happened.

"That damned Sergei is a rare 'un for the skirts," Aksinya the cook was saying as she plodded along behind her mistress. "He gets 'em all ways—he's tall an' handsome an' he has the sort of face they like. Take any woman—why that scoundrel flatters an' flatters her an' leads her to sin. And as for being inconstant, the scoundrel's as inconstant as inconstant can be!"

"And you, Aksinya. . . . That . . . boy of yours," said the young mistress as she walked ahead, "is he still alive?"

"Of course, he's alive, ma'am, why shouldn't he be? Them as aren't wanted always go on living."

"Where did you get him from?"

"Hm-m. Just like that, I live amongst people, don't I—they all want their bit of fun."

"And that young fellow, has he been with us long?"

"Who d'you mean? Sergei?"

"Yes."

"About a month. He used to work for the Konchonovs but the old man kicked him out." Aksinya lowered her voice and continued: "They say he had an affair with the mistress. . . . There's how bold he is, the thrice anathematized soul!"

III

Warm, hazy twilight settled on the town. Zinovy Borisich had not yet returned from the mill-dam. Boris Timofeyich, the father-in-law, was also away: he was visiting an old friend on the occasion of a name-day celebration and had ordered Katerina Lvovna not to wait supper for him. Having nothing better to do, Katrina Lvovna supped early, opened the little window of her attic and sat there shelling sunflower seeds. The house servants had their meal in the kitchen and then went away to sleep—some in the shed, some in the storehouses and others to the high, fragrant haylofts. The last to leave the kitchen was Sergei. He went about the yard, unleased the watch-dogs and, whistling as he went, walked past Katerina Lvovna's window, looked up at her, and bowed low.

"Good evening," she said softly from her attic window, but the yard remained as quiet as a wilderness.

"Madam!" somebody breathed outside her locked door some two minutes later.

"Who's that?" she asked in frightened tones.

"You don't have to be afraid, madam: it's me, Sergei," answered the clerk.

"What do you want, Sergei?"

"There's a little bit of business I want to talk over, madam: just a small matter for which I crave your kindness: allow me to come in for a moment."

Katerina Lvovna turned the key and let Sergei in.

"What do you want?" she asked, backing towards the window.

"I've come to ask you whether you haven't got a book for me to read, Katerina Lvovna. I'm bored to tears here."

"I haven't got any books, Sergei, I don't read them," she answered.

"It's so boring here, I'm sick of it," complained Sergei.

"You're a fine one to say it boring!"

"God bless me, why shouldn't I be bored here: I'm young and this here place is no better than a monastery. It looks as how there's nothing coming but lonesomeness to the very grave. Sometimes I even get desperate."

"Why don't you get married?"

"That's easy to say, madam, get married. Who can I marry? I'm an insignificant man: a rich girl won't have me and the poor, you know yourself, Katerina Lvovna, have no education because of their poverty. What do they know about real love? And what do rich people think about this business, anyway? You, for instance, would be a comfort to any other man, to one with feelings, and they keep you locked up like a canary in a cage."

"Yes, I'm bored."

The admission burst from her lips.

"How not be bored, ma'am, with such a life! If you had someone on the side like all the others have—but you don't even get a chance to see anyone."

"Now you're going a bit too far. It's this way: If I had a baby I think I might be happy with him."

"But let me tell you, ma'am, there's a reason, too, for babies coming, they don't just arrive. Living all these years with different masters and seeing how the merchants' wives all lead miserable lives, I also, you understand, know a thing or two. There's a song that says: 'Life is dull when the sweetheart's gone. . . .' and that's why, believe me, Katerina Lvovna, my heart's heavy, it's on account of it feeling for you in your boredom—I could take a knife and cut it out and throw it at your feet. It would be easier, a hundred times easier, for me if I did. . . ."

Sergei's voice had begun to shake.

"What are you telling me all this about your heart for? That's got nothing to do with me. Go away. . . ."

"No, forgive me, ma'am," whispered Sergei, taking a step towards Katerina Lvovna, his whole body trembling. "I know and see and I feel for you and I understand; you don't lead any better life than I do: only now," here his voice sank so low that he scarcely breathed the last words, "now, at this very moment, everything's in your hands, it's in your power. . . ."

"What are you saying? Why did you come to me? I'll throw myself out of the window," said Katerina Lvovna, feeling herself seized by an indescribable terror and clutching the window-sill.

"You are all my life to me. Why do such a silly thing?" whispered Sergei boldly, and pulling the young mistress away from the window embraced her firmly.

"Oh, oh, let me go," she groaned softly, weakening under Sergei's burning kisses and pressing herself involuntarily to his powerful body.

Sergei lifted the mistress like a child and carried her in his arms to a dark corner.

The silence that fell on the room was disturbed only by the rhythmic ticking of her husband's watch that hung at the head of her bed: but that hindered nothing.

"Go," said Katerina Lvovna half an hour later without looking at Sergei and straightening her dishevelled hair before a small mirror.

"Why should I go away now?" asked Sergei in a happy voice.

"My father-in-law will lock the doors."

"Oh, my darling, what sort of people have you lived among if they only know how to get to a woman through doors? To get to you I come and go as I please, there are doors everywhere," answered the young man pointing to the posts that supported the gallery.

IV

Another week passed and still Zinovy Borisich did not return home and all that week, night after night until the white dawn broke, his wife enjoyed the company of Sergei.

And on those nights in Zinovy Borisich's bedroom much wine from the father-in-law's cellar was drunk, many were the tidbits eaten, and the kisses implanted on the mistress's sweet lips, and much playing with black curls was there on a soft pillow. But not all of the road is as smooth as a tablecloth, there are potholes along the way too.

Boris Timofeyich could not sleep: in his cotton shirt of many colors the old man roamed about the silent house and, lo and behold, what did he see but merry Sergei in his red shirt sliding as quiet as quiet down the post under his daughter-in-law's window. Here was a fine surprise! Boris Timofeyich rushed out at the young fellow and grabbed him by the legs. Sergei turned to give his master one of the best in the ear but stopped as he remembered that he might cause a commotion.

"And where," said Boris Timofeyich, "have you been, thief that you are?"

"Where I've been, Boris Timofeyich, there, sir, I no longer am," answered Sergei.

"Did you spend the night with my daughter-in-law?"

"There again, sir. I know where I spent the night; but you, Boris Timofeyich, you, sir, mark my words—what has been done can't be undone. At any rate, don't you bring shame on your merchant's house. Now tell me what you want from me? What do you expect to get out of me?"

"I want to give you five hundred lashes, you viper," answered Boris Timofeyich.

"I'm in the wrong, so do what you like," agreed the young fellow. "Tell me where to go; amuse yourself, drink my blood."

Boris Timofeyich led the way to his stone storehouse and thrashed Sergei with a horsewhip until his own arms ached. Not a groan escaped Sergei's lips but his teeth gnawed away half his shirt-sleeve.

Boris Timofeyich left Sergei for his flayed back to heal; he gave

him an earthenware jug of water, hung a huge padlock on the door
and sent for his son.

Even today a journey of a hundred versts over Russia's country
roads is no light undertaking and Katerina Lvovna felt she would
not be able to live another hour without her Sergei. Suddenly her
dormant nature developed in all its fullness, and she became so
determined there was no holding her back. She found out where
Sergei was and talked to him through the iron door and then dashed
off to look for the keys. "Let him out, let Sergei out," she said to
her father-in-law.

The old man turned green. He had never expected such brazen
impertinence from a daughter-in-law who, even if she had sinned,
had always, until now, been submissive.

"What are you talking about, you so-and-so?" he began calling
Katerina Lvovna shameful names.

"Let him out," she said. "I tell you honestly there has been
nothing bad between us yet."

"Nothing bad," he said, gritting his teeth. "And what were you
doing with him all those nights? Fluffing up your husband's
pillows?"

But she wanted to have her own way: let him out, that's all.

"If that's the way it is," said Boris Timofeyich, "I'll tell you
something: when your husband comes we'll take you, you faithful
wife, to the stables and flay you with our own hands and that
scoundrel I'll have sent to prison tomorrow."

That was what Boris Timofeyich decided: but it was not to be.

v

At supper Boris Timofeyich ate salted mushrooms and buckwheat porridge which gave him heartburn; then came a sudden
pain in the pit of his stomach; he vomited terribly and by morning
he died in the same way as those rats in his storehouses for which
Katerina Lvovna with her own hands prepared special food with a
dangerous white powder that had been entrusted to her care.

Katerina Lvovna released her Sergei from the old man's stone
storeroom and, never worrying about what people might say, let
him recover from her father-in-law's blows in her husband's bed;

and without suspecting anything, they buried her father-in-law, Boris Timofeyich, with Christian rites. There was nothing remarkable about the matter, and nobody gave it a second thought. Boris Timofeyich had died, and he died after eating salted mushrooms, as many others who have eaten them died. They buried Boris Timofeyich hurriedly without even waiting for his son, for the weather was warm and the messenger had not found Zinovy Borisich at the mill. He had happened to hear of some timber going cheap another hundred versts or so away and had gone to take a look at it without telling anybody exactly where he had gone.

Once she had got this business off her hands Katerina Lvovna let herself go. She was no timid woman and there was no knowing what to expect from her; she paraded about the house giving orders right and left and would not let Sergei leave her side for a moment. This caused wonderment in the household but Katerina Lvovna's generous hand soon found everyone, and all of this wonderment suddenly stopped all at once. "The mistress is sweet on Sergei," they surmised, "that's all. It's her own look-out," they said, "she's the one who'll have to answer for it."

In the meantime Sergei got better, was soon in his old form and was again strutting around Katerina Lvovna for all the world like a turkey-cock, and again their life of love began. Not for them alone, however, did time roll on: after a long absence, Zinovy Borisich, the wronged husband, was hurrying home.

VI

It grew terribly hot after dinner and the nimble flies were an unbearable torment. Katerina Lvovna closed the shutters of her bedroom window, hung a woollen shawl on the inside and then lay down beside Sergei to rest on her husband's high bed. She was asleep and at the same time not quite asleep, she was simply exhausted; the perspiration streamed down her face and it was so hot and hard to breathe. She felt it was time to rouse herself; it was time to go into the garden for tea but still she could not get up. At last the cook came and knocked at the door: "The samovar's under the apple-tree and it's getting cold." Katerina Lvovna forced herself to roll over and began stroking the cat. And that cat was rubbing itself against them, between her and Sergei, such a wonderful, big grey cat, as fat as fat can be, with whiskers like a tax assessor. Katerina Lvovna ran her fingers through its thick coat and it came closer and rubbed its head against her; it pushed its snub nose against her firm bosom and was all the time softly singing a song as though it were telling her a tale of love.

"How did that huge cat get in here," wondered Katerina Lvovna. "I put the cream on the window-sill in here: sure enough he'll guzzle it all up. I'll chase him out," she decided and tried to get hold of the cat to throw it out but it slipped through her fingers like mist.

"But where could that cat have come from?" wondered Katerina Lvovna in the middle of her nightmare. "We never had any cat in the bedroom and see what a big brute has got in here now."

Again she tried to get hold of the cat but once more it was not there to take hold of.

"Now whatever can it be? Is it really a cat or what?" Katerina Lvovna asked herself. Fright drove the dream and the sleepiness away. She looked round the room—there was no cat anywhere, only handsome Sergei was lying there, his strong arm pressing her breast to his hot face.

Katerina Lvovna got up, sat on the bed, kissed and fondled Sergei time and again, then straightened the crumpled quilt on the bed and went into the garden for tea; the sun had gone down and a wonderful, enchanted evening breeze waited over the heated earth.

"I overslept," Katerina Lvovna told Aksinya as she sat down to tea on a carpet spread under an apple-tree in blossom.

"And what does it all mean, Aksinya?" she began questioning the cook and at the same time wiped a saucer on the tea-cloth.

"What does what mean?"

"It wasn't like a dream, it was just real, a cat came rubbing against me. What could it be?"

"What are you talking about?"

"I mean it, a cat came."

Katerina Lvovna told her about the cat.

"Why did you want to stroke it?"

"Don't be silly. I don't know why I stroked it."

"It's strange enough, I'm sure."

"It's something I can't make out."

"It sure enough means someone's going to be close to you or something else, maybe, something else will come of it."

"But what?"

"Exactly *what* nobody can tell you, madam, but something's sure enough going to happen."

"I keep seeing the moon in my dreams, and now there's that cat," she continued.

"The moon means a baby."

Katerina Lvovna blushed.

"Should I send Sergei here to you, madam?" asked Aksinya, who hoped to become her mistress's confidante.

"I don't know," answered Katerina Lvovna, "all right, go and get him; I'll give him tea here."

"That's what I think, I'd better send him here," decided Aksinya and waddled away towards the garden gate.

Katerina Lvovna also told Sergei about the cat.

"Idle dreams, that's all," Sergei answered.

"Then why is it I never had any idle dreams about a cat before, Sergei?"

"There's lots of things we didn't have before! I used to get all moony when I saw you out of the corner of my eye, and now what? I possess all of your white body."

Sergei put his arms round her, turned her head over heels in the air and jokingly threw her on to the soft carpet.

"Oh, you make me dizzy," exclaimed Katerina Lvovna. "Sergei, come and sit here close to me," she called him lazily, stretching herself in a voluptuous pose.

The young man bent down to get under the low branches of the apple-tree, which was overflowing with white blossoms, and sat down on the carpet at Katerina Lvovna's feet.

"Did you always long for me, Sergei?"

"Of course I did. . . ."

"But how did it feel? Tell me all about it."

"What is there to tell? How can I explain what longing is? I yearned. . . ."

"Then why didn't I feel it, Sergei, why didn't I get to know you were moony about me? They say you can feel that sort of thing."

Sergei was silent.

"If you were yearning for me so much why were you always singing songs? Eh? You know, I heard you singing on the gallery," she continued, all the while fondling him.

"What if I did sing? D'you think mosquitoes hum all their lives because they're happy?" answered Sergei drily.

A short pause followed. Katerina Lvovna was filled with the highest ecstasy by Sergei's admissions.

She wanted to talk on but Sergei only frowned and sat silent.

"Look, Sergei, it's paradise, what a paradise!" she exclaimed, looking through the flower-laden branches of the apple-tree that completely covered her; she looked straight up to the deep blue sky in which hung a full, bright moon.

The moonlight slanted down through the leaves and blossoms of the apple tree making whimsical colored patterns that flickered over the face and body of Katerina Lvovna as she lay there on her back; there was silence in the air; a faint, warm breeze stirred the sleepy leaves, bringing with it the fragrance of flowering grasses and trees and a breath of something languid, inducing idleness, voluptuousness and dark desires.

As Katerina Lvovna was not answered, she lay back in silence, gazing through the pale-rose of the apple blossoms at the sky above. Sergei was silent too, although he was not interested in the sky. With his arms clasped round his knees he stared fixedly at his boots.

A golden night! Silence, moonlight, fragrance and a precious life-giving warmth! Away beyond the gully, on the far side of the orchard, somebody began singing a sweet melody, in the bird-cherry thicket by the fence a nightingale called and then burst into loud song, a quail in a cage on a high pole murmured in its sleep, a well-fed horse in the stable sighed deeply and some dogs raced noiselessly across the common by the orchard fence and disappeared into the ugly black shadows of the old half-ruined salt warehouses.

Katerina Lvovna raised herself on one elbow and gazed at the high grass in the orchard; the grass seemed to be playing in moonlight, broken into checkered patches by the leaves and flowers of the trees. The grass was all turned to gold by those dainty patches of light that flickered and quivered as though they were living, fire-colored butterflies or as though all the grass under the trees had been caught up in a net of moonlight and was swaying from side to side.

"Oh, Sergei, it's gorgeous!" exclaimed Katerina Lvovna as she looked round.

Sergei glanced round indifferently.

"Why are you so miserable, Sergei? Perhaps you've had enough of my love?"

"Why talk so silly?" Sergei answered drily, stooped down, and lazily kissed her cheek.

"You're not true to me," said Katerina Lvovna, jealously, "you're fickle."

"I can't get angry, even at them words," answered Sergei in calm tones.

"Then why did you kiss me like that?"

Sergei did not say another word.

"That's the way husbands kiss their wives," she continued, playing with his curls, "that's how they blow the dust off each other's lips. You ought to kiss me so that the young flowers fall off this tree we're sitting under."

"Like this, like this," she whispered winding her arms round her lover and kissing him with passionate abandon.

"Listen, Sergei," said Katerina Lvovna a little while later, "why do they all call you fickle, why do they all say the same thing?"

"Who's been telling lies about me?"

"That's what people say."

"May be I did throw over them as weren't worth keeping."

"Why were you fool enough to get mixed up with them if they weren't worth it? You didn't ought to make love to them that aren't worth while."

"It's all right for you to talk. Is it something you do in your right mind? You get tempted, that's all. Sinning with a wench comes quite simple, and then she goes and hangs herself round your neck. That's all there is to it!"

"You listen to me, Sergei! I don't know and don't want to know how it was with the others, but you yourself led me on to this love of ours and you know just how much I started of my own free will and how much was temptation on your part, so if you, Sergei, betray me, if you think you can jilt me for anybody else, whoever she may be, then remember, Sergei, my friend, I won't be alive when we part."

Sergei gave a start.

"How can you, Katerina Lvovna!" began Sergei. "You are every-thing to me. And just you look how things stand with us. You say you can see I'm sulky today but you don't try to think what the reason is. For all you know my heart may be bleeding."

"Tell me, Sergei, tell me your sorrow."

"What is there to tell? The first thing that's going to happen, the Lord be praised, is your husband will be back and then it's all up with Sergei Filippich. He'll have to go back to the yard with the musicians and sit under the shed and watch the candle burning in Katerina Lvovna's bedroom while she shakes up the feather bed and gets into it with her lawful spouse, Zinovy Borisich.

"That will never be!" drawled Katerina Lvovna merrily and waved her hand.

"How can it not be? As far as I can see you can't do anything to stop it happening. But, Katerina Lvovna, I've got a heart, too, and I can see I'm going to have a bad time soon."

"All right, let's not talk about it."

Katerina Lvovna liked to feel that Sergei was jealous and with a laugh again gave herself up to kissing him.

"And then, again," continued Sergei, quietly freeing his head from her arms, which were bare to the shoulders, "again I must say that I've got such a modest position that I think ten times, one way or another, and not just once. If I were, so to say, your equal, if I were some gentleman or merchant, then, Katerina Lvovna, never in my life would I part with you. But you must know how it is, what it's like for me to be with you. When I see that old man of yours take you by your lily-white hands and lead you into the bed-room, my heart will have to bear it all and maybe, even, all my life I shall be a man to despise on account of it. Katerina Lvovna! After all, I'm not like other men, who are satisfied enough to get their fill of a woman. I know what real love is, I feel it eating into my heart like a black serpent. . . ."

"What are you telling me all this for?" Katerina Lvovna inter-rupted him.

She felt very sorry for Sergei.

"Katerina Lvovna! What else can I do but tell you? How can I keep silent? Perhaps everything has been told to your old man with all the details; perhaps it won't be some time in the future but even tomorrow that Sergei will have to clear out and there won't be a sign of him left in the house."

"No, no, don't say that, Sergei! Never, never, not for anything will I part from you!" exclaimed Katerina Lvovna, soothing him with more of her caresses. "If it comes to that pass . . . either he won't live or I won't, but I intend to have you."

"That can't be, not by no means, Katerina Lvovna," answered Sergei, shaking his head sadly and sorrowfully. "It's a dog's life for me, too, on account of this love. If I hadn't loved somebody above my station I'd have been satisfied. D'you think you can always have me to make love to? Is it an honor for you to be my mistress? I'd like to be your husband and marry you before the altar and then, even though I'll always consider myself beneath you, I can at least tell the world how much I respect my wife. . . ."

These words of Sergei's, his jealousy, his anxiety to wed her, put Katerina Lvovna in a daze; it is always pleasant for a woman to have somebody want to marry her, even if her connections with the man before marriage were of the shortest. For Sergei's sake she was now prepared to go through fire and water, into prison or on the cross. He had made her so much in love with himself that there was no limit to her loyalty to him. She was beside herself from happiness. Her blood was seething and she would hear nothing more. With a swift movement she placed her hand over Sergei's lips, pressed his head to her bosom and said:

"And I know now how I'll make a merchant of you and live with you in the proper way. Only don't make me sad about nothing before the proper time."

Again the kissing and fondling began.

An old clerk who slept in the shed heard through his sound sleep how the silence of the night was broken by whispering and soft laughter, as though mischievous children were conferring together how best to make fun of an old man; then came roars of laughter and merriment as though saucy mermaids were tickling somebody. All this came from where Katerina Lvovna, bathed in moonlight and rolling on the soft carpet, played and frolicked with her husband's young clerk. And the white flowers kept falling, falling, from the old apple-tree until at last they ceased to fall. In the meantime the short summer night had passed, the moon hid itself behind the steep, high roofs of the warehouses and stared more and more wanly at the earth; from the kitchen roof came a piercing feline duet; this was followed by spitting and angry snorts after which two or three tom-cats crashed noisily from the roof onto a heap of boards nearby.

"Let's go to bed," said Katerina Lvovna slowly, as though she were worn out; she got up from the carpet and just as she had lain there, in her shift and petticoat, walked across the silent, deathly silent merchant yard and Sergei followed her carrying the carpet and the blouse which she, in her playfulness, had thrown off.

VII

Katerina Lvovna had only just blown out the candle and, fully undressed, lain down on her feather bed, when sleep overtook her. After playing and amusing herself to her heart's content she slept so soundly that her legs were asleep and so were her arms; and again through her sleep she seemed to hear the door open and the cat that had recently visited her fall on the bed in a heavy heap.

"Now what sort of punishment is that cat?" she wondered wearily. "This time I made sure the door was locked, I locked it myself, and the window's closed tight but it's there again. I'll throw it out right now," and Katerina Lvovna wanted to get up but her sleeping arms and legs would not obey her; and the cat walked up and down her whole body purring strangely, as though it were saying human words. And shivers ran over her, ran over her whole body.

"No," she thought, "there's nothing else for it but to get holy water tomorrow and sprinkle the bed because it's a strange cat that's in the habit of coming to haunt me."

And the purring was right by her ear and a nose pushed against her and the cat said, "What sort of a cat am I? Why d'you call me a cat? That's smart of you, Katerina Lvovna, calling me a cat when you know I'm Boris Timofeyich, a merchant of standing. Only I'm feeling bad now because all my insides are cracking up from what my kind daughter-in-law has treated me to. That's why I got small," he purred, "and look like a cat to those who know little about me, about who I really am. How are you getting on nowadays, Katerina Lvovna? How are you faithfully observing the law? I came from the graveyard specially to see how you and Sergei Filippich are keeping your husband's bed warm. Purr, purr, purr. . . . I don't see anything. Don't you be afraid of me: you see my eyes have fallen out from your food. Look me straight in the eyes, girlie, don't be afraid!"

Katerina Lvovna looked and screamed at the top of her voice. The cat was again lying between her and Sergei but this cat had the head of Boris Timofeyich, full size, and instead of eyes there were two circles of fire that kept turning and turning in different directions.

Sergei woke up. He soothed Katerina Lvovna, but all sleep had left her and it was as well for her that it had.

As she lay wide-eyed, she suddenly heard what she thought was somebody climbing over the gate. The dogs started dashing about but soon fell silent. They must have been fondling up to somebody. Another minute passed and the iron latch on the door below rattled and the door opened. "Either I'm dreaming all this or it's my Zinovy Borisich come back, because that door was opened with his spare key," thought Katerina Lvovna and hurriedly shook Sergei.

"Listen, Sergei," she said, propping herself up on one elbow and listening intently.

Somebody was coming carefully up the staircase, treading warily, one foot at a time, and approaching the locked bedroom door.

Katerina Lvovna jumped from the bed in her shift and opened the window. That same moment Sergei jumped barefoot out of the window on to the gallery and wound his legs round the post that he had used so often as the way out of the mistress's bedroom.

"No, don't, don't. You lie down here and don't go too far away," whispered Katerina Lvovna; she threw Sergei's clothes and boots out of the window and herself darted back under the covers to wait.

Sergei obeyed her: instead of sliding down the post he found a place for himself under a basket on the gallery.

Meanwhile Katerina Lvovna heard her husband approach the door and stand listening, holding his breath. She could even sense the quickened beating of his jealous heart; it was not, however, pity that Katerina Lvovna felt, but an evil joy.

"Go and look for yesterday," she thought, smiling and breathing as gently as an innocent babe.

This lasted for about ten minutes: at last Zinovy Borisich grew tired of waiting and listening to his wife's slumber, and tapped at the door.

"Who's that?" called Katerina Lvovna in a sleepy voice after a while.

"Me," answered Zinovy Borisich.

"Is it you, Zinovy Borisich?"

"Yes, me, as if you can't hear!"

Katerina Lvovna jumped out of bed just as she had been lying, in her shift, let her husband in and dived back into the warm bed.

"It's chilly before dawn," she said, wrapping herself up in the blanket.

Zinovy Borisich entered, looked round, prayed at the icons, lit a candle and again looked round the room.

"How are you getting along?" he asked his wife.

"All right," she answered; sitting up in bed she began to put on a wide cotton blouse.

"Shall I go and get the samovar started?" she asked her husband.

"No, you can call Aksinya, let her light it."

She slipped her bare feet into her shoes, ran out and did not return for half an hour. In that time she had lit the samovar herself and had gone quietly out on to the gallery to talk to Sergei.

"Stay where you are," she whispered.

"How long?" asked Sergei, also in a whisper.

"You've got no sense. Stay here till I call you." And Katerina Lvovna pushed him back into his old place.

Sitting on the gallery, Sergei could hear all that was happening in the bedroom. He heard the door bang as Katerina Lvovna came back to her husband and could hear every word they said.

"What have you been doing so long?" Zinovy Borisich asked his wife.

"I've been putting up the samovar," she answered calmly.

A pause followed. Sergei heard Zinovy Borisich hang his coat on the hook. Now he was washing himself, snorting and splashing the water all round him; then he asked for a towel; the conversation began again.

"How did you bury Father?" inquired the husband.

"Well, he died and so we buried him."

"Isn't that strange?"

"Maybe it is," answered Katerina Lvovna, rattling the cups.

Zinovy Borisich walked sadly up and down the room.

"What have you been doing to pass the time here?" he again inquired of his wife.

"Everybody knows what pleasures we have: we never go to a ball at all and to theaters just as often."

"You don't seem to be very pleased to welcome your husband," began Zinovy Borisich, giving her a side glance.

"We're not so young, you and I, to go crazy on meeting each other. What else do you want? I'm running about, doing things for you."

Katerina Lvovna again ran out of the room to fetch the samovar and again she visited Sergei, shook him and said, "Keep your eyes open, Sergei!"

Sergei had no very clear idea of what all this was going to lead to, but nevertheless he held himself in readiness.

When Katerina Lvovna returned Zinovy Borisich was kneeling on the bed hanging a silver watch with a bead chain on a nail over the head of the bed.

"Why is it, Katerina Lvovna, that when you are alone you make a bed for two?" he asked his wife slily.

"I was expecting you all the time," answered Katerina Lvovna looking calmly at him.

"For which we humbly thank you. . . . And how did this thing come to be lying on the bed?"

Zinovy Borisich picked up Sergei's thin woollen belt from the bedsheet and held it by one end in front of his wife's eyes.

Katerina Lvovna was not in the least put out.

"I picked it up in the garden," she said, "and used it to hold up my skirt."

"Yes," said Zinovy Borisich with emphasis. "I've also heard a few things about your skirts."

"What have you heard?"

"About all your goings on."

"There haven't been any goings on."

"I'll find out all about that, I'll find out all right," answered Zinovy Borisich, pushing his empty cup to his wife.

She did not answer him.

"All those goings on of yours, Katerina Lvovna, we'll bring out into the light of day," he continued after a long pause, frowning at his wife.

"Your Katerina Lvovna isn't so terribly scared. She's not awfully afraid of that," she answered.

"What? What?" shouted Zinovy Borisich, raising his voice.

"Nothing much, get on with it," answered his wife.

"Here, you, look out. You've got too talkative while I've been away!"

"And why shouldn't I be talkative?" asked Katerina Lvovna.

"You ought to look after yourself better."

"I've no need to look after myself. It's not enough for long tongues to talk scandal to you, on top of it all I have to put up with insults!"

"It's got nothing to do with long tongues, I know the truth about your love affair."

"About what love affair?" shouted Katerina Lvovna, flashing up, this time without any pretence.

"I know all about it."

"If you know, then tell me straight out!"

Zinovy Borisich sat silent for a while and again pushed his empty cup towards his wife.

"I can see there's nothing to talk about," snapped Katerina Lvovna contemptuously, throwing a spoon excitedly into her husband's saucer. "Come on, tell me what the informers have told you about. Who's this lover of mine you know about?"

"You'll know in time, don't be in too much of a hurry."

"They've told you some lies about Sergei, haven't they?"

"I'll find out, I'll find out, Katerina Lvovna. Nobody has taken away my power over you and nobody can . . . I'll make you tell me yourself. . . ."

"Ee-ee! I've had enough of this," screamed Katerina Lvovna, grinding her teeth; white as a sheet she suddenly jumped up and disappeared through the door.

"Here he is," she said a few seconds later, returning and leading Sergei by the sleeve. "Ask him and me together about what you know. Maybe you'll learn something more, something you didn't bargain for."

Zinovy Borsich was bewildered. He looked first at Sergei who was standing in the doorway, then at his wife who sat calmly on the edge of the bed with her arms folded, and didn't know what was going to happen next.

"What are you doing, you viper," he managed to blurt out, still sitting in his chair.

"Ask us about what you say you know so well," said Katerina Lvovna, insolently. "You thought you were going to scare me with threats of a club," she continued, winking significantly, "but there won't ever be anything of the sort: maybe I knew what to do with you before I heard those promises of yours, and, anyway, I'll do it."

"What's that? Get out!" roared Zinovy Borisich at Sergei.

"How so?" Katerina Lvovna mocked him.

Adroitly she locked the door, put the key in her pocket and again flopped on the bed in her wrap.

"Come along, Sergei, come here, to me, dearest," she motioned the clerk to her side.

Sergei shook his curls and boldly sat down beside the mistress.

"Oh, Lord! Good God! What are you doing? What are you up to, you savages?!" screamed Zinovy Borisich, his face red with anger as he got up from his chair.

"Say now, isn't it wonderful! Look, look my pretty boy, how wonderful it is!"

Katerina Lvovna laughed and kissed Sergei passionately right in front of her husband.

At that very moment a stinging slap resounded on her cheek and Zinovy Borisich made for the open window.

VIII

"Ah . . . ah . . . so! . . . All right, old friend, many thanks. That's all I was waiting for!" shrieked Katerina Lvovna. "Now I see all right . . . it won't be as you want but as I want. . . ."

With a single movement she pushed Sergei away from her and sprang swiftly at her husband so that before Zinovy Borisich had time to reach the window she had seized him from behind, grasping his throat in her slim fingers, and threw him to the floor like a sheaf of damp hemp.

As Zinovy Borisich went down he banged the back of his head on the floor and fell into complete panic. He had not expected such a sudden climax. His wife's first attack showed him that she was determined to go to any length to get rid of him and that his present position was one of extreme danger. Zinovy Borisich realized all this in a flash, at the very moment when he fell, and, therefore, did not cry out, knowing that his voice would not reach anybody's ear but would only speed matters up. In silence he looked round and brought his eyes, filled with rage, reproach and suffering, to rest on his wife whose slim fingers were firmly gripping his throat.

Zinovy Borisich did not defend himself; his arms with their tightly clenched fists were stretched full length and jerked spasmodically. One of them was quite free but the other Katerina Lvovna held pressed to the floor with her knee.

"Hold him," she whispered indifferently to Sergei and turned towards her husband.

Sergei sat on his master, pressed both his arms down with his knees and was going to put his hands under Katerina Lvovna's on Zinovy Borisich's throat but instead he suddenly let out a scream. At the sight of the man who had wronged him the idea of vengeance aroused in Zinovy Borisich a last effort: fiercely he tore himself away, pulled his arms from under Sergei's knees, seized Sergei's curls in his liberated hands, and, like a wild animal, bit him in the throat. It was over in a moment, however, for Zinovy Borisich immediately dropped his head with a heavy groan.

Katerina Lvovna, pale and hardly breathing at all, stood over her husband and her lover; in her right hand was a heavy metal candlestick which she held by the upper end, the heavy base downwards. A thin stream of crimson blood flowed down Zinovy Borisich's cheek.

"Get a priest . . ." groaned Zinovy Borisich, dully, in disgust throwing his head as far back as possible from Sergei who was sitting on him. "Confession . . ." he muttered still less audibly, shuddering, his eyes fixed sideways on the blood that was clotting under his hair.

"You'll be all right as you are," whispered Katerina Lvovna.

"We've wasted enough time on him already," she said to Sergei, "take a good hold of his throat."

Zinovy Borisich croaked.

Katerina Lvovna bent down and pressed her hands on Sergei's as they lay on her husband's throat and pressed one ear to his chest. Five silent minutes later she got up and said:

"Enough, he's had it."

Sergei also stood up to get his breath. Zinovy Borisich lay strangled, his head cut open. At the back of his head, on the left side, there was a small patch of blood which had stopped flowing since it had coagulated under the matted hair.

Sergei carried the body to a cellar in that same stone-built warehouse where he had recently been locked up by the late Boris Timofeyich and then returned to the attic room. In the meantime Katerina Lvovna had rolled up her sleeves, tucked her petticoats up high and was carefully washing away, with soap and a bast scrubber, the pool of Zinovy Borisich's blood on the floor of his bedroom. The water was still warm in the samovar from which Zinovy Borisich had soothed his masterful spirit with poisoned tea and so the blood was washed away without leaving any trace.

Katerina Lvovna took up the copper washbowl and bast scrubber.

"Show me a light," she said to Sergei, as she walked towards the door, "lower, lower down," she said, carefully examining the floorboards over which Sergei had dragged the body all the way to the cellar.

In two places only there were specks no bigger than cherries on the painted floor. Katerina Lvovna wiped them with her scrubber and they vanished.

"That's what you get for creeping up on your wife like a thief," said Katerina Lvovna, straightening up and looking towards the warehouse.

"Now it's all over," said Sergei, shuddering at the sound of his own voice.

When they returned to the bedroom a faint rosy streak of dawn had appeared in the east, turning the light blossoms of the appletree golden and peeping through the green stakes of the garden fence into Katerina Lvovna's room.

The old clerk was plodding slowly across the yard from the shed to the kitchen, a sheepskin coat thrown over his shoulders.

Katerina Lvovna carefully pulled the cord opening the shutters, and examined Sergei attentively as though trying to peer into his soul.

"Now you're the merchant," she said, placing her white hands on his shoulders.

Sergei did not answer her.

Sergei's lips trembled, and he was in a fever. Katerina Lvovna's lips were cold, and that was all.

Two days later big calluses appeared on Sergei's hands from the crowbar and spade he had been using; they had helped to pack away Zinovy Borisich so well in his cellar that without the aid of his widow or her lover nobody could have found him until Judgment Day.

I X

Sergei went about with a red kerchief round his neck, complaining of a sore throat. But before the toothmarks implanted by Zinovy Borisich on Sergei's throat had time to heal, people began to ask after Katerina Lvovna's husband. Sergei himself began to talk about him more than anybody else. In the evening he would sit with the other young men on the garden seat near the gate and would start the talk going: "What can have happened to the old man? Why hasn't he got back yet?"

The other young people also wondered why.

Then came the news from the mill that the merchant had hired horses and had set out for home long ago. The driver who had brought him said that Zinovy Borisich had seemed to be upset about something and paid him off in a strange fashion: he had stopped the cart near the monastery, about three versts from the town, taken his bag and walked off. The story only made people wonder all the more.

Zinovy Borisich had disappeared and that was the end of it.

A search was made but nothing was discovered: the merchant might have vanished into thin air. The deposition made by the arrested driver stated that the merchant had got out of the cart above the river near the monastery and had walked off. No explanation was forthcoming and the widow lived openly with Sergei. Conjectures were made that Zinovy Borisich was in one place or another, but he did not return, and Katerina Lvovna knew better than anybody else that he never would.

A month passed, then a second and a third and Katerina Lvovna felt herself heavy with child.

"We'll get all the money, Sergei: I have an heir," she said and then went to the municipality to complain: things are so and so, she was pregnant, and business was at a standstill: they should let her take control of everything.

A commercial undertaking could not be allowed to run to ruin. Katerina Lvovna was her husband's lawful wife, there were no debts and so there was no reason why she should not take over. She did.

Katerina Lvovna ruled the place with a firm hand and Sergei was called Sergei Filippich on account of her. Then, suddenly, like a bolt from the blue, came more trouble. The mayor received a letter from Livni to the effect that Boris Timofeyich had been using not only his own capital to trade with, but money belonging to a young nephew, a minor, Fyodor Zakharov Lyamin, and that the matter should be investigated and control not given to Katerina Lvovna alone. First this news came, the mayor spoke to Katerina Lvovna about it, and then, about a week later, an old woman arrived from Livni with a little boy.

"I'm the late Boris Timofeyich's cousin," she said, "and this is my nephew, Fyodor Lyamin."

Katerina Lvovna received them herself.

Sergei, who saw the arrival and Katerina Lvovna's reception, went as white as a sheet.

"What's wrong with you?" asked the mistress, seeing his deadly pallor when he entered the house immediately after the newcomers, then stared at them and remained in the hall.

"Nothing," said the clerk, turning from the hall into the outer room. "I was just thinking how fine it all is," he added with a sigh, closing the door behind him.

"What are we going to do now?" Sergei asked Katerina Lvovna that evening as they sat at the samovar. "That's put paid to us as far as the business is concerned."

"Why do you think that, Sergei?"

"Because everything will have to be shared now. What are we going to get out of it, for ourselves?"

"Surely there'll be enough for you, Sergei?"

"I'm not thinking about myself; only I don't think there'll be any happiness for us."

"Why not? Why shouldn't we be happy?"

"Because, Katerina Lvovna, I love you so much I want to see you a real lady, and not living like you've been doing till now," answered Sergei Filippich. "And now it seems there'll be less capital and we'll have to put up with being worse off than we were before."

"But surely you don't think it's money I need, Sergei?"

"That's right, maybe you're not exactly interested but I am, because I respect you and in the eyes of the common, envious people it'll be painful. You can have your own way, of course, but I can never be happy with things as they are. I have my own ideas on the subject."

And so Sergei went on and on, harping on the theme, that he had become the most unfortunate man on account of this Fyodor Lyamin, that he had been deprived of the opportunity of elevating and honoring her above all the other merchant people. Each time Sergei led up to the same subject: were it not for this Fyodor, Katerina Lvovna, who would bear a son before her husband had been missing nine months, would get all the capital and their happiness would know no bounds.

X

But then Sergei suddenly stopped talking about the heir. As soon as such speeches ceased coming from Sergei's lips, Fyodor Lyamin became fixed in Katerina Lvovna's mind and heart. She even became moody and unaffectionate to Sergei. Whether she was sleeping or busy in the household or saying her prayers, she always had the same thing on her mind: "How can such things be? Why should I lose capital on account of him? How much I have suffered, how many sins I have to answer for, and here he comes along and takes it away from me without any trouble. . . . It wasn't as if it was a grown-up man, he's only a boy, a little babe. . . ."

The early frosts had set in. It goes without saying that no word of Zinovy Borisich had been heard from anywhere. Katerina Lvovna grew stouter and walked about deep in thought; there was a lot of talk about her in the town—how came it that this young Izmailova, who till then had been childless and pining away, had suddenly started to swell in front. Meanwhile the co-heir, the minor, Fyodor Lyamin, played about the yard in his little squirrel coat, breaking the thin ice that had formed on the puddles.

"Now then, Fyodor," Aksinya the cook would shout at him as she ran across the yard, "is that the way for a merchant's son to behave, stamping in puddles?"

And the co-heir, who bothered Katerina Lvovna and her lover, romped about as carefree as a young kid, and slept just as carefree opposite the old woman who had charge of his upbringing, never dreaming that he had crossed anybody's path or cut short anybody's happiness.

At last Fyodor caught chicken pox, which was made worse by a cold on the chest, so the boy was put to bed. At first they treated him with herbs and things, but later sent for a doctor.

The doctor began to call regularly, prescribed some medicine which was given to the boy hourly by his aunt or by Katerina Lvovna when she was asked to.

"Be so kind," the old woman would say, "Katerina, you are in the family way yourself and are awaiting God's judgement: be so kind."

Katerina Lvovna did not refuse the old woman. When the latter went to evening mass to pray for "the youth Fyodor lying on his bed of sickness" or to early mass again to pray for him, Katerina Lvovna would sit with the sick child, would give him a drink when he needed it and his medicine at the proper time.

Once, the old woman, who was going to evening and late service on the occasion of the Presentation of the Blessed Virgin Mary, asked Katerina Lvovna to look after Fyodor, who was getting better.

Katerina Lvovna went into Fyodor's room and he was sitting up in bed in his little squirrel coat, reading the *Lives of the Christian Fathers*.

"What are you reading, Fyodor?" she asked as she sat down in a chair.

"*Lives*, auntie, I'm reading the *Lives*."

"Are they interesting?"

"Very interesting, auntie."

Katerina Lvovna rested her chin on her hand and began to watch his whispering lips and suddenly it seemed as though demons had broken loose from their chains and she fell prey to her former thoughts of the wrong this boy was doing her and how good it would be if he did not exist.

"And what's more," thought Katerina Lvovna, "he's sick; they give him medicine . . . anything might happen to a sick person. . . . The doctor didn't make the right medicine, that's all."

"Isn't it time for your medicine, Fyodor?"

"If you please, auntie," answered the boy and after sipping the medicine from the spoon, added, "it's very interesting, auntie, the way the saints are described."

"All right, go on reading," said Katerina Lvovna and casting a cold glance over the room stopped at the frost-covered windows.

"I must tell them to close the shutters," she said and went into the drawing-room, from there to the hall and then to her own room upstairs where she sat down.

Five minutes later Sergei in a sheepskin coat trimmed with seal came up to her room and entered without saying a word.

"Have they closed the shutters?" Katerina Lvovna asked him.

"Yes, they have," answered Sergei, brusquely, snuffing the candle with the scissors.

A silence followed.

"Will late mass last long tonight?" asked Katerina Lvovna.

"Yes, it's a big holiday tomorrow: it'll be a long service," answered Sergei.

Another pause.

"I'll go to Fyodor. He's alone in there," muttered Katerina Lvovna, getting up.

"Alone?" he asked her, frowning.

"Alone," she answered in a whisper, "what about it?"

Something like a lightning flash passed from her eyes to his but not another word was spoken.

Katerina Lvovna went downstairs and walked through the empty rooms; it was silent everywhere; the icon-lamps burnt peacefully; her own shadow flittered across the walls; now that the windows were covered by shutters, the frost on them began to melt and water was dripping from them. Fyodor was sitting up and reading. When he saw Katerina Lvovna he only said to her:

"Auntie, please take this book and give me the one that's on the icon cabinet."

Katerina Lvovna acceded to his request and gave him the book.

"Wouldn't you like to sleep, Fyodor?"

"No, I'll wait for auntie."

"Why wait for her?"

"She promised to bring me some holy bread from church."

Katerina Lvovna suddenly turned pale; for the first time her own child had turned below her heart, and she felt cold in her bosom. She stood for a while in the middle of the room and then went out rubbing her chilly hands.

"Well?" she whispered as she silently entered her bedroom and found Sergei still in the same position beside the stove.

"What?" asked Sergei in a scarcely audible voice and choked.

"He's alone."

Sergei raised his brows and began to breathe heavily.

"Come on," said Katerina Lvovna and turned sharply to the door.

Sergei quickly pulled off his boots and asked:

"What shall I take?"

"Nothing," breathed Katerina Lvovna and led him quietly after her by the hand.

XI

The sick boy shuddered and dropped the book on to his knees when Katerina Lvovna came into the room for the third time.

"What's the matter, Fyodor?"

"Oh, something frightened me, auntie," he answered smiling fearfully and cringing into one corner of the bed.

"What frightened you?"

"Who was that with you, auntie?"

"Where? Nobody came with me, dearest."

"Nobody?"

The boy stretched toward the foot of the bed, screwed up his eyes, looked towards the door through which his aunt had come, and grew calmer.

"I suppose I must have imagined it," he said.

Katerina Lvovna stood still, leaning on the rail at the head of her nephew's bed.

Fyodor looked at his aunt and remarked that for some reason or other she was very pale.

In answer to that remark Katerina Lvovna forced a cough and looked in expectation towards the door of the drawing-room. In there only a floor-board creaked.

"I'm reading the life of my patron saint, Feodosiy, the Soldier of God, auntie. He served God well."

Katerina Lvovna stood there in silence.

"If you like, auntie, sit down here and I'll read it again for you," said the nephew, fondly.

"Wait a minute while I trim the icon-lamp in the drawing-room," answered Katerina Lvovna and hurried out of the room.

There came a very faint whisper from the drawing-room: but in the dead silence of the house it reached the boy's sharp ears.

"Auntie! What are you doing? Who are you whispering to?" he screamed in a tearful voice. "Come back here, auntie: I'm afraid," he called still more tearfully a second later and heard Katerina Lvovna say, "All right" in the drawing-room and thought it was said to him.

"What are you afraid of?" Katerina Lvovna asked him in a somewhat hoarse voice as she walked into the room with bold, determined steps and stood beside his bed so that the drawing-room door was hidden from the sick boy by her body. "Lie down," she said immediately afterwards.

"I don't want to, auntie."

"Now then, Fyodor, do as I tell you, lie down, it's late . . ." repeated Katerina Lvovna.

"But why, auntie? I'm not at all sleepy."

"No, you lie down, lie down," said Katerina Lvovna, her voice changing again, so that it was no longer firm; she took the boy under the arms and laid him down at the head of the bed.

At that moment Fyodor let out a frantic scream: he had seen the pale, barefooted Sergei entering the room.

With her hand Katerina Lvovna covered the mouth the frightened boy opened in his terror and shouted:

"Come on, hurry up, hold him out straight so that he can't struggle!"

Sergei seized Fyodor by the arms and legs and Katerina Lvovna, with a single movement, covered the babyish face of the sufferer with a big down pillow and pressed her strong, firm bosom on top of it.

Some four minutes the room was as silent as the grave.

"He's dead," whispered Katerina Lvovna and had only just stood up to put everything in order when the walls of that old house that had seen so many crimes trembled under deafening blows: the windows rattled, the floors shook, the vibrating chains of the hanging icon-lamps cast fantastic shadows on the walls.

Sergei shuddered and ran away as fast as his legs would carry him; Katerina Lvovna went after him and the noise and uproar followed them. It seemed as though some unearthly forces were shaking the sinful house to the foundations.

Katerina Lvovna was afraid that, in his terror, Sergei would run out into the yard and betray himself by his fright; but he made his way to the attic bedroom.

Sergei ran full pelt up the stairs and in the darkness banged his head on the half-open door; with a groan he rolled down the stairs, completely out of his mind from superstitious terror.

"Zinovy Borisich, Zinovy Borisich!" he muttered, flying headlong downstairs, knocking Katerina Lvovna off her feet and dragging her with him.

"Where?" she asked.

"He flew over us on an iron sheet. There, there he is again! Ai, ai . . ." screamed Sergei. "Listen to him rattling, he's rattling again."

It was now quite clear that many hands were banging at the windows from the outside and that somebody was trying to break open the door.

"You fool! Get up, you fool!" screamed Katerina Lvovna, and with those words darted back to Fyodor, laid his dead head on the pillows in the most natural pose as though he were asleep and then with a firm hand opened the door which the crowd was trying to break down.

A terrible scene met her eyes. Katerina Lvovna looked out over the crowd that was besieging the porch and saw row after row of unfamiliar people climbing over the fence into the yard while in the street there was a hum of human speech.

Before Katerina Lvovna realized what had happened, the people surrounding the porch forced her back and threw her into the room.

XII

And this is how the alarm was raised: on the eve of the festival of the Presentation people crowded all the churches of the town Katerina Lvovna lived in, which, although it was only a district town, was quite big and had some factories; the church that was to celebrate its saint's day on the morrow was not only full of people, but even the churchyard was packed for midnight mass. The church boasted a choir of merchants' apprentices led by a choir master who was also an amateur in the vocal art.

Our people are pious and assiduous churchgoers. In addition, they have an artistic temperament; the grandeur of the solemn church chorals is one of the loftiest and purest forms of enjoyment known to our people. Wherever a choir is singing almost a half of the town is certain to gather, especially the younger men from the trading establishments: shop assistants, shop boys, clerks, artisans from the factories and mills, as well as the owners and their wives—they all crush into one church; everybody wants at least to stand on the porch, at least to stand under a window in the fierce heat or biting frost to hear how the octaves are rolled out or how a bold tenor handles the most capricious fugues.

The Izmailovs' parish church was dedicated to the Presentation of the Blessed Virgin Mary and on the eve of that festival, therefore, at the time of the incident with Fyodor described above, the youth of the whole town had been in that church; leaving church in a noisy crowd, they discussed the merits of a well-known tenor and the accidental flukes of an equally well-known bass.

Not all of them, however, were interested in matters musical: there were those in the crowd who were interested in other questions.

"You know, you chaps, they're saying funny things about that young Izmailova woman," said, as they approached the house, a young mechanic brought from St. Petersburg by a merchant to run his steam mill; "they say she's at her amours with their clerk Sergei every minute of the day. . . ."

"Everybody knows it," answered another in a sheepskin, cloth-covered coat. "She wasn't in church today, either."

"Church! She's such a dirty bitch and she doesn't fear God, or her conscience or the public eye."

"Look, they've got a light up there," said the mechanic, pointing to a crack between the shutters.

"Let's have a look through the crack and see what they're up to," muttered a number of voices.

The mechanic climbed on to the shoulders of two of his associates and had no sooner applied his eye to the crack than he screamed at the top of his voice:

"Brothers, friends! They're smothering somebody in there,

smothering him!" And the man battered desperately at the shutter with his fists. A dozen other men followed his example, climbed up to the windows and began banging at the shutters.

Every second the crowd grew and the siege of the Izmailov house, which we already know of, began.

"I saw it myself, I saw it with my own eyes," testified the mechanic standing over Fyodor's dead body. "The boy was stretched out on the bed and those two were smothering him."

Sergei was taken to the police station that same night, while Katerina Lvovna was removed to her upper room and two guards were placed there to watch her.

The cold in the Izmailov house was unbearable for the doors were open most of the time. One dense crowd of curious sightseers followed another. They all came to see the body of Fyodor lying in his coffin and to view another big coffin covered with a heavy pall. On Fyodor's forehead lay a strip of white satin covering the red scar left by the postmortem examination of the skull. The examination by the police doctor showed that Fyodor had died of asphyxiation and when Sergei was confronted with the body, at the priest's first words about the last judgement and the awful punishment awaiting unrepentant sinners, he wept and not only frankly confessed the murder of Fyodor but also asked that the body of Zinovy Borisich that he had buried without a proper funeral service, be dug up. The body of Katerina Lvovna's husband, which had been buried in dry sand, was not fully decomposed: it was disinterred and placed in a big coffin. To the horror of all, Sergei named the young mistress as his accomplice in both these crimes. To all questions Katerina Lvovna answered, "I know nothing about anything like that." Sergei was confronted with her and forced to expose her. Katerina Lvovna listened to his confession, stared at him in dumb amazement but without anger, and then said indifferently, "If he's so anxious to say all that, there's no reason for me to be stubborn: I killed them."

"What for?" she was asked.

"For him," she answered pointing to Sergei who sat with his head hanging.

The criminals were kept in prison and the case that had aroused public attention and indignation was dealt with very quickly. At the end of February the court announced to Sergei and to widow

Katerina Lvovna, of the Third Guild of Merchants, that the sentence was punishment by public flogging on the market square and exile to penal servitude. At the beginning of March, on a cold frosty morning, the executioner raised the allotted number of reddish-blue welts on Katerina Lvovna's naked white back, then administered Sergei's portion on his shoulders and branded his handsome face with three criminal brands.

All this time Sergei, for some reason or another, aroused more popular sympathy than Katerina Lvovna. Covered in blood and dirt he staggered as he descended the black scaffold but Katerina Lvovna walked away quietly, striving only to prevent the thick shift and coarse prison coat from touching her lacerated back.

Even when her baby was brought to her in the prison hospital she only said, "Don't bother me with it!" and turning towards the wall, without a groan, without a complaint, slumped face downwards on the hard bunk.

XIII

The convict party to which Sergei and Katerina Lvovna were detailed set out when spring had just begun by the calendar but when the sun, as the saying goes, "shines brightly but gives no warmth."

Katerina Lvovna's child was given to be brought up by the old woman, Boris Timofeyich's sister, and as he was regarded as the legitimate son of the murderess's dead husband he now remained the sole heir to the entire Izmailov property. Katerina Lvovna was very satisfied with this arrangement and gave up the child with complete indifference. Her love for the child's father, like that of many excessively passionate women, did not by one particle pass over to the child.

Incidentally, light and darkness, good and evil, joy and boredom did not exist for her; she did not understand anything, or love anybody, not even herself. She only waited impatiently for the party to set out on the road, when she hoped to see her Sergei again, and she even forgot to think of the child.

Katerina Lvovna's hopes were not in vain: fettered with heavy chains, the branded Sergei passed through the prison gates in the same group.

Man gets used to any situation, even the most abominable, in any situation he retains, as far as possible, his ability to pursue his own few joys; Katerina Lvovna did not have to adapt herself in any way: she would see Sergei again and with him even the convict's road promised happiness.

Katerina Lvovna had not brought many things of value with her in her canvas bag and still less ready money. But long before they reached Nizhny-Novgorod all of it, however, had been distributed amongst the sergeants of the escort for an opportunity to walk beside Sergei on the road and to embrace him for an hour or so at night in the cold, dark, narrow corridors of the transit prisons.

Katerina Lvovna's branded friend, however, did not seem so very amiable towards her: he did not greatly value these secret meetings with her, meetings for which she, foregoing food and drink, paid 25 kopeks from her scanty purse, and he often said, "Instead of coming to hide in corners with me it would be better to give the money to me and not the sergeant."

"I only gave him 25 kopeks, Sergei, dear," said Katerina Lvovna in justification.

"Isn't that money? D'you find 'em lying about in the road, those 25 kopeks, and you've paid a lot of 'em already, anyway."

"But still, we've been able to meet."

"And d'you think it's so wonderful to meet after all this suffering? I'm ready to curse my very life, not only these meetings."

"But I don't care, Sergei, as long as I can see you."

"That's all nonsense," answered Sergei.

At times Katerina Lvovna bit her lips till they bled when she heard such answers and in eyes unused to weeping there appeared tears of rage and chagrin during those meetings in the dark of night; still she put up with it all, kept her silence and tried to deceive herself.

In this way, with their relations on this new footing, they went as far as Nizhny-Novgorod. Here they were joined by a party on its way to Siberia along the Moscow highway.

In this big party, containing many people of all sorts, there were two interesting characters in the women's section: one of them, Fiona, a soldier's wife from Yaroslavl, was a fine, luscious woman, tall, with a thick braid of black hair and languid hazel eyes shaded, as with a mysterious veil, by thick lashes; the other was a

17-year-old, thin-faced blonde with dainty, pink skin, a tiny mouth, dimples on her fresh cheeks and light golden curls that escaped capriciously from under her coarse convict's kerchief. This girl was known as little Sonya in the party.

The beautiful Fiona was of gentle and lazy disposition. In their party everybody knew her well and none of the men were particularly glad when they had success with her just as none of them were very much upset when they saw that she bestowed those same favors on others who sought them.

"Our Aunt Fiona is a kindly woman, generous to all," the convicts agreed jokingly.

Little Sonya, however, had a different character.

"She's slippery, she's always close by but you can't get your hands on her," was what they said of her.

Little Sonya had taste, she liked to pick and choose and was, in fact, very finical. She did not want passion dished up to her uncooked; she wanted it served with a piquant sauce, with suffering and sacrifice; while Fiona had a Russian simplicity too lazy even to say, "Go away" to anybody and knew only one thing—that she was a woman. Such women are highly valued in gangs of thieves, in convict parties and St. Petersburg Social-Democratic Communes.

The appearance of these two women in a combined party together with Sergei and Katerina Lvovna had tragic significance for the latter.

XIV

From the first days of the journey from Nizhny-Novgorod to Kazan, Sergei began very obviously seeking favors of Fiona, and not without success. The languid, beautiful Fiona did not repulse Sergei any more than she, in her kindness of heart, rejected anybody else. On the third or fourth stage Katerina Lvovna had, by bribery, arranged a meeting with Sergei at early dusk and was lying awake, waiting all the time for the sergeant on duty to come into the room, nudge her and whisper, "Run quick!" The door opened once and a woman darted out into the corridor; the door opened a second time and another woman slipped down from the bed of boards and ran into the corridor after her escort; at last somebody tugged at the coat that covered Katerina Lvovna. The young woman rose quickly from the shelf bed polished by the sides of countless convicts, threw the coat over her shoulders and pushed the escort standing in front of her.

When Katerina Lvovna went down the corridor, which was feebly lit at one place only by a wick in a saucer of oil, she came across two or three couples who were scarcely discernible from any distance. As she passed the men's room she could hear subdued laughter coming through the observation hole cut in the door.

"Ugh, playing the fool," mumbled Katerina Lvovna's escort and, holding her by the shoulders, pushed her into a corner and went away.

With one hand Katerina Lvovna felt a coat and a beard; her other hand touched a woman's hot face.

"Who's that?" asked Sergei in a low voice.

"What are you doing here? Who's that with you?"

In the darkness Katerina Lvovna pulled the kerchief off her rival's head. The woman slipped away to one side and, stumbling over somebody, ran off down the corridor.

Hearty laughter came from the men's cell.

"You swine," whispered Katerina Lvovna and struck Sergei across the face with the ends of the kerchief she had torn off the head of his new friend.

Sergei would have raised his hand but Katerina Lvovna ran lightly down the corridor and entered her own door. The laughter from the men's cell was repeated as she ran, and so loudly that the sentry standing apathetically in front of the dim lamp and spitting at the toe of his boot, raised his head and growled, "Quiet, there!"

Katerina Lvovna lay down without a word to tell herself, "I don't love him," but felt that she loved him more ardently than ever. And before her eyes she kept seeing his hand trembling under *that woman's* head and his other arm embracing her warm shoulders.

The poor woman wept and involuntarily yearned for that same hand to place itself under her head, for that same arm to embrace her hysterically trembling shoulders.

"Well, anyway, are you going to give me my kerchief back?" asked the soldier's wife Fiona, waking her next morning.

"And so that was you, was it?"

"Give it back to me, please."

"Why did you separate us?"

"How did I separate you? Surely you don't think I'm so much in love or need him so badly that you should get angry about it."

Katerina Lvovna thought for a second and then pulled from under her pillow the kerchief she had captured the night before, threw it to Fiona and turned to the wall. She felt easier at heart.

"T-Foo," she said to herself, "surely I'm not going to get jealous of that painted swill-tub? May she rot in hell. It's disgusting even to compare myself with her."

"And you, Katerina Lvovna, just listen here," said Sergei when they were on the road next day, "please get it into your head once and for all that I'm not Zinovy Borisich, and secondly that you're no high and mighty merchant any more; so don't get huffy, I ask you. I got no use for a she-goat's horns."

Katerina Lvovna made no reply and for a week walked beside Sergei without exchanging a word or a glance. As the offended party she stood on her dignity and did not want to make the first step towards reconciliation after her first quarrel with Sergei.

While Katerina Lvovna was still angry with Sergei, the latter began trying to preen himself and make up to white little Sonya. He would bow to her "with our best respects," smile at her and when they met would try to get his arms round her and squeeze her. Katerina Lvovna saw it all and it only made her heart seeth all the more.

"Perhaps I ought to make it up with him?" she wondered, stumbling along as though she did not see the ground before her.

But now, more than ever before, her pride would not allow her to be the first to go to him to make up. In the meantime Sergei was getting more and more entangled with little Sonya and the general opinion was that the unapproachable blonde, who was so elusive and never gave herself into anybody's hands, was suddenly being tamed.

"You shed tears about me," said Fiona one day to Katerina Lvovna, "and what did I do to you? I took the chance when I had it and now it's gone, but you keep your eye on that Sonya."

"My pride has gone. I simply must make up with him today," decided Katerina Lvovna at last and her only thought was of how to effect the reconciliation in the best possible manner.

Sergei himself got her out of this difficult situation.

"Lvovna," called Sergei to her during a halt. "Come out to me tonight. There's something I want to talk about."

At first Katerina Lvovna did not answer.

"Are you still angry? Won't you come?"

Again Katerina Lvovna did not answer.

But Sergei and everybody else who watched Katerina Lvovna saw her edge her way towards the senior sergeant as they neared the transit prison and push into his hand seventeen kopeks that she had saved from money given as alms on the way.

"As soon as I can, I'll give you another ten," Katerina Lvovna promised.

"All right," said the sergeant and hid the money in his coat cuff.

When these negotiations had been completed Sergei gave a short cough and winked to Sonya.

"Oh, Katerina Lvovna," he said, taking her in his arms on the steps at the entrance to the prison, "there's no one in the whole world to compare with you."

Katerina Lvovna blushed and almost choked with joy.

As soon as night fell, the door opened slightly and she immediately slipped out; she trembled as she felt with her hands for Sergei in the dark corridor.

"Katya, darling," whispered Sergei, embracing her.

"My own bad boy!" answered Katerina Lvovna through her tears and pressed her lips against his.

The sentry passed down the corridor, halted, spat on his boots and walked on; worn-out convicts snored in their cells, a mouse gnawed at a quill pen, crickets under the stove tried to outchirp each other, and Katerina Lvovna was in the seventh heaven.

But the raptures came to an end, and the inevitable prose made itself heard.

"It hurts so much: from my ankles right up to the very knees, the bones are aching," complained Sergei sitting beside Katerina Lvovna on the floor in the corridor.

"What can I do about it, Sergei?" asked Katerina Lvovna, snuggling under a fold of his coat.

"Should I ask to be sent to the hospital in Kazan?"

"Don't say that, Sergei."

"They hurt so much, I'll die, then."

"How can you remain behind while they drive me on?"

"What else can I do? They keep rubbing and rubbing and soon the chains will cut me to the bone. If only I had woolen stockings to put on, maybe. . . ." continued Sergei a moment later.

"Stockings? I've got some new stockings, Sergei."

"Well, what could be better?" answered Sergei.

Without a further word, Katerina Lvovna darted back into her cell, emptied her bag out on the shelf bed, then hurried back to Sergei in the corridor with a pair of thick blue woollen stockings with brightly colored clocks on the sides.

"Now everything will be all right," whispered Sergei, saying good-bye to Katerina Lvovna and taking her last pair of stockings.

The happy Katerina Lvovna went back to her place and fell sound asleep.

She did not hear Sonya leave the room after she returned, nor did she see her return just before morning.

All this happened just two stages before Kazan.

XV

A cold, inclement day with gusts of wind and rain mixed with snow inhospitably greeted the convict party as they left the gates of the stuffy transit prison. Katerina Lvovna left smartly enough but she had no sooner taken her place in the ranks than she began to tremble and turned green. Everything went dark before her eyes: she felt a pain in all her joints and they refused to support her. In front of Katerina Lvovna stood Sonya in the well-known blue woolen stockings with the bright clocks up the sides.

Katerina Lvovna moved off more than half dead: only her eyes stared terrifyingly at Sergei and never once left him.

At the first halt Katerina Lvovna walked calmly up to Sergei, whispered, "You villain" and unexpectedly spat straight into his eyes.

Sergei wanted to spring at her, but he was held back.

"Just you wait," he muttered as he wiped his face.

"She's got guts enough to tackle you, all right," the other convicts mocked at Sergei, and Sonya's laughter poured out merriest of all.

The little intrigue she had got mixed up in was exactly to Sonya's taste.

"You won't get away with that," Sergei threatened Katerina Lvovna.

Exhausted by the march and the bad weather and broken in spirit, Katerina Lvovna fell into a troubled sleep at the next transit prison and did not hear two men come into the women's cell in the dark.

When they entered, Sonya sat up, pointed Katerina Lvovna out to them, lay down again and covered herself with her coat.

The next moment Katerina Lvovna's coat was pulled over her head and the heavy end of a doubled rope wielded by a man's heavy hand lashed across her back, covered only by the coarse cotton shift.

Katerina Lvovna screamed out but her voice could not be heard under the coat that had been thrown over her head. She struggled but also without avail; a burly convict was sitting on her shoulders and holding her arms in a firm grip.

"Fifty," counted a voice at last, a voice which nobody would have had difficulty in recognizing as Sergei's, and the night visitors disappeared through the door.

Katerina Lvovna freed her head and jumped up; there was nobody there, only not far away somebody giggled maliciously under cover of a coat. Katerina Lvovna recognized Sonya's laugh.

Never had she felt so mortified; there was no limit to the malice that boiled at that moment in Katerina Lvovna's soul. She surged forward out of her senses, and out of her senses she fell unconscious on to the breast of Fiona who caught her up.

On the full bosom that had but recently comforted Katerina Lvovna's faithless lover with the pleasures of lust, she now wept out her unbearable sorrow and snuggled up to her foolish and flabby rival like a child snuggling up to its mother. Now they were equals: they had been reduced to the same value and both had been thrown over.

They are equals! . . . Fiona, submissive to the first suggestion, and Katerina Lvovna, ending a drama of love!

There was now nothing that could give offence to Katerina Lvovna. When she had exhausted her tears she seemed turned to stone and with wooden calm got ready to go out for the roll-call.

The drum was beating: boom, boom, boom—convicts, fettered and unfettered, poured out into the yard: Sergei and Fiona, Sonya and Katerina Lvovna, an Old Believer shackled to a Jew, a Pole shackled to a Tatar. . . .

At first they massed together in a crowd, then got into some sort of order and marched off.

The most sorrowful of sights: a handful of people, torn from the world and deprived of any hope of a better future, plod their way through the thick, black mud of the dirt road. Their whole surroundings are horrible in their ugliness: the endless mud, the grey sky, the wet, leafless willows and the tousled crows on their gaunt branches. The wind groans and rages, roars and howls.

The hellish, soul-rending sounds that complete the horror of the picture seem to recall the advice of Job's wife in the Bible: "Curse the day thou wast born, and die."

Whoever does not want to listen to these words, whoever is afraid of death, must, in this difficult situation, strive to drown out the howling voices with something still more ugly. The common man knows this very well: on such occasions he gives free play to all his simple bestiality and begins to mock himself, other people and their feelings. Under ordinary circumstances he is not particularly gentle, but in conditions such as these he becomes the very essence of evil.

* * *

"Hullo, Mrs. Merchant, do I find your honor in good health?" asked Sergei impertinently of Katerina Lvovna as soon as the party was out of sight of the village in which they had spent the night.

With these words he turned round to Sonya, covered her with the skirts of his coat and sang in a high falsetto:

> I see through the window your sweet golden head,
> I see that you sleep not, my darling,
> I'll throw my cloak o'er you to hide your sweet head . . .

At this point Sergei put his arms round Sonya and kissed her loudly in full view of the whole party. . . .

Katerina Lvovna saw it all and yet saw nothing: she walked like one no longer alive. People began to nudge her, call her attention to the way Sergei was carrying on so disgustingly with Sonya, and make her the butt of their coarse jokes.

"Leave her alone," said Fiona, taking her part when somebody in the party tried to poke fun at Katerina Lvovna, as she stumbled along. "Can't you see the woman's very ill?"

"She must have got her poor little tootsies wet," this from a young convict.

"Of course, she's from the merchant class, been brought up tenderly," responded Sergei.

"If she had warm stockings she'd be all right, of course," he continued.

Katerina Lvovna seemed suddenly to wake up.

"You dirty snake!" she said, "go on, laugh, you scoundrel, laugh!"

"Oh, no, Mrs. Merchant, I don't mean that as a joke at all: only Sonya here has some very fine stockings to sell and I just thought perhaps our merchant lady might buy them."

Many of them laughed. Katerina Lvovna marched on like a wound-up automaton.

The weather grew worse all the time. Large flakes of wet snow began to fall from the grey clouds that covered the sky but they melted almost before they reached the ground and helped swell the sea of heavy mud. At last a dark, leaden strip appeared; the far side of it was out of sight. This was the Volga. A fairly strong wind was blowing across the Volga driving back and forth the broad, dark, slowly rising waves.

The party of wet and shivering convicts moved slowly towards the landing-stage and stood there awaiting the ferry.

When the dark ferry arrived, the crew began to accommodate the convicts.

"They say you can get vodka on this ferry," said one of the convicts when the ferry, covered with flakes of wet snow, put off from the shore and tossed on the waves of the raging river.

"Yes, it wouldn't be at all bad to have a small drop right now," answered Sergei and, continuing to bait Katerina Lvovna for Sonya's amusement, said, "Mrs. Merchant, for the sake of our old friendship, buy us a drop of vodka. Don't be stingy. Remember, my sweetheart, our former love, remember what good times we had together, my love, how we sat out the long autumn nights together, how we sent all your relatives to kingdom come without the benefit of book and clergy."

Katerina Lvovna was shivering with cold. Apart from the cold that penetrated to the very marrow under her wet clothes, something else was happening in Katerina Lvovna. Her head was on fire; the pupils of her eyes were wildly distended, animated by the sharp, wandering glitter and fixed motionlessly on the rolling waves.

"I'd like a drop of vodka, too," chirped little Sonya. "It's so cold I can't stand it any longer."

"Aren't you going to treat us, Mrs. Merchant?" Sergei continued to pester her.

"Haven't you got any conscience?" said Fiona, shaking her head. She was supported by the convict Gordyushka.

"Yes, it doesn't show you up at all well," he said. "Even if you aren't ashamed as far as she's concerned you ought to be in front of the others."

"Ugh, you're anybody's snuffbox!" shouted Sergei to Fiona. "You're a fine one to talk about conscience. What's it got to do with my conscience? Maybe I never did love her at all and now . . . Sonya's old shoe is prettier to me than her mug, the ragged old cat; what have you got to say about that? Let her make love to Gordyushka there with his twisted mouth; or to . . ." he looked towards a mounted officer in a long black cloak and military cap with cockade and added, "or still better make yourself nice to the officer: at any rate the rain doesn't get under his cloak."

"And everybody would call her Mrs. Officer," Sonya put in.

"I should say so! And she'd easily get what to buy stockings with, too!"

Katerina Lvovna did not attempt to defend herself: she stared even more fixedly at the waves, and her lips moved. She seemed to hear, between Sergei's foul remarks, howls and groans coming from the waves as they gaped open and slapped to again. Suddenly in one of the breaking waves she seemed to see the blue head of Boris Timofeyich, out of another appeared her husband embracing Fyodor whose head was hanging down. Katerina Lvovna tried to remember a prayer and moved her lips to repeat it but her lips kept saying, "How we had good times together, how we sat out the long autumn nights together and sent people out of this world with violent death."

Katerina Lvovna shuddered. Her wandering eyes became fixed and wild. Her arms once or twice stretched out nobody knew where into space and then dropped to her sides again. Another minute and she swayed and, without taking her eyes off the dark waters, bent down, caught Sonya by the legs and with one single leap went overboard with her.

Everybody was petrified with amazement.

Katerina Lvovna appeared on the surface and then disappeared again; another wave brought little Sonya to the top.

"A boathook! Throw them a boathook!" shouted the people on the ferry.

A heavy boathook with a long rope attached flew through the air and splashed in the water. Sonya had disappeared again. Two seconds later, carried swiftly away from the ferry by the current, she again waved her arms; but at that very moment Katerina Lvovna appeared out of another wave, rose almost to her waist above the water, hurled herself at Sonya like a big pike at a soft little perch and neither of them appeared again.

FYODOR DOSTOEVSKY

The Dream
of a Ridiculous Man:

A FANTASTIC STORY

I

I AM A RIDICULOUS MAN. They call me a madman now. It would have been a promotion for me had I not appeared as ridiculous to them as ever. But I no longer mind—they are all dear to me now, even when they are laughing at me, something endears them to me particularly then. I would laugh with them—not at myself, that is, but because I love them—I would laugh if I did not feel so sad looking at them. What saddens me is that they do not know the truth, and I know the truth. Oh, how hard it is to be the only one to know the truth! But they will not understand this. No, they will not.

Translated by OLGA SHARTSE. *Reprinted from* A Funny Man's Dream. Moscow, [n.d.].

It used to hurt me very much that I seemed ridiculous. I did not seem it, I was. I have always been ridiculous and I think I've known it since the day I was born. I believe I realized it when I was seven. Then I went to school and then to the university, but what of it? The more I studied the more I came to realize that I was ridiculous. And so, as far as I was concerned, the ultimate meaning of university learning was to prove and explain to me, the more I probed it, that I was indeed ridiculous. Life taught me the same thing. With every year my awareness of how ridiculous I was in every respect grew and developed. I was laughed at by everyone and all the time. But none of them knew or guessed that of all the people in the world I knew best how ridiculous I was, and it was the fact that they did not know this that hurt me most of all, but the fault was entirely mine: I was always so proud that I would never admit this knowledge to anyone. My pride swelled in me with the years, and had I allowed myself to admit to anyone that I was ridiculous, I believe I would have blown my brains out with a revolver that same night. Oh, the torment I went through in my adolescence for fear that I would weaken and make the admission to my friends! As I grew to manhood I learned more and more of this awful shortcoming of mine with every year, but in spite of this I took it a little more calmly for some reason. I repeat—for some reason, because to this day I have been unable to give it a clear definition. Perhaps it was because of that hopeless sadness that was mounting in my soul about something that was infinitely greater than myself: this something was a mounting conviction that *nothing mattered*. I had begun to suspect this long ago, but positive conviction came to me all at once, one day last year. I suddenly felt that *I would not have cared* if the world existed at all or if there was nothing anywhere. I began to know and feel with all my being that *there has been nothing* since I have been there. At first I kept thinking that there must have been a great deal before, but then I realized that there had not been anything before either, and that it only seemed so for some reason. Gradually, I became convinced that there would never be anything at all. It was then I suddenly ceased getting angry with people and no longer noticed them at all. It was quite true, even in the merest trifles: for instance, I would walk into people as I went along the street. Not that I was lost in thought either, for what was there to think about, I had given up thinking altogether then: I did not care. Neither did I solve any problems; no, not a single one, and yet there was a host of them. But I *did not care* now, and all the problems receded into the background.

And it was much later that I learned the Truth. It was last November, the third of November to be exact, that I learned the Truth, and since then I remember every moment of my life. It happened on a gloomy night, the gloomiest night that could ever be. I was walking home, the time being after ten, and I remember thinking that no hour could be gloomier. It was so even physically. It had been raining all day, and it was the coldest and gloomiest rain, even an ominous rain, I remember, obviously hostile to people, and suddenly after ten it stopped and a horrible dampness set in, which was colder and damper than during the rain, and steam rose from everything, from every cobble-stone, from every alleyway if you peered into its deepest and darkest recesses. I suddenly fancied that if all the gas-lights were to go out it would be more cheerful, for gas-light, showing up all this, made one feel even sadder. I had hardly eaten anything that day, and since late afternoon I had been at an engineer's I knew, with two other friends of his. I said nothing all evening and I believe I bored them. They were discussing something exciting and actually lost their tempers over it. But they did not care, I could see; they lost their tempers just for form. I went and blurted it out to them: "Gentlemen," I said, "you don't really care, you know." They took no offence, they just laughed at me. That was because there was no reproach in my remark, I simply made it because I did not care. They saw that I did not care and it made them laugh.

When, walking home, I thought of the gas-light, I glanced up at the sky. The sky was terribly dark, but I could clearly make out the ragged clouds and the fathomless black pits between them. Suddenly I noticed a tiny star twinkling in one of those pits and I stopped to stare at it. That was because the tiny star gave me an idea: I made up my mind to kill myself that night. I had made up my mind to do it fully two months before, and poor though I am I had bought a splendid revolver and had loaded it that same day. Two months had already passed, however, and it was still lying in my desk drawer; my feeling of not caring had been so strong then that I wanted to choose a moment when it would be a little less so to do it in, why—I do not know. And so every night, for two months, I had gone home with the thought of killing myself. I was waiting for the right moment. And now this star gave me the idea, and I made up my mind that *it had to be* that night. But why the tiny star gave me the idea, I do not know.

There I stood staring at the sky when suddenly the little girl clutched at my arm. The street was already deserted and there was hardly a soul about. A droshky was standing some way off with the driver dozing in it. The girl must have been about eight; all she wore in this cold was a poor cotton frock and a kerchief, she was drenched through, but I particularly noticed her sodden, broken shoes, and I remember them even now. They struck me particularly. She suddenly began to tug at my elbow and cry. She was not weeping, but was crying out snatches of words which she could not articulate properly because she was shivering all over as in a fever. Something had frightened her, and she called out desperately: "My mummy, my mummy!" I half-turned towards her but said not a word and continued on my way, while she kept running after me, tugging at my coat, and her voice rang with that peculiar sound which in badly frightened children means despair. I know that sound. Though her words were incoherent, I understood that her mother lay dying somewhere, or perhaps it was some other disaster that had befallen them, and she had rushed out into the street to find someone or something to help her mother. But I did not go with her; on the contrary, it suddenly occurred to me to drive her away. I told her to go and look for a policeman. But she folded her hands in entreaty and, sobbing and panting, ran along at my side and would not leave me alone. It was then I stamped my feet at her and shouted. All she cried was: "Sir, oh sir!" but, abandoning me abruptly, she darted across the street: another passer-by appeared there and it was to him she must have run from me.

I climbed my five flights of stairs. I live in a lodging house. My room is wretched and small, with just one attic window in it, a semi-circular one. The furniture consists of an oilcloth-covered sofa, two chairs, a table with my books on it, and an armchair, a very, very old one but a Voltaire armchair for all that. I sat down, lighted my candle, and gave myself up to thought. The room next door was a real Bedlam. It has been going on since the day before yesterday. The man who lives there is a discharged captain and he was having guests, about six of them—castaways on the sea of life—drinking vodka and playings *stoss* with an old deck of cards. There had been a fight the night before, and I know that two of them had torn at one another's hair for quite a long time. The landlady wanted to put in a complaint against them, but she is terribly afraid of the captain. The only other lodger is a thin little lady, an officer's wife, a newcomer to the town with three small children, who have all been ill since they came here. The lady and the children live in deadly fear of the captain, they spend their nights shaking with fear and crossing themselves, and as for the youngest baby, it was even frightened into a fit once. The captain, I know for a fact, sometimes accosts people on the Nevsky and begs alms. He won't be given a post anywhere, but strangely (this is why I am telling all this), in all the months he has been staying with us, he never once roused any resentment in me. I naturally shunned his company from the outset, but then he too thought me a bore the very first time we met, and no matter how loudly they shout in their room or how many they are—I never care. I sit up all night and, honestly, I never even hear them, so utterly do I forget them. I cannot get to sleep until dawn, you know; it has been like that for a year now. I spend the whole night sitting in my armchair and doing nothing. I only read in the daytime. I just sit there, without even thinking. My thoughts are vague and stray, and I let them wander. My candle burns down every night. I calmly settled down in my chair, took out my revolver and placed it on the table before me. I remember asking myself as I put it down: "Are you sure?" and answering quite firmly: "I *am* sure." That is, I would kill myself. I knew that I would definitely kill myself that night, but how much longer I would sit thus at the table before I did it I did not know. And I would have certainly killed myself if it had not been for that little girl.

II

You see how it was: though I did not care, I was still sensitive to pain, for instance. If someone struck me I would feel the pain. Mentally it was exactly the same: if something very pathetic happened I would feel pity, just as I would have felt pity in the days before I had ceased caring for anything in the world. And I did feel pity earlier that night: surely, I should have helped a child in distress? Why had I not helped the girl then? Because of an idea that had occurred to me; when she was tugging at my coat and crying out, a problem suddenly confronted me and I was unable to solve it. It was an idle problem but it had angered me. I got angry because, having definitely decided to commit suicide that very night, I ought to have cared less than ever for anything in the world. Then why had I suddenly felt that I did care and was sorry for the little girl? I remember I was frightfully sorry for her, my pity was strangely poignant and incongruous in my position. I really cannot give a better description of that fleeting feeling of mine, but it remained with me even after I had reached my room and had seated myself in my chair, and it vexed me more than anything else had done for a long time. One argument followed another. It was perfectly clear to me that if I was a man and not yet a nought, and had not yet become a nought, I was therefore alive and, consequently, able to suffer, resent, and feel shame for my actions. Very well. But if I was going to kill myself in a couple of hours from then, why should I be concerned with the girl and what did I care for shame or anything else in the world? I would become a nought, an absolute nought. And could it be that my ability to feel pity for the girl and shame for my vile action was not in the least affected by the certainty that I would soon become *completely* non-existent, and therefore nothing would exist. Why, the reason I had stamped my feet and shouted so brutally at the poor child was to assert that: "Not only don't I feel pity, I can even afford to do something inhumanly vile now, because two hours from now all will be extinguished." Do you believe me when I say that this was the reason why I had shouted? I am almost convinced of it now. It had seemed clear to me that life and the world were from then on dependent on me, as it were. I should even say that the world seemed specially made for me alone: if I killed myself the world would be no more, at least as far as I was concerned. To say nothing of the possibility that there would really be nothing for anyone after I was gone, and the moment my consciousness dimmed the whole world, being a mere attribute of my consciousness, would instantly dim too, fade like a mirage and be no more, for it may be that all this world of ours and all these people are merely part of myself, are just myself. I remember that as I sat there and reasoned, I gave an entirely different twist to all these new problems that were thronging my mind, and conceived some perfectly new ideas. For instance, a strange notion like this occurred to me: supposing I had once lived on the moon or Mars and had there committed the foulest and scurviest of deeds imaginable, for which I had been made to suffer all the scorn and dishonor conceivable in nothing less than in a dream, in a nightmare, and supposing I later found myself on the earth, with the crime committed on that other planet alive in my consciousness and, besides, knowing there was no return for me, ever, under any circumstances—would *I have cared* or not as I gazed at the moon from this earth? Would I have felt shame for that deed or not? All these questions were idle and superfluous since the revolver was already lying in front of me and I knew with all my being that *it* was bound to happen, and yet the questions excited me and roused me to a frenzy. I no longer seemed able to die before I had solved something first. In short, that little girl saved me because the unsolved questions put off the shot. Meanwhile, the noise at the captain's began to subside too: they had finished their game and were now settling down to sleep, grumbling, and sleepily rounding off their mutual abuse. It was then that I suddenly fell asleep in my chair in front of the table, a thing that never happened to me before. I dropped off without knowing it at all. Dreams, we all know, are extremely queer things: one will be appallingly vivid, with the greatest imaginable precision in every minutely finished detail, while in another you skip, for example, through time and space so swiftly that you hardly notice. Dreams, I believe, are directed by desire, not reason, by the heart and not the mind, and yet what fantastic tricks my reason sometimes plays on me in dreams! The things that happen to my reason in sleep are quite incredible. For example, my brother died five years ago. I dream of him sometimes: he takes an active interest in my affairs, we are very fond of one another, yet all through my dream I know and remember perfectly well that my brother has long been dead and buried. Why does it not surprise me then that though dead he is still there beside me, worrying about my affairs? Why does my reason reconcile itself to all this so willingly? But enough. To return to my dream. Yes, my dream of November the 3rd. They all tease me now that, after all, it was nothing but a dream. But surely it makes no difference whether it was a dream or not since it did reveal the Truth to me? Because if you have come to know it once and to see it, you will know it is the Truth and that there is not, there cannot be any other, whether you are dreaming or living. Very well, it was a dream—let it be a dream, but the fact remains that I was going to snuff out the life which you all extol so, whereas my dream, my dream—oh, my dream revealed to me another life, a life revived, magnificent and potent.

Listen then.

III

I said that I fell asleep without knowing it and even continuing with my musings on the same matters as it were. Suddenly I dreamed that I picked up my revolver and, still keeping my chair, pressed it to my heart—my heart and not my head, whereas I had definitely decided to shoot myself through the head, and the right temple it had to be. With the revolver pressed to my heart I waited a moment or two, and suddenly my candle, the table and the wall in front of me all began to rock and sway. I quickly pulled the trigger.

In dreams you sometimes fall from a great height or you are stabbed or beaten, but you never feel the pain unless you jerk and actually hurt yourself against the bedpost; you do feel the pain then, and it is almost certain to wake you up. It was the same in my dream: I felt no pain but with the sound of the report my whole being seemed to be shaken up and suddenly everything was extinguished and there was a horrible blackness all around me. I seemed to have gone blind and mute, I was lying on something very hard, stretched out on my back, seeing nothing and unable to make the slightest movement. Voices shouted and feet tramped all about me; there was the captain's low rumble and the landlady's shrill screech —and suddenly there was a blank again, and now they were carrying me in a coffin with the lid nailed down. I could feel the coffin swaying and I was reflecting upon it, when all of a sudden the thought struck me for the first time: I was dead, quite dead. I knew it without a doubt, I could neither see nor move, and yet I could feel and reason. But soon I reconciled myself to this and, as usual in dreams, accepted the fact without demur.

And now they were piling earth over my grave. Everyone left, I was alone, utterly alone. I did not stir. Whenever I used to imagine what it would be like to be buried, I generally associated but one sensation with the grave: the feeling of damp and cold. And now too I felt very cold, the tips of my toes were the worst, and that was all the sensation I had.

I lay there and, strangely, expected nothing, resigning myself to the fact that the dead have nothing to expect. But it was damp. I do not know how long I lay there—whether it was an hour, or a day, or many days. All of a sudden a drop of water, which had seeped through the lid of the coffin, fell on my left closed eye; a minute later there was another drop, a minute more and there was a third, and so on, drops falling at regular one-minute intervals. Profound indignation suddenly mounted in my heart, and suddenly I felt a physical pain in it. "It's my wound," I thought. "My shot, the bullet's there. . . ." And the water kept dripping, a drop a minute, straight down on my closed eye. I suddenly invoked, not with my voice for I lay inert, but with the whole of my being, the Ruler of all that was befalling me:

"Whoever Thou may be, but if Thou art and if there does exist any wisdom greater than the present, suffer it to descend upon this too. But if Thou art imposing vengeance upon me for my unwise suicide, with all the ugliness and absurdity of the life to come, then know Thee that no tortures I could ever be made to suffer could compare with the contempt I shall always feel in silence, be it through millions of years of martyrdom!"

I invoked and fell silent. Deep silence reigned for almost a full minute, and one more drop even fell, but I knew with infinite and profound faith, that all would certainly be different now. And suddenly my grave was rent open. That is, I do not know if it was dug open, but a dark and strange being picked me up and bore me away into space. I suddenly recovered sight. It was deep night, and never, never had there been such darkness yet! We were flying through space, the earth was already far behind us. I asked the one that bore me nothing at all, I waited, I was proud. I made myself believe I was not afraid, and my breath caught with admiration at the thought that I was not afraid. I do not remember how long we flew nor can I venture a guess: everything was happening the way it usually happens in dreams when you leap over space and time, over all laws of existence and reason, and only pause where your heart's desire bids you pause. I remember I suddenly saw a tiny star in the darkness. "Is it Sirius?" I could not hold back the question, although I did not want to ask anything at all. "No, that is the star you saw between the clouds on your way home," replied the one that bore me away. I knew the being was somewhat human in likeness. Strangely enough, I had no love for that being, I rather felt a deep aversion for it. I had expected complete non-existence and with that thought I had shot myself. And now I was in the hands of a being, not a human being of course, but a being nonetheless that *was*, that existed. "It just shows that there is life hereafter," I thought with the peculiar flippancy of dreams, but the essence of my spirit remained with me intact. "If I must *be* again," I thought, "and again live by someone's inescapable will, I do not want to be beaten and humiliated!" "You know that I am afraid of you, and for this you despise me," I suddenly said, unable to hold back my cringing words which held an admission, and feeling the pin-prick of humiliation in my heart. He did not answer my question, but all at once I knew that I was not being despised; I was not being laughed at nor even pitied; I knew that our flight through space had a purpose, mysterious and strange, concerning me alone. Fear mounted in my heart. Something was being mutely but painfully transmitted to me by my silent companion, piercing me through as it were. We flew through dark and unfamiliar space. I no longer saw the constellations my eyes were used to seeing. I knew that there were certain stars in the vastness of the sky whose rays took thousands and millions of years to reach the earth. Perhaps we were already flying through those regions. I waited for I knew not what, my tormented heart gripped with a terrible anguish. And suddenly I was shaken with a feeling that was familiar and so stirring: I saw our sun! I knew it could not be *our* sun which had begotten *our* earth, and also that we were infinitely far away from our sun, but my whole being told me that this was a sun exactly like our own, a duplicate of it, its twin. My soul rang with sweet and stirring ecstasy: this familiar source of light, the same light that had given me life, evoked an echo in my heart and resurrected it, and for the first time since my burial I sensed life, the same life as before.

"But if this is the sun, if this is a sun exactly like ours, then where is the earth?" I cried. And my companion pointed to a star sparkling in the darkness like emerald. We were flying straight towards it.

"Are such duplications really possible in the universe, is this really the law of nature? And if that star is an earth, can it be an earth like ours . . . exactly like ours, wretched and poor but dear and ever beloved, inspiring even in its most ungrateful children a love as poignant for it as our own earth inspires?" I cried out, trembling with rapturous, boundless love for that dear, old earth I had deserted. A vision of the poor little girl I had hurt flashed past me.

"You shall see everything," my companion said, and I sensed a peculiar sorrow in his words. But now we were quickly nearing the planet. It grew as we approached, I could already distinguish the oceans, the outline of Europe, and suddenly my heart was ablaze with a great and holy jealousy. "How can such a duplication be and what for? I do love and can love only the earth I have left behind, the earth bespattered with my blood when I in my ingratitude snuffed out my life with a shot through the heart. But I never, never ceased to love that earth, and the night I parted with it I think I loved it even more poignantly than ever before. Does this new earth hold suffering? On our earth we can only love truly by suffering and only through suffering. We can love in no other way and know no other love. I want suffering so I can love. I want, I long this instant to kiss that one and only earth I left behind me, and weep, and I do not want, I defy, life on any other!"

But my companion had already left me. I do not know how it came about but suddenly I found myself upon this other earth in the bright sunlight of a day as lovely as paradise. I believe I was on one of those islands which on our earth comprise the Greek Archipelago, or it may have been on the mainland somewhere, on the shore which the Archipelago adjoins. Everything was exactly the same as on our earth, but it all seemed to wear the splendor of a holiday, and shone with the glory of a great and holy triumph at last attained. A gentle emerald-green sea softly lapped the shores and caressed them with a love that was undisguised, visible, and almost conscious. Tall and beautiful trees stood in flowering splendor, while their countless little leaves welcomed me (I'm certain of it) with their gentle and soothing rustling, and they seemed to be murmuring words of love to me. The meadow was ablaze with bright, fragrant flowers. Birds fluttered above in flocks and unafraid of me alighted on my shoulders and hands and happily beat me with their sweet, tremulous wings. And finally I saw and came to know the people of this joyous land. They came to me themselves, they surrounded me and kissed me. Children of the sun, of their own sun—oh how beautiful they were! I have never seen such beauty in man on our planet. Only in our youngest children could one, perhaps, detect a distant and very faint reflection of this beauty. The eyes of these happy people shone with a clear light. Their faces were aglow with wisdom and intelligence matured into serenity, but their expression was gay; their words and voices rang with child-like joy. Oh, I instantly understood all, all, the moment I looked into their faces! This was an earth undefiled by sin, inhabited by people who had not sinned; they dwelt in a paradise just like the one in which our ancestors, so the legends of all mankind say, had once dwelt before they knew sin, with the only difference that the whole of this earth was one great paradise. These people, laughing happily, clung to me and caressed me; they led me away and every one of them showed eagerness to comfort me. They did not question me about anything at all, they seemed to know all, and were anxious to drive the suffering from my face.

IV

I repeat, you see: let it be nothing but a dream. But the sensation of being loved by those innocent and beautiful people will remain with me for ever, and even now I can feel their love pouring down on me from up there. I have seen them with my own eyes, have known them and been convinced; I have loved them and, afterwards, suffered for them. Oh, I realized from the first that I should never be able to understand them at all in many things; for instance, it appeared inexplicable to me, a modern Russian progressive and wretched citizen of St. Petersburg, that, knowing so much, they did not possess our science. But I soon realized that their knowledge was enriched and stimulated by other penetrations than ours, and that their aspirations were also quite different from ours. They desired nothing and were content, they did not strive to know life the way we strive to probe its depths, because their life was consummate. But their knowledge was finer and more profound than our science, for our science attempts to explain the meaning of life. Science itself strives to fathom it in order to teach others how to live; while *they* knew how to live without the help of science, I saw it but I could not understand this knowledge of theirs. They showed their trees to me, and I failed to appreciate the depth of the love with which they gazed at them: it was as if they were speaking to beings like themselves. And do you know, I may not be wrong if I tell you that they did speak to them. Yes, they had found a common tongue and I am convinced the trees understood them. This was the way they treated all Nature—the beasts who lived in peace with them, never attacking them and loving them, conquered by the people's own love for them. They pointed out the stars to me and spoke to me about them, saying things I could not understand, but I am positive they had some tie with those heavenly bodies, a living tie, not spiritual alone. Oh no, these people did not insist that I should understand them, they loved me as it was, but then I knew that they, too, would never understand me and so hardly spoke to them about our earth. I only kissed the earth they lived on and without words adored them, and they saw it and permitted themselves to be adored, unashamed of my adoration, for their own love was great. They felt no pang for me when, moved to tears, I sometimes kissed their feet, joyfully certain in my heart of the infinite love with which they would reciprocate my emotion. I sometimes asked myself in bewilderment: how was it that they never insulted one like me, never roused one like me to feelings of jealousy or envy? I asked myself again and again, how did I, a braggart and a liar, refrain from telling them of all my acquired knowledge of which they naturally had no inkling, from wishing to impress them with it, if only because I loved them? They were gay and frolicsome like children. They wandered about their beautiful groves and forests, singing their beautiful songs, eating light food—the fruit of their trees, the honey of their woods, and the milk of the beasts devoted to them. They toiled but little to procure their food and clothing. They loved and begot children, but never did I detect any signs of that *cruel* sensuality in them, which almost everyone falls victim to on our earth, one and all, and which serves as the sole source of almost all the sins of mankind on our earth. They welcomed the children born to them as new participants in their bliss. There were no quarrels or jealousy among them, and they did not even understand the meaning of these words. Their children were the children of all of them, for they formed one family. Sickness was very rare, though there was death; but their old people died peacefully; they seemed to fall asleep, blessing and smiling upon the ones they were taking leave of, themselves carrying away the clear smiles of those surrounding them in farewell. I saw no grief or tears then, only love multiplied as it were to ecstasy, but an ecstasy that was serene, contemplative and consummate. It was as if they kept in touch with their dead even after their death, and that their earthly ties were unsevered by death. They hardly understood me when I asked them if they believed in life eternal, for evidently their faith in it was so implicit it presented no problem to them. They had no churches, but they had a vital, close and constant association with the Sum of the universe; they had no creed, but instead they had the unshakable knowledge that, when their earthly bliss was consummated to the ultimate extent of its earthly nature, all of them—the living and the dead—would come into even closer contact with the Sum of the universe. They looked forward to that day with eagerness but with no impatience or morbid longing. It seemed rather that they were already carrying a foretaste of it in their hearts, sharing it with one another. Before going to sleep at night they would sing, their voices blending in true and blissful harmony. Their songs spoke of all that the passing day had granted them to feel, they hallowed it and bid it farewell. They hallowed nature, earth, sea and woods. They were fond of making up songs about one another, praising one another like children; they were the simplest of songs, but they came from the heart and stirred other hearts. Why songs alone? Their very lives were spent admiring one another. It was a sort of infatuation with one another, universal and complete. However, some of their other songs, solemn and exultant, I hardly understood at all. While understanding the words, I could never grasp their full meaning. It remained inaccessible to my intellect, as it were, yet instinctively my heart grew more and more responsive to it. I often told them that I had foreglimpsed this long, long ago; that all this happiness and glory had stirred a chord of anguished longing in me while on our own planet, mounting at times to unbearable sorrow; that I had foreglimpsed all of them and their glory in the dreams of my heart and the visions of my mind; that often I could not watch the sun go down on our earth without tears. . . . That my hatred for the people on our earth always held sadness: why could I not hate them without loving them, why could I not help forgiving them, and why was there sadness in my love for them;

why could I not love them without hating them? They listened to me, and I saw that they could not comprehend what I was telling them, but I was not sorry I had told them for I knew that they appreciated to the full the great yearning I felt for the ones I had left behind. When they turned their dear, loving gaze on me, when I felt that with them my heart became as innocent and truthful as theirs, it sufficed me, and I was not sorry I did not understand them. I was speechless with the fulness of life, and could only worship them in silence.

Oh, everyone laughs in my face now and says that one could never dream of all those details I am narrating now, that in my dream I could have seen and felt nothing but a mere sensation of something conceived by my own heart in delirium, and as for the details I must have made them up on awakening. And when I admitted to them that it may really have been so—oh Lord, the way they laughed in my face, the fun they had at my expense! Yes, of course, I was overcome by the mere sensation of my dream, and that alone survived in my wounded, bleeding heart: as for the actual images and shapes, that is, those I had really seen in my dream, they were so perfect in their harmony, charm and beauty and were so true, that our feeble words naturally failed me to describe them on awakening, and they were bound to become blurred in my mind. Therefore, I may indeed have been compelled to make up the details afterwards though unconsciously, distorting them of course, especially since I was so impatient and eager to give them some sort of expression. But then how could I doubt the truth of my words? It was a thousand times better perhaps, brighter and happier than I am telling it. Granted it was a dream, but all of this had been, it had to be. Do you know, I shall tell you a secret: it may not have been a dream at all! Because something happened next, something so horribly true that it could never come to one even in a dream. Granted, my heart conceived that dream, but could my heart alone have been able to conceive that appalling reality which befell me next? How could I have made it up by myself, how could my heart prompt that dream? Surely my shallow heart and my whimsical, wretched mind could not have been elevated to such revelations of the truth? Oh, judge for yourselves: I have concealed it until now, but now I shall disclose this truth as well. The fact is that I . . . I corrupted them all!

V

Yes, yes, it ended in my corrupting them all! I do not know how it could have happened, but I remember perfectly that it did. My dream sped across thousands of years and left with me only an impression of it as a whole. I only know that it was I who caused their downfall. Like a malignant trichina, an atom of the plague afflicting whole kingdoms, so I spread contamination through all that happy earth, sinless before I came to it. They learned to lie and came to love lying and came to know the beauty of lies. Oh, it may have begun quite *innocently*, with laughter, coquetry, playful love, or it really may have been the atom of lying seeping into their hearts and appealing to them. Soon after, sensuality was born, sensuality conceived jealousy, and jealousy conceived cruelty. . . . Oh, I don't know, I can't remember, but soon, very soon blood was spilt for the first time: they were astounded and horrified, and began to separate and go different ways. They formed unions, but the unions were inimical to one another. Reproaches and recriminations began. They came to know shame and shame was made a virtue. They learned the meaning of honor, and each union flew its own colors. They became cruel to their beasts who retreated from them into the forests and turned hostile. A struggle ensued for division, for sovereignty, for personal prominence, for thine and mine. They now spoke different tongues. They tasted of sorrow and came to love sorrow, they thirsted for sufferings and said that only through suffering could Truth be attained. And then science was introduced. When they grew evil, they began to talk of fraternity and humanity, and they understood these ideas. When they grew criminal they invented justice and in order to maintain it prescribed for themselves voluminous codes of law, and to add security to these codes they erected a guillotine. They had but a vague memory of what they had lost, and even refused to believe that once they had been innocent and happy. The very thought that they could have once been so happy made them laugh, and they called it a dream. They could not even envisage it in images and shapes, but strangely and miraculously, though they had lost all faith in their former happiness, calling it a fairy-tale, they so wanted to become innocent and happy again that they succumbed to their heartfelt wish like children and, deifying this wish, they put up numerous temples and began to pray to their own idea, or rather their "wish," knowing full well that it could never come true or be granted to them, but adoring and worshipping it in tears none the less. And yet, if it had been possible to restore them to the innocent and happy realm they had lost, or if someone could have given them a glimpse of it again and asked them whether they would like to come back to it, they would have probably refused. They told me: "Let us be deceitful, evil and unjust, but we *know* it, we weep over it, and torment ourselves for it, and the punishment we inflict upon ourselves is even harsher perhaps than that which will be meted out to us by the merciful Judge who will sit in judgement over us and whose name we do not know. We possess science, and through it we shall seek and find the Truth once again, and this time we shall apprehend it consciously. Knowledge is superior to feeling, consciousness of life is superior to life. Science will give us wisdom, wisdom will determine the laws, and knowledge of the laws of happiness is superior to happiness." This is what they said to me, and after saying it each one loved himself above all others, nor could he have done differently. Each one protected his ego so jealously, that he directed all his strivings towards humiliating and belittling the ego of others: and this became his life work. Next came slavery, there was even voluntary slavery: the weak willingly submitted to the strong only so they should help them to crush those even weaker than themselves. There were the righteous who came to these people and in tears spoke to them of their arrogance, of their loss of all sense of measure and harmony, all shame. But the righteous were mocked and stoned. Holy blood dyed the thresholds of temples. Men appeared in their stead who began to contrive how best to unite everyone once again but in such a manner that each should continue loving himself above all others and yet should not stand in the others' way, so that all could once more live together in apparently good agreement. Great wars were fought because of this idea. Though engaged in warfare, the fighters firmly believed that science, wisdom and the instinct of self-preservation would eventually force mankind to unite into a society that was concordant and sensible, and in the meantime, to speed matters up, the "wise" tried to exterminate the unbelievers in their idea and the "unwise" as quickly as possible so they should not impede the idea's triumph. But the instinct of self-preservation soon began to weaken, and men pandering to their arrogance or sensuality demanded outright: all or nothing. To acquire all they resorted to crime and if that failed— to suicide. Religions were next introduced with a cult of non-existence and self-destruction for the sake of eternal peace in non-entity. The people were at last worn out with their senseless toil, and suffering shadowed their faces; and they proclaimed that suffering was beauty, for in suffering alone lay thought. They extolled suffering in their songs. I walked among them, wringing my hands and weeping over them; my love for them was even greater perhaps than before when their faces showed no suffering and they were innocent and so beautiful. I came to love the earth defiled by them even more than I did when it was a paradise, solely because grief had come to it. Alas, I have always loved sorrow and grief, but for my own self, for myself alone, while over them I wept in pity. I held my arms out to them in despair, accusing, cursing and despising myself. I told them that I had done it all, I alone; that it was I who brought them this germ of corruption, iniquity and deceit. I implored them to crucify me, I taught them how to make the cross. I could not, I had not the strength to kill myself, but I wanted to suffer at their hands, I longed for suffering, longed for my blood to be drained—drop by drop in these sufferings. But they just laughed at me and finally came to regard me as a saintly fool. They made excuses for me, saying that they had received only what they had been asking for, and that all they had now could not have been otherwise. At last they declared that I was becoming a danger to them, and that they would lock me up in the mad-house if I did not keep quiet. At this, sorrow gripped my heart so fiercely that I could not breathe, I felt that I was dying, and then . . . that was when I woke up.

It was already morning, or rather day had not yet dawned but it was after five. I awoke in my armchair; my candle had burnt out, the captain's room was locked in sleep, and a silence unusual for our house reigned about me. I instantly leapt to my feet in amazement: nothing even remotely like this had ever happened to me before, not in any of the trifling details that did not really matter such as falling asleep in my chair, for instance. And suddenly, as I stood there recovering my senses, I saw my revolver lying all ready and loaded before me. With a quick thrust I pushed it away. No, give me life now, life! I raised my arms and invoked the eternal Truth, or rather wept, for all my being was roused to exultation, immeasurable exultation. Yes, I wanted to live and spread the word. My resolution to preach came on the instant, to preach now and for ever, of course. I shall preach, I must preach—what? Truth. For I have seen it, seen it with my own eyes, seen it in all its glory.

And so I have been spreading the word ever since! What is more, the ones who laugh at me are dearer to me now than all the others. Why it is so I do not know nor can explain, but let it be so. They say that I am floundering already, that is, if I am floundering so badly now how do I expect to go on? It's perfectly true, I am floundering and it may become even worse as I go on. There is no doubt that I will indeed flounder and lose my way more than once before I learn how best to preach, that is with what words and by what deeds, for it is a very difficult mission. It's all as clear as day to me even now, you know; but, listen, who of us does not flounder? And yet everyone is going towards the same thing, at least all strive for the same thing, all—from the wise man to the meanest wretch —only all follow different paths. It's an old truth, but here's something new: I cannot flounder too badly, you know. Because I have seen the Truth, I have seen it and I know that people can be beautiful and happy without losing their ability to dwell on this earth. I cannot and will not believe that evil is man's natural state. And yet it's just this conviction of mine that makes them all laugh at me. How can I help believing it, though: I have seen the Truth, it was not a figment of my imagination or my mind, I have seen it, seen it, and its *living image* has taken hold of my soul for ever. I have seen it in such consummate wholeness that I refuse to believe that it cannot live among men. And so, how could I lose my way? I shall stray once or twice of course, I shall perhaps even use the words of others sometimes, but not for long: the living image of what I have seen will remain with me always, it will always correct me and put me straight. I am full of vigor and strength. I shall go and preach, be it for a thousand years. Do you know, I first wanted to conceal the fact that I had corrupted them all, but that would have been a mistake—a mistake already, you see. Truth whispered in my ear that I was *lying*, Truth saved me and showed me the way. But I do not know how to build a paradise, for I do not know how to put it in words. I lost the words on awakening. At least all the most important words, the most essential. Never mind; I shall go on my way and preach tirelessly, because I have seen it with my own eyes, even though I cannot describe what I have seen. That is something the mockers fail to understand. They say: "It was just a dream, ravings and hallucinations." Oh dear! Is that clever? And they are so proud of themselves, too. A dream, they say. But what is a dream? Isn't our life a dream? I shall go further: let it never, never come true, let paradise never be (after all, I do realise that!) I shall go and spread the word anyway. And yet it could be done so simply: in a single day, in a *single hour* everything would be settled! One should love others as one loves oneself, that is the main thing, that is all, nothing else, absolutely nothing else is needed, and then one would instantly know how to go about it. It's nothing but an old truth, repeated and read billions of times, and yet it has not taken root. "Consciousness of life is superior to life, knowledge of the laws of happiness is superior to happiness"—this is what we must fight against. And I shall. If only everyone wanted it, it could be all done at once.

* * *

As for that little girl, I have found her . . . I shall go! Yes, I shall go!

LEO TOLSTOY

God Sees the Truth, but Waits

I N THE CITY OF VLADIMIR lived a young merchant, Aksenov. He had two shops and a house.

Aksenov was brown-haired, curly-headed, and handsome, very fond of fun and singing. From youth Aksenov drank a lot, and when he got drunk he was riotous, but since he got married he had given up drinking and such things happened to him only rarely.

One summer Aksenov went to the fair in Nizhny. When he began to say good-bye to his family, his wife said to him:

"Ivan Dmitrievich, don't go today; I had a bad dream about you."

Aksenov laughed and said:

"You're always afraid I'll go carousing at the fair."

His wife said:

"I don't know myself what I fear, but I had a bad dream—I dreamed that you were returning from town, took off your hat, and I look: your head is all grey."

Aksenov laughed.

"Well, that's lucky. You watch, when I sell out everything I'll bring expensive gifts."

Translated by CARL R. PROFFER.

And he said good-bye to his family and left.

Halfway there he met a merchant he knew and stopped to spend the night with him. They drank some tea together and went to bed in two adjoining rooms. Aksenov did not like to sleep long; he woke up in the middle of the night, and since it would be easier to travel while it was cool he woke up his driver and ordered the horses harnessed. Then he went to the owner's small black hut, settled accounts, and left.

Having driven about forty versts he again stopped to feed the horses, he rested in the entry of the inn, and at dinner he went out onto the porch and ordered the samovar set up; he got out his guitar and started to play; suddenly a troika with a bell drives into the yard, and an official and two soldiers get out of the carriage; he walks up to Aksenov and asks who he is and where he's from. Aksenov tells him everything and asks him if he wouldn't like to drink some tea with him. Only the official persists with his interrogation: "Where did you spend last night? Alone or with a merchant? Did you see the merchant in the morning? Why did you leave the inn early?" Aksenov wondered why he was questioning him about everything; he told him everything as it was and then says, "Why are you interrogating me like this? I'm not a thief, not some robber. I'm traveling on my business, and there's no reason to question me."

Then the official called the soldiers and said:

"I'm the district police officer and I'm questioning you because the merchant with whom you spent last night had his throat cut. Show your things; you two search him."

They went into the hut, took his trunk and a bag, started unstrapping it and searching. Suddenly the police officer took a knife out of the bag and shouted:

"Whose knife is this?"

Aksenov looked and saw that they had gotten a bloody knife from his bag, and he was frightened.

"And why is there blood on the knife?"

Aksenov wanted to answer, but he could not utter a word.

"I . . . I don't know . . . I . . . knife . . . I . . . not mine. . . ."

Then the police officer said:

"In the morning the merchant was found in bed with his throat cut. There was no one besides you to do it. The hut was locked from the inside, and there was no one except you in the hut. Here's this bloody knife in your bag, and one can tell from your face. Tell how you killed him and how much money you stole."

Aksenov swore that it was not he that did it, that he had not seen the merchant after he drank tea with him, that he had his own 8000 rubles, that the knife was not his. But his voice broke, his face was pale, and like a guilty person he shook all over from fear.

The police officer called the soldiers, ordered him tied and carried in the cart. When they dumped him in the cart with his feet tied, Aksenov crossed himself and began to cry. They confiscated Aksenov's goods and money, sent him to prison in the nearest town. They sent to Vladimir to find out what kind of person Aksenov was, and all of the merchants and other inhabitants of Vladimir attested that from youth Aksenov had drunk and caroused, but he was a good man. Then they began to try him. They tried him for killing a Ryazan merchant and stealing 20,000 rubles.

His wife despaired over him and did not know what to think. All of her children were still small, and one was still at breast. She took them all with her and went to the town where her husband was kept in prison. At first they did not admit her, but then she petitioned the chief officials, and she was taken to her husband. When she saw him in prison clothes, in chains, together with robbers, she fell to the ground and could not come to her senses for a long time. Then she placed her children around her, sat down beside him, and started telling him about domestic matters and asking him about everything that had happened to him. He told her everything. She said:

"What will we do now?"

He said:

"We must petition the Tsar. It is impossible to ruin an innocent man!"

The wife said that she had already submitted a petition to the Tsar, but that the petition had not gone through. Aksenov said nothing and just lowered his head. Then his wife said:

"It wasn't for nothing, remember, I had that dream then, that you had gotten grey. Now you really have turned grey—from grief. You shouldn't have gone then."

And she began to run her fingers through his hair and said:

"Vanya, dearest friend, tell your wife the truth: wasn't it you that did it?"

Aksenov said: "And you suspect me too!" He covered his face with his hands and began to cry. Then a soldier came and said that the wife and children had to leave. And Aksenov said good-bye to his family for the last time.

When his wife left Aksenov began to remember what they had said. When he remembered that his wife suspected him too and asked him if he had killed the merchant, he said to himself: "It's obvious that except God no one can know the truth, and I only had to ask Him and expect mercy only from Him." And after that time Aksenov ceased submitting petitions, ceased hoping, and only prayed to God.

Aksenov was sentenced to be punished with the lash and exiled to penal servitude. And they did this.

He was flogged with a lash and then, when the wounds from the lash healed, he was marched to Siberia with other convicts.

Aksenov lived in Siberia as a convict for twenty-six years. The hair on his head got as white as snow, and his beard grew long, thin, and grey. All of his joviality disappeared. He got hunched over, started walking quietly, spoke little, never laughed, and often prayed to God.

In prison Aksenov learned to sew boots, and with the money he earned he bought the *Lives of the Saints* and read them when it was light in the prison; and on holidays he went to the prison church, read the Apostles, and sang in the choir—his voice was still good. The authorities liked Aksenov for his meekness, and his fellow prisoners respected him and called him "grandfather" and "a man of God." When there were petitions from the prison, his comrades always sent Aksenov to ask the authorities, and when there were quarrels among the convicts they always came to Aksenov to judge them.

No one wrote Aksenov letters from home, and he did not know whether his wife and children were alive.

Once new convicts were brought to prison. In the evening all of the old convicts gathered around the new ones and started asking them who was from what town or village and what they were sentenced for. Aksenov also sat down on a plank-bed near the newcomers and, his head lowered, listened to what they were saying. One of the new convicts was a tall, healthy old man of about sixty, with a trimmed grey beard. He told what they had taken him for. He said:

"Right, brothers, I ended up here for no reason. I untied a coachman's horse from his sledge. Caught me and said I stole it. But I said: 'I just wanted to get home faster, I let the horse go. And the coachman is my friend. All right?' I said. 'No,' they say, 'you stole it.' But they didn't know how or why I stole it. There were things I should long ago have ended up here for, but they couldn't convict me, and now they've marched me here illegally. But I'm lying; I've been in Siberia before, but I didn't hang around long."

"And where are you from?" asked one of the convicts.

"My family's from the city of Vladimir, we're small merchants there. My name's Makar, Semyonovich to be formal."

Aksenov raised his head and asked:

"Tell me, Semyonych, have you heard tell of the Aksenovs in Vladimir? Are they alive?"

"How could I not hear? They're rich merchants, though their father's in Siberia. Apparently he's just like us, a sinner. And you, grandfather, why are you here?"

Aksenov did not like to talk about his misfortune; he sighed and said:

"For my sins I've been in penal servitude for twenty-six years."

Makar Semyonov said:

"But for what kind of sins?"

Aksenov said: "They must merit this," and did not want to tell anything more, but his other fellow prisoners told the new one how Aksenov came to be in Siberia. They told how on the road someone had killed a merchant and planted a knife on Aksenov, and how he had been unjustly condemned for that.

When Makar Semyonov heard this, he looked at Aksenov, banged his hands on his knees and said:

"Well, a miracle! That's a miracle! You've gotten old, grandfather!"

They started asking him why he was surprised and where he had seen Aksenov; but Makar Semyonov did not answer, he said only:

"Fellows, it's a miracle we've had to meet here!"

And with those words it occurred to Aksenov that this man might know who killed the merchant. He said:

"Maybe you've heard about this affair before, Semyonych, or you've seen me before?"

"How could I not hear? The world's full of rumors. But the affair was long ago, what I heard I've forgotten," said Makar Semyonov.

"Maybe you heard who killed the merchant?" asked Aksenov.

Makar Semyonov laughed and said:

"Why, apparently, the one in whose bag the knife was found killed him. If someone planted the knife on you, he's not a thief till he's caught. And anyhow how could he plant a knife in your bag? Why it was under your head. You would have heard."

As soon as Aksenov heard these words he thought that this man himself killed the merchant. He got up and walked away. Aksenov could not sleep all that night. He became very depressed and he started to imagine things; first he imagined his wife as she was when she saw him off to the fair for the last time. So he saw her as if before him; he saw her face and eyes, and he heard her talking to him and laughing. Then he imagined his children as they were then—small, one in a fur coat, the other at breast. And he remembered himself as he was then—jovial, young; he remembered how he sat on the little porch of the inn where he was arrested and played his guitar, and how jovial he felt then. And he recalled the punishment place where he was flogged and the executioner, and the people around, the chains, and the convicts, and his entire twenty-six year prison life, and he recalled his old age. And Aksenov became so depressed that he was ready to kill himself.

"And all because of this villain!" thought Aksenov.

And he felt such fury against Makar Semyonov that even if he undid himself he wanted to avenge himself. During the day he did not go near Makar Semyonov and he did not look at him.

Two weeks passed like this. Aksenov could not sleep at night, and he was so depressed he did not know what to do with himself.

Once, at night, he was walking around the prison and saw some earth pour out from under one of the plank-beds. He stopped to look. Suddenly Makar Semyonov hopped out from under the plank-bed and with a frightened face looked at Aksenov. Aksenov wanted to walk on so as not to see him; but Makar grabbed him by the arm and told him how he was digging a tunnel under the wall and how he carried out the dirt in his boot tops every day and dropped it on the street when they were being driven out to work. He said:

"Just be quiet old man, and I'll take you out too. But if you tell, they'll flog me, and I won't let you off, I'll kill you."

When Aksenov saw his villain, he trembled all over from fury, yanked his arm away and said:

"I've no reason to leave, and you've none to kill me—you killed me a long time ago. And whether I inform on you or not—I'll do as God disposes me."

When they were leading the convicts out to work the next day, the soldiers noticed that Makar Semyonov was dropping dirt, started searching the prison and found the hole. The warden came to the prison and started questioning everyone: who had dug the hole? Everyone denied knowing anything. Those who knew did not give Makar Semyonov away because they knew that they would flog him half to death for it. Then the warden turned to Aksenov. He knew that Aksenov was an honest man and said:

"Old man, you are truthful; tell me before God who did this."

Makar Semyonov stood as if there was nothing the matter, and he looked at the warden, and he did not glance around at Aksenov. Aksenov's hands and lips were trembling, and for a long time he could not utter a word. He was thinking: "Why should I forgive him and protect him when he ruined me? Let him pay for my torments. But if I tell on him, they really will flog him. And what if I suspect him wrongly? And so what? Will it make me feel any better?"

The warden said again: "Well, old man, tell the truth. Who dug it?"

Aksenov glanced at Makar Semyonov and said:

"I did not see and do not know."

So they did not find out who dug it.

The next night when Aksenov lay down on his plank-bed and was just dozing off, he heard someone come up and sit down at his feet. He looked into the darkness and recognized Makar.

Aksenov said:

"What else do you need from me? What are you doing here?"

Makar Semyonov remained silent. Aksenov raised up and said.

"What do you want? Go away! Or else I'll call a soldier."

Makar Semyonov bent close to Aksenov and said in a whisper: "Ivan Dmitrievich, forgive me!"

Aksenov said:

"What is there to forgive you?"

"I killed the merchant and I planted the knife on you. I intended to kill you too, but there was a noise outside. I planted the knife in your bag and climbed out the window." Aksenov remained silent and did not know what to say. Makar Semyonov got down off the bed, bowed down to the earth and said:

"Ivan Dmitrievich, forgive me, for the sake of God, forgive me. I will confess that I killed the merchant—you will be pardoned. You will return home."

Aksenov said:

"It's easy for you to talk, but what is it like for me to suffer! Where will I go now? My wife has died, the children forgotten; there's nowhere for me to go. . . ."

Makar Semyonov did not get up from the floor; he beat his head against the ground and said:

"Ivan Dmitrych, forgive me! It would be easier for me to be flogged with a lash than to look at you now. . . . And you still pitied me—you didn't tell on me. Forgive me, for the sake of Christ. Forgive me, cursed villain that I am!" and he began to sob.

When Aksenov heard Makar Semyonov crying, he began to cry himself and said:

"God will forgive you; perhaps I am a hundred times worse than you!" And suddenly his soul felt lighter. And he ceased being homesick, and he did not want to go anywhere outside the prison, but he just thought about his last hour.

Makar Semyonov did not obey Aksenov and confessed to the crime. When permission came for Aksenov to return, Aksenov had already died.

LEO TOLSTOY

The Death of Ivan Ilych

I

D URING A RECESS in the Melvinsky case in the large building of
the Law Courts, the members and prosecutor gathered in
Ivan Egorovich Shebek's office, and a conversation about the celebrated Krasov case began. Fedor Vasilievich grew angry, demon-
strating that it was not in their jurisdiction; Ivan Egorovich main-
tained his own position, while Peter Ivanovich, who had not gotten
into the argument in the beginning, took no part in it—he was
looking through the *News* which had just been delivered.

"Gentleman!" he said, "Ivan Ilych has died."

"Really?"

"Here, read it," he said to Fedor Vasilievich, handing him the
fresh paper which still smelled of ink.

Printed in a black border was: 'With profound sorrow Praskovia
Fedorovna Golovina informs relatives and acquaintances of the
passing of her beloved husband, member of the Department of
Justice, Ivan Ilych Golovin, which occurred on February 4, 1882.
The funeral will be at one o'clock in the afternoon Friday.'

Translated by CARL R. PROFFER.

Ivan Ilych had been a colleague of the assembled gentlemen and they all liked him. He had been ill for several weeks already and it was said his disease was incurable. His position was held open for him, but it was thought that in case of his death Alekseev would perhaps be appointed to his position, and to Alekseev's position— either Vinnikov or Shtabel. Thus, on hearing about the death of Ivan Ilych, the first thought of each of the gentlemen assembled in the office was about what significance this death could have for the transfer or promotion of the members themselves or their acquaintances.

"Now I will surely get Shtabel's position or Vinnikov's," thought Fedor Vasilievich. "It was promised me long ago, and the promotion means a raise of eight hundred rubles besides the expense account."

"Now I will have to apply for my brother-in-law's move from Kaluga," thought Peter Ivanovich. "My wife will be very happy. Now she won't be able to say that I've never done anything for her relatives."

"I didn't think he would ever make it out of bed," said Peter Ivanovich aloud. "It's a pity."

"Just what was it he had?"

"The doctors couldn't diagnose it. That is, they diagnosed it, but differently. When I saw him last time, it seemed to me he would recover."

"And I hadn't visited him since the holidays. I kept intending to go."

"Did he have any property?"

"I think his wife had something small. But something insignificant."

"And now it'll be necessary to go there. They lived so terribly far away."

"Far from you that is. Everything is far from you."

"He cannot forgive me for living on the other side of the river," said Peter Ivanovich, smiling at Shebek. And they began to talk about the distances between various parts of the city, and they went back to the meeting.

Besides the considerations aroused by this death in each about transfers and possible changes in duties which could result from it, the fact itself of the death of a close acquaintance aroused in all of those who had learned of it, as always, a feeling of gladness that "he died and not I."

Each one thought or felt, "How about that; he died, and I didn't." But at the same time the closer acquaintances, the so-called friends of Ivan Ilych, involuntarily thought also of the fact that now they would have to fulfill the very boring duties of decorum and go to the funeral service and make a visit of condolence to the widow.

Closest of all were Fedor Vasilievich and Peter Ivanovich.

Peter Ivanovich had been a fellow student at law school and considered himself indebted to Ivan Ilych.

Having informed his wife at dinner of the news of Ivan Ilych's death and the consideration about the possibility of moving his brother-in-law to their district, Peter Ivanovich, without lying down to take a rest, put on his frock-coat and drove to Ivan Ilych's.

At the entrance to Ivan Ilych's apartment stood a carriage and two cabs. Downstairs near the cloak-stand in the hall stood a gilded coffin-lid decorated with tassels and cord which had been polished with metal powder. Two ladies in black were taking off their fur coats. One, Ivan Ilych's sister, was familiar; the other lady was not. Peter Ivanovich's comrade Schwartz was coming downstairs and seeing Peter Ivanovich enter, he stopped on the top step and winked at him as if saying, "Ivan Ilych stupidly arranged things, not like you and I would do."

Schwartz's face with its English side whiskers and his whole body in a frock-coat had, as always, an air of elegant solemnity; and this solemnity, which always contradicted the character of Schwartz's playfulness, had a special salt here. So thought Peter Ivanovich.

Peter Ivanovich let the ladies go ahead of him and slowly followed them up the stairs. Schwartz did not start down, but remained upstairs. Peter Ivanovich understood why: he obviously wanted to arrange where to play bridge that evening. The ladies went up the stairs to the widow, but Schwartz with firm, seriously pursed lips and a playful glance, indicated with a movement of the eyebrows that Peter Ivanovich should go to the right into the dead man's room.

Peter Ivanovich entered, as is always the case, with uncertainty about what he was supposed to do there. The one thing he knew was that it never hurts to cross oneself in these cases. He wasn't quite sure whether one is also supposed to make obeisances at the same time, and therefore chose a middle course: entering the room he began to cross himself and made a slight movement resembling an obeisance. At the same time, so far as the movements of his arms and head allowed, he glanced around the room. Two young men, one a high-school student, probably nephews, were walking out of the room crossing themselves. An old woman was standing motionless. And a lady with strangely raised eyebrows was saying something to her in a whisper. A vigorous, resolute subdeacon in a coat was reading something loudly, with an expression which precluded any contradiction; the peasant, Gerasim, crossing in front of Peter Ivanovich with light steps, was spreading something on the floor. Seeing this Peter Ivanovich immediately became aware of the slight odor of the decomposing body. During his last visit to Ivan Ilych, Peter Ivanovich had seen this peasant in the study; he was performing the duty of sick nurse, and Ivan Ilych especially loved him. Peter Ivanovich kept on crossing himself and making slight obeisances in a middle direction between the coffin, the subdeacon, and the ikons on the table in the corner. Then, when this movement of crossing the hand seemed to have gone on too long, he paused and began to examine the dead man.

The dead man lay, as dead men always lie, especially heavily, his stiffened limbs sunk dead in the cushions of the coffin, with his head forever bowed on the pillow; and sticking out, as they stick out on all dead men, were his yellow waxen forehead with bald spots on the sunken temples and his protruding nose which seemed to be pressing on the upper lip. He had changed much, had grown even thinner since Peter Ivanovich had seen him, but like all dead men his face was more handsome and, this is the main thing, more significant. On his face was an expression which said that what was supposed to have been done had been done, and had been done correctly. Besides that there was in his expression a reproach and a reminder to the living. This reminder seemed out of place to Peter Ivanovich, or at least inapplicable to him. Something became unpleasant to him, and therefore Peter Ivanovich hurriedly crossed himself and, as it seemed to him, too hurriedly, inconsonantly with the rules of decorum, turned around and walked to the door. Schwartz was waiting for him in the next room, his legs spread wide apart and both hands playing with his top hat behind his back. One glance at the playful, well-groomed, and elegant figure of Schwartz refreshed Peter Ivanovich. Peter Ivanovich understood that he, Schwartz, stood above this and would not surrender to depressing impressions. Just his look said: the incident of Ivan Ilych's funeral can in no way serve as sufficient cause for calling the order of the session broken, that is, that nothing can prevent us from snapping through a deck of cards as we unseal it and the servant sets up four unburned candles; in general there is no basis for supposing that this incident could prevent us from spending this evening pleasantly too. Indeed, he said this in a whisper to Peter Ivanovich as he was passing, suggesting that they get together for a game at Fedor Vasilievich's. But, apparently, it was not Peter Ivanovich's fate to play bridge that evening. Praskovia Fedorovna, a short, fat woman who in spite of all her efforts to the contrary grew broader from the shoulders downward, dressed all in black, with her head covered with lace and the same strangely raised eyebrows as the woman who had been standing opposite the coffin, emerged from her room with some other ladies; and having accompanied them to the door of the dead man's room, she said:

"The service will begin immediately; go in."

Bowing indefinitely, Schwartz stopped, evidently neither accepting nor declining this proposal. Recognizing Peter Ivanovich, Praskovia Fedorovna sighed, walked right up to him, took his hand and said:

"I know that you were a true friend of Ivan Ilych . . ." and looked at him expecting him to make some action consonant with these words.

Peter Ivanovich knew that just as there one was supposed to cross oneself, so here one was supposed to shake her hand, sigh, and say, "Believe me. . . ." And he did this. And having done it he felt that the desired result had been achieved: that he was touched and she was touched.

"Let us go before they begin in there; I have to talk to you," said the widow. "Give me your arm."

Peter Ivanovich offered his arm, and they headed for the inner rooms, past Schwartz who winked sadly at Peter Ivanovich. "There goes the bridge! Don't object, we'll find another partner. Maybe you can be fifth when you get away," said his playful glance.

Peter Ivanovich sighed even more deeply and sadly, and Praskovia Fedorovna pressed his hand gratefully. When they entered her drawing room, which was upholstered in pink cretonne and dimly lit, they sat down by a table—she on the divan, Peter Ivanovich on a low pouffe with broken springs which yielded spasmodically under his weight. Praskovia Fedorovna wanted to warn him to sit on another chair, but she found the warning inconsonant with her situation and changed her mind. Sitting down on the pouffe Peter Ivanovich recalled how Ivan Ilych had decorated this drawing room and had consulted with him about this very same pink cretonne with green leaves. Passing the table and sitting down (in general the whole drawing room was full of knick-knacks and furniture), the widow caught the black lace of her black mantilla on the carved edge of the table. Peter Ivanovich rose to detach it, and the freed pouffe under him began to shake and push him. The widow began to detach her lace herself, and Peter Ivanovich again sat down, pressing down the rebellious pouffe under him. But the widow did not get completely detached and Peter Ivanovich again rose and again the pouffe began to rebel and even creaked. When all this was over, she took out a clean cambric handkerchief and began to cry. But the episode of the lace and the battle with the pouffe had cooled his emotions, and he sat there grown sullen. Ivan Ilych's butler Sokolov interrupted this awkward situation with a report that the location in the cemetery which Praskovia Fedorovna had designated would cost two hundred rubles. She stopped crying, and having glanced at Peter Ivanovich with the air of a victim, said in French that it was very difficult for her. Peter Ivanovich made a silent sign which expressed undoubting assurance that it could not be otherwise.

"Please smoke," she said with a voice which was at once magnanimous and crushed, and she busied herself questioning Sokolov about the price of the location. Lighting a cigarette, Peter Ivanovich listened as she interrogated him very circumstantially about different prices of ground and decided which should be taken. Besides that, when she finished on the location, she also made arrangements for the singers. Sokolov left.

"I do everything myself," she told Peter Ivanovich, moving to one side the albums which lay on the table; and noticing that his ashes threatened the table, she quickly moved an ashtray in front of Peter Ivanovich and began to speak, "I find it a pretense to assure people that because of my grief I cannot occupy myself with practical matters. On the contrary if anything can if not console, at least distract me—it is taking care of things which concern him." She again reached for her handkerchief as if she intended to cry, and suddenly, as if mastering her emotion, shook herself and began to speak calmly.

"However, I have one matter which concerns you."

Peter Ivanovich bowed, keeping control of the pouffe springs which immediately shook beneath him.

"The last days he suffered terribly."

"He suffered much?" asked Peter Ivanovich.

"Oh, terribly! Not the last minutes, but the last hours he screamed incessantly. For three days in a row he screamed unceasingly. It was unbearable. I cannot understand how I bore it; you could hear him behind three closed doors. Oh, what I bore!"

"And was he really conscious?" asked Peter Ivanovich.

"Yes," she whispered, "until the last minute. He said good-bye to us a quarter of an hour before his death and also asked that Volodya be taken away."

The thought of the suffering of a man whom he had known so closely, first as a merry little boy, as a schoolmate, then as a grown-up partner, suddenly terrified Peter Ivanovich in spite of the unpleasant awareness of his and this woman's pretense. Again he saw the forehead, the nose pressing on the lips, and he became afraid for himself.

"Three days of terrible sufferings and death. Why it could happen to me now, at any minute," he thought, and for a moment he became afraid. But immediately, he himself did not know how, the usual thought came to his rescue—that it had happened to Ivan Ilych, and not to him and that this should and could not happen to him, that in thinking this way he was surrendering to a gloomy mood which one ought not do, as was obvious from Schwartz's face. And having thus reflected, Peter Ivanovich felt reassured and began to ask with interest for details about the demise of Ivan Ilych, as if death were an event peculiar only to Ivan Ilych, and not at all peculiar to him.

After various remarks about the details of the truly terrible physical sufferings which Ivan Ilych had born (Peter Ivanovich learned of these details only from the way in which Ivan Ilych's torments acted on Praskovia Fedorovna's nerves), the widow, evidently, found it necessary to get down to business.

"Oh, Peter Ivanovich, it's so difficult, so terribly difficult, so terribly difficult,"—and she again burst out crying.

Peter Ivanovich sighed and waited while she blew her nose. When she had blown her nose he said, "Believe me . . ." and again she began talking and expressed what was evidently her main business with him. This business consisted of questions about how to get money from the government treasury on the occasion of her husband's death. She made it appear she was asking Peter Ivanovich's advice about a pension; but he saw that she already knew the smallest details, even things that he did not know—everything that could be extracted from the government treasury on the occasion of this death, but that she wanted to find out if it weren't somehow possible to extract even more money. Peter Ivanovich tried to think of some way, but when he had thought a little and out of decorum slightly upbraided our government for its niggardliness, he said that it seemed impossible to get more. Then she sighed and, evidently, began trying to think of a way to free herself of her visitor. He understood this, extinguished his cigarette, stood up, shook her hand, and went into the anteroom.

In the dining room where stood the clock which had made Ivan Ilych so happy when he bought it in an antique shop, Peter Ivanovich met a priest and a few other acquaintances who had come for the service, and he saw a pretty young woman he recognized—Ivan Ilych's daughter. She was all in black. Her waist, which was very thin, seemed even thinner. She looked gloomy, determined, almost angry. She bowed to Peter Ivanovich as if he were guilty of something. Behind the daughter, with the same offended look, stood a rich young man Peter Ivanovich knew, a court investigator, her fiancé, as he had heard. He bowed mournfully to them and wanted to go into the dead man's room when from under the stairway the figure of the schoolboy son appeared—he looked terribly much like Ivan Ilych. It was little Ivan Ilych, as Peter Ivanovich remembered him in Law School. His eyes were red from tears, and like those of all dirty-minded boys of thirteen or fourteen. When he saw Peter vanovich the little boy began to frown morosely and shamefacedly. Peter Ivanovich nodded to him and entered the dead man's room.

The service had begun—candles, moans, incense, tears, sobbing. Frowning, Peter Ivanovich stood looking down at his feet. He did not glance at the dead man once, and right to the end did not surrender to depressing influences, and he was one of the first to leave. There was no one in the anteroom. Gerasim, the butler's assistant, darted out of the deceased's room; with his strong hands he rummaged through all of the coats to find Peter Ivanovich's coat, and handed it to him.

"Well, friend Gerasim?" said Peter Ivanovich in order to say something, "It's a pity isn't it?"

"God's will. We will all be there," said Gerasim, baring his white, strong peasant's teeth, and like a man in the heat of strenuous work, he opened the door briskly, called the coachman, seated Peter Ivanovich, and jumped back to the porch as if deciding what else he should do.

It was especially pleasant for Peter Ivanovich to breathe pure air after the odor of incense, the corpse, and carbolic acid.

"Where to?" asked the coachman.

"It's not too late. I'll still drop by Fedor Vasilievich's."

And Peter Ivanovich went there. And he actually caught them at the end of the first rubber, so that it was convenient for him to sit in as the fifth.

II

The past history of Ivan Ilych's life was most simple and ordinary and most terrible.

Ivan Ilych died at forty-five, a member of the Court of Justice. He was the son of an official who had been in various ministries and departments in Petersburg and had the sort of career that gets people into a position from which, because of long past service and rank, they cannot be dismissed, even though it becomes clear that they are no good for any real responsibility; and therefore they receive specially invented fictitious places and unfictitious thousands (from six to ten) on which they live to very old ages.

Such was the privy councillor, Ilya Efimovich Golovin, the unnecessary member of various unnecessary institutions.

He had three sons. Ivan Ilych was the second son. The eldest had the same sort of career as his father, only in a different ministry, and

he had already closely approached the service age at which the sine-
cure is received. The third son was a failure. He had ruined himself
in several jobs and was now serving in the railway division: his
father and his brothers, and especially their wives, not only disliked
meeting him—they did not even remember his existence unless
it was absolutely unavoidable. His sister married Baron Gref, the
same kind of Petersburg official as his father-in-law. Ivan Ilych was
le phénix de la famille, as they said. He was not as cold and efficient
as the eldest and not as desperate as the youngest. He was the mean
between them—an intelligent, lively, pleasant and decorous man.
He was educated in Law School along with his younger brother.
The younger one did not finish; he was dismissed from the fifth
class, but Ivan Ilych finished the course well. In Law School he
was just what he was subsequently in all his life: a capable, merrily
goodhearted and sociable man who, however, was strict about ful-
filling what he considered his duty; and he considered his duty to
be what was so considered by people placed higher than he. He was
not servile either as a boy nor later as an adult, but there was the
fact that from earliest years, like a fly to light, he was attracted to
people placed higher in society; he assimilated their ways, their
views on life, and he established friendly relations with them. All
of the enthusiasms of boyhood and adolescence passed without leaving much trace; he had surrendered to both sensuality and vanity,
and—near the end, in upper classes—to liberalism, but always within
acceptable limits which his instinct accurately indicated to him.

In Law School he had committed acts which he had formerly
considered vile and which filled him with self-revulsion even as he
was committing them; but subsequently, seeing that these acts were
also committed by people of high standing and were not considered
bad by them, he didn't exactly call them good, but he completely
forgot them and was not bothered by reminiscences about them.

Having graduated from Law School in the tenth rank of the
civil service and received money for his uniforms from his father,
Ivan Ilych ordered clothes from Scharmer's, hung a medallion in-
scribed *respice finem* on his watch-chain, said good-bye to his prince
and patron, had dinner at Donon's with his comrades, and with a
fashionable new suitcase, linen, clothes, shaving and toilet appur-
tenances, and a travelling rug—all bought in the best stores—he

left for the provinces and an official position of special service to the governor which his father had gotten him.

In the provinces Ivan Ilych immediately established an easy and pleasant situation—the same as his situation at Law School. He served, made a career, and at the same time amused himself pleasantly and decorously; from time to time he traveled to country districts with commissions from his chiefs, there he comported himself with dignity both with superiors and with inferiors; and with precision and incorruptible honesty, of which he could not but feel proud, he carried out the commissions, primarily cases involving the Old Believers, which had been placed in his hands.

In official matters, in spite of his youth and proclivity for easy amusement, he was extremely reserved, punctilious, and even severe; but in society matters he was often playful and witty and always a good-natured, decorous and *bon enfant*, as his superior and his wife—with whom he was like one of the family—used to say of him.

In the provinces there was a liason with one of the women who made advances to the foppish young lawyer; and there was a milliner; and there were carousals with visiting aides-de-camp and trips to a certain outlying street after supper; and there was obsequiousness to his superior and even to the superior's wife, but all of this bore such a high tone of propriety that all of this simply came under the rubric of the French saying: *il faut que jeunesse se passe*. Everything happened with clean hands, in clean shirts, with French phrases, and—the main thing—in the highest society, consequently with the approval of people of high standing.

Thus Ivan Ilych served for five years, and then came a change in duty. New judicial institutions appeared; new people were needed.

An Ivan Ilych became this new man.

Ivan Ilych was offered the position of Court Examiner, and Ivan Ilych accepted it in spite of the fact that the position was in another district and he had to give up the relations he had established and establish new ones. Ivan Ilych's friends saw him off; they made a group photograph, handed him a silver cigarette case, and he left for his new position.

As a Court Examiner Ivan Ilych was just as *comme il faut*, decorous, able to separate his official duties from private life and inspire general respect as he had been when he was a special service official. As for the service as Examiner, it was far more interesting and attractive to Ivan Ilych than his previous job. In his previous service it had been pleasant to put on a Scharmer uniform and, with a swinging gait, walk past the trembling petitioners who were awaiting an audience and minor officials who envied him directly into his chief's office and sit down with him for tea and a cigarette; but there were few people who were directly dependent on his will. These people were police officials and Old Believers when he was sent on special commissions; and he liked to treat people who were dependent on him politely, almost as comrades, he liked to make them feel that he, who could crush them, was treating them in a simple, friendly way. There were few such people then. But now, as Court Examiner Ivan Ilych felt that everyone, everyone without exception, the most important, self-satisfied people—everyone was in his hands; and all he had to do was to write certain well-known words on a paper with a certain heading, and that important, self-satisfied person would be brought to him as an accused or a witness, and he would, if Ivan Ilych did not want to have him sit down, stand before him and answer his questions. Ivan Ilych never misused this power of his, on the contrary, he tried to soften its expression; but the consciousness of this power and the possibility of softening it were the things which created the main interest and attractiveness of his new service. In the service itself, especially during examinations, Ivan Ilych quickly acquired a way of eliminating all considerations which did not touch on his service and placing any case, no matter how complicated, in a form in which the external sides of the case would be reflected on paper and in which his personal view was totally eliminated and, most important, all required formality was observed. This work was new. And he was one of the first men to apply in practice the Code of 1864.

On moving to the new town for the position of Court Examiner Ivan Ilych made new acquaintances, connections; he held himself a new way and assumed a somewhat different tone. He held himself at a certain respectable distance from the district authorities and chose the best circle of court officials and rich gentry who lived in the town; and he assumed a tone of slight dissatisfaction with the government, of moderate liberalism and enlightened citizenship. At the same time, without changing the elegance of his toilet at all, he ceased shaving his chin and gave his beard freedom to grow wherever it pleased.

Ivan Ilych's life in the new town was very pleasant: the society which was rebelling against the Governor was genial and good, his salary was larger, and not the smallest of these pleasant things was bridge—which Ivan Ilych began to play; he had the ability to play gaily, while calculating quickly and very cleverly so that on the whole he always won.

After two years of service in the new town Ivan Ilych met his future wife. Praskovia Fedorovna Mikhel was the most attractive, intelligent, brilliant girl of the circle in which Ivan Ilych moved. Along with other amusements and diversions from his work as Examiner, Ivan Ilych established playful, easy relations with Praskovia Fedorovna.

When he was special service official Ivan Ilych usually danced, but as Court Examiner he danced as an exception. He danced in the sense that "even though there are new institutions and I am in the fifth rank, if it comes to dances I can show that in this area too I can do it better than other people." Thus, at the end of the evening he occasionally danced with Praskovia Fedorovna, and it was primarily during these dances that he conquered Praskovia Fedorovna. She fell in love with him. Ivan Ilych did not have a clear, definite intention of getting married, but when the girl fell in love with him he asked himself this question. "Indeed, why not get married?" he said to himself.

The maiden Praskovia Fedorovna was not bad looking, she was from a good gentry family; there was a bit of property. Ivan Ilych could have aspired to a more brilliant match, but this was a good match. Ivan Ilych had his salary; she, he hoped, would have as much. A good background, she was a nice, pretty and completely respectable woman. It would be as unjust to say that Ivan Ilych got married because he fell in love with his fiancée and found her sympathetic to his views on life as it would be to say that he got married because the people of his society approved of the match. Ivan Ilych got married with both considerations in mind: he was doing something pleasant for himself by acquiring such a wife, and along with that he was doing something which the most highly placed people considered correct.

And Ivan Ilych got married.

The process of marriage itself and the first period of married life, with its conjugal caresses, new furniture, new dishes, and new linen, went very well—until his wife's pregnancy—so that Ivan Ilych had already begun to think that marriage not only does not destroy the character of an easy, pleasant, gay and always decorous life approved by society—a character which Ivan Ilych considered natural to life in general—but that marriage would even improve it. But then, with the first months of his wife's pregnancy, there appeared something new, undefined, unpleasant, difficult, and indecorous which could not have been expected and from which it was absolutely impossible to escape.

Without, as it seemed to Ivan Ilych, any cause, *de gaité de coeur* as he said to himself, his wife began to destroy the pleasantness and decorum of life; for no reason at all she became jealous of him, demanded that he devote all his attention to her, found fault with everything, and made unpleasant and coarse scenes for him.

At first Ivan Ilych hoped to free himself from the unpleasantness of this situation by the same easy and decorous relation to life which had saved him before—he tried to ignore his wife's mood, he continued to live easily and pleasantly as before: he invited friends in for bridge games, he himself tried to go out to the club or to acquaintances' homes. But his wife began to curse him with such energy and coarse words that Ivan Ilych was horrified—and she continued to curse him every time he did not carry out her demands; evidently she had firmly decided not to cease until he submitted, that is until he would sit home and not, like her, mope. He realized that married life—at least with his wife—is not always conducive to the pleasures and decorum of life, but on the contrary often destroys them, and that therefore it was essential to build barriers against this destruction. And Ivan Ilych started to look for ways to do this. The service was the one thing which imposed on Praskovia Fedorovna; and using the service and the duties it entailed, Ivan Ilych started to fight with his wife, fencing off his own independent world.

With the birth of the baby, attempts at feeding it and various failures in this, with the real and imaginary sicknesses of baby and mother in which Ivan Ilych's help was demanded even though he understood nothing about them, the demand for Ivan Ilych to fence himself off a world outside of his family became even more insistent. As his wife became more irritable and demanding, Ivan Ilych transferred his life's center of gravity to the service more and more. He started to like the service more and became more ambitious than he was before.

Very soon, not more than a year after his marriage, Ivan Ilych realized that conjugal life, while it offers certain comforts in life, is essentially a very complicated and difficult matter toward which—in order to perform one's duty, that is to lead a decorous life approved by society—one must work out a definite attitude, just as toward the service.

And Ivan Ilych worked out such an attitude toward conjugal life. From family life he demanded only those comforts of domestic dinner, housekeeper, and bed which it could give him, and most important, that decorum of external forms which had been established by social opinion. For the rest he sought gay pleasure and if he found it was very thankful; but if he met antagonism and querulousness he immediately retired to his separate fenced-off world in the service, and in it he found pleasure.

Ivan Ilych was valued as a good official, and within three years he was made the prosecutor's assistant. The new responsibilities, their importance, the possibility of indicting people and putting them in prison, the public speeches, the success which Ivan Ilych had in this job—all this attracted him to the service even more.

Children came. His wife became progressively more querulous and ill-tempered, but the attitudes toward domestic life which Ivan Ilych had worked out made him almost immune to her querulousness.

After seven years' service in one town Ivan Ilych was transferred to another province as prosecutor. They moved, there was little money, and his wife did not like the place to which they had moved. Although his salary was larger than the previous one, life was more expensive; besides that two children died, and therefore family life became even more unpleasant for Ivan Ilych.

Praskovia Fedorovna blamed her husband for all the inconveniences that happened in this new place of residence. The majority of topics of conversation between husband and wife, especially the upbringing of the children, led to questions which recalled past quarrels; and the quarrels were ready to flare up at any moment. There remained only those rare periods of amorousness which the couple sometimes found, but they did not last long. These were islets at which they anchored for a time, but then again set out on a sea of hidden enmity which was expressed by their alienation from each other. This alienation could have disturbed Ivan Ilych if he had considered that it should not be thus; but now he accepted this situation as not only normal, but as the goal of his activity in the family. His goal consisted of progressively freeing himself more and more from these unpleasantnesses and giving them a character of harmlessness and decorum; and he achieved this by spending progressively less time with his family; and when he was forced to do this he tried to secure his position by the presence of outsiders. But the main thing was that Ivan Ilych had the service. For Ivan Ilych the entire interest of life was concentrated in the world of the service. The consciousness of his power, the possibility of ruining any person whom he might want to ruin, even the external dignity of his entrance into court and meetings and subordinates, his success with superiors and subordinates, and most important, the mastery (he felt this) with which he conducted cases—all this made him happy, and together with chats with comrades, dinners, and bridge, it filled his life. Thus in general Ivan Ilych's life went on just as he considered it should go: pleasantly and decorously.

Thus he lived seven more years. His eldest daughter was already sixteen, one more baby died; and a young boy student, the object of dissension, remained. Ivan Ilych wanted to enter him in Law School, and to spite him Praskovia Fedorovna put him in the gymnasium. The daughter studied at home and turned out well; the boy was not a bad student either.

III

Thus went Ivan Ilych's life during the course of seventeen years from the time of his marriage. He was already an old prosecutor who had refused several transfers, waiting for a more desirable position, when unexpectedly a certain unpleasant event happened which almost destroyed his peaceful life. Ivan Ilych had been expecting the position of chairman in a university city, but somehow Hoppe ran ahead and received this position. Ivan Ilych got irritable, started making reproaches and quarreled with him and with his immediate superiors; they became cold to him and when the next appointment came up, they passed over him again.

This was in 1880. That was the most difficult year in Ivan Ilych's life. In that year it turned out that on the one hand his salary was not sufficient to live on, on the other that everyone had forgotten him and that what seemed to him the greatest and cruelest injustice toward him seemed a quite ordinary matter to others. Even his father did not consider it his responsibility to help him. He felt that everyone had abandoned him, considering his position with a 3500 ruble salary quite normal and even fortunate. He alone knew that considering those injustices which had been committed against him, the eternal nagging of his wife, and the debts which he started to make by living beyond his resources—he alone knew that his position was far from normal.

In the summer of that year, to save resources, he took a leave and went to spend the summer with his wife at Praskovia Fedorovna's brother's.

In the country, without the service, Ivan Ilych for the first time felt not only boredom, but unbearable depression; and he decided that it was impossible to live thus and essential to take some decisive steps.

After spending a sleepless night during which he paced up and down on the terrace, Ivan Ilych decided to go to Petersburg to lobby, and in order to punish *them*—the people who were unable to appreciate him—to transfer to another ministry.

The next day, in spite of all the protests of his wife and brother-in-law, he left for Petersburg.

He went for one thing: to get a position with a salary of 5000 rubles. He was no longer predisposed to any ministry, tendency, or kind of work. He needed only a position, a position with five thousand, in the administration, in banking, in railroads, in Empress Maria's institutions, even in customs, but certainly with five thousand and certainly to leave the ministry where they were unable to appreciate him.

And lo and behold Ivan Ilych's trip was crowned with amazing, unexpected success. At Kursk an acquaintance, F. S. Ilin, got in the first-class carriage and informed him of a telegram just received by the Governor of Kursk saying that in a few days there would be a reshuffling in the ministry: Ivan Semyonovich was being appointed to Peter Ivanovich's place.

The proposed reshuffling, apart from its significance for Russia, had special significance for Ivan Ilych, because it advanced a new person, Peter Petrovich, and, probably, his friend Zekhar Ivanovich, which was highly favorable for Ivan Ilych. Zakhar Ivanovich was Ivan Ilych's friend and comrade.

In Moscow the news was confirmed. And when he arrived in Petersburg Ivan Ilych found Zakhar Ivanovich and received a promise of a sure position in his former ministry of justice.

A week later he telegraphed his wife:

"Zakhar in Miller's place. I will get the appointment at the first report."

Thanks to this change of personnel Ivan Ilych had unexpectedly received an appointment in his former ministry in which he stood two steps higher than his comrades: a salary of five thousand and three thousand five hundred moving expenses. All vexation at his former enemies and the entire ministry was forgotten, and Ivan Ilych was completely happy.

Ivan Ilych returned to the country happier and more satisfied than he had been in a long time. Praskovia Fedorovna also cheered up, and a truce was concluded between them. Ivan Ilych told stories about how everyone feted him in Petersburg, how all of those who were his enemies had been shamed and now fawned before him, how they envied him his position, and especially how everyone loved him in Petersburg.

Praskovia Fedorovna listened to all of this and acted as if she believed it, and did not contradict it in any way, but simply made plans for the new way of life in the city to which they were moving. And with joy Ivan Ilych saw that these plans were his plans, that they agreed, and that his life, which had stumbled, was again assuming the real character of gay pleasure and decorum natural to it.

Ivan Ilych returned for a short time. He had to take over his new duty on the tenth of September, and besides time was needed to get settled in the new place, to move everything from the provinces, to order and purchase many other things—in a word, to get settled the way he had decided in his mind, and almost exactly as it had been decided in Praskovia Fedorovna's soul.

And now when everything had been settled so successfully and when he and his wife agreed on their goal and, besides, they lived together very little, they got along more genially than they had gotten along since the first years of their married life. Ivan Ilych had intended to take his family away immediately, but the insistence of his sister and brother-in-law (who had suddenly become especially amiable and friendly to Ivan Ilych and his family) made Ivan Ilych depart alone.

Ivan Ilych departed, and the gay mood caused by success and by agreement with his wife, the one intensifying the other, did not leave him the whole time. A charming apartment was found, the very one about which husband and wife had dreamed. Spacious high-ceilinged reception rooms, a grand and comfortable study, rooms for his wife and daughter, a classroom for his son—everything as if conceived especially for them. Ivan Ilych himself undertook the furnishing; he picked out the wallpaper, he purchased upholstery and furniture, especially antiques the style of which he considered especially *comme il faut*; and everything grew and grew and approached the ideal which he had set himself. When he had half furnished it, his furnishings surpassed his expectation. He understood the character—*comme il faut*, elegant, not vulgar—which everything would take on when it was ready. Falling asleep, he imagined the completed reception-hall. Looking at the still unfinished living room he already saw the fireplace, the screen, the what-not, and the little chairs here and there, the dishes and plates on the walls, and the bronzes when all these would stand in their places. He was made happy by the thought that he would surprise Pasha and Lizanka who also had a taste for this. They would not expect it at all. He had special success in finding and buying cheaply old things, which lent everything an especially noble character. In his letter he purposely presented everything worse than it was in order to surprise them. All of this so interested him that even his new service—though he liked the work—interested him less than he had expected. During his court sessions there were moments of absent-mindedness: he would drift into thought about whether the cornices over the curtains should be straight or curved. He was so interested in this that he often did things himself; he even moved the furniture around and he re-hung the curtains himself. Once he climbed up a ladder to show an uncomprehending upholsterer how he wanted the drapes; he missed a step and fell, but being a strong and agile man he grabbed hold so that he only knocked his side against the knob on the window frame. The bruise hurt, but it quickly went away. All this time Ivan Ilych felt especially gay and healthy. He wrote: "I feel as if fifteen years of my life have been taken off." He thought he could finish in September, but things dragged on until the middle of October. Still, it was charming—not only he said so, everyone who saw it said so.

In essence it was the same thing that is owned by all of the people who are not really rich but who want to look like rich people and therefore only look like each other: damasks, black wood, flowers, carpets, and bronzes, dark things and shiny things—everything that people of a certain type have in order to look like people of a certain type. And in his place everything looked like this so much that it could not attract one's attention, but all of it seemed somehow special to him. When he met his family at the railroad station, he drove them to the apartment; it was light and ready and a lackey in a white tie opened the door into an anteroom decorated with flowers; next they walked into the living room, the study, oohing and ahing with pleasure—he was very happy, he led them everywhere, drinking in their praises and beaming with pleasure. When, that same evening at tea, Praskovia Fedorovna asked him, among other things, how he fell, he laughed and showed them how he had gone flying and frightened the upholsterer.

"I'm not a gymnast for nothing. Someone else would have killed himself, but I just barely got hit right here; when you touch it, it hurts, but it's already going away; just a bruise."

And they began living in the new residence (in which, as always, when they got thoroughly settled, they were short only one room) on the new salary which lacked only a little (some five hundred rubles) of being enough; and it was very good. It was especially good at first, when everything had not yet been furnished and it was still necessary to furnish some things—to buy this, order that, move this, adjust that. Although there were a few disagreements between husband and wife, they were both so satisfied and there was so much work that it all ended without big quarrels. When there was nothing more to furnish it got a little boring, began to lack something; but then new acquaintances and habits were made and life was filled up.

After spending the morning at court Ivan Ilych would return

for dinner, and at first his mood was good, even though it suffered a bit precisely from using the apartment. (Every spot on the table-cloth or the damask, every broken drawstring on the curtain disturbed him; he had put in so much work on the furnishings that any breakage was painful for him.) But in general Ivan Ilych's life went as, in his belief, life should go: easily, pleasantly, and decorously. He got up at nine, drank coffee, read the newspapers, then put on his undress uniform and went to court. There the yoke in which he worked was put on; he immediately fit into it. Petitioners, inquiries at the chancery, the chancery itself, sessions—both public and administrative. In all this one had to know how to exclude everything fresh and vital—that which always destroys the smooth flow of judicial cases: one must not permit any relations to people except official ones; the reason for any relations should only be official, and the relations themselves are only official. For example, a person comes and wants to find out something. Ivan Ilych, as one in whose sphere the matter does not lie, can have no relations to such a person; but if the person has some relation to him as a member of the court, one which can be expressed on a paper with a heading—within the limits of these relations Ivan Ilych does everything which can be done, he does it decisively, and while doing it he observes a semblance of friendly human relations, i.e. courtesy. As soon as the official relation ends, any other one does too. It was this ability to separate the official side and not mix it with his real life that Ivan Ilych possessed in the highest degree, and with long practice and talent he polished it to such a degree that occasionally, like a virtuoso, he would even allow himself, as if jokingly, to mix human and official relations. He allowed himself this because he felt that if necessary he always had the strength to resume the official attitude again and drop the human one. For Ivan Ilych this business went along easily, pleasantly, and decorously, and even with virtuosity. Between sessions he smoked, drank tea, chatted a little about politics, a little about things in general, a little about cards, and most of all about appointments. And tired, but with the feeling of a virtuoso who has played his part—one of the first violins in an orchestra—with precision, he would return home. At home someone was visiting his daughter and wife or they had gone somewhere; the son was in the gymnasium, he was preparing lessons with his tutors, and he studied hard that which is taught in the gymnasium. Everything was good. After dinner, if there were no guests, Ivan Ilych sometimes read a book about which people were talking a lot; and in the evening he sat down to work, i.e. he read papers, checked laws—compared witnesses' depositions and noted the applicable laws. This neither bored nor amused him. It was boring when he could have been playing bridge, but if there was no bridge game it was at least better than sitting alone or with his wife. Ivan Ilych's pleasures were small dinners to which he invited ladies and men important because of their social position, and just as his drawing room resembled all drawing rooms, the way he passed the time with them resembled the usual way such people pass the time.

Once they even had a party; they danced. And Ivan Ilych was gay, and everything was good, only there was a big quarrel with his wife over the tarts and candy: Praskovia Fedorovna had her plan, and Ivan Ilych insisted on getting everything from an expensive confectioner, and he got many tarts, and the quarrel was over the fact that there were tarts left over, and the confectioner's bill was forty-five rubles. The quarrel was big and unpleasant; "Fool, imbecile." Then he grabbed himself by the head and in his anger mentioned something about divorce. But the party itself was gay. The best society was there, and Ivan Ilych danced with Princess Trufonova, the sister of the one famous for founding the charity "Bear my Burden." His official joys were the joys of egotism, his social joys were the joys of vanity, but Ivan Ilych's real joys were the joys of playing bridge. He admitted that after anything, after any disagreeable events in his life at all, the joy which, like a candle, burned before all others—was to sit down for bridge with good players and undemonstrative partners, definitely a foursome (with five it is very annoying to sit out, although one pretends that he likes it very much), and to have a serious, intelligent game (when the cards are coming); then to have supper and drink a glass of wine. And after bridge, especially when he won a little (a large win is unpleasant), he went to bed in an especially good mood.

Thus they lived. Their social circle was the best; important people and young people came to visit.

Husband, wife, and daughter were in complete agreement in their view of their circle of acquaintances; and in the same way they all tacitly repulsed and rejected any of the various shabby friends or relatives who with many endearments flew into their drawing room with the Japanese dishes on the walls. Soon these shabby friends ceased flying, and the Golovins were left with one of the best societies. Young men courted Lizanka, and Petrishchev, the son of Dmitri Ivanovich Petrishchev and the sole heir of his property, a court examiner, started to court Lizanka, so that Ivan Ilych already talked to Praskovia Fedorovna about it: shouldn't they take them for a troika ride or arrange a play? Thus they lived. And everything went along thus, without changing, and everything was very good.

IV

Everyone was healthy. That Ivan Ilych sometimes said he had a strange taste in his mouth and something felt uncomfortable in the left side of his stomach could not be called bad health.

But it happened that this discomfort began to intensify and turn into not exactly pain yet, but into a consciousness of a constant weight in the side and into a bad mood. This bad mood, which kept getting worse and worse, began to spoil the pleasantness of an easy and decorous life which had been established in the Golovin family. Husband and wife began to quarrel more and more often; and the easiness and pleasantness quickly fell away, and it was with difficulty that even the decorum held on. Again scenes began more often. Again only the islets remained, and there were few of those on which husband and wife could meet without an explosion.

And Praskovia Fedorovna now said, not without basis, that her husband had a bilious character. With her typical habit of exaggerating, she said that he had always had such a horrible character that she had to have goodness in her to bear it for twenty years. It was true that the quarrels now began from his side. His gripes always began just before dinner and often precisely when he began to eat, during the soup course. He would remark that one of the dishes was ruined, or that something was wrong with the food, or that his son had put his elbow on the table, or that his daughter's hairdo was bad. And he blamed Praskovia Fedorovna for everything. At first Praskovia Fedorovna objected and said unpleasant things to him, but once or twice he became so infuriated during dinner that she realized it was a state of sickness caused by his eating food, and she restrained herself; she no longer objected, but just hurried to finish dinner. Praskovia Fedorovna considered her restraint a great virtue. Having decided that her husband had a horrible character and had made her life unhappy, she began to feel sorry for herself. And the more she felt sorry for herself, the more she hated her husband. She began to wish that he would die, but she could not wish that, because then there would be no salary. And that made her even more irritated toward him. She considered herself terribly unhappy precisely because even his death could not save her, and she would get irritated; she concealed this, and this concealed irritation of hers intensified his irritation.

After one scene in which Ivan Ilych was especially unjust and after which he, explaining things, said that he was indeed irritable, but that it was from his illness; she told him that if he was sick, he should treat himself and demanded that he go to a celebrated physician.

He went. Everything was as he expected; everything was as it always is. The waiting and the solemnity with which he was admitted—the doctor's solemnity—was familiar to him (it was the same which he knew he used in court), and the pounding, and the listening, and the questions demanding answers which were foregone conclusions and evidently unnecessary, and the significant air which said, "You just put yourself in our hands, and we will arrange everything, always in the same manner for every man alike." Everything was exactly like in court. The celebrated doctor adopted the same air toward him that he had assumed toward a defendant.

The doctor said: such-and-such and such-and-such show that inside you have such-and-such and such-and-such; but if this is not confirmed by test for such-and-such and such-and-such, one must assume you have such-and-such and such-and-such. If we assume such-and-such, then . . . etc. For Ivan Ilych only one question was important: was his condition dangerous or not? But the doctor ignored this inappropriate question. From the doctor's point of view this question was idle and not worth discussion; all that existed was a weighing of probabilities—a floating kidney, a chronic catarrh, and appendicitis. It was not a matter of Ivan Ilych's life, but an argument between a floating kidney and appendicitis. And before

Ivan Ilych's eyes the doctor resolved this argument in favor of appendicitis, making the reservation that a test of the urine might give new clues and then the matter would be re-examined. All this was precisely what Ivan Ilych himself had done to defendants a thousand times in just such a brilliant manner. Just as brilliantly the doctor made his resumé, glancing triumphantly, even gaily over his spectacles at the defendant. From the doctor's resumé Ivan Ilych drew the conclusion that it was bad, but that it made no difference to the doctor, or perhaps, anyone; but it was bad for him. And this conclusion struck Ivan Ilych painfully, giving rise to a feeling of great pity for himself and great malice towards the doctor who was indifferent to such an important question.

But he did not say anything, but stood up, put money on the table, and having sighed, said, "We sick people, probably, often ask you inappropriate questions," he said. "In general, is this a dangerous disease or not?"

The doctor glanced at him sternly over his spectacles with one eye, as if saying, "Defendant, if you do not remain within the bounds of the questions put to you, I will be forced to have you removed from the courtroom."

"I have already told you what I consider necessary and appropriate," said the doctor, "What follows the test will show." And the doctor bowed.

Ivan Ilych walked out slowly and got dejectedly into his sleigh and drove home. The whole way he kept going over everything the doctor had said, trying to translate all these confused, vague, scientific words and to read an answer to his question in them: bad—is it very bad for me, or is there nothing yet? And it seemed to him that the sense of everything the doctor had said was that it was very bad. Everything in the streets seemed gloomy to Ivan Ilych. The cab-drivers were gloomy, the houses gloomy, the passers-by and shops gloomy. This pain, dull gnawing pain which did not cease for a second, seemed to be acquiring another, more serious, meaning in connection with the doctor's vague speeches. With a new oppressive feeling Ivan Ilych now began to keep track of this pain.

He arrived home and began to tell his wife about it. His wife listened, but in the middle of his story his daughter came in wearing a hat—she and her mother had been planning to go somewhere.

Making an effort she sat down to listen to this boring thing, but she could not stand it for long, and her mother did not wait for the end.

"Well, I'm very happy," said his wife, "so now you just watch out and take your medicine regularly. Give me the prescription; I'll send Gerasim to the drugstore." And she went to get dressed.

He had hardly stopped for a breath while she was in the room, and he sighed heavily when she went out.

"Well, so what," he said, "perhaps there really isn't anything yet. . . ."

He began to take medicine, to carry out the doctor's directions, which changed after the urine test. But then it happened that there was some confusion in this test and what was supposed to have followed it. He could not get to the doctor himself, and it was turning out that what was going on was not what the doctor had told him. Either he had forgotten, or he had lied, or he was concealing something from him.

But nevertheless Ivan Ilych began to carry out the directions precisely, and at first he found comfort in carrying them out.

From the time of his visit to the doctor Ivan Ilych's main occupation became the precise carrying out of the doctor's directions regarding hygiene and taking medicine, and keeping track of his pain, of all the excretions of his body. People's illnesses and people's health became Ivan Ilych's main interests. When in his presence anyone talked about sick people, about people who had died or about those who had recovered—especially from an illness which resembled his, he would listen carefully, trying to conceal his agitation, ask questions, and apply them to his own illness.

The pain did not abate, but Ivan Ilych made an effort to force himself to think he was better. And he could deceive himself as long as nothing upset him. But as soon as there was some unpleasant incident with his wife, a failure in the service, bad cards at bridge, he immediately felt the whole force of his illness; it used to be that he bore these failures expecting that "pretty soon now I'll get better, I'll fight, I'll wait for success or a grand slam." But now every failure disturbed him and plunged him into despair. He would say to himself: "No sooner did I start to get better and the medicine was beginning to work than there was a damned failure or unpleasantness. . . ." And he was furious with bad luck, or with the people who had caused him unpleasantnesses, who were killing him; and he felt that this fury would kill him, but he could not restrain himself from it. It might seem that it should have been clear to him that his infuriation with circumstances and people made his illness worse and that therefore he should have paid no attention to unpleasant chances; but he reasoned quite the opposite way: he said that he needed peace, that he kept track of everything that disturbed this peace, and at every disturbance, no matter how small, he got irritated. That he read medical books and conferred with doctors worsened his condition. This worsening progressed so evenly that he could deceive himself by comparing one day to the next— the difference was slight. But when he conferred with doctors it seemed to him things were going worse and even very rapidly. And in spite of this he was constantly conferring with doctors.

This month he had gone to another celebrity; the other celebrity said almost the same thing the first one had, but he put the questions a different way. And the advice of this celebrity only deepened Ivan Ilych's doubt and fear. A friend of a friend—a very good doctor —diagnosed the illness in a completely different way, and in spite of the fact that he promised recovery, with his questions and hypotheses he confused Ivan Ilych even more and strengthened his doubt. A homeopathist diagnosed the illness in still another way and gave him medicine, and secretly from everyone, Ivan Ilych took it for a week. But after the week he felt no improvement, and having lost his faith in the previous medicine and in this, he fell even deeper into dejection. Once a lady he knew was telling him about healing by ikons. Ivan Ilych caught himself listening attentively and believing the reality of the fact. This incident frightened him. "Can I have become so weak intellectually?" he said to himself. "Nonsense! It's all foolishness, I mustn't surrender to nervous fears, but choose one physician and strictly keep to his treatment. That's what I will do. Now it's over. I'm not going to think about it; I'm going to carry out the treatment strictly until summer. And then we'll see what's what. Now an end to this vacillation!" It was easy to say this, but impossible to carry it out. The pain in his side kept aching, it seemed to intensify progressively, to become constant; the taste in his mouth kept becoming stranger—it seemed to him his mouth smelled of something repulsive—and his appetite and strength kept getting weaker. It was impossible to deceive himself: something terrible, new, and more significant than anything significant in Ivan Ilych's life before was going on in him. And he alone knew about it; no one around him understood or they didn't want to understand, and they thought that everything on earth was going along as before. It was this which tormented Ivan Ilych most of all. He saw that the people in his house—most of all his wife and daughter, who were in the midst of their visits—did not understand anything, they were vexed that he was so depressed and demanding, as if he were to blame for it. Although they tried to conceal it, he saw that he was an obstacle to them, but that his wife had worked out a definite attitude toward his illness and was maintaining it irrespective of what he said or did. The attitude was like this:

"You know," she would say to her acquaintances, "unlike all kind people Ivan Ilych cannot strictly carry out the prescribed treatment. Today he'll take the drops and eat what has been ordered and he'll go to bed on time; tomorrow suddenly, if I don't see to it, he'll forget to take them, eat sturgeon (though he's been ordered not to), and sit at bridge until one o'clock."

"Just when did I?" Ivan Ilych will say angrily. "Once—at Peter Ivanovich's."

"And yesterday at Schebek's."

"It made no difference, I couldn't sleep from the pain."

"Be that as it may, this way you'll never recover and you are tormenting us."

Praskovia Fedorovna's external attitude toward her husband's illness, one she had expressed to others and to him, was that Ivan Ilych was to blame for the illness, and the whole illness was a new unpleasantness which he was inflicting on his wife. Ivan Ilych felt that this came out of her involuntarily, but that did not make him feel better.

At court Ivan Ilych noticed, or thought that he noticed, the same strange attitude toward him: sometimes it seemed to him they were watching him as if he were a person who would soon vacate his position; sometimes his friends suddenly began to jest amiably about his nervous fears, as if that horrible and terrifying, unheard of something which was taking place within him and never ceased to gnaw at him and was irresistibly drawing him away somewhere were a most pleasant topic for jests. He was especially irritated by Schwartz with his playfulness, liveliness, and *comme il faut* manner which reminded Ivan Ilych of himself ten years ago.

Friends would come to make a foursome and they would sit down to play. They dealt, the new cards were bent to soften them; the diamonds were placed with the diamonds, he had seven. His partner said, "No trumps" and supported him with two diamonds. What more could he want? He ought to feel gay and brisk—a grand slam. And suddenly Ivan Ilych feels that gnawing pain, that taste in his mouth, and that he can be made happy by the slam strikes him as somehow bizarre.

He looks at Mikhail Mikhailovich, his partner, as he raps the table with his sanguine hand and politely and indulgently restrains himself from grabbing up the trick, pushing the cards toward Ivan Ilych to give him the pleasure of gathering them without going to any trouble, without stretching his arms out. "Does he think I am so weak that I can't stretch my arm out?" thinks Ivan Ilych, and he forgets trumps and overtrumps his partner and loses the slam by three tricks; and most horrible of all is that he sees how Mikhail Mikhailovich is suffering and he does not care. And it is horrible to think why he does not care.

They all see that he is in pain and say to him, "We can quit if you are tired. You rest." Rest? No, he is not tired at all and they will play out the rubber. They are all gloomy and silent. Ivan Ilych feels that he has lowered his gloom on them and cannot dispel it. They have supper and go home, and Ivan Ilych remains alone with this consciousness that his life has been poisoned for him and is poisoning the lives of others, and that this poison is not getting weaker, but is penetrating his being more and more.

And with this consciousness, as well as with the physical pain, as well as the horror, he had to go to bed and often not to sleep the greater part of the night because of the pain. Still, in the morning he had to get up again, get dressed, go to court, talk, write, and if he didn't go—to remain at home with those same twenty-four hours a day, each one of which was torment. And he had to live thus on the brink of destruction alone, without a single person who would understand or pity him.

v

Thus it went for a month, then two. Before New Year's Day his brother-in-law arrived in the city and stopped at their house.

Ivan Ilych was at court. Praskovia Fedorovna went out to make some purchases. Entering his study, he found his brother-in-law there unpacking his suitcase himself—he was a strong and healthy man. He raised his head at Ivan Ilych's footsteps and looked at him for a second without saying anything. This look revealed everything for Ivan Ilych. His brother-in-law opened his mouth to gasp, but restrained himself. This gesture confirmed everything.

"Well, have I changed?"

"Yes . . . there is a change."

And after this no matter how much Ivan Ilych turned the conversation to his external appearance, his brother-in-law would not say anything about it. Praskovia Fedorovna came home and the brother-in-law went to see her. Ivan Ilych locked his door with a key and started looking into the mirror—straight, then from the side. He got a picture of himself and his wife, and he compared the picture with what he saw in the mirror. The change was enormous. Then he bared his arms to the elbow, looked at them, lowered his sleeves, sat down on the ottoman, and got blacker than night.

"No, no," he said to himself; he jumped up, walked to the table, opened a case and started to read it, but could not. He unlocked the door and went into the reception room. The door into the drawing room was closed. He walked up to it on tiptoes and started listening.

"No, you are exaggerating," Praskovia Fedorovna was saying.

"What do you mean I'm exaggerating? Can't you see? He's a dead man—look at his eyes! There's no light. What does he have?"

"No one knows. Nikolaev (this was another doctor) said something, but I don't know. Leshchetitsky (this was a celebrated doctor) said something different."

Ivan Ilych walked away, went to his room, lay down and started thinking: "Kidney, floating kidney." He remembered everything the doctors had told him, how it had torn loose and was floating. And with an effort of imagination he tried to catch the kidney and stop it, make it firm; it seemed to him so little was needed. "No, I'll go to Peter Ivanovich again." (This was the friend who had a friend who was a doctor.) He rang, ordered the horse hitched up, and got ready to go.

"Where are you going, *Jean*?" asked his wife with an especially gloomy and exceptionally kind expression.

This exceptional kindness infuriated him. He gave her a saturnine look.

"I have to go to Peter Ivanovich's."

He went to the friend who had the friend who was a doctor. And they went to the doctor together. He caught him at home and talked to him for a long time.

Examining anatomically and physiologically the details about what, in the opinion of the doctor, was going on inside him, he understood everything.

There was something, one small thing, in his vermiform appendix. All this might correct itself. Strengthen the energy of one organ, weaken the activity of another, absorption will take place and everything will be corrected. He was a little late for dinner. He had dinner, chatted merrily, and for a long time he didn't feel like going in to work. Finally he went to his study and immediately sat down to work. He read the cases and worked, but consciousness that he had put something aside—an intimately important matter which he would work on when he finished—did not leave him. When he finished the cases he remembered that this intimate matter was the thought of his vermiform appendix. But he did not surrender to it; he went into the drawing room for tea. Guests were there; they talked, played the piano, and sang—the Court Examiner, the desired fiancé for his daughter, was there. According to Praskovia Fedorovna, Ivan Ilych had a merrier time that evening than usual, but he did not forget for a moment that he had important thoughts about his vermiform appendix which he had put off. At eleven o'clock he said goodnight and went to his room. He had slept alone since the time of his illness, in a small room near the study. He went in, undressed, and picked up a novel by Zola, but he did not read it—he was thinking. And the desired recovery of his vermiform appendix took place in his imagination. There was absorption, there was evacuation, and normal activity was reestablished. "Yes, that's how it will be," he said to himself. "Only nature needs to be helped." He remembered the medicine, got up, took it, lay down on his back trying to feel the beneficient action of the medicine destroying the pain. "I need only take it regularly and avoid harmful influences; I already feel somewhat better—much better." He started touching his side, it was not painful to the touch. "Yes, I don't feel it; really, it's already much better." He extinguished the candle and lay down on his side. . . . The vermiform appendix is recovering, the absorption is going on. Suddenly he felt the old, familiar, dull, gnawing pain, insistent, quiet, serious. In his mouth the same familiar nastiness. His heart sank, his head began to spin. "My God, my God!" he muttered, "Again, again, and it will never stop." And suddenly he saw the whole matter from another viewpoint. "The vermiform appendix! The kidney!" he said to himself. "The point is not in the vermiform appendix, not in the kidney—it's in life and . . . death. Yes, there was life, and now it's leaving, leaving, and I cannot stop it. Yes. Why deceive myself? Isn't it evident to everyone except me that I am dying, and the only question is the number of weeks, days—right now perhaps. There was light, and now there is darkness. I was here, and now I'll go there. Where?" Cold enveloped him, his breathing stopped. He felt only his heartbeats.

"When I am not, what will there be? There won't be anything. So where will I be when I am not? Can that be death? No, I don't want that." He jumped up, wanted to light the candle, grabbed for it with trembling hands, knocked the candle and candleholder onto the floor, and again fell back on the pillow. "Why? It makes no difference," he said to himself, opening his eyes and staring into the dark. "Death. Yes, death. And none of them knows, and they don't want to know, and they don't feel sorry. They are playing. (From beyond the door he heard the distant rattle of a voice and its accompaniment.) It makes no difference to them, but they'll die too. Morons! I'll go early, but they'll go later, and the same thing will happen to them. And they're making merry. Beasts!" Spite choked him. And it became tormenting for him, unbearably miserable. It cannot be that everyone is always doomed to this horrible terror. He got up.

"Something is wrong. I must calm down, I must consider it all over from the beginning." And then he began to consider it. "Yes, the beginning of the illness. I hit my side, and I was still the same that day and the next; it ached a little, then more, then the doctors, then depression, anguish, again doctors; and I kept getting closer and closer to the abyss. Less strength. Closer, closer. And then I dried up; I have no light in my eyes. And death, but I think about my appendix. I think about it in order to fix the appendix, but it is death. Can it be death?" Again horror seized him; he gasped for breath, bent over, started trying to find the candle, and pressed his elbow on a stand beside the bed. It was in his way and it began to hurt; he grew furious with it, pressed down harder in anger and made the stand fall over. And in despair, gasping for breath, he fell onto his back, expecting death momentarily.

At this time the guests were leaving. Praskovia Fedorovna was seeing them off. She heard the fall and came in.

"What's wrong?"

"Nothing. I accidentally knocked it over."

She went out, brought a candle. He lay breathing heavily and quickly, like a man who has run a half mile, with his fixed eyes staring at her.

"What's wrong, *Jean?*"

"No . . . o . . . thing. Kno . . . o . . . cked." —What's the point of talking, she won't understand, he thought.

She really didn't understand. She picked up the stand, lit him a candle, and hurriedly went out: she had to see off a guest.

When she returned, he was still lying on his back staring up.

"How are you, is it worse?"

"Yes."

She shook her head and sat down.

"You know *Jean*, I think maybe Leshchetitsky should be invited here to the house."

This meant inviting a celebrated doctor regardless of the money. He smiled malignantly and said, "No." She sat for a minute, then walked up and kissed him on the forehead.

While she was kissing him he hated her with all the strength of his soul, and he made an effort not to push her away.

"Good-bye. Please God you'll fall asleep."

"Yes."

VI

Ivan Ilych saw that he was dying, and he was in constant despair.

In the depth of his soul Ivan Ilych knew that he was dying; but not only did he not get used to it, he simply did not understand it, and there was no way he could understand it.

The syllogism he had learned in Kiesewetter's logic: "Caius is a man, men are mortal, therefore Caius is mortal" had always seemed to him a correct example only as applied to Caius and not man in the abstract—he had always been a being quite, quite distinct from all of the others: he was Vanya with mama, with papa, with Mitya and Volodya, with toys, with a coachman, with nanna, then with Katenka, with all the joys, woes, raptures of childhood, boyhood, and youth. Did Caius know about the odor of the striped leather ball which Vanya had so loved? Did Caius kiss his mother's hand like that and did the silk in the folds of his mother's dress rustle like that for Caius? Had he rioted at Law School because of the meat pies? Was Caius so in love? Could Caius conduct a court session like he could?

And Caius really is mortal, and it is correct for him to die; but me, Vanya, Ivan Ilych, with all my feelings and thoughts—I am another matter. And it cannot be that I am supposed to die. That would be too terrible.

Such was his feeling.

"If I am supposed to die like Caius, I would have known it; an inner voice would have told me, but there was nothing like that in me. All of my friends and I—we understood that it is not at all as with Caius. And now look what's happened!" he said to himself. "It cannot be. It cannot be, but it is. How can that be? How does one understand it?"

And he could not understand and tried to banish the thought as false, incorrect, sick—and to squeeze it out with other correct, healthy thoughts. But this thought, and not only the thought, but the reality, kept coming and standing in front of him.

And in place of that thought he called up in turn other thoughts in hope of finding support in them. He attempted to return to his former currents of thought, the ones which formerly had blotted out the thought of death for him. But, strange thing, everything that formerly had blotted out, concealed, destroyed the consciousness of death was no longer able to produce this effect. Of late Ivan Ilych was spending most of his time in these attempts to reestablish the former currents of feeling which had blotted out death. He would say to himself, "I'll occupy myself with service duties—why I once lived only in them." And he went to court, banishing all doubts; he got into conversations with his colleagues and sat down absentmindedly, as was his old habit, scanning the crowd with a pensive look and leaning both of his emaciated arms on the arms of the oaken chair, just as usual leaning toward a colleague, moving the papers closer, whispering back and forth, and then, suddenly raising his eyes and sitting erect, he uttered familiar words and began the case. But suddenly in the middle of this the pain in his side, paying no attention to the stage the case had reached, began *Its* gnawing case. Ivan Ilych would heed it, banish the thought of it; but it continued its work, and *It* would come and stand right in front of him and look at him; and he was petrified, the fire in his eyes went out, and he would again begin to ask himself, "Can *It* really be the only truth?" And with surprise and disappointment his colleagues and subordinates saw how he, so brilliant and clever a judge, got mixed up, made mistakes. He would shake himself, try to come to his senses, and somehow he got the session to its end; and he would return home with the sorrowful consciousness that his court cases could not, as they used to, conceal from him that which he wanted to conceal, that he could not use court cases to free himself from *It*. And what was worst of all was that *It* attracted him not in order that he should do something, but only so that he would look at it, straight in its eyes, look at it and without doing anything be tormented inexpressibly.

And to save himself from this condition Ivan Ilych looked for consolations, new screens; and these new screens were found and for a short time they seemed to save him; but soon again they not so much fell apart as let the light through, as if *It* were piercing through everything, and nothing could blot it out.

During this last period he would enter the drawing room he had decorated, the same drawing room where he fell, for which— as it was malignantly amusing for him to think—for the furniture of which he had sacrificed his life, because he knew that his illness began with that fall. He would enter and see that there was a cut scratched on the polished table by something. He would look for the cause of this and find it in the bronze ornamentation of the album which was bent at the edge. He would take up the expensive album which he had lovingly compiled and feel vexed with the sloppiness of his daughter and her friends—in one place it would be torn, in another the photographs turned upside down. He would put it carefully in order, bend the ornamentation back into place.

Then the thought occurred to him of moving all of the albums and this *établissement* to another corner, near the flowers. He would call the lackey; either his daughter or wife would come to his aid— they would disagree, contradict each other, he argued and got angry; but it was all good because he did not remember about *It*, *It* was not visible.

But then when he was moving something himself his wife said, "Please, the servants will do it; you are hurting yourself again," and suddenly *It* flashed through the screens, he caught sight of *It*. *It* flashed, he still hoped *It* would disappear; but involuntarily he concentrated on his side—it still sits there as before, it still gnaws the same way; and he can no longer forget that he distinctly sees *It* looking at him from behind the flowers. What's the point of anything?

"And it is true that here, over that curtain—as if while storming a fort—I lost my life. Can that be? How horrible and how stupid! It cannot be! Cannot be, but is."

He would go into his study, lie down, and again remain alone with *It*. Eye to eye with *It*, and nothing could be done about *It*. Just look at *It* and go cold.

VII

How this happened it is impossible to say because it happened step by step, unnoticeably, but in the third month of Ivan Ilych's illness it happened that his wife, and his daughter, and his son, and his servants, and his acquaintances, and his doctors, and—most important—he himself knew that the whole interest he had for other people was whether he would soon vacate his position and at last free the living from the uneasiness caused by his presence and himself be freed from his sufferings.

He slept less and less; they gave him opium and began to inject morphine. But this did not relieve him. The dull anguish which he experienced in his semi-conscious state relieved him only at first because it was something new, but then it became just as torment- ing as open pain or even more.

At the prescription of the physicians special foods were prepared for him, but these foods became gradually more and more tasteless, more and more disgusting to him.

Special arrangements also had to be made for his excretions, and this was a torment every time. Torment from the filth, absence of decorum, and the smell, from the consciousness that another person had to take part in it.

But there was a consolation just in this unpleasant matter. The butler's assistant Gerasim always came to carry the things out.

Gerasim was a clean, fresh, young peasant who had grown stout on town vittles. Always cheerful and bright. At first Ivan Ilych was embarrassed by the sight of this man—he was always clean, dressed in the Russian fashion, and doing this repulsive chore.

Once when he had gotten up from the commode and was too weak to pull up his pants he fell into a soft chair and looked with horror at his bare, enfeebled thighs with the sharply marked muscle lines.

Wearing heavy boots, spreading around the pleasant odor of tar from his boots and the freshness of winter air, Gerasim entered with a light, firm gait. He was wearing a clean Hessian apron and a clean print shirt with the sleeves rolled up over his strong, naked, young arms; and without looking at Ivan Ilych, obviously restraining the joy of life which beamed on his face so as not to offend the sick man, he went up to the commode.

"Gerasim," said Ivan Ilych weakly.

Gerasim trembled, evidently frightened that he had perhaps made some blunder, and with a quick move he turned toward the sick man with his fresh, simple young face which was just beginning to grow a beard.

"Yes, sir?"

"I think this is unpleasant for you. Excuse me. I cannot."

"Oh no, sir." And Gerasim's eyes flashed and he bared his young white teeth. "Why not go to a little trouble? You're sick."

And with quick adroit hands he did his usual chore and went out walking lightly. And five minutes later, stepping just as lightly, he returned.

Ivan Ilych was still sitting the same way in the chair.

"Gerasim," he said, when he had set down the clean, washed commode, "please come here, help me." Gerasim went up to him. "Lift me up. It's difficult for me alone, and I sent Dmitri away."

Gerasim went up to him; with strong arms, just as he stepped lightly, he grasped Ivan Ilych, adroitly and softly raised him up, and supporting him he pulled up his pants with the other hand.

He wanted to set him down, but Ivan Ilych asked him to carry him to the divan. Gerasim, without effort and without apparent pressure, led him, almost carrying him, to the divan and sat him down.

"Thanks. How adroitly, how well . . . you do everything."

Gerasim smiled again and wanted to leave. But Ivan Ilych felt so good with him, that he did not want to dismiss him.

"Now here, move that chair over to me, please. No, that one, under my legs. It's easier for me when my legs are higher."

Gerasim brought the chair, set it down without banging it; in one motion he lowered it evenly to the floor and raised Ivan Ilych's legs onto the chair; it seemed to Ivan Ilych that it got easier for him while Gerasim was raising his legs up high.

"I feel better when my legs are high," said Ivan Ilych. "Put the pillow there under me."

Gerasim did this. Again he raised the legs and put them down. Again Ivan Ilych felt better while Gerasim was supporting his legs. When he lowered them, it seemed worse to him.

"Gerasim," he said to him, "are you busy now?"

"Not at all, sir," said Gerasim, who had learned how to talk to masters from city serfs.

"What else do you have to do?"

"Why what else is there to do? I've done everything except cut wood for tomorrow."

"Then hold my legs a little higher, can you?"

"Why not, I can." Gerasim raised the legs higher, and it seemed to Ivan Ilych that in that position he did not feel the pain at all.

"But what about the wood?"

"Don't worry, sir. I'll manage."

Ivan Ilych ordered Gerasim to sit down and hold his legs, and he talked to him. And, strange thing, it seemed to him that he felt better while Gerasim was holding his legs.

After that Ivan Ilych began to call Gerasim occasionally and had him hold his legs on his shoulders, and he liked to talk to him. Gerasim did this easily, willingly, simply, and with kindness which touched Ivan Ilych. In all other people health, strength, and vitality offended Ivan Ilych; only Gerasim's strength and vitality calmed Ivan Ilych rather than annoying him.

Ivan Ilych's main torment was the falsehood, the falsehood which for some reason had been accepted by everyone that he was only sick, and was not dying, and that he had only to be calm and take medicine and then something very good would happen. But he knew that no matter what they did nothing would happen except even more tormenting sufferings and death. And this falsehood tormented him; it tormented him that they did not want to admit what everyone knew, including him, but wanted to lie to him on the occasion of his horrible position; they wanted to and they forced him to take part in this falsehood. Falsehood, this falsehood perpetrated on him on the eve of his death, falsehood which was intended to reduce this terrible solemn act of his death to the level of all their visits, curtains, and sturgeon for dinner—this was horribly tormenting for Ivan Ilych. And, strangely, many times when they were making their little jokes at him he was within a hair of screaming at them; stop lying, both you and I know that I am dying, so at least stop lying. But he never had the spirit to do it. He saw that everyone around him had reduced the terrible, horrible act of his dying to the level of an accidental unpleasantness, partly a lack of decorum (something like what happens to a person who walks into a drawing room and breaks wind), and they did this using the same "decorum" which had served all his life; he saw that no one pitied him, because no one wanted even to understand his position. Only Gerasim understood this position and pitied him. And therefore Ivan Ilych felt good only with Gerasim. He felt good when, sometimes all night long, Gerasim held his legs and did not want to leave, saying, "Don't worry, Ivan Ilych, I'll still get enough sleep," or when suddenly shifting to the familiar "thou" he would add, "If you weren't sick it would be another matter, but as it is why shouldn't I work a bit extra?" Only Gerasim did not lie, from everything it was evident that he alone understood what was happening and did not consider it necessary to conceal it, and simply pitied his weak, emaciated master. Once he even said this straight out when Ivan Ilych was sending him away:

"We're all going to die. Why shouldn't I work a bit extra?" he said, meaning by this that he was not enburdened by his work precisely because he was doing it for a dying man and hoped that at his time someone would do the same work for him.

Apart from the falsehood, or as a consequence of it, the most tormenting thing for Ivan Ilych was that no one pitied him as he wanted that he should be pitied. At certain moments, after long sufferings, Ivan Ilych wanted nothing more, no matter how ashamed he was to admit it, than for someone to pity him like a sick child. He wanted to be petted and kissed, for them to cry over him as people pet and comfort children. He knew that he was an important member of court, that he had a graying beard, and that therefore this was impossible; but he still wanted it. And there was something close to this in his relations with Gerasim, and therefore his relations with Gerasim comforted him. Ivan Ilych wants to cry, wants them to pet and cry over him, and then his colleague, court official Shebek comes, and instead of crying and petting himself Ivan Ilych makes a serious, stern, profound face and from inertia gives his opinion on the insignificance of a Court of Cassation decision and stubbornly insists on it. This falsehood around him and in him too poisoned the last days of Ivan Ilych's life more than anything else.

VIII

It was morning. It was only morning because Gerasim had left and the lackey Peter had come, put out the candles, opened one curtain, and quietly started cleaning up. Whether it was morning or evening, whether it was Friday or Sunday made no difference to Ivan Ilych, there was only one thing for him: gnawing, tormenting pain which did not ease for a moment; consciousness of life which was hopelessly and gradually leaving, but which had not left completely; always that same approaching, terrible, odious death which was the one reality; and still the same falsehood. What days, weeks, or hours of the day are there under such circumstances?

"Will you have some tea?"

'He needs routine order, so the masters have to drink tea in the morning,' he thought, and said only,

"No."

"Would you like to move to the divan?"

'He needs to get the room in order, and I'm in the way. I am uncleanliness, disorder,' he thought and said only,

"No, leave me here."

The lackey bustled around some more. Ivan Ilych stretched out his hand. Peter walked up obligingly.

"What do you want, sir?"

"My watch."

Peter got the watch which was close at hand and gave it to him.

"Half past eight. Have they gotten up yet?"

"No, sir. Vasily Ivanovich (this was his son) has gone to the gymnasium, but Praskovia Fedorovna just ordered me to wake her if you asked. Should I?"

"No, it's not necessary," 'Should I try some tea?' he thought. "Yes, some tea . . . bring it."

Peter walked to the door. Ivan Ilych was terrified of remaining alone. 'How could I keep him here? Yes, the medicine.' "Peter, get me my medicine," 'Why not, maybe even the medicine will still help.' He took the spoon, drank it. 'No, it won't help. It's all rubbish, deception,' he decided, as soon as he felt the familiar, cloying, and hopeless taste. 'No, I can't believe any more. But the pain, the pain; if only it would let up for a minute.' And he moaned. Peter returned. "No, go, bring the tea."

Peter went out. Left alone Ivan Ilych moaned not so much from the pain, no matter how horrible it was, as from anguish. 'Always the same thing, the same thing, always these endless days and nights. If only it would be faster. What should be faster? Death, darkness. No, no. Anything's better than death!'

When Peter came in with the tea on a tray, Ivan Ilych looked at him absently for a long while, without understanding who and what he was. Peter was disconcerted by this look. And when Peter looked disconcerted, Ivan Ilych came to his senses.

"Yes," he said, "tea . . . good, put it down. Just help me wash up and get a clean shirt."

And Ivan Ilych started to wash up. With pauses for rest he washed his hands and face, cleaned his teeth, started to comb his hair and looked in the mirror. He was terrified; the way his hair stuck limply to his pale forehead was especially terrifying.

When his shirt was being changed he knew he would be even more terrified if he glanced at his body, so he did not look at himself. But then everything was over. He put on his robe, wrapped himself in a plaid, and sat down in a chair for tea. For one minute he felt refreshed, but no sooner had he started to drink the tea—again the same taste, the same pain. He forced himself to finish it and lay down, stretching his legs out. He lay down and dismissed Peter.

Still the same. One minute there would be a drop of hope, the next a sea of despair would rage; and always pain, always pain, always anguish, always the very same thing. It is horribly depressing to be alone; he wants to call to someone, but he knows in advance that it is even worse when others are present. 'If only I could have morphine again, I could lose consciousness. I'll tell him, the doctor, to think up something else. It is impossible like this, impossible.'

An hour, two pass like this. But there's a ring in the anteroom. Maybe the doctor. Precisely, it's the doctor—fresh, brisk, corpulent, merry, with an expression which says, "There you've been frightened by something, and now we'll fix everything up for you." The doctor knows this expression is unsuitable here, but he has already put it on once and for all, and he cannot take it off—like a man who put on a frock-coat in the morning to pay some calls.

The doctor rubs his hands briskly, reassuringly.

"I'm cold. There is a biting frost. Let me get warmed up," he says with an expression which seemed to say 'you just have to wait a little until I get warmed up, and when I'm warm, I'll correct everything.'

"Well, how is it?"

Ivan Ilych feels that the doctor wants to say, "How's every little thing?" but that even the doctor feels that he cannot say that, and he says, "How did you pass the night?"

Ivan Ilych looks at the doctor with a questioning expression: 'Won't you ever be ashamed to lie?' But the doctor does not want to understand the question.

And Ivan Ilych says:

"It's just as horrible as always. The pain isn't going away, it isn't subsiding. If only something would happen!"

"Yes, you sick people are always like that. Well, now I seem to have warmed up; even Praskovia Fedorovna, who is so particular, couldn't say anything against my temperature. Well, good morning." And the doctor shakes his hand.

And dropping all of his former playfulness the doctor begins to examine the sick man with a serious mien, the pulse, the temperature; and the sounding, the listening begin.

Ivan Ilych knows firmly and indubitably that all this is rubbish and empty deception, but when the doctor gets down on his knees and stretches out toward him, pressing his ear first high then low, and performs various gymnastic exercises over him with a very meaningful face—Ivan Ilych submits to this just as he used to submit to the speeches of the attorneys, and, as then, he knew very well that they were lying and why they were lying.

The doctor was still on his knees on the divan and sounding something when Praskovia Fedorovna's silk dress rustled in the door, and they heard her reproach Peter for not informing her of the doctor's arrival.

She walks in, kisses her husband, and immediately begins proving that she had gotten up a long time ago and that it was only through a misunderstanding that she was not here when the doctor arrived.

Ivan Ilych looks at her, scans her all over, and mentally reproaches her for the whiteness and the plumpness and the cleaniness of her hands and neck, for the gloss of her hair and the glitter of her eyes—which were full of life. With all the strength of his soul he hates here. And her touch makes him suffer from the swelling hatred for her.

Her attitude toward him and his illness is still the same. As the doctor had worked out one attitude toward the sick which he could no longer give up, so she had worked out one attitude toward him —that he was not doing what he should be doing, and was to blame himself, and she was lovingly rebuking him for this—and she could no longer give up this attitude toward him.

"Why he just doesn't listen to me! Doesn't take his medicine on time. And the main thing—he goes to bed in a position which is surely harmful for him—his legs up high."

She told how he made Gerasim hold his legs.

The doctor smiled contemptuously but gently, as if to say, "What's to be done, these sick people sometimes think up such stupidities; but one can forgive them."

When the examination was finished the doctor glanced at his watch, and then Praskovia Fedorovna announced to Ivan Ilych that no matter what he wanted, she had invited a celebrated doctor to come today; and together with Mikhail Danilovich (this was the name of the regular doctor), he would examine him and they would hold a consultation.

"So please don't put up any opposition. I am doing this for myself," she said ironically, giving him to feel that she was doing it all for him—and that alone meant he had no right to refuse her. He frowned and remained silent. He felt that the falsehood surrounding him was so tangled that it was difficult to unravel anything.

She was doing everything to him only for herself; and she told him that she was doing for herself that which she really was doing for herself—as if this were so incredible that he would have to believe the reverse.

The celebrated doctor did in fact appear at eleven thirty. Again there were soundings and significant conversations in his presence and in the other room about the kidney, about the vermiform appendix; and there were questions and answers with such significant looks that again instead of the real question about life and death, which was the only thing that stood before him now, the question arose of the kidney and veriform appendix which were doing something improperly, and which, because of this, would now be attacked and made to work properly by Mikhail Danilovich and the celebrity.

The celebrated doctor took his leave with a serious but not a hopeless mien. And to the timid question which Ivan Ilych asked him, eyes shining with terror and hope raised toward him—whether there was a possibility he would recover—the doctor replied that he could not guarantee it, but there was a possibility. The look of hope with which Ivan Ilych followed the doctor out was so pitiful that seeing it Praskovia Fedorovna even burst out crying as she walked through the study door to give the celebrated doctor his fee.

The lift in spirits produced by the doctor's encouragement did not last long. Again the same room, the same pictures, curtains, wallpaper, medicine bottles, and the same aching, suffering body. And Ivan Ilych began to moan; he was given an injection and fell asleep.

When he came to it was getting dark; his dinner was brought in. With an effort he ate some bouillon; and again the same thing, and again night setting in.

After dinner, at eight o'clock, Praskovia Fedorovna walked into his room in evening dress, her fat breasts pushed up by her corset, with traces of powder on her face. That morning she had already reminded him of their trip to the theater. Sarah Bernhardt was visiting and they had a box which he had insisted they take. Now he had forgotten about it, and her outfit offended him. But he concealed his offense when he recalled that he himself had insisted that they get the box and go because it would be an aesthetic and educational pleasure for the children.

Praskovia Fedorovna walked in, self-satisfied, but with a guilty air. She sat down, asked how he was; he saw this was done only to ask him, not to find out anything, because she knew there was nothing to find out; and she began to say what she had to: that she would not have gone for anything, but the box had been taken, and Helene and their daughter and Petrishchev (the court examiner, their daughter's fiancé), and it was impossible to let them go alone. But that it would be much more pleasant for her to visit with him. Only he should be sure to follow the doctor's instructions while she was gone.

"Yes, and Fedor Petrovich (the fiancé) wanted to come in. May he? And Liza."

"Let them come in."

The daughter came in all dressed up, with her young body exposed, the body which made him suffer so much. And she was showing it off to him. She was strong, healthy, obviously in love and vexed at his illness, sufferings, and death which were interfering with her happiness.

Fedor Petrovich came in too, hair curled *à la Capoul*, dressed in a frock-coat, his long sinewy neck tightly surrounded by a white collar, an enormous white shirtfront and narrow black trousers encasing his strong thighs, one white glove stretched over his hand, and carrying an opera hat.

Following him, the schoolboy crept in unnoticed, wearing a new little uniform, poor little fellow, and gloves; he had horrible blueness under his eyes and Ivan Ilych knew what that meant.

He had always felt sorry for his son. And now it was terrible to see his frightened, pitying look. It seemed to Ivan Ilych that besides Gerasim only Vasya understood and pitied him.

Everyone sat down. Again they asked him how he was. There was a silence. Liza asked her mother about the opera-glasses. There was an altercation between mother and daughter about who had put them where. It ended unpleasantly.

Fedor Petrovich asked Ivan Ilych if he had seen Sarah Bern-hardt. Ivan Ilych did not at first understand what he was being asked, but then he said, "No, have you see her already?"

"Yes, in *Adrienne Lecouvreur*."

Praskovia Fedorovna said she was especially good in such-and-such. Her daughter disagreed. A conversation about the elegance and realism of her acting began—the same conversation which is always repeated and is always the same.

In the middle of the conversation Fedor Petrovich glanced at Ivan Ilych and fell silent. The others glanced at him and fell silent. Ivan Ilych stared ahead with shining eyes, obviously angry at them. This had to be corrected, but there was no way to correct it. The silence had to be broken somehow. No one could manage to do it, and they all became terrified that suddenly the decorous falsehood would somehow fall apart, and the truth would be clear to every-one. Liza was the first to manage it. She interrupted the silence. She wanted to conceal what everyone was thinking, but she be-trayed it.

"Well, *if we are going*, it's time," she said glancing at her watch, a gift from her father; and barely noticeably she smiled meaningfully to the young man about something which they alone knew; and she got up rustling her dress.

Everyone got up, said good-bye and left.

When they went out it seemed to Ivan Ilych that he felt more at ease; there was no falsehood—it had gone with them, but the pain remained. Always the same pain, always the same terror— these things fixed it so that nothing was harder, nothing easier. Everything was worse.

Again minute followed minute, hour followed hour, and it was still the same, and still there was no end, and the inevitable end became still more terrifying.

"Yes, send Gerasim in," he replied to a question from Peter.

IX

His wife returned late at night. She came in on tiptoes, but he heard her; he opened his eyes and hurriedly closed them again. She wanted to send Gerasim away and sit with him herself. He opened his eyes and said:

"No. Go away."

"Are you suffering very much?"

"It makes no difference."

"Take some opium."

He agreed and drank it. She went out.

Until around three he was in a tormented delirium. It seemed to him that he and his pain were being shoved somewhere into a narrow black sack, and it is deep and they keep pushing further and further and they cannot push him through. And this horrible act is done while he is suffering. And he is afraid, and yet wants to fall through there, and struggles, and helps. And then suddenly he broke through and fell, and he came to his senses. Gerasim is still sitting at the foot of the bed, dozing peacefully, patiently. But he is lying with his emaciated legs in stockings raised on his shoulders, and still the same never-ceasing pain.

"Go away, Gerasim," he whispered.

"It's all right. I'll sit a while, sir."

"No, go away."

He took his legs down, lay with his side on his arm, and he felt sorry for himself. He waited only until Gerasim had gone out into the next room, and he no longer kept restraining himself, and he cried like a baby. He cried about his helplessness, about his horrible loneliness, about the cruelty of God, about the absence of God.

"Why hast Thou done all this? Why hast Thou brought me here? Why, why dost Thou torment me so horribly?"

He did not expect an answer, and he cried because there is and can be no answer. The pain intensified again, but he did not stir; did not call out. He said to himself, "Well, go on, well, strike me! But why? What have I done to Thee, why?"

Then he quieted down, not only ceased crying but ceased breathing and turned into total attention: as if he were listening not to a voice speaking in sounds, but to a voice of the soul, to a current of thoughts rising in him.

"What do you need?" was the first clear idea he heard which could be expressed in words, "What do you need? What do you need?" he repeated to himself. "What? Not to suffer. To live," he answered.

And again he gave himself to such intense attention that even the pain did not distract him.

"Live? Live how?" asked the voice of his soul.

"Yes, live, as I lived before: well, pleasantly."

"As you lived before, well and pleasantly?" asked the voice. And he started going over the best moments of his pleasant life in his imagination. But, strange thing, all these best moments of the pleasant life now seemed quite different than they seemed then. Everything—except the first reminiscences of childhood. There, in childhood, there was something really pleasant with which one could live if it returned. But the person who experienced that pleasantness no longer existed: it was as if a reminiscence of someone else.

As soon as the period which had produced him, the present Ivan Ilych, began, everything which had then seemed joyful now melted before his eyes and turned into something trivial and often nasty.

And the further away from childhood, the closer to the present, the more trivial and dubious the joys were. This began with Law School. There were still a few things that were truly good: he had gaiety there, he had friendships there, he had hopes there. But in the higher classes these good moments were already rarer. Then, during his first service for the governor, there were again good moments: these were the reminiscences of love for a woman. Then it got all mixed up and there was even less that was good. Later still less good, and the further he went, the less there was.

Marriage . . . so accidentally, and disillusionment, and the odor from his wife's mouth, and sensuality, pretense! And the dead service, and the worries about money, and so it went for a year, and two, and ten, and twenty—and always the same thing. And the further he went, the more deadly it got. "It is precisely as if I had been walking downhill while imagining I was walking uphill. Thus it was. In social opinion I was walking uphill, and to that extent life was running away from under me. . . . And now it's done, die!"

"So what does it mean? Why? It cannot be. It cannot be that life was so senseless and nasty. But if it really was so nasty and senseless, then why die and die suffering? Something's wrong."

"Maybe I didn't live as I should have," it suddenly occurred to him. "But how could it be so, when I did everything as one ought?" he said to himself and immediately dismissed this single solution of the entire riddle of life and death as something entirely impossible.

"What do you want now? To live? Live how? Live as you live at court when the bailiff proclaims, 'Court is in session!' Court is in session, in session is court," he repeated to himself, "So this is court! But I am not guilty!" he proclaimed with malice, "Guilty of what?" And he ceased crying, and turning his face to the wall, he started thinking about just one thing: why, what is the purpose of all this horror?

But no matter how much he thought, he found no answer. And whenever the thought occurred to him, and it occurred to him often, that all of this was happening because he had lived wrong, he immediately recalled all the correctness of his life and dismissed this strange thought.

x

Two more weeks passed. Ivan Ilych no longer got up from the divan. He did not want to lie in bed so he lay on the divan. And lying with his face to the wall almost all the time, he kept suffering alone through the same unresolved sufferings and, alone, kept thinking the same unresolved thought. "What is this? Can this really be death?" And an inner voice would reply: "Yes, it's true." —"Why all these torments?" And the voice would reply: "Just so, for no particular reason." Above and beyond this there was nothing.

From the very beginning of his illness, from the time when Ivan Ilych went to the doctor for the first time, his life was divided into two opposite moods which kept replacing each other: first there was despair and the expectation of incomprehensible and horrible death, then there was hope and interest-filled observation of his body's functions. First before his eyes there was just his kidney and appendix which were temporarily evading the carrying out of of their responsibilities; then there was just incomprehensible, horrible death from which it was impossible to escape.

These two moods kept replacing each other from the very beginning of his illness; but the further the illness progressed, the more dubious and fantastic became the conception of the kidney, and the more real the consciousness of approaching death.

All he had to do was to recall what he was three months ago and what he was now, recall how steadily he had gone downhill, and any possibility of hope was destroyed.

In the last period of the loneliness in which he found himself, lying with his face to the back of the divan, loneliness in the midst of a populous city and his numerous acquaintances and his family, loneliness more complete than any which can exist—either on the bottom of the sea or on earth—in the last period of this horrible loneliness Ivan Ilych lived only in memories of the past. One after another he imagined scenes from his past. It always began with the closest in time and extended back to what was most distant, to childhood, and it would stop on that. If he recalled the stewed prunes he had been given to eat today, he remembered the raw, shrivelled French prunes of his childhood, their special taste, and the abundance of saliva when he got down to the stones, and along with this reminiscence of taste there arose a whole series of reminiscences from the same time: nanna, his brother, toys. "I shouldn't think of it . . . hurts too much," said Ivan Ilych to himself and again brought himself back to the present. The button on the back of the divan and the creases in its morocco. "Morocco is expensive, doesn't last; there was a quarrel about it. But it was some other morocco and some other quarrel—when we tore father's briefcase and were punished, but mama brought us meat pies." And again it would stop on childhood, and again it would be painful for Ivan Ilych; and he tried to dismiss it and think about something else.

And again, at this very moment, along with this current of reminiscences running through his soul—about how his illness was growing and getting worse. The same was true here—the further back he went, the more life there was. There was more good in life, and there was more life itself. The two merged together. "Just as these torments keep getting worse and worse, so life itself was getting worse and worse," he thought. One bright spot there, behind, in the beginning of life, and then it kept getting blacker and blacker, faster and faster. "In inverse ratio to the square of the distance from death," thought Ivan Ilych. And this image of a stone flying downwards with increasing velocity stuck in his soul. Life, a series of increasing sufferings, flies faster and faster toward its end, the most terrible suffering. "I am flying. . . ." He shuddered, moved above, wanted to resist it; but he already knew it was impossible to resist, and again tired of looking but unable to avoid looking at what was in front of him, he fixed his eyes on the back of the divan and waited—waited for the terrible fall, shock, and destruction. "It is impossible to resist," he said to himself. "But if only I could understand why this is. That is impossible too. It could be explained if I said that I did not live as I should have. But it is impossible to stipulate that," he said to himself, twisting his lips into a smile as if someone could see this smile of his and be deceived by it. "There is no explanation! Torment. Death. . . . Why?"

XI

Thus passed two weeks. During these weeks an event desirable to Ivan Ilych and his wife took place: Petrishchev made a formal proposal. This happened in the evening. The next day Praskovia Fedorovna came in to see her husband considering how she should inform him of Fedor Petrovich's proposal, but that very night Ivan Ilych had taken a new turn for the worse. Praskovia Fedorovna found him on the same divan but in a new position. He was lying on his back, moaning, and staring fixedly straight in front of him.

She started talking about his medicines. He shifted his gaze to her. She did not finish what she had begun—there was such malice, directed at her, expressed in his look.

"For God's sake, let me die in peace," he said.

She wanted to leave, but then her daughter entered and went up to say good morning. He looked at his daughter the same way he had at his wife, and to her questions about how he was he said drily that he would soon free them all from himself. They both fell silent, sat there for a moment, and then went out.

"What are we guilty of?" Liza said to her mother. "As if we had done it! I feel sorry for papa, but why does he torment us?"

The doctor came at the usual time. Ivan Ilych answered "Yes," and "No," never taking his angry eyes off him; and at the end said, "You know very well that you can't help anything, so leave me alone."

"We can lessen the suffering," said the doctor.

"You can't do that either, leave me alone."

The doctor went out into the drawing room and informed Praskovia Fedorovna that it was very bad and there was one way—opium—to lessen the sufferings which would be horrible.

The doctor said his physical sufferings were horrible and this was true, but more horrible than his physical sufferings were his moral sufferings, and this was his main torment.

That night his moral sufferings consisted of staring at Gerasim's sleepy, good-natured face with its high cheekbones and having it suddenly occur to him: "And what if, in fact, my whole life, my conscious life has been wrong."

It occurred to him that what he had formerly imagined to be completely impossible—that he had not lived his life as he should have—might be true. It occurred to him that his scarcely perceptible impulses to struggle against what was considered good by the most highly placed people, scarcely perceptible impulses which he had immediately resisted—that it was precisely these which might have been the real thing, and all the rest might be wrong. His service, and his way of life, and his family, and the interests of society and the service—all that could be wrong. He tried to defend all this to himself. And suddenly he felt all the weakness of what he was defending. And there was nothing to defend.

"But if this is so," he said to himself, "and I am leaving life conscious that I ruined everything that was given me and cannot correct it, what then?" He lay on his back and started going over his whole life in a completely new way. In the morning when he saw the lackey, then his wife, then his daughter, then the doctor, their every movement, their every word confirmed the horrible truth which had been revealed to him at night. He saw himself in them, everything that he had lived by; and he saw clearly that all of this was wrong, all of this was a horrible, enormous deception hiding both life and death. This consciousness intensified, increased tenfold his physical sufferings. He moaned and tossed about and grabbed at his clothing—it seemed to him it was choking and stifling him. And he hated them on that account.

They gave him a large dose of opium, and he lost consciousness; but at dinner the same thing began again. He drove them all away and tossed from place to place.

His wife came to him and said, "*Jean*, my dear, do this for me (for me?). It can't hurt anything, and it often helps. What does it matter, it's nothing. And often one's health. . . ."

He opened his eyes wide.

"What? Take communion? Why? It's not necessary! However...."

She began to cry.

"Yes, my friend? I'll call our priest. He's such a nice man."

"Fine, very good," he muttered.

When the priest came and heard his confession Ivan Ilych was softened and seemed to feel relief from his doubts and therefore from his sufferings, and he found a moment of hope. He again started to think of his vermiform appendix and the possibility of correcting it. He took communion with tears in his eyes.

When they laid him down after communion he felt better for a moment, and hope for life appeared again. He started to think about the operation which they had proposed to him. "To live, I want to live," he said to himself. His wife came to congratulate him; she said the usual words and added, "You feel better, don't you?"

Without looking at her he muttered, "Yes."

Her dress, her figure, the expression of her face, the sound of her voice—everything told him one thing: "Wrong. Everything you lived and live by is falsehood, deceit which hides life and death from you." And as soon as he thought this, his hate rose up and, together with his hate, tormenting physical sufferings, and with these sufferings consciousness of the end—close, inevitable. Something new happened: the pain started to grind, shoot, and constrict his breathing.

The expression on his face when he said "yes" was horrible. Having muttered this "yes" while looking her right in the face, he turned over onto his face with rapidity extraordinary for his weakness and shouted:

"Go away, go away, leave me alone!"

XII

From that moment began the scream which did not cease for three days, which was so horrible that one could not hear it through two closed doors without horror. At the moment he answered his wife he realized that he was lost, that there was no return, that the end had come, the absolute end, and doubt not resolved remains doubt.

"Oh! Ooh! Oh!" he screamed in various intonations. He had began by screaming: "I won't!" and thus continued screaming on the letter "o."

For the whole three days, during which there was no time for him, he struggled in the black bag into which an unseen, irresistible force was shoving him. He fought as a man condemned to death fights in the hands of the executioner, knowing that he cannot save himself; and with every minute he felt that in spite of all his efforts to resist, he was getting closer and closer to that which horrified him. He felt that his torment was in the fact that he was being shoved into that black hole and even more in the fact that he couldn't crawl right into it. He was prevented from crawling into it by his conviction that his life had been good. This justification of his life got him stuck and prevented him from moving forward and tormented him more than anything else.

Suddenly some force struck him in his chest and side, constricted his breathing even more, he fell through into the hole and there, at the end of the hole, there was something light. What happened to him was what you experience when you are in a railroad car when you think you are going forward and you are going backward—and you suddenly realize the real direction.

"Yes, everything was wrong," he said to himself, "but that doesn't matter. One can, one can do the 'right thing.' But what is the 'right thing?'" he asked himself and suddenly grew quiet.

This was at the end of the third day, an hour before his death. At that very moment the schoolboy son quietly crept into his father's room and approached his bed. The dying man kept screaming desperately and flailing about with his arms. His hand fell on the schoolboy's head. The schoolboy grabbed it, pressed it to his lips, and began crying.

At that very moment Ivan Ilych fell through, saw the light, and it was revealed to him that his life was not what it should have been, but that this could still be corrected. He asked himself: "What is that 'right thing?'" and he grew silent, listening. At this point he felt that someone was kissing his hand. He opened his eyes and looked at his son. He felt sorry for him. His wife came in. He looked at her. She was looking at him with an open mouth, unwiped tears on her nose and cheeks, and a desperate expression. He felt sorry for her.

"Yes, I am tormenting them," he thought. "They are sorry, but it will be better for them when I die." He wanted to say this but did not have the strength to utter it. "However, why say it, I must act," he thought. With his eyes he indicated his son to his wife and said:

"Take him away . . . sorry . . . and for you. . . ." He wanted to say 'forgive me' too, but said 'forego,' and no longer strong enough to correct it, waved his hand, knowing that the one who should understand would understand.

And suddenly it became clear to him that what was oppressing him and not going away would suddenly all go away at once—from two sides, from ten sides, from all sides. He was sorry for them, he had to act so as not to hurt them. Relieve them and relieve himself from these sufferings. "How good and how simple," he thought. "But the pain?" he asked himself. "Where did it go? Well, where are you, pain?"

He turned his attention to it.

"Yes, there it is. Well, so what? Let the pain be."

"And death? Where is it?"

He searched for his former customary terror of death and did not find it. Where is it? What death? There was no terror because there was no death.

In place of death there was light.

"So that's what it is!" he suddenly muttered aloud. "What joy!"

All of this happened to him in one instant, and the significance of this instant did not change. For those present his agony continued another two hours. Something rattled in his chest; his exhausted body twitched. Then the rattling and gasping became less and less frequent.

"It is over!" said someone over him.

He heard those words and repeated them in his soul. "Death is over," he said to himself. "It is no more."

He drew in some air, stopped halfway through the breath, stretched out, and died.

VSEVOLOD GARSHIN

The Red Flower

[TO THE MEMORY OF I. TURGENEV]

I

"IN THE NAME OF HIS IMPERIAL MAJESTY and Sovereign Monarch Tsar Peter the First I declare this madhouse open for inspection!"

This speech was uttered in a loud, cutting, ringing voice. The hospital clerk who was registering the patient in a big dog-eared book that lay on an ink-stained desk, could not help smiling. But the two young attendants did not laugh: after two days and sleepless nights spent alone with the madman, whom they had just brought down by railway, they could barely stand on their feet. At the last station but one he had become so violent that he had to be put in a straight jacket, for which purpose they called the conductors and a policeman. Thus bound he was brought to town and delivered at the hospital.

He looked ghastly. Over his grey garment, which had been torn to shreds during his outburst of violence, was a tightly laced jacket

Translated by BERNARD ISAACS. *Reprinted from* The Red Flower. *Moscow*, [n.d.].

of coarse canvas cut low at the neck; the long sleeves pinioned his crossed arms over his chest and were tied behind his back. His bloodshot dilated eyes (he had not slept for ten days) glittered with a feverish blazing light; his lower lip twitched with a nervous spasm; his curly matted hair hung over his forehead like a mane; he paced from corner to corner of the office with swift heavy strides, staring fixedly at the old file cabinets and the oilcloth-covered chairs, and throwing an occasional glance at his companions.

"Take him in. The building on the right."

"I know, I know. I was here last year. We were inspecting the hospital. I know all about it, it will be difficult to deceive me," said the patient.

He turned towards the door. The door-keeper opened it to let him pass through; he walked out of the office with the same swift, heavy, resolute stride, his demented head held high, and made for the mental department on the right almost at a run. His attendants were barely able to keep up with him.

"Ring the bell. I can't do it, you have tied my hands."

The door-keeper opened the door, and the patient and his attendants entered the hospital.

It was a large stone building of old-fashioned construction. Two large halls—one a dining-room, the other a common room for the quiet inmates—a wide passage with a glass door leading into the garden, and about twenty separate rooms where the inmates lived, occupied the ground floor; on the same floor were two dark rooms, one padded, the other boarded, where the violent patients were kept, and a great gloomy room with a vaulted ceiling which was the bath-room. The upper floor was occupied by the women. A confused hum, punctuated by howls and screeches, came from there. The hospital had been built for eighty patients, but as it was the only one serving several adjacent districts, it accommodated up to three hundred. The tiny rooms contained as many as four and five beds; in the winter, when the patients were not allowed out into the garden, and all the windows behind their iron bars were shut tight, the air in the hospital became unbearably stuffy.

The new patient was led into the room containing the baths. This room was a depressing sight even to a sane man, and all the more painful was it to a sick disordered mind. It was a large vaulted room with a sticky stone floor illuminated by a single corner window; the walls and arches were painted with dark-red oil paint; two built-in stone baths, like two oval holes filled with water, were sunk into the ground on a level with the floor, which was black with dirt. A huge copper stove with a cylindrical boiler for heating the water and a maze of copper pipes and taps occupied a corner facing the window; to a sick brain all this had an extraordinarily sinister fantastic appearance, and the bath attendant himself, a burly, dour-faced, taciturn Ukrainian, only tended to heighten this impression.

When the patient was taken into this terrible room to have his bath, and, in accordance with the system of treatment introduced by the house physician, to have a large blister plaster put on the back of his neck, he was beside himself with terror and fury. Ridiculous thoughts, one more monstrous than the other, whirled in his brain. What was this? The Inquisition? A secret place of execution where his enemies had decided to do away with him? Or was this Hell itself? It then occurred to him that this was a kind of ordeal. He was undressed despite his desperate resistance. With an energy redoubled by sickness he easily wrenched himself out of the hands of the attendants, who fell sprawling on the floor; finally the four of them threw him down, and seizing him by the arms and legs, lowered him into the warm water. It seemed boiling hot to him, and wild crazy thoughts of ordeal by boiling water and red-hot iron thronged his sick head. Choking with water, struggling furiously in the grip of the attendants, he shouted out in a half-strangled voice an incoherent speech, the nature of which one cannot possibly imagine unless one has actually heard it. It was a mixture of prayers and curses. He screamed and fought until he was utterly exhausted, and then quietly, with hot tears pouring down his face, he uttered a phrase that was oddly at variance with his previous speech.

"Holy martyr St. George! Into thy hands I give my body. But my soul—no, oh no!"

The attendants were still holding him, although he had calmed down. The warm bath and the ice bag applied to his head had done their work. But when, almost senseless, he was taken out of the water and seated on a stool to have a blister plaster applied, he mustered his last ounce of strength and his crazed brain in a fresh outburst.

"What have I done?" he shrieked. "I did not wish anyone any

evil. Why do you want to kill me? O-o-o! Oh, my God! Oh, the souls of all those tortured before me! Deliver me, I pray. . . ."

The burning touch of the plaster to the nape of his neck made him struggle furiously. The attendants could not manage him and did not know what to do.

"It cannot be helped," said the soldier who was performing the operation, "it will have to be rubbed off."

These simple words, misconstrued by the sick man as "rubbed out," made him shudder. "Rubbed out? Rub what out? Rub who out? Me?" he thought, and shut his eyes in deadly terror. The soldier took a rough towel by its two ends and rubbed it hard across the back of the man's neck, tearing off the blister plaster and leaving a livid patch where the skin had come away with it. The pain of that operation, unbearable even to a calm and sane person, seemed the end of everything to the patient. He wrenched himself free with a frantic effort, and his naked body went rolling over the flagstones. He thought he had had his head cut off. He wanted to cry out but he could not. He was carried senseless to his bed, where, without coming to, he fell into a long, deep, dead sleep.

II

He awoke in the night. All was quiet; in the large room next door one could hear the breathing of the sleeping patients. Somewhere far away an inmate of the dark padded room was talking to himself in a strange monotonous voice, while upstairs, in the women's department, a hoarse contralto was singing a wild song. The sick man lay listening to these sounds. He felt terribly weak in all his aching limbs, and his neck was causing him great pain.

"Where am I? What has happened?" he wondered. And suddenly the last month of his life came back to him with extraordinary vividness, and he realized that he was ill and what his illness was. He recalled various crazy thoughts, words, and actions of his, and a shudder ran through his body.

"That is over now. Thank God, that is all over!" he whispered, and fell asleep again.

The iron-barred open window gave upon a small area between the big buildings and the stone fence; no one ever used that area,

and it was covered with a rank growth of wild shrubs and lilac
bushes, which were in full blossom at that time of the year. On
the other side of the shrubbery directly facing the window rose a
high dark wall, from behind which peeped the tops of the trees
growing in the large garden, all bathed and steeped in moonlight.
On the right rose the white building of the hospital, its barred
windows lighted up from within; on the left was the blank of the
mortuary, dazzling white under the moon. The moonlight poured
into the room through the barred window and lit up part of the
bed and the gaunt pallid face of the sick man with closed eyes;
there was not a trace of madness in it now. It was the deep heavy
sleep of an exhausted man, a sleep without dreams, without the
slightest movement, almost without breathing. He awoke for several seconds perfectly sane and seemingly healthy, only to get up
in the morning as insane as ever.

III

"How do you feel?" the doctor asked him the next day.

The patient, who had just woken up, still lay under his blanket.

"Splendid!" he answered, jumping up, putting on his slippers
and snatching his dressing-gown. "Splendid! The only trouble is
this!" And he pointed to the back of his head. "I cannot turn my
head, it hurts me. But that is nothing. Everything is good when
you understand it; and I understand."

"Do you know where you are?"

"Of course I do, doctor! In a madhouse. But once you understand it makes absolutely no difference. Absolutely no difference."

The doctor looked into his eyes searchingly. His smooth handsome face with its perfectly groomed golden beard and steady blue
eyes behind a pair of gold-rimmed spectacles was inscrutable and
observant.

"What are you staring at me for? You will not be able to read
my soul," the patient continued, "but I can clearly read yours! Why
are you doing evil? Why have you herded together all these unfortunate people, why do you keep them here? I don't care: I understand what it's all about and so I take it calmly; but they? Why
these tortures? To a man who has had a great idea, a common idea,
brought home to him, it makes no difference where he lives, what

he feels. He does not even care whether he lives or not. . . . Isn't that so?"

"Possibly," the doctor answered, sitting down on a chair in a corner of the room the better to be able to watch the patient, who was pacing swiftly from corner to corner in his huge shuffling horse-hide slippers and his fluttering cotton gown with broad red stripes and large flowers. The medical assistant and the attendant accompanying the doctor continued to stand at attention by the door.

"And I have it!" the patient cried. "When I discovered it I felt myself a new man. My senses were sharpened, and my brain functions as never before. What I used to arrive at by a long process of guess-work and inference, I now realize intuitively. I have attained in reality what philosophy has evolved in theory. I experience through myself the great ideas that space and time are but a fiction. I dwell in all the ages. I live beyond space, everywhere or nowhere, as you like. And therefore I do not care whether you keep me here or let me go, whether I am free or bound. I notice that there are one or two more like me here. But for the rest of the crowd such a situation is terrible. Why don't you set them free? Who wants—"

"You said," the doctor interrupted him, "that you live beyond space and time. But surely you will agree with me that you and I are both in this room, and that it is now"—the doctor consulted his watch—"half past ten on May the sixth, eighteen hundred and—. What do you say to that?"

"Nothing. I do not care where I am and when I live. If I do not care, does not that signify that I am everywhere and always?"

The doctor smiled.

"Sound logic," he said. "I daresay you are right. Good day. Would you care for a cigar?"

"Thank you." He stopped, took a cigar, and bit off the tip with nervous impatience. "It helps you to think," he said. "This world is a microcosm. At one end—alkalis, at the other—acids. . . . Such is the equilibrium of the world in which opposite bases are neutralized. Good-bye, doctor!"

The doctor proceeded on his round. Many of the patients stood stiffly at their cots, waiting for him. No chief enjoys such respect from his subordinates as a psychiatrist does from his insane patients.

The sick man, left alone, continued to pace feverishly from corner to corner. Tea was brought him; without sitting down, he emptied the large cup in two gulps, and ate up the chunk of white bread in the twinkling of an eye. Then he went out, and for several hours in succession, without stopping, he walked from one end of the building to the other with his swift heavy stride. It was a rainy day and the inmates were not allowed out into the garden. When the doctor's assistant looked for the new patient, someone pointed him out at the end of the passage; he was standing there with his face pressed against the glass pane of the garden door, staring at the flower-bed. His attention was attracted by an unusually vivid scarlet flower, a variety of the poppy.

"Please come and be weighed," the doctor's assistant said, touching his shoulder.

When the patient turned his face to him, he recoiled with a stab of fear—such a look of maniacal malignity and hatred was reflected in the patient's blazing eyes. At the sight of the doctor's assistant, however, he instantly changed his expression and followed him meekly without uttering a word, as though sunk deep in thought. They went into the consulting-room; the patient stepped on to the platform of the small decimal scales without waiting to be invited; the doctor's assistant checked his weight, and wrote "109 pounds" against his name in the book. The next day it was 107, and the day after that 106.

"If he keeps on like this he will not last long," the doctor said, and gave orders for him to be fed well.

But despite the doctor's orders and the patient's prodigious appetite, the latter lost weight day by day, and the figure which the assistant wrote down in the book dwindled steadily. The patient hardly slept and spent whole days in ceaseless movement.

IV

He realized that he was in a madhouse; he even realized that he was ill. Sometimes, as on that first night, he would wake up in the stillness of the night after a whole day of violent movement, aching in all his limbs, and with a weight of lead in his head, but otherwise perfectly sane. It may have been the absence of impressions induced by the still night and the semi-darkness, or the sluggish work of a brain roused from sleep that made him clearly realize his position at such moments with what seemed to be perfect sanity. Then, with daybreak, the hospital came to life, and a wave of impressions engulfed him; his sick brain could not cope with them, and he succumbed again. His condition was a peculiar mixture of sane reasoning and nonsense. He understood that all these people around him were hospital patients, yet he saw in every one of them some incognito or secretly disguised person whom he had known before, or about whom he had heard or read. The hospital was tenanted by people of all ages and all countries, dead and living. Here, resurrected, were the famous and the strong of all the world, and soldiers killed in the last war. He saw himself in a kind of enchanted circle in which was gathered all the might of the earth, and in a frenzy of pride, believed himself to be the centre of that circle. All his hospital mates had gathered here with him to fulfil a task which he vaguely envisaged as a gigantic enterprise aimed at destroying the evil of the world. He did not know what form it would take, but he felt that he had it in him to carry it out. He could read people's minds; things revealed to him their whole history; the great elms in the hospital garden told him legends of the past; the building, which was really fairly old, he considered to have been erected under Peter the Great, and was convinced that the Tsar had lived in it at the time of the Poltava Battle. He read this on the walls, on pieces of chipped off plaster, on the fragments of bricks and tiles that he found in the garden; the whole history of this house and its garden was written on them. He peopled the small building of the mortuary with scores and hundreds of individuals long since dead, and he stared through its little basement window, seeing in the shadowy light reflected in the old, iridescent and dirty glass the familiar lineaments which he had once seen in life or on portraits.

Meanwhile the weather had turned fine and sunny, and the inmates spent all day in the garden. Their part of the garden was a small space, thickly overgrown with trees, which had flowers planted over it wherever possible. The warden made everyone work in it who was at all fit to do anything; day in day out the patients pottered about sweeping the paths, strewing sand on them, weeding and watering the flower-beds, the cucumbers, melons and watermelons, which they had planted with their own hands. The corner of the garden was overgrown with cherry-trees; avenues of elm-

trees ran down it; in the middle, on a small artificial mound, a
flower-bed had been laid out, the most beautiful flower-bed in the
whole garden; bright flowers grew round the borders of the upper
ledge, while the center was adorned by a gorgeous yellow dahlia
with red spots. It was the centerpiece of the whole garden, which
it dominated, and it was to be observed that many of the inmates
attached a kind of mysterious significance to it. It struck the new
patient, too, as being rather remarkable, a palladium of the garden
and building, as it were. All the garden walks, too, had been planted
by the inmates with all kinds of flowers such as are usually met with
in Ukrainian homes: tall roses, brilliant petunias, clumps of tall
tobacco plants with small pink blossoms, mint, marigolds, nastur-
tiums, and poppies. Right near the doorstep grew three clusters of
poppies of some peculiar variety; they were much smaller than the
ordinary poppy, from which they were distinguished, however, by
their extraordinarily brilliant scarlet hue. It was this flower that had
arrested the patient's attention on his first day at the hopsital, when
he had been found looking out into the garden through the glass
door.

On coming out into the garden, the first thing he had done
before descending the steps was to look at those brilliant flowers.
There were only two of them, growing somewhat apart from the
rest on an unweeded spot, half-buried in rank goose-foot and dock.

The inmates came through the door one by one, and the door-
keeper gave each of them a thick, white knitted cap with a red cross
on the front of it. These caps had been in the war and had been
purchased by auction. But the patient, naturally, attached a special
mysterious significance to that red cross. He took his cap off and
looked at the cross, then at the poppies. The flowers were brighter.

"He is winning," said the patient, "but we shall see."

And he descended the steps. Looking round and not seeing the
attendant, who was standing behind him, he stepped over the
flower-bed and stretched his hand out towards the flower, but could
not bring himself to pluck it. He felt a hot stab of pain in his out-
stretched arm, and then throughout his body, as though some
powerful secret current emanating from the red petals had shot
through his body. He went closer, his hand almost touching the
flower, but it seemed to him as if the flower were defending itself,
exhaling a poisonous deadly breath. His head reeled; making a last

desperate effort, he seized it by its stem when suddenly a heavy hand dropped on his shoulder. The attendant had caught him.

"You must not pick the flowers," the old man said. "And you should not walk on the flower beds. There are a lot of you lunatics here; if every one took a flower there would be nothing left of the garden," he pointed out persuasively, his hand still on the patient's shoulder.

The patient looked him in the face, removed his hand in silence, and walked away down the garden path deeply perturbed. "Poor wretches!" he thought. "You see nothing, you are so blind that you defend it. But come what may, I shall put an end to it. Soon now we shall cross swords. And if I die in the attempt, what does it matter. . . ."

He walked about the garden till late in the evening, striking up acquaintances and starting strange conversations in which each of his interlocutors found only the answers to his own crazy thoughts expressed in absurd mysterious words. The patient walked about first with one companion, then another, and towards the end of the day he was more convinced than ever that "all was ready," as he put it to himself. Soon now, soon, the iron bars would fall apart, and all the people imprisoned here would be set free and rush to all corners of the earth, and the world, with a shudder, would throw off its shabby old covering and appear in all its glorious and shining new beauty. He had almost forgotten about the flower until he mounted the steps on his way out of the garden, when he saw the two red coals glowing amid the dense, darkened and already dewy grass. The patient lagged behind the crowd, and when the door-keeper's back was turned, he jumped over the flower-bed, snatched the flower and hid it away hastily under his shirt. When the fresh dewy leaves touched his body he grew as pale as death, and his eyes dilated in terror. A cold sweat broke out on his forehead.

The lamps were lit in the hospital; while waiting for their supper most of the inmates lay down on their beds, and only a few restless souls hurriedly paced the passage and the halls. Among them was the patient with the flower. He walked about with his clasped hands convulsively crossed on his chest as if he would crush and destroy the plant that lay hidden there. He gave everyone he met a wide berth, taking care not to touch them with the hem of his garment. "Keep away, keep away!" he shouted. But such exclamations in the hospital hardly attracted attention. He walked faster and faster, making longer and longer strides; he walked for an hour, two hours, in a kind of frenzy.

"I'll wear you out! I'll strangle you!" he muttered savagely.

At times he gnashed his teeth.

Supper was served in the dining-room. Several painted and gilt wooden bowls containing a thin millet gruel were set out on large bare tables; the patients took their seats on the benches; they were each given a lump of black bread. They ate with wooden spoons, eight men out of one bowl. Some of them—those who were on an improved diet—were served separately. Our patient quickly swallowed his portion, which the attendant had brought him in his room, and not satisfied with this, he went into the common dining-room.

"May I sit here?" he asked the warden.

"Haven't you had your supper yet?" the latter asked as he dished out extra portions of porridge.

"I am very hungry. Besides, I have to keep my strength up. Food is my only support; I don't sleep at all, you know."

"My dear man, you're welcome to it. Taras, give him a spoon and some bread."

He sat down before one of the common bowls and ate a vast quantity of porridge.

"That'll do, now, that'll do," the warden said at length, when all had finished supper while our patient was still sitting over his bowl, eating out of it with one hand, while the other he held clutched to his breast. "You'll overeat."

"Ah, if you only knew what a lot of strength I need! Farewell, Nikolai Nikolayevich," the patient said, getting up from the table and wringing the warden's hand. "Farewell."

"Where are you off to?" the warden said with a smile.

"I? Nowhere. I am staying here. But tomorrow, perhaps, we shall see each other no more. Thank you for all your kindness."

And he gripped the warden's hand once more. His voice shook and there were tears in his eyes.

"Now, don't upset yourself, my dear," said the warden. "Why these gloomy thoughts? Go and lie down and have a good sleep. You ought to sleep more; if you sleep well, you'll get well quickly."

The patient was sobbing. The warden turned away and told the attendants to hurry up and clear the table. Within half an hour everyone in the hospital was asleep—all except one man, who lay fully dressed on his bed in the corner room. He was shivering as if with the fever, clutching convulsively at his breast, which, so it seemed to him, was impregnated with a dread and deadly poison.

v

He did not sleep all night. He had plucked that flower because he regarded the act as a deed of valor which he was obliged to perform. The scarlet petals had attracted his attention the moment he had looked through the glass door, and it seemed to him that it was from that very moment that he had come at last to realize what his task was in this world. All the world's evil was concentrated in that brilliant red flower. He knew that opium was obtained from the poppy; it was perhaps this thought, magnified in his mind to grotesque dimensions, that had made him create that grim fantastic spectre. To him the flower was the embodiment of all evil; it had soaked up all the innocently spilt blood (that was why it was so red), all the tears, and all the bile of humanity. It was a mysterious, sinister creature, the opposite of God, Ahriman in a modest innocent guise. It had to be torn out and killed. More, it had to be prevented, in dying, from spreading its evil through the world. And that is why he had concealed it in his bosom. He hoped that by the morning the flower would have lost all its malign power. The evil that was in it would pass into his breast, his soul, and there it would either be conquered or would conquer—and then he himself would perish, die, but he would die an honest fighter, the first fighter of mankind, because no one up till then had dared single-handed to grapple with all the evil of the world.

"They have not seen it. I have. How can I let it live? Better death."

And he lay fainting, exhausted by the unreal shadowy struggle that he was waging. In the morning the doctor's assistant found him almost half-dead. Nevertheless, excitation presently got the upper hand; he sprang from his bed and began to run about the hospital again, talking to the patients and to himself louder and more wildly than ever. He was not allowed to go out into the garden. Seeing that he was losing weight, not sleeping, and walking about all the time, the doctor ordered him an injection of a large dose of morphium. He offered no resistance: fortunately, his crazy thoughts at the time happened to fit in with this operation. He soon fell asleep; the frenzied movement ceased, and the loud maddening tune produced by the time-beat of his quick nervous steps died out of his ears. He dropped off and no longer thought of anything, not even of the second flower that remained to be plucked.

He plucked it three days later under the eye of the old door-keeper and before the latter could prevent him. The door-keeper ran after him. The patient ran into the hospital with a triumphant yell and dashed into his room where he hid the flower in his bosom.

"Why do you pluck the flowers?" demanded the door-keeper, running in after him. But the patient, who was now lying on his bed with his arms folded on his chest in his customary pose, began to talk such nonsense that the doorkeeper, saying nothing more, took off his head the cap with the red cross which he had forgotten in his precipitate flight, and went away. And the phantom struggle began again. The sick man felt the evil gushing from the flower in long, wriggling, snake-like jets; they wrapped themselves around him, squeezed and crushed his limbs, sunk their deadly venom into him. Between curses directed against his enemy he wept and prayed to God. By the evening the flower had withered. The sick man trampled on the blackened plant, picked the remnants of it up from the floor and carried them into the bath-room. He threw the squashed shapeless scraps on to the blazing coals of the stove, and stood for a long time watching his enemy hiss and shrivel until he had turned at last into a soft little heap of snow-white ashes. He blew at it, and it all disappeared.

The next day the patient was worse. Deathly pale and haggard, with glittering eyes sunk deep in their sockets, he continued his violent pacing with a reeling stumbling gait and talked and talked without a stop.

"I should not like to resort to force," the head physician told his assistant. "But this activity must be stopped. Today his weight is ninety-three pounds. At this rate he won't last more than two days."

The physician became lost in thought.

"Morphine? Chloral?" he said half-questioningly.

"The morphine didn't work yesterday."

"Have him bound. I doubt, though, whether he will survive."

VI

The patient was bound. He lay on his bed in a strait jacket, tightly strapped down to the iron cross-pieces of the bedstead with broad strips of canvas. But the furious activity, if anything, increased rather than abated. He struggled hard for hours to free himself from his fetters. At last, with a violent wrench, he tore one of the bands, and freed his leg, then, slipping out from under the rest, began to pace the room with arms bound, shouting out wild unintelligible speeches.

"Daze my eyes!" cried the door-keeper coming in. "The devils must ha' been helping you! Gritsko! Ivan! Quick, he's got loose."

The three of them fell upon the patient, and there began a long struggle, a tiring one for the attackers, and an agonizing one for the attacked, who spent the last of his exhausted strength. At last he was overcome, and bound down to his bed more securely than ever.

"You don't understand what you are doing!" the sick man panted. "You are perishing! I saw a third, just beginning to blossom. It's ready now. Let me finish my work! I have to kill it! Kill it! Then it will all be over, everything will be saved. I would send you, but this is a thing I can only do myself. You would die from the mere touch."

"Keep quiet, sir!" said the old door-keeper, who was left to watch at his bedside.

The patient suddenly fell silent. He had decided to trick his keepers. He was kept tied down all day and left in that position for the night. After giving him his supper, the caretaker made his bed on the floor near the patient's cot and lay down. In a minute he was fast asleep, and the patient fell to work again.

He twisted his whole body over to reach the iron bar that ran lengthwise down the bedstead, and feeling for it with his wrist, which was concealed in the long sleeve of the strait jacket, he began to rub the sleeve hard against the iron bar. In due course the thick canvas gave way and he freed his forefinger. After that things went faster. With a dexterity and suppleness that would have been incredible in a healthy man, he untied the knot behind his back which pinioned the sleeves, and unlaced the jacket, after which he sat for a long time listening to the snores of the caretaker. But the old man slept soundly. The patient took off the strait jacket and untied the bands that strapped him to the bed. He was now free. He tried the door; it was locked from the inside, and the key, no doubt, lay in the caretaker's pocket. He did not dare to search his pockets for fear of wakening him, so he decided to go out through the window.

The night was still, warm, and dark; the window was open; stars shone in the black sky. He looked at them, distinguishing familiar constellations and feeling glad that they seemed to understand him and sympathize with him. Narrowing his eyes, he saw the endless rays which they sent him, and his mad resolve was strengthened. The thing was to bend aside one of the thick rods on the barred window, crawl through the narrow opening into the area, and climb over the high stone wall. There he would fight his last battle, and after that—death might come for all he cared.

He tried to bend the thick bar with his bare hands, but the iron refused to yield. Then he twisted the strong sleeves of the strait jacket into a rope, hitched it to the spearhead hammered out at the bottom of the bar, and threw his whole weight upon it. After desperate efforts, which almost exhausted his last remaining strength, the rod bent, offering a narrow opening. He squeezed himself through it, grazing the skin of his shoulders, elbows and knees, crept through the bushes and stopped before the wall. All was quiet. The windows of the great building were dimly lit up by the night lamps. There was not a soul about. No one had noticed him; the old man set to watch at his bedside was probably fast asleep. The stars twinkled kindly and their rays went straight to his heart.

"I am coming," he whispered, gazing at the sky.

At his first attempt he lost his footing, and with broken fingernails and bleeding hands and knees, he began to seek a more convenient spot. At a point where the garden wall joined the wall of the mortuary several bricks were missing. The patient found these holes in the wall and used them for a foothold. He climbed up the wall, seized the branch of an elm growing on the other side, and quietly lowered himself to the ground by means of the tree trunk.

He rushed to the familiar spot near the doorstep. The flower, a dark little patch with folded petals, stood out clearly in the dewy grass.

"The last!" whispered the patient. "The last! Today victory or death. But that does not matter any more. Wait," he said, looking up at the sky, "I shall be with you soon."

He pulled out the plant, crushed it, squashed it, and clutching it in his hand, returned to his room the way he had come. The old man was sleeping. The patient dropped senseless on his bed the moment he reached it.

In the morning he was found dead. His face was calm and serene; the emaciated features with the thin lips and closed sunken eyes expressed a kind of proud elation. When he was placed on the stretcher they tried to unclench his hand to take the red flower out. But his hand had stiffened in death, and he carried his trophy away with him to the grave.

VLADIMIR KOROLENKO

Makar's Dream:

A CHRISTMAS STORY

POOR MAKAR HAD THIS DREAM, the one who drove his calves to gloomy far-off lands, the same Makar upon whose head, as the proverb says, all troubles fall.

His birthplace—the backwoods settlement of Chalgan—was lost in the remote Yakut taiga. Makar's father and grandfather had fought and won a piece of frozen ground from the taiga, and though the gloomy forest still stood around like a hostile wall, they did not despair. Fences ran across the cleared space, there were stacks of hay and straw, small smoky huts grew up; finally, like a victory banner, a bell-tower shot up from a little hill in the center of the village. Chalgan became a large settlement.

But while Makar's father and grandfather were fighting with the taiga, burning it with fire, cutting it with iron, they themselves grew wild without realizing it. Marrying Yakut girls they adopted the Yakut language and Yakut customs. The characteristic features of the Great Russian tribe were expunged and disappeared.

Translated by CARL R. PROFFER.

However that may be, my Makar still firmly remembered that he was a native Chalgan Russian peasant. He was born here, had lived here, and he planned to die here. He was very proud of his background and sometimes abused the other "pagan Yakuts" although, to tell the truth, he himself was no different than the Yakuts either in his habits or in his way of life. He spoke Russian little and rather poorly, he dressed in animal skins, wore *torbasa** on his feet, usually ate only a flat cake mixed with brick-tea, and on holidays and other special occasions he consumed precisely as much boiled butter as was on the table in front of him. He rode the backs of oxen very adroitly, and in case of an illness he called a shaman who would go mad and leap at him gnashing his teeth, trying to frighten the ailment and drive it out of Makar.

He worked terribly hard, lived poorly, bore hunger and cold. Did he have any thoughts besides his constant worries about flat cakes and tea?

Yes, he did.

When he was drunk, he would cry. "How hard our life is," he would say, "my Lord!" Besides that he sometimes said that he would like to abandon everything and go away to "the mountain." There he would not plough, nor sow; he would not cut and haul wood, he would not even grind grain on a hand millstone. He would just save himself. What this mountain was, where it was, he did not know exactly; he knew only that, first, this mountain existed, and second, that it was somewhere far away—so far away that even *Toyon's*** policeman could not get him there. . . . Also, of course, he would not pay taxes there. . . .

When sober he abandoned these thoughts, perhaps admitting the impossibility of finding such a mountain; but when drunk he became braver. He would grant that he might not find the real mountain and end up on another, "In that case I would die," he would say, but nevertheless he intended to go; if he did not carry out this intention it was probably because the settlement Tatars always sold him rotten vodka which was mixed with cheap tobacco to make it stronger, and from this he quickly became weak and got sick.

---

* Deerskin moccasins.
** Toyon—the Yakut word for God. Also applied to officials and superiors.

II

It was Christmas Eve, and Makar was aware that tomorrow was a big holiday. On this occasion he was tormented by a desire to drink, but there was no money to drink on—he had little flour left, and Makar was already in debt to the local merchants and Tatars. However, tomorrow was a big holiday, so it was impossible to work —what would he do if he did not get drunk? This thought made him unhappy. What a life he had! Even on a big holiday he would not have a bottle of vodka to drink.

A happy thought occurred to him. He got up and put on his torn *sona* (fur coat). His wife, a solid, sinewy, remarkably strong and just as remarkably ugly woman, who knew all of his guileless impulses through and through, guessed his intention this time too.

"Where are you going, you devil? You want to drink vodka alone again?"

"Shut up! I'll buy one bottle. We'll drink it together tomorrow." He banged her on the shoulder so hard she staggered, and he winked slyly. Such is the female heart: she knew that Makar would definitely trick her, but she gave in to the warmth of a conjugal caress.

He went out, caught his old piebald pony in an *alas**, led it to the sled by the mane and started harnessing. Soon after, the piebald carried its master through the gates. It stopped there, and turning its head, looked questioningly at Makar, who was sunk in thought. Then Makar pulled the left rein and headed the horse toward the edge of the settlement.

On the very edge of the settlement stood a small hut. Out of it, as out of the other huts, rose smoke from a fireplace—high, high, veiling the cold stars and bright moon in its white billowing mass. The fire crackled merrily, reflecting through pellucid circles. Outside it was quiet.

Here lived foreigners from a distant land. How they got here, what tempest cast them into this remote region Makar did not know and was not interested in knowing, but he liked to do business with them, because they neither harrassed him nor insisted too much on payment.

* Plot of grass in the woods.

Entering the hut, Makar immediately went to the fireplace and stretched his frozen hands out toward the fire.

"Cha!" he said, thus expressing the sensation of cold.

The foreigners were home. A candle was burning on the table, although they were not working. One lay in bed blowing smoke rings and pensively following their winding curves, apparently tying them to the long threads of his own thoughts. The other was sitting in front of the fireplace, and he too was thoughtfully following something—the flames running back and forth across the burning wood.

"Hello!" said Makar to break the oppressive silence. Of course, he did not know what sadness lay on the hearts of foreign people, what reminiscences were thronging in their minds that evening, what images they imagined in the fantastic interplay of fire and smoke. Besides, he had his own trouble.

The young man sitting in front of the fireplace raised his head and gave Makar a vague look as if not recognizing him. Then he shook his head and quickly got up from the chair.

"Oh, hello, hello, Makar! That's just fine! Will you have some tea with us?"

Makar liked the proposition.

"Some tea?" he asked. "That's good! Yes, brother, good. . . . Fine!"

He started taking off his things hurriedly. When he had removed his fur coat and hat he felt more at ease, and seeing the hot coals already burning in the samovar, he turned to the young man effusively:

"I love you, really! I love you so much, so much. . . . I can't sleep at night. . . ."

The foreigner turned around and a bitter smile appeared on his face.

"So, you love me?" he said. "What do you need?"

Makar faltered.

"There is one matter," he answered. "But how did you know? O.K. I'll have some tea and then tell you."

Since the tea had been offered to Makar by the hosts themselves, he considered it appropriate to go further.

"Is there any roast meat? I love it," he said.

"No."

"Well, it doesn't matter," said Makar in a soothing tone, "I'll have it another time. . . . O.K.?," he asked, "another time?"

"O.K."

Now Makar considered the foreigners indebted to him for a piece of roast meat, and he never let such debts pass unpaid.

In an hour he again got in his lumber cart. He had gotten a whole ruble by selling in advance five loads of wood on comparatively good terms. True, he took an oath and swore he would not drink up this money until the next day, but he intended to do so immediately. But what could he do? The pleasure ahead deafened the rebukes from his conscience. He did not even think about how, when he got drunk, he would be faced with a cruel drubbing from his deceived, faithful wife.

"Where are you going, Makar?" shouted the foreigner, laughing, seeing that instead of going straight Makar's horse turned left in the direction of the Tatars.

"Whoa! . . . Whoa! . . . You see, what a damned horse it is. . . . Where is he going?" said Makar to justify himself—still pulling the left rein firmly and imperceptibly switching the piebald with his right.

Waving his tail reproachfully, the clever nag quietly stumbled off in the required direction, and before long the scraping of Makar's runners stopped at the gates of a Tatar house.

III

Several horses with high Yakut saddles were tied by these gates.

It was stifling in the stuffy hut. The acrid smoke of cheap tobacco hung in a cloud, which was slowly being drawn up the fireplace. Yakut visitors were sitting on benches and at tables; there were cups of vodka on the tables; here and there small groups were playing cards. Their faces were sweaty and red. The gamblers' eyes followed the cards wildly. Money was taken out and then immediately hidden in other pockets. A drunken Yakut was sitting on the straw in a corner, weaving back and forth and droning an endless song.

Makar put out his money and they gave him a bottle. He shoved it into his coat and unnoticed by the others walked into a dark corner. There he poured cup after cup and drank them one after the other. The vodka was bitter, diluted by more than three-quarters water because of the holiday. But evidently they had not spared the cheap tobacco. Every time he drank, Makar's breath caught for a moment, and crimson circles spun before his eyes.

Before long he was drunk. He also sank down on the straw, and putting his arms around his knees laid his heavy head on them. The same absurd rasping sounds flowed from his throat by themselves. He sang that tomorrow was a holiday and he had drunk up five loads of wood.

Meanwhile it is getting stuffier and stuffier in the hut. New visitors walked in—Yakuts who had come to pray and drink Tatar vodka. The host saw that soon there would not be room for all. He got up from the table and glanced over the crowd. His glance pierced into the dark corner and saw the Yakut and Makar there.

He went up to the Yakut, and grabbing him by the collar threw him out of the hut. Then he went up to Makar. Because he was a local person, the Tatar showed him more respect: opening the door wide he used his foot to give the poor fellow such a jolt from behind that Makar flew out of the hut and landed with his nose right in a snowdrift.

It is difficult to say whether he was offended by such treatment. He did feel the snow in his sleeves, the snow on his face. Extricating himself from the snowdrift, he made his way toward the piebald.

The moon was already high. The Great Bear had begun to dip its tail downward. The frost was getting heavier. In the north from time to time the fiery shafts of the beginning northern lights rose up, playing softly, from a dark hemispherical cloud.

The piebald, evidently understanding his master's condition, made his way home cautiously and sensibly. Makar sat on the wood-cart, weaving back and forth and continuing his song. He sang that he had drunk up five loads of wood and that his old lady was going to pound him. The sounds which tore from his throat rattled and moaned in the evening air so mournfully and plaintively that the foreigner who at that moment was climbing to the top of his hut to close the fireplace chimney felt his heart sink even lower from Makar's song. Meanwhile the piebald had drawn the wood-cart onto a small hill from which the surrounding areas were visible. Suffused with moonlight, the snow was glittering brightly. At times the light of the moon seemed to fade, the snow darkened, and the reflection of the northern lights immediately poured across it. Then it seemed that the snowy hills and the taiga were first drawing close, then moving away. Across the taiga Makar clearly saw the snowy bald spot of Yamalakh hill, beyond which, in the taiga, he had set his traps for all kinds of forest animals and birds.

This changed the direction of his thoughts. He began to sing that a fox had fallen into his trap. Tomorrow he would sell the fur and his old lady would not pound him.

The first stroke from the bell-tower was ringing out in the frosty air when Makar entered his hut. With his first words he informed his old lady that a fox had fallen into their snare. He had completely forgotten that his old lady had not drunk the vodka with him, and he was quite surprised when in spite of the joyous news she immediately gave him a cruel kick in the seat of his pants. After that, when he had fallen into the bed, she managed to sock him in the neck with her fist.

Meanwhile, floating far far into the distance, the solemn holiday tolling of bells rolled over Chalgan.

IV

He was lying in bed. His head burned. Inside it burned like fire. A pungent mixture of vodka and tobacco was spreading through his veins. Cold streams of melting ice flowed across his face; the same kind of streams were dripping down his back too.

The old woman thought he was sleeping. But he was not sleeping. The fox would not leave his mind. He had managed to completely convince himself that it had fallen into a trap; he even knew just which one it was. He saw it—saw it as, pinned by a heavy log, it dug at the snow with its claws and tried to pull itself out. Moonbeams piercing through the thicket of trees were playing on its golden fur. The beast's eyes glittered straight at him.

He could stand it no longer, and getting up from bed he started for his faithful piebald to drive out on the taiga.

What's that? Had the strong hands of his old woman grabbed the collar of his *sona* and thrown him onto the bed again?

No, he is already outside the settlement. The runners crunch evenly along the firm snow. Chalgan has been left behind. The solemn tone of the church bell floats behind, and against the light sky above the dark line of the horizon flash the black silhouettes of bands of Yakut riders in tall sharp-pointed caps. The Yakuts are hurrying to church.

Meanwhile the moon had gone down, and up high, at the very zenith, there was a small whitish cloud shining with a suffused, phosphorescent luster. Then it seemed to break, stretch out, flicker; and streaks of varicolored fires spread swiftly from it in various directions, while a small, dark hemispherical cloud in the north got even darker. It got black—blacker than the taiga which Makar was approaching.

The road wound through low, dense underbrush. Hills rose up on the left and right. The further he went, the higher the trees became. The taiga got thicker. It stood there silent and full of mystery. The naked branches of the larches drooped under a silver hoarfrost. Piercing through their summits, the soft glow of the northern lights strayed along the earth revealing a snowy glade here and there, or the fallen bodies of smashed forest giants buried in the snow. . . . A moment—and again everything was shrouded in darkness full of silence and mystery.

Makar stopped. At this place, almost on the road itself, was the beginning of a whole system of traps. In the phosphorescent light he could clearly see a low stockade of fallen timber; he even saw the first snare—three long heavy logs resting on an upright stake and supported by a rather clever system of levers with horsehair strings.

True, these were someone else's traps, but of course the fox might fall in someone else's. Makar got down from the sled, left the intelligent piebald on the road, and started listening carefully.

Not a sound on the taiga. Just the solemn tolling from the distant, now invisible settlement came floating as before.

There was no reason to be afraid. The owner of the traps, Alyoshka, a Chalganin, a neighbor, and a blood enemy of Makar was no doubt in church now. He could not see a single track on the smooth surface of the recently fallen snow.

He set off toward the thicket—nothing there. Snow crunches under his feet. The log traps stand in rows, like rows of cannon with open maws, in silent anticipation.

He walked back and forth—in vain. He struck out toward the road again.

But, hey! ... A light rustle. ... Reddish fur flashed on the taiga, this time in a lighted place, so close. ... Makar clearly saw the sharp ears of a fox; its fluffy tail flicked from side to side as if enticing Makar into the thicket. It disappeared among the tree-trunks in the direction of Makar's traps, and soon after a dull but heavy thud resounded in the forest. At first it rang out abruptly, dully—then as if echoing under the canopy of the taiga, and it died quietly in a distant ravine.

Makar's heart began to pound. That was a log trap falling.

He started to run, pushing his way through the thicket. Cold branches struck him across the eyes, poured snow in his face. He stumbled; his breath caught.

Then he ran out on a clearing which he himself had once cut. White from hoarfrost, trees stood on both sides; a shrinking path loomed across it, and its end was guarded by the throat of a large log trap. ... It wasn't far. ...

But there on the path, near the trap, flashed a figure, flashed and disappeared. Makar recognized the Chalganin Alyoshka; he could clearly see his small, stumpy figure, bent forward, with the gait of a bear. It seemed to Makar that Alyoshka's dark face got even darker and his big teeth were bared even more than usual.

Makar felt sincere indignation. "The rat! He is walking my trapline." True, Makar had just walked past Alyoshka's log traps himself, but there was a difference. ... To be precise, the difference was that when he himself had walked by someone else's traps he felt afraid of being caught; but when others walked past his traps he felt indignation and a desire to catch the violater of his rights.

He started running across toward the trap which had fallen. The fox was there. In his shuffling ursine gait Alyoshka was heading there too. He had to get there first.

There's the fallen trap. The red fur of the pinned animal shows under it. The fox has dug in the snow with its claws exactly as he had seen it before, and it was looking straight at him with its sharp burning eyes just as before.

"*Tytymá* (don't touch it)! It's mine!" Makar shouted at Alyoshka.

"*Tytymá!*" Alyoshka's voice rang out like an echo, "Mine!"

They both ran up at the same time and hurriedly, fighting each other, began to raise the log trap freeing the animal from beneath.

When the trap was raised up, the fox got up too. It gave a jump, then stopped, glanced at both of the Chalganins with a kind of sarcastic look; then lowering its nose, it licked the place that had been pinned by the log and merrily ran on, waving its tail in greeting.

Alyoshka was going to run after it, but Makar grabbed him from behind by the tail of his *sona*.

"*Tytymá!*" he shouted, "It's mine!" And he ran after the fox himself.

"*Tytymá!*" again rang the echo of Alyoshka's voice, and Makar felt him, in turn, grab him by the *sona*; and in one second Alyoshka again ran forward.

Makar was infuriated. He forgot the fox and headed for Alyoshka.

They kept running faster and faster. A branch of a larch tore the hat off Alyoshka's head, but he had no time to pick it up; Makar had already overtaken him with a ferocious shout. But Alyoshka had always been slyer than poor Makar. He stopped suddenly, turned around, and lowered his head. Makar hit it with his stomach and somersaulted into the snow. As he was falling, the cursed Alyoshka grabbed the cap from Makar's head and disappeared in the taiga.

Makar got up slowly. He felt totally beaten and unhappy. His state of mind was hateful. The fox had been in his hands, but now. . . . It seemed to him that in the darkened thicket it had again waved its tail sarcastically and disappeared completely.

It got dark. The whitish cloud could barely be seen in the zenith. It seemed to be quietly melting, and beams of fading light were still streaming from it, somehow wearily and languidly.

Whole streams of cutting rivulets of melted snow were running down Makar's overheated body. Snow had fallen down his sleeves, the collar of his *sona*; it was dripping down his back, pouring into his boots. Cursed Alyoshka had carried off his cap with him. He had lost his gloves somewhere during the chase. Things were bad. Makar knew that the fierce frost does not joke with men who go out into the taiga without gloves and without a cap.

He had already been walking for a long time. According to his calculations he should have come out of Yamalakh and seen the bell-tower long ago, but he kept circling in the taiga. The forest, as if enchanted, held him in its embrace. The same solemn tolling still reached him from the distance. It seemed to Makar that he was going toward it, but the tolling kept getting further away, and as its reverberations reached him more and more softly, dull despair crept into Makar's heart.

He got tired. He was crushed. His legs were shaking. His battered body ached with dull pain. His breath was catching in his throat. His hands and feet were frozen. His bared head felt as if red-hot bands were tightening around it.

"I'm going to die!" kept flashing through his mind more and more often. But he kept walking.

The taiga was silent. It just closed around him with a kind of stubborn hostility and gave no hope and no light anywhere.

"I'm going to die nevertheless!" Makar kept thinking.

He lost all his strength. Now the young trees struck him straight in the face without any restraint, mocking his helpless position. In one place, in a glade, a white *ushkan* (hare) ran out, sat on its haunches, waved its long ears with black markings on the tips, and started washing itself, making the most impudent faces at Makar. It was giving him to understand that it knew him, Makar, perfectly well—knew that he was the same Makar that had built clever contraptions in the taiga for his, the hare's, destruction. But now it was making fun of him.

Makar felt bitter. Meanwhile, the taiga was becoming more animated, but animated in a hostile way. Now even the distant trees were stretching their long branches into his way and grabbing him by the hair, beating his eyes and face. The ptarmigans were coming out of their secret coverts and fixing their curious round eyes on him; and grouse were running among them with drooping tails and angrily spread wings, and were loudly telling their mates of him, Makar, and of his snares. Finally, in the distant thickets, thousands of foxes' muzzles began to flash. They sniffed the air, and looked at Makar sarcastically, twitching their sharp ears. And the hares stood in front of him on their hind legs, and they laughed, announcing that he had gotten lost and would not get out of the taiga.

This was too much.

"I'm going to die!" thought Makar, and he decided to do it immediately.

He lay down in the snow.

It was getting colder. The last rays of the northern lights flickered faintly and stretched across the sky, peeping at Makar through the treetops. The last echoes of the bell reached him from faraway Chalgan.

The northern lights flared up and went out. The tolling ceased. And Makar died.

v

How it happened, he did not notice. He knew that something should go out of him, and he waited for it to go out at any moment. . . . But nothing went out.

Meantime, he realized that he had already died, and therefore he lay quietly, without moving. He lay for a long time—so long that he got bored.

It was totally dark when Makar felt someone poke him with a foot. He turned his head and opened his closed eyes.

Now the larches were standing over him peacefully, quietly, as if ashamed of the earlier pranks. The shaggy firs stretched out their broad, snow-covered paws and rocked quietly, quietly. Just as quietly radiant snowflakes settled through the air.

From the blue sky bright, kind stars peeped through the thick branches and seemed to be saying: "There, you see, a poor man died." Right over Makar's body, poking it with his foot, stood the old priest Ivan. His long cassock was covered with snow; snow could be seen on his fur *begres* (cap), on his shoulders, in Father Ivan's long beard. Most surprising of all was the fact that this was the same Father Ivan who had died four years earlier.

He had been a good priest. He never pressed Makar for the tithes, never even demanded money for the services. Makar had set his own fees for christenings and requiems, and now he recalled with shame that he sometimes paid rather little, and on occasion had not paid at all. Father Ivan still did not take offense; he demanded only one thing: he had to be given a bottle of vodka every time. If Makar had no money, Father Ivan sent for the bottle himself, and they drank it together. Without fail the priest got as drunk as suited his position, but he rarely got into fights and then not bad ones. Makar would deliver him, helpless and defenseless, home into the care of his old wife.

Yes, he was a good priest, but he died a bad death. Once when everyone had left the house and the drunken priest was left lying in bed alone, he decided to smoke. He got up, and went staggering up to the huge fiercely heated fireplace to light his pipe from the fire. He was already too drunk; he tripped and fell into the fire. When his family returned all that was left of the priest were his legs.

Everyone felt sorry for the kind Father Ivan; but since all that was left of him were his legs, no doctor in the world could cure him. They buried the legs and another priest was appointed to Ivan's place.

Now Ivan, whole, was standing over Makar and prodding him with his foot.

"Get up, Makar old fellow," he said, "Let's go."

"Where am I going?" asked Makar with dissatisfaction.

He supposed that once he had died it was his obligation to lie peacefully, and he had no need of going into the taiga again, wandering without a road. Otherwise why should he die?

"Let us go to the *Great Toyon*."

"Why am I going to him?" asked Makar.

"He is going to judge you," said the priest in a sorrowful and somewhat tender voice.

Makar remembered that after death one really did have to go somewhere for judgment. He had heard this in church once. That meant the priest was right. He would have to get up.

And Makar got up, muttering to himself that there is no peace for a man even after death.

The priest walked ahead, Makar behind him. They kept walking straight. The larches moved aside meekly, making way. They walked to the east.

With surprise Makar noticed that there were no tracks in the snow behind Father Ivan. Glancing under his feet he saw no tracks there either; the snow was as clean and smooth as a tablecloth.

He thought that now it would be very easy for him to walk other people's traps since no one could find out about it; but evidently guessing his secret thought, the priest turned around to him and said:

"*Kabys* (quit it, stop)! Don't you know what you'll get for every thought like that?"

"Well, well!" Makar answered, dissatisfied, "Now I can't even think! What's made you so strict nowadays? Just shut up!"

The priest shook his head and walked on.

"Do we have a long way to go?" asked Makar.

"A long way," answered the priest sadly.

"And what are we going to eat?" asked Makar again, worriedly.

"You have forgotten," answered the priest, turning around to him, "that you are dead and now you don't need to eat or drink."

Makar did not like that very much. Of course, it is good in case there is nothing to eat, but then one should lie just as he was lying immediately after his death. But to walk, and then to walk even further and not to eat anything seemed to him totally illogical. He started grumbling again.

"Don't gripe!" said the priest.

"O.K." answered Makar in a hurt tone, but he continued complaining to himself and grumbling about the bad rules: "They make a man walk, but he doesn't have to eat. Who ever heard of such a thing?"

He was dissatisfied the whole time he was following the priest. And they apparently walked for a long time. True, Makar had not seen the dawn; but judging by the distance, it seemed to him that they had already been walking for a whole week: they had left behind so many ravines and cliffs, rivers and lakes, they had passed by so many forests and plains. When Makar looked back it seemed to him the dark taiga itself was running away from them, and the high snowy mountains seemed to melt into the murky night and quickly hide beyond the horizon.

They seemed to be rising higher and higher. The stars kept getting bigger and brighter. Then the rim of the moon, which had set long ago, appeared from beyond the crest of the height to which they had risen. It seemed to be hurrying to leave, but Makar and the priest were overtaking it. Finally it started to rise above the horizon again. They walked across a smooth, extremely elevated plain.

Now it got light—much lighter than at the beginning of the night. Of course this happened because they were much closer to the stars. The stars, each the size of an apple, fairly glittered; and the moon, as big as the bottom of a large golden barrel, shone like the sun, illuminating the plain from edge to edge.

Every snowflake on the plain was sharply discernible. A multitude of roads lay across it, and they all converged toward one place in the east. People of various aspects in various kinds of clothes were walking and riding along the roads.

Carefully scrutinizing one rider, Makar suddenly turned off the road and ran after him.

"Wait, wait!" shouted the priest, but Makar did not even hear. He had recognized a Tatar he knew who six years ago had stolen a piebald horse from him, and who had died five years ago. Now the Tatar was riding the same piebald horse. The horse was skimming along rapidly. From under its hooves flew whole clouds of snowy dust which glittered with the various flashes of twinkling stars. At the right of this mad gallop Makar was surprised that he, a pedestrian, could so easily overtake the mounted Tatar. However, seeing Makar several steps away, the Tatar stopped quite willingly. Makar attacked him vehemently.

"Let's go to the village elder," he shouted, "that's my horse, His right ear is slit. Look how smart he is! . . . He rides another man's horse, and his owner goes on foot like a beggar."

"Wait!" said the Tatar to this. "There's no need to go to the elder. It's your horse, you say? . . . Well, take it then! The damned beast! I've been riding it for five years, and it still seems not to have moved. . . . Men on foot are overtaking me constantly; it's even shameful for a good Tatar."

And he threw his leg over as if to get down from the saddle, but at that moment the gasping priest ran up to him and grabbed Makar by the arm.

"Unhappy fellow!" he exclaimed. "What are you doing? Don't you see the Tatar wants to trick you?"

"Of course he's tricking me," exclaimed Makar, waving his arms, "it was a good horse, a real gentleman's. . . . I was offered forty rubles for it when it was only three years old. . . . No-oo, brother! If you've ruined the horse, I'll cut it up for meat, and you'll pay me hard cash. Do you think that there's no law for you because your're a Tatar?"

Makar was getting angry and shouting on purpose, so as to attract some more people, because he was used to being afraid of Tatars. But the priest stopped him.

"Quiet, quiet. Makar! You keep forgetting that you have already died. . . . Why do you need a horse? And besides, don't you see that on foot you are moving much faster than the Tatar? Do you want to have to ride for thousands of years?"

Makar realized why the Tatar was giving up the horse so willingly.

"Sly people!" he thought, and turned to the Tatar:

"O.K. then! Ride the horse, and I'll forgive you, brother."

The Tatar angrily pulled his cap down over his ears and whipped the horse. The horse whirled into action, chunks of snow poured out from under its hooves; but though Makar and the priest had not moved, the Tatar did not draw even an inch away.

He spit angrily and turned to Makar:

"Listen, *dorog* (friend), you don't have a twist of *makhorka* (tobacco) do you? I want a smoke awfully, but I smoked up all my own tobacco four years ago."

"A dog's your friend, not I!" Makar answered angrily. "You see —he stole my horse and asks for tobacco! You could go to hell altogether and I still wouldn't feel sorry for you!"

And with these words Makar moved on.

"Well, it's too bad you didn't give him a twist of *makhorka*," Father Ivan said to him. "No fewer than a hundred sins would have been forgiven you at Toyon's judgment."

"So why didn't you tell me that before?" snapped Makar.

"Well, now it's too late to teach you. You should have learned about this from your priests in life."

Makar grew angry. He saw no sense in priests: they took their tithes and didn't even teach you when to give a Tatar a twist of tobacco in order to receive forgiveness of sins. A hundred sins is no joke . . . and all just for one twist! . . . That had really cost him!

"Wait!" he said. "I'll keep one twist with me, and I'll give the other four to the Tatar right now. That will be four hundred sins."

"Look back," said the priest.

Makar looked back. Only a white deserted plain stretched out behind. For one second the Tatar flashed like a distant dot. It seemed to Makar he had seen the white dust flying out from under his piebald's hooves, but in a second this dot disappeared too.

"Well, well," said Makar. "The Tatar will be O.K. without the tobacco. You see, he ruined the horse, the damned guy!"

"No," said the priest, "he did not ruin your horse, but it is the stolen horse. Haven't you heard from old men that one can't ride far on a stolen horse?"

Makar actually had heard that from old men, but since during his life he had often seen Tatars ride as far as the city itself on stolen horses, it is understandable that he put no faith in the old men. But now he came to the conclusion that even old men sometimes tell the truth.

And he began overtaking many riders on the plain. They were all running just as fast as the first one. The horses were flying like birds, the riders were sweating, and nevertheless Makar kept overtaking and leaving them behind.

For the most part they were Tatars, but there were a few native Chalgan Russians too; a few of the latter were sitting on stolen oxen and goading them with lumps of ice.

Makar looked at the Tatars with hostility, and every time he grumbled that that was still not enough for them. But when he met Chalganins he would stop and chat amiably with them: they were still friends, even though thieves. At times he even expressed his sympathy by picking up a lump of ice on the road and zealously goading the oxen and horses from behind; but as soon as he took a few steps himself the riders would be left behind, as barely visible dots.

The plain seemed infinite. They kept overtaking riders and men walking, but nevertheless everything around seemed empty. Hundreds or even thousands of versts seemed to lie between each two travelers.

Among other people Makar came across an unfamiliar old man; he was evidently from Chalgan; this could be seen from his face, from his clothing, even from his walk, but Makar could not remember ever seeing him before. The old man had a torn *sona*, a big hat with earflaps, also torn, old leather pants, and torn calfskin *torbasa* (boots). But, worst of all, in spite of his old age he was carrying an even more ancient old woman on his shoulders, her feet dragging along the ground. The old man was breathing hard, staggering, and leaning heavily on his stick. Makar felt sorry for him. He stopped. The old man stopped too.

"*Kapse* (speak)!" said Makar amiably.

"No," said the old man.

"What've you heard?"

"Ain't heard nothin'."

"What've you seen?"

"Ain't seen nothin'."

Makar was silent for a minute, and then he considered it possible to ask the old man who he was and where he was crawling from.

The old man gave his name. Long ago—how long he did not know himself—he had left Chalgan and gone away "to the mountain" to save himself. He did not do anything there; he ate only berries and roots, he did not plough, did not sow, did not grind wheat, and did not pay taxes. When he died he went to Toyon for judgment. Toyon asked who he was and what he had done. He said he had gone away "to the mountain" and saved himself. "Good," said Toyon, "but where is your woman? Go, bring your old woman here." And he went after his old woman, but she had been forced to beg before her death—and there had been no one to feed her, and she had neither a house, nor a cow, nor breed. She grew weak and could not move her legs. And now he had to drag the old lady to Toyon on his back.

The old man began to cry, but the old woman goaded him with her foot, like an ox, and said in a weak but angry voice:

"Get going!"

Makar felt even sorrier for the old man, but he was heartily glad that he had not managed to go away "to the mountain." His old woman was a huge stout woman, and it would be even harder for him to carry her. And if besides this she started prodding him with her foot like an ox, she would surely ride him to a second death.

From compassion he was going to pick up the old woman's legs in order to help his friend, but he had taken scarcely two or three steps when he was forced to let go of the old woman's legs so they would not be left in his hands. In a minute the old man and his burden disappeared from view.

The rest of the way they met no more people whom Makar would honor with special attention. There were thieves loaded like beasts of burden with stolen goods, moving along step by step; fat Yakut chiefs rode along mounted on high saddles, like towers, their tall caps brushing the clouds. Skipping right beside him ran poor *komnochity* (workmen), as lean and light as hares. A saturnine murderer all covered with blood was walking along with a wildly wandering gaze. In vain he would throw himself into the pure snow to wash away the bloody spots. The snow turned to crimson foam instantly, and the spots on the murderer stood out more clearly; and one could see wild despair and horror in his eyes. And he kept walking on, avoiding the frightened looks of other people.

And now and then the small souls of children flashed by in the air like little birds. They flew in large flocks, and this did not surprise Makar. The bad, coarse food, the filth, the heat of the fireplaces, and the cold lights in the huts drove them out of Chalgan alone almost by the hundreds. When they overtook the murderer they rushed far off to the side in a frightened flock, and the quick, agitated whirring of their small wings could be heard for a long time after that.

Makar could not help noticing that he was moving quite rapidly in comparison with the others, and he hurried to ascribe this to his virtue.

"Listen, *agabyt* (Father)," he said, "What do you think? Even though in life I liked to drink, I was a good man. God loves me. . . ."

He glanced at Father Ivan inquiringly. He had an ulterior motive: to get some information out of the old priest. But he said tersely:

"Don't be proud! It's not far now. You'll soon find out for yourself."

Makar had not noticed earlier that it seemed to be getting light on the plain. First a few rays of light shot up from beyond the horizon. They ran quickly across the sky and extinguished the bright stars. And the stars went out; the moon set. And the snowy plain grew dark.

Then mists arose and stood around the plain like an honor-guard.

And in one place, in the east, the mists grew lighter, like warriors dressed in gold.

And then the mists stirred, the gold warriors bowed down to the ground.

And then the sun rose from behind them and rested on their golden ranks and looked across the plain.

And the whole plain shone with a marvelous blinding light.

And the mists rose up triumphantly in an enormous line; it parted in the west, and, swaying, swept upwards.

And it seemed to Makar that he heard a wonderful song. It was somehow the same long familiar song with which the earth greets the sun every time. But Makar had never paid sufficient attention to it before, and for the first time he understood what a wonderful song it was.

He stood and listened and did not want to walk on, but he wanted to stand here eternally and listen. . . .

* * *

But Father Ivan touched his sleeve.

"Let's go in," he said, "We have arrived."

Then Makar saw that they were standing at a large door which the mists had concealed earlier.

He was very loath to go in, but there was nothing to be done, and he submitted.

V I

They entered a handsome and spacious hut, and just as they were entering Makar noticed that it was extremely cold outside. In the middle of the hut stood a fireplace made of pure silver with marvelous carved decorations, and in it burned golden logs suffusing an even heat which immediately penetrated the entire body. The fire in this marvelous fireplace did not cut or burn the eyes; it just warmed, and again Makar wanted to stand here eternally and warm himself. Father Ivan also walked up to the fireplace and stretched out his frozen hands to it.

There were four doors into the room, only one of which led outside; and young men in long white shirts walked in and out of them from time to time. Makar thought that they must be the workers of Toyon. It seemed to him that he had seen them somewhere already, but he could not remember precisely where. He was not a little surprised by the fact that large white wings flopped on the back of each worker, and he thought that Toyon probably had still other workers since with their wings these surely could not get through the thicket of the taiga to cut wood or poles.

One of the workers walked up to the fireplace too, and turning his back to him, started talking to Father Ivan:

"Speak!"

"There's nothing to say," answered the priest.

"What did you hear on earth?"

"Didn't hear anything."

"What did you see?"

"Didn't see anything."

They were both silent a bit, and then the priest said:

"I brought that one there."

"He's from Chalgan?" asked the worker.

"Yes, from Chalgan."

"Well, that means we'll have to get the big scales ready."

And he went out one of the doors to make arrangements; Makar asked the priest why scales were needed, particularly large ones.

"You see," replied the priest somewhat embarrassedly, "scales are needed to weigh the good and evil which you did in life. For all other people evil and good approximately balance each other, but people from Chalgan have so many sins that Toyon ordered special scales made with huge bowls for the sins."

At these words Makar's heart seemed to skip a beat. He began to quail.

Workers brought in and set up the big scales. One bowl was gold and small, the other was wooden, of huge proportions. A deep black hole suddenly opened under the latter.

Makar walked up and examined the scales assiduously to make sure they were true. They were true. The scales stood evenly, without wavering.

However, he did not fully understand their construction and would have preferred to use a simple balance on which in the course of a long life he had learned how to sell or buy with a certain profit to himself.

"Toyon is coming," Father Ivan said suddenly and he hastily started straightening his cassock.

The middle door opened and in walked ancient, venerable Toyon with a big silver beard that reached below his waist. He was dressed in rich furs and fabrics unfamiliar to Makar, and on his feet were warm boots lined with velvet such as Makar had seen on an old ikon-painter.

And at the first glance at old Toyon, Makar realized that he was the same old man whose picture he had seen in church. Only there was no son with him here; Makar thought that he had probably gone off to work. But a dove flew into the room, and after circling around the old man's head, it perched on his knee. And old Toyon stroked the dove with his hand, while sitting on a chair especially prepared for him.

Old Toyon's face was kind, and when Makar's heart had become too heavy, he looked at this face and he felt better.

But his heart had become heavy because he had suddenly remembered his whole life, to the last details, remembered his every step, and every stroke of the ax, every tree he had cut, and every deceit, and every glass of vodka drunk.

And he became ashamed and afraid. But having looked at Toyon's face, he took heart.

But when he had done so, he decided that perhaps he would manage to conceal a few things.

Old Toyon looked at him and asked him who he was and where he was from, his name and how old he was.

When Makar had answered Toyon asked:

"What did you do in your life?"

"You know yourself," answered Makar, "you must have it written down."

Makar was testing old Toyon, wanting to find out if he really did have everything written down.

"Tell me yourself, don't be silent!" said old Toyon.

And Makar again took heart.

He started to enumerate his jobs, and although he remembered every stroke of the ax and every pole he had cut, and every furrow he had ploughed, he added thousands of poles and hundreds of loads of wood, and hundreds of logs, and hundreds of pounds of sown seed.

When he had enumerated everything, old Toyon turned to Father Ivan:

"Bring the book here."

Then Makar saw that Father Ivan served as Toyon's *suruksut* (clerk), and got very angry that he had not told him about this before in a friendly way.

Father Ivan brought a large book, opened it, and started to read.

"Look and see," said old Toyon, "how many poles."

Father Ivan looked and said with sorrow:

"He added thirteen thousand."

"He's lying!" shouted Makar vehemently. "He's probably made a mistake, because he is a drunk and died a bad death!"

"Be quiet!" said old Toyon. "Did he take extra from you for christenings and weddings? Did he ever squeeze you for tithes?"

"Why speak in vain," replied Makar.

"There, you see," said Toyon, "I know myself that he liked to drink. . . ."

And old Toyon got angry.

"Now read his sins from the book, because he is a deceiver and I do not believe him," he said to Father Ivan.

And meanwhile the workers had thrown Makar's poles, and his firewood, and his furrows, and all of his works into the golden bowl. And altogether there turned out to be so much that the golden bowl of the scales descended, so the wooden one raised very very high; and it was impossible to reach it by hand, and the divine young workers flew up on their wings and a whole hundred of them dragged it down with ropes.

Heavy was the work of a man from Chalgan!

But Father Ivan started reading off the frauds, and it turned out there were twenty-one thousand nine hundred and thirty-three frauds; and the priest started reading off how many bottles of vodka Makar had drunk, and there were four hundred bottles; and the priest read further, and Makar saw that the wooden bowl was outweighing the golden one, and that it was already descending into a pit, and while the priest was reading it kept descending.

Then Makar thought to himself that his case was bad, and approaching the scales he tried to support the bowl with his foot unnoticed. But one of the workers saw this and it caused an uproar.

"What's going on there?" asked old Toyon.

"Why he wanted to hold up the scales with his foot," replied the worker.

Then Toyon turned angrily to Makar and said:

"I see that you are a cheat, a sluggard and drunkard. . . . And you left your arrears unpaid, and you owe your tithes to the priest, and the police officer is sinning for you by cursing you every time with nasty words! . . ."

And turning to Father Ivan, old Toyon asked:

"Who in Chalgan puts the biggest loads on horses and who drives them harder than anyone else?"

Father Ivan replied:

"The church beadle. He carries the mail and drives the police officer around."

Then old Toyon said:

"Hand over this sluggard to the church beadle as a gelding, and let him carry the police officer until he collapses. . . . And then we will see."

And just as old Toyon was saying these words the door opened and old Toyon's son walked into the hut and sat down at his right hand.

And the son said:

"I heard your sentence. . . . I lived in the world for a long time and I know things there: it will be hard for the poor man to carry the police officer! But . . . so be it! . . . Only perhaps he has something else to say. Speak, *baraksan* (poor fellow)!"

Then something strange happened. Makar, the same Makar who never in his life had uttered more than ten words in a row, suddenly felt the gift of words in himself. He began to speak and was amazed himself. It was as if there were two Makars: one was talking, the other was listening and surprised. He did not believe his ears. His speech flowed smoothly and passionately; the words ran out one after the other and then stood in long harmonious rows. He was not timid. If he happened to stutter, he immediately corrected himself and shouted out twice as loud. But the main think was that he himself felt he was speaking convincingly.

Old Toyon, who was at first rather angry at his audacity, soon began to listen with close attention as if he were convinced that Makar was not such a fool as he seemed at first. In the first moment Father Ivan was even frightened and started pulling Makar by the tail of his *sona*, but Makar waved him away and continued as before. But then the priest stopped being afraid and he burst into a smile, seeing that his parishioner was hitting on the truth and that the truth warmed the heart of old Toyon. Even the young men in long shirts and white wings who lived with old Toyon as workers came to the doors from their quarters, and they listened to Makar's speech with amazement, pushing each other with their elbows.

He began by saying he did not want to be the beadle's gelding. And not because he was afraid of hard work, but because the decision was wrong. And since the decision was wrong, he would not submit; he would not even lift a finger, not move a foot. Let them do what they want to him! Let them even give him to the devils for eternal torment—he would not carry the police officer because it was wrong. And let them not think that he was afraid of being a gelding: the beadle goads the gelding, but he feeds him oats, but he had been driven all his life and had never been fed oats.

"Who goaded you?" asked old Toyon hotly.

Yes, he had been goaded all his life! He had been goaded by elders and bailiffs, magistrates and police officers demanding taxes; he had been goaded by priests demanding tithes; he had been goaded by privation and hunger, and he had been goaded by freezing weather and heat waves, rain and drought; he had been goaded by the frozen earth and the evil taiga! A beast of burden goes forward looking at the ground not knowing where it is being goaded. . . . And he too. . . . Could he know what the priest was reading in church and why he had to pay tithes? Could he know why and where his eldest son had been taken when he was conscripted into the army, or where he had died, or where his poor bones lay now?

They charged he had drunk a lot of vodka? Of course that is true, his heart craved vodka. . . .

"How many bottles did you say he drank?"

"Four hundred," replied Father Ivan glancing into the book.

"All right! But was that really vodka? Three-quarters was water and only one-quarter real vodka, and even that was mixed with tobacco. Therefore three hundred bottles should be thrown from the tally.

"Is everything he is saying true?" old Toyon asked Father Ivan, and it was obvious that he was still angry.

"Pure truth," Father Ivan replied quickly, and Makar continued.

He had added thirteen thousand poles? So what? What if he had cut only sixteen thousand? Is that too little? And besides he had cut two thousand when his first wife was ill. . . . And his heart was heavy, and he wanted to sit by his woman, but necessity drove him out into the taiga. . . . And in the taiga he wept, and the tears froze on his eyelashes, and cold from his grief pierced right to his heart. . . . But he had gone on cutting!

But then his wife died. She had to be buried, but he had no money. And he hired himself out to cut firewood in order to pay for his wife's house in the other world. . . . But the merchant saw that he had to have the work, so he gave only twenty kopecks per load. . . . And his woman lay alone in the unheated, frozen hut, but he again went on cutting and weeping. He thought these loads should be counted five times and even more.

Tears appeared in old Toyon's eyes, and Makar saw the bowls of the scales shake, and the wooden one was rising up while the golden one sank down.

And Makar continued: they had everything noted down in the book. . . . Let them look a little more—when had he ever been given affection, kindness, or joy? Where were his children? When they were dying he was bitter and sorrowful; but when they grew up, they left him in order to fight onerous privation alone. And he and his second wife had grown old alone; and he had seen his strength leaving him and evil, homeless decrepitude approaching. They had stood alone, like two orphaned fir trees in the steppe, pounded from all sides by cruel storms.

"Is it true?" old Toyon asked again.

And the priest hurried to reply:

"Pure truth!"

And then the scales shuddered again. . . . But old Toyon began thinking.

"How is this," he said, "on earth I have truly righteous people. . . . Their eyes are clear, and their faces bright, and their clothes are without stains. . . . Their hearts are as soft as good soil; they receive the good seed and send back fragrant shoots whose odor pleases me. But look at yourself. . . ."

And all glances were fixed on Makar, and he was ashamed. He felt that his eyes were dim and his face dark, his hair and beard unkempt, his clothing torn. And though long before his death he kept intending to buy boots to wear at the judgment, as a good peasant should do, he kept drinking up the money, and now he stood before Toyon, like the poorest Yakut, in wretched *torbasy*. . . . And he wanted to fall through the earth.

"Your face is dark," continued old Toyon, "your eyes dim and clothing torn. And your heart has grown over with burdock and thistles and bitter wormwood. That is why I love my righteous and turn my face away from ungodly men such as you."

Makar's heart contracted. He felt the shame of his existence. He was going to lower his head, but suddenly he raised it and began to speak again.

Of what righteous men was Toyon speaking? If it was those who lived on earth at the same time Makar had in rich homes, then he knew them. . . . Their eyes are clear because they had not poured as many tears as Makar had, and their faces bright because they were bathed in perfumes and their clean clothes were made by hands other than their own.

Makar again lowered his head, but immediately raised it again.

But could it be that Toyon did not see that he, like others, had been born with clear, open eyes which reflected the earth and the sky, and with pure heart ready to open up to all that is beautiful in the world? And if now he wanted to hide his dark and shameful face under the earth, it was not his fault. . . . Whose then? That he did not know. . . . But he did know only that the patience of his heart had been exhausted.

VII

Of course if Makar could have seen what effect his speech was having on old Toyon, if he had seen that every one of his angry words fell in the golden bowl like a plummet of lead, he would have calmed his heart. But he did not see any of this, because blind despair was pouring into his heart.

He had surveyed his whole bitter life. How could he have borne this horrible burden until now? He had carried it because hope kept beckoning ahead, like a small star in the fog. He was alive, therefore it could be that he should experience a better lot. . . . Now he was standing at the end, and hope was snuffed out. . . .

Then it grew dark in his soul, and fury raged in it as a tempest breaks over the empty steppe in the black of night. He forgot where he was, before whom he was standing—he forgot everything except his anger. . . .

* * *

But old Toyon said to him:

"Wait, *baraksan*! You are not on earth. . . . Here there is justice for you too. . . ."

And Makar trembled. Into his heart fell the awareness that they felt sorry for him, and it grew softer; and because his poor life, from the first day to the last, was still before his eyes, he began to feel unbearably sorry for himself. And he began to weep. . . .

And old Toyon wept too. . . . And old Father Ivan wept, and the young workers of God shed tears, wiping them away with their wide white sleeves.

And the scales kept shuddering, and the wooden bowl was rising ever higher and higher!

*   *   *

ANTON CHEKHOV

Heartache

E VENING TWILIGHT. Large wet flakes of snow circle lazily around
the just lighted streetlamps and lie on roofs, horses' backs,
caps, and shoulders in a thin, soft layer. Cabby Iona Potapov is all
white as a ghost. As hunched over as a living body can be hunched,
he sits on the box and does not stir. If a whole snowdrift were to
fall on him, even then, it seems, he would not find it necessary to
shake the snow off himself . . . His nag, too, is white and motionless. In her motionlessness, angularity of shape, and stick-like
straightness, even up close she looks like a penny gingerbread horse.
In all probability she is sunk in thought. One who has been torn
away from the plow, from the customary grey scenes, and been cast
here, into this whirlpool of monstrous light, unceasing din, and
rushing people, cannot help thinking . . .

It has been a long time since Iona and his horse have moved
from their place. They left the stable before supper, and still there
is no fare. But now evening darkness is descending on the city. The

Translated by CARL R. PROFFER.

pale light of the streetlamps is surrendering its place to vivid color, and the bustle in the street is becoming noisier.

"Cabby, to the Vyborg District!" hears Iona, "Cabby!"

Iona starts, and through eyelashes pasted over with snow he sees an officer in a cloak with a hood.

"To the Vyborg District!" repeats the officer. "What's the matter, are you asleep? To the Vyborg District!"

As a sign of assent Iona tugs the reins, causing the layers of snow to pour off the horse's back and his own shoulders . . . The officer gets in. The cabby clucks to the horse, stretches his neck out swan-like, raises up, and more from habit than need, waves his whip. The nag stretches her neck too, crooks her stick-like legs, and moves irresolutely from her place . . .

"Where are you heading, you gnome!" almost immediately Iona hears shouts from the dark mass of people moving back and forth. "Where the hell are you going? Keep to the r-r-right!"

"You don't know how to drive! Keep to the right!" says the officer angrily.

The driver of a carriage curses him; a passer-by who was crossing the road and has his shoulder bumped by the nag's muzzle looks at him fiercely and shakes the snow from his sleeve. Iona fidgets on the box, as if on pins and needles, shoves his elbows out to the side and rolls his eyes like a madman, as if he does not understand where he is and why he is here.

"What scoundrels they all are!" jokes the officer. "They are all trying to bump into you or fall under the horse. They're conspiring."

Iona looks around at the passenger and moves his lips . . . Apparently he wants to say something, but nothing comes from his throat except a wheeze.

"What?" asks the officer.

Iona twists his mouth with a smile, strains his throat and wheezes:

"My son, sir . . . er, he died this week."

"Hm! What did he die of?"

Iona turns his whole body around toward the passenger and says:

"Well who knows? From fever, probably . . . He lay in the hospital three days and died . . . God's will."

"Turn off, you devil!" rings out in the dark. "Where yah crawled out of, you old dog? Use your eyes!"

"Get going, get going . . ." says the passenger. "At this rate we won't get there before tomorrow. Use the whip!"

The cabby again stretches out his neck, raises up, and waves the whip with ponderous grace. Then he looks back at the passenger, but he has closed his eyes and apparently is not disposed to listen. When he has let him out in the Vyborg District, Iona stops by a tavern, hunches over on the box, and again he does not stir . . . The wet snow again paints him and his nag white. One hour passes, another . . .

Cursing each other and stomping their boots loudly on the sidewalk, three young men walk by: two of them are tall and thin, the third is short and hunchbacked.

"Driver, to Policemen's Bridge!" shouts the hunchback in a cracking voice. "Three of us . . . a twenty-kopek piece!"

Iona tugs the reins and clucks. A twenty-kopek piece is not a proper fare, but he's not interested in the price . . . A ruble or a five-kopek piece, it's all the same to him, as long as he has passengers . . . Bumping into each other and swearing, the young men walk up to the sleigh and all three immediately try to sit down. They begin to solve the question of which two are to sit and which one to stand. After lengthy abuse, capriciousness, and rebukes, they reach the conclusion that since the hunchback is the smallest, he ought to stand.

"Well, drive on," cracks the hunchback, taking his place and breathing down Iona's neck. "Shove off! And, brother, your cap! A worse one couldn't be found in all of Petersburg . . ."

"He, he . . . He, he . . ." laughs Iona. "Whatever you say . . ."

"Well, you 'whatever you say,' drive on! You gonna drive like this the whole way? Yes? And how about a sock in the neck? . . ."

"My head is bursting . . ." says one of the gangly ones. "Yesterday at the Dukmasovs' Vaska and I drank four bottles of cognac between the two of us."

"I don't see why he lies!" the other gangly one says angrily. "He lies like a pig!"

"Really, God punish me . . ."

"That's about as true as that louse's coughs."

"He, he!" snickers Iona. "Gay fellows!"

"Faugh, go to Hell!" says the hunchback indignantly. "Are you going to get going or not, you old rat? Is this the way to drive?"

Behind his back Iona can feel the twisting body and quavering voice of the hunchback. He hears the abuse directed at him, he sees the men, and little by little the feeling of loneliness begins to lift from his heart. The hunchback goes on abusing him until he is choked by a six-story-high oath and breaks off coughing. The gangly ones begin to talk about a certain Nadezhda Petrovna. Iona looks around at them. Waiting for a short pause, he looks around again and mutters:

"And this week my . . . er . . . son died!"

"We'll all die . . ." sighs the hunchback, wiping his lips after the coughing. "Well, drive on, drive on! Gentlemen, I absolutely cannot go any further like this! When will he get us there?"

"You encourage him a little—in the neck!"

"Hear that you old rat? Why I'll whack your neck! . . . If we're going to stand on ceremony with your kind, we might as well go on foot . . . You hear, Snake Gorynych? Or do you spit on your words?"

And Iona hears more than feels the thud of a blow on the neck.

"He, he . . ." he laughs. "Gay fellows . . . God grant you health!"

"Driver, are you married?" asks a tall one.

"Me? He, he . . . Ga-a-ay fellows! Now I got one wife—the damp earth . . . Ho, ho, ho . . . The grave, that is! . . . My son's died now, and I'm alive . . . Queer thing, death knocked at the wrong door . . . Instead of coming to me, it went to my son . . ."

And Iona turns around to tell how his son died, but the hunchback sighs lightly and announces that, thank God, they've finally arrived. Receiving his twenty-kopek piece, Iona looks after the carousers disappearing in a dark entrance for a long time. Again he is alone, and again there is silence for him . . . The heartache which had eased for a while, appears again and rends the breast with even greater force. Iona's eyes run anxiously and tormentedly over the crowd surging along both sides of the street: from these thousands of people, can't even one be found who would hear him out? But the crowds run along, not noticing him or his heartache . . . Vast, boundless heartache. If Iona's breast burst and the heartache poured out, it seems it would flood the entire world—but nevertheless people do not see it. It managed to fit into such an insignificant shell that you would not see it in the daylight with a torch . . .

Iona sees a doorkeeper with a sack and decides to talk to him.

"What time would it be now, friend?" he asks.

"After nine . . . Why you stopping here? Move along!"

Iona drives a few steps away, hunches up and surrenders to the heartache . . . He considers it useless to turn to people. But five minutes do not pass before he straightens up, shakes his head as if he felt a sharp pain, and yanks the reins . . . He can't bear it.

"To the stable," he thinks, "to the stable."

And as if she has understood his thought, the nag begins to run at a trot. An hour and a half later Iona is already sitting by a big dirty stove. On the stove, floor, and benches people are snoring. The air is stuffy and smells of cheap vodka . . . Iona looks at the sleepers, scratches himself and regrets returning home so early . . .

"And I didn't make enough for oats," he thinks. "That's the reason for the heartache. A man who knows his stuff . . . who's full himself and whose horse is full, is always at ease."

In one of the corners a young driver gets up, croaks sleepily, and heads for the waterbucket.

"You want a drink?" asks Iona.

"Obviously!"

"So . . . Your health . . . And, friend, my son died. Did you hear? This week in the hospital . . . A story!"

Iona looks for what effect his words have produced, but sees nothing. The young man has covered his head and is already sleeping. The old man sighs and scratches himself . . . He wants to talk, just as the young man wanted to drink. It will soon be a week since his son died, and he still hasn't talked to anyone about it properly . . . He should speak with good sense, in measured tones . . . He must tell how his son got sick, how he suffered, what he said before death, how he died . . . He should describe the funeral and the trip to the hospital for the deceased's clothes. A daughter, Anisya, remained in the country . . . He should talk about her too . . . Does he have any dearth of things he can talk about now? The listener should moan, sigh, lament . . . And it's even better to talk to women. Even though they are fools, they wail after two words.

"Go see after the horse," thinks Iona. "You'll always manage some sleep . . . You'll probably get enough sleep."

He gets dressed and goes into the stable where his horse is standing. He thinks about oats, hay, about the weather . . . About his son, when he is alone, he cannot think . . . It is possible to talk to someone about him, but by himself it is unbearably painful to think about him and draw his picture.

"Chewing?" Iona asks his horse, seeing her shining eyes. "Well, chew, chew . . . If we didn't get enough for oats, we'll eat hay . . . Yes . . . I've already got too old to go out . . . My son should drive, not me . . . He was a real driver . . . If only he were alive . . ."

Iona is silent for a while and continues:

"So, my girl . . . Kozma Ionych is gone . . . He left this life . . . Went and died for nothing . . . Now, let's say, you have a little colt, and you are the natural mother of this little colt . . . And suddenly, let's say, this little colt left this life . . . Wouldn't you be sorry?"

The nag chews, listens, and breathes on the hands of her master . . .

Iona is carried away and tells her everything . . .

ANTON CHEKHOV

Gooseberries

THE SKY HAD BEEN COVERED WITH RAIN CLOUDS since early morning; it was calm, not hot and oppressive as it is on grey overcast days when clouds have been hanging over the fields for a long time and you wait for rain but it does not come. Ivan Ivanych, a veterinarian, and Burkin, a high-school teacher, were already weary of walking, and the field seemed endless to them. Far ahead the windmills of the village of Mironositzky were barely visible; to the right a row of hills stretched out and then disappeared far beyond the village, and they both knew that the bank of the river was there, and meadows, green willows, homesteads, and that if you stood on one of the hills, you could see a vast field from there, and telegraph poles, and a train which from a distance looked like a caterpillar crawling, and in clear weather even the city was visible from there. Now, in calm weather, when all of nature seemed meek and pensive, Ivan Ivanych and Burkin were filled with love for this field, and they were both thinking what a big and beautiful land this was.

Translated by CARL R. PROFFER.

"Last time, when we were in the Elder Prokofy's barn," said Burkin, "you were going to tell some story."

"Yes, I wanted to tell about my brother then."

Ivan Ivanych sighed heavily and lit up his pipe in order to begin the story, but just at that time it started to rain. And five minutes later a heavy rain was pouring down, and it was hard to foresee when it would end. Ivan Ivanych and Burkin stopped to decide what to do; the dogs, already wet, were standing with their tails between their legs and looking at them feelingly.

"We have to take cover somewhere," said Burkin. "Let's go to Alyokhin's. It's not far."

"Let's go."

They turned aside and kept walking across a mown field, first straight, then bearing to the right until they came out on the road. Soon poplars came into view, a garden, then the red roofs of barns; the river gleamed, and the view opened out on a broad expanse of water with a mill and a white bath-house. This was Sofino, where Alyokhin lived.

The mill was working, drowning out the sound of the rain; the dam was shaking. Near some carts stood wet horses, heads lowered; and men loaded with bags were walking around. It was damp, muddy, uncomfortable; and the water had a cold, evil look. Ivan Ivanych and Burkin were already feeling the cold, dirt, and discomfort all through their bodies; their feet had grown heavy with mud, and when, after crossing the dam, they walked up toward the owner's barns, they remained silent as if they were angry with each other.

In one of the barns there was noise from a winnowing-machine; the door was open, and dust was pouring from it. Alyokhin himself was standing on the threshold, a man of about forty, tall, stout, with long hair, resembling a professor or an artist more than a gentleman farmer. He had on a white shirt, belted with a rope, which had not been washed for a long time, loose pantaloons instead of trousers; and mud and straw were sticking to his boots. His nose and eyes were black from dust. He recognized Ivan Ivanych and Burkin and, apparently, was happy to see them.

"Please, gentlemen, go into the house," he said, smiling, "I'll be there immediately, in a minute."

It was a large two-storied house. Alyokhin lived downstairs in two rooms with low arches and small windows where the stewards had once lived; the furniture here was simple, and it smelled of rye bread, cheap vodka, and harnessing. But he went upstairs, to the showy rooms, rarely, only when guests came. Ivan Ivanych and Burkin met a maid in the house, a young woman, so beautiful that they both stopped at once and glanced at each other.

"You can't imagine how happy I am to see you, gentlemen," said Alyokhin, entering the hall behind them. "What a surprise! Pelageya," he turned to the maid, "give our guests something to change into. And, come to think of it, I'll change too. Only first I have to go wash up, and I don't think I've washed since spring. Gentlemen, would you like to go to the bath-house, and meantime they'll get things ready here."

Beautiful Pelageya, so delicate and so soft in appearance, brought towels and soap, and Alyokhin went to the bath-house with his guests.

"Yes, it's been a long time since I've washed," he said, undressing. As you see I have a good bath-house; my father built it, and somehow there's never any time to wash."

Alyokhin sat down on the steps and lathered up his long hair, and neck, and the water around him turned brown.

"Yes, I confess . . ." said Ivan Ivanych meaningfully, looking at his head.

"It's been a long time since I've washed . . ." repeated Alyokhin embarrassedly, and he again lathered up, and the water around him turned dark blue, like ink.

Ivan Ivanych went outside, leaped into the water with a splash, and swam in the rain, throwing his arms far out, and he made waves, and on the waves rode white lilies; he swam to the very middle of the pond and dove down, and after a minute he appeared in another place and swam further, and he kept diving, trying to touch the bottom. "Oh! My God . . ." he kept repeating, enjoying himself, "Oh! My God . . ." He swam to the mill, chatted about something with a peasant there, and turned back, and in the middle of the pond he lay on his back, exposing his face to the rain. Burkin and Alyokhin were already dressed and ready to leave, but he kept swimming and diving.

"Oh! My God . . ." he was saying. "Ah, Lord have mercy on me."

"You've had enough!" Burkin shouted to him.

They returned to the house. And only when the lamp was lit in the large drawing-room upstairs, and Burkin and Ivan Ivanych, dressed in silk dressing-gowns and warm slippers were sitting in armchairs, and Alyokhin himself, scrubbed, combed, in a new frock-coat, was walking around the drawing-room, evidently enjoying the feeling of warmth, cleanliness, dry clothing, and light footwear, and when beautiful Pelageya, sliding noiselessly across the rug and smiling softly, had served tea and jam on a platter, only then did Ivan Ivanych proceed to his story; and it seemed that not only Burkin and Alyokhin were listening to him, but also the old and young ladies and soldiers staring calmly and sternly from gold frames.

"We are two brothers," he began, "myself, Ivan Ivanych, and the other Nikolai Ivanych, two years or so younger. I went in for science, became a veterinarian, but at nineteen Nikolai was already sitting in a government office. Our father, Chimsha-Himalayski, was a *kantonist*, but he earned an officer's rank and left us hereditary nobility and a small estate. After his death the small estate was taken away from us for debts, but, however that may be, we spent our childhood free in the country, just like peasant children we spent days and nights in the field, in the woods, tended horses, stripped bast from trees, caught fish, and did other such things . . . And you know, anyone who has ever caught a perch or seen migrating thrushes on clear cool days in the autumn when flocks of them sweep over the village, is no longer a city dweller, and he will have a longing for freedom until his very death. My brother was melancholy in the government office. The years passed, and he kept sitting in the same place, writing the same papers, and always thinking about the same thing—how to get to the country. And little by little this melancholy of his took the form of a definite desire, a dream to buy himself a little property somewhere on the bank of a river or lake.

"He was a kind, meek person, I loved him; but I never sympathized with this desire to shut himself up on his own little property for his whole life. It is an accepted saying that a man needs only

six feet of earth. But it is a corpse that needs six feet, not a man.
And now they also say that if our intelligentsia is drawn to the land
and is striving to get on farms, then that is a good thing. But these
farms are the same six feet. To retire from the city, from struggle,
from the hubbub of life, to retire and hide on one's own farm—
that is not life, it is egotism, laziness; it is a kind of monasticism,
but monasticism without effort. A man does not need six feet of
earth, not a farm, but the entire globe, all of nature where un-
hindered he can display all the characteristics and peculiarities of
his free spirit.

"Sitting in his chancellery, my brother Nikolai dreamed how
he would eat his own cabbage soup, from which a delicious odor
would spread all over the yard, how he would eat on the green
grass, sleep in the sun, sit for hours on a bench outside the gate and
look at the field and the wood. Agricultural books and all kinds
of advice in almanacs were his joy, his spiritual food; he loved to
read newspapers too, but he read only the advertisements that such
and such number of acres of tillable land and meadows, with house,
river, garden, mill and millpond. And in his mind he pictured
garden paths, flowers, fruits, starling-houses, crucians in the ponds,
and you know, all kinds of things like that. These imaginary pictures differed according to the advertisements he happened to find,
but for some reason there had to be gooseberries in each of them.
Not a single farm, not a single poetic corner could he imagine without having gooseberries there.

"'Country life has its comforts,' he used to say. 'You sit on
the balcony, you drink tea, and your ducklings swim in the pond,
it smells so good, and . . . and the gooseberries are growing.'

"He would draw a plan of his estate and every time the plan
came out the same: a) master's house, b) servants' house, c) garden,
d) gooseberries. He lived meagerly, did not eat enough, did not
drink enough, dressed God knows how, like a beggar, and he saved
everything and put it in the bank. He was terribly stingy. It was
painful for me to look at him and I would give him something,
send it for the holidays, and he would hide that too. Once an idea
has hold of a man, there's nothing you can do.

"The years passed, he was transferred to another province, he
had already passed forty; but he kept reading advertisements in
newspapers and saving up! Then I hear he's got married. Still with

the same goal of buying himself a farm with gooseberries he married a homely old widow, without any feeling, just because she had some money. He lived starving, and put her money in the bank in his own name. She had formerly been married to the postmaster, and with him had gotten accustomed to pies and cordials; but with her second husband she didn't even see enough black bread; she started to dry up from such a life, and within three years she took sick and gave her soul to God. And, of course, not for a moment did my brother think that he was to blame for her death. Money, like vodka, makes a man eccentric. In our town a merchant was dying. Before his death he ordered himself given a plate of honey, and he ate all his money and lottery tickets with the honey so that no one would get it. Once when I was examining droves of cattle at the stations, a cattle seller fell under a locomotive, and his leg was cut off. We carry him into the waiting room, blood is pouring out—a terrible thing, and he keeps asking that his leg be found, and he kept worrying about it: there were twenty rubles in the boot on that leg, and he was afraid they would be lost.

"Now you are telling another story," said Burkin.

"After his wife's death," continued Ivan Ivanych, after thinking for a moment, "my brother started searching for an estate. Of course, even if you search for five years, you'll still end up making a mistake and buying something completely different than what you had dreamed of. Through an agent my brother Nikolai bought a mortgaged estate of three hundred acres with a house for the master, quarters for the servants, a park, but with no orchard, no gooseberries, no ponds with ducklings; there was a river, but the water in it was the color of coffee, because on one side of the estate there was a brickyard and on the other a glue factory. But my Nikolai Ivanych was little saddened; he ordered himself twenty gooseberry bushes, planted them, and settled down as a landowner.

"Last year I went to check on him. I thought, I'll go and see how things are there. In his letters my brother called his estate, 'Chumbaroklov Waste, Himalayskoe.' I arrived at Himalayskoe after mid-day. It was hot. Everywhere there were ditches, fences, hedgerows, fir-trees set in rows—and you didn't know how to enter the yard, where to leave the horse. I walk up to the house, and a fat red dog that looks like a pig comes to meet me. It wants to bark but is too lazy. A fat, bare-legged woman cook, who also looked like a pig, comes out of the kitchen and says that the master was resting after dinner. I go in to see my brother, he's sitting in bed, his knees covered with a blanket; he had grown old, corpulent, and flabby; his cheeks, nose, and lips jutted forward—it looked as if he might grunt into the blanket at any moment.

"We embraced and wept from joy and the sad thought that we had once been young, but now we were both grey and it was time to die. He got dressed and took me out to show me his estate.

" 'Well, how are you getting along here?' I asked.

" 'Not bad, thank God, I live well.' "

"This was no longer the former poor timid clerk, but a real landowner, a gentleman. He had already settled in here; he had developed a taste for it and grown used to it; he ate much, washed in a bath-house, had grown stout; he already had lawsuits going against the village commune and both of the factories, and he was very offended if the peasants did not call him "your honor." And he worried about his soul in a solid, gentlemanly manner, so he performed good deeds not simply, but with pomposity. And what kind of good deeds? He treated the peasants for all diseases with soda and castor oil, and on his nameday he had a thanksgiving prayer service held in the middle of the village, and afterwards he treated them to a half-bucket of vodka, which he thought was the necessary thing. Oh, those horrible half-buckets! Today a fat landowner drags the peasants before the district police office for trespassing, and tomorrow, a holiday, he treats them to a half-bucket; and they drink and shout "hurrah" and drunk they bow down at his feet. A change for the better in life, satiety, and idleness develop the most insolent self-conceit in a Russian. Nikolai Ivanych, who at one time in the government office was afraid to have his own views, even if he told no one, now spoke nothing but verities, and these in the tone of a government minister: 'Education is essential, but for the peasants it is premature,' 'Corporal punishments are generally harmful, but in some cases they are useful and irreplaceable.'

" 'I know the peasants and how to treat them,' he would say. 'The peasants love me. All I have to do is move my finger, and the peasants will do everything I want.' "

"And all this, note, was said with a kind, intelligent smile. He repeated twenty times, 'We of the gentry,' 'I as a gentleman;' evidently he no longer remembered that our grandfather was a peasant and our father a soldier. Even our last name, Chimsha-Himalayski, which is basically grotesque, now seemed to him sonorous, distinguished and very delightful.

"But the point is not him, it is me myself. I want to tell you what a change took place in me during those few hours I was at his farm. In the evening when we were drinking tea, the cook put a plateful of gooseberries on the table. They were not store-bought, but his very own gooseberries, picked for the first time since the bushes were planted. Nikolai Ivanych laughed, and he stared at the gooseberries silently for a moment, with tears in his eyes; and he could not speak from the excitement, then he put one berry in his mouth, looked at me triumphantly, like a child who has finally gotten his favorite toy, and said:

'How tasty!'

And he ate greedily and kept repeating:

'Oh, how tasty! You try some!'

"They were hard and sour, but as Pushkin said, 'the falsehood which exalts us is dearer to us than a thousand truths!' I saw a happy man whose cherished dream had been so obviously realized, who had attained his goal in life, who had gotten what he wanted, who was satisfied with his fate and himself. For some reason something sad has always been mingled with my thoughts about human happiness, and now, at the sight of a happy man, an oppressive feeling close to despair overcame me. It was especially oppressive at night. My bed was set up in the room next to my brother's bedroom, and I could hear how he did not sleep, and how he would get up and walk to the plate with the gooseberries on it and take one berry at a time. I mused: really, how many happy, satisfied people there are! What an overwhelming force! You look at this life: the insolence and idleness of the strong, the ignorance and bestiality of the weak, all around there is impossible poverty, overcrowding, degeneration, drunkenness, hypocrisy, lying . . . Meanwhile there is peace and quiet in all the houses and streets; of the fifty thousand who live in the city there is not one who will cry out, loudly express his indignation. We see those who go to the market for provisions, eat by day, sleep by night, those who speak their nonsense, marry, grow old, and good-naturedly carry their dead to the cemetery; but we do not see and do not hear those who are suffering; and that which is terrible in life takes place somewhere behind the scenes. All is quiet, peaceful, and only mute statistics protest: so many went insane, so many buckets were drunk, so many children died of malnutrition . . . And, evidently, this order of things is necessary; evidently the happy person feels good only because the unhappy bear their burdens silently, and without this silence happiness would be impossible. This is a general hypothesis. Behind the door of every happy, satisfied man there should be someone standing with a hammer and constantly reminding him with the pounding that there are unhappy people, that however happy he is, sooner or later life will show him its claws and misfortune will befall him—sickness, poverty, losses, and no one will see or hear him, just as he does not see or hear others. But there is no man with a hammer; the happy person lives in himself, and minor daily cares disturb him slightly as the wind does an aspen, and then everything is all right.

"That night I realized how I too was satisfied and happy," continued Ivan Ivanych getting up. "After dinner and out hunting I too preached how to live, how to believe, how to govern the peasants. I too said that learning is light, that education essential, but for the present simple literacy was enough for the common people. Freedom is good, I would say, it is as impossible to go on without it as without air, but we must wait a bit. Yes, that's what I used to say, but now I ask: 'Wait for what?' said Ivan Ivanych looking angrily at Burkin. "Wait for what, I ask you? For what reasons? They tell me that everything doesn't happen at once, every idea is realized in life gradually, in its own time. But who says this? Where is the proof that this is just? You cite the natural order of things, on the law governing phenomena, but is there any order or law that I a living, thinking person, should stand beside a ditch and wait for its sides to grow together themselves or for silt to fill it, when perhaps I could jump over it or build a bridge across it? And again, wait for what? Wait when there is no strength to live, but it is necessary to live and you want to live!

"I left my brother's early in the morning that time, and since then it has grown unbearable for me to stay in the city. The peace and quiet weigh upon me; I am afraid to look at the windows because now there is no more oppressive sight for me than a happy family sitting around a table and drinking tea. I am already old and not fit for struggle; I am not even capable of hating. I just grieve mentally, get irritated, vexed; at night my head burns from the rush of thoughts, and I cannot sleep . . . Oh, if only I were young!"

Ivan Ivanych walked from corner to corner in agitation and repeated:

"If only I were young!"

He suddenly went up to Alyokhin and started to press first one of his hands, then the other.

"Pavel Konstantinovich!" he uttered in an imploring voice, "do not calm down, do not let yourself go to sleep! While you are young, strong, brisk, don't cease doing good! There is no happiness, and there should not be any, but if there is any sense and aim to life, this sense and aim are not in our happiness at all, but in something greater and more sensible. Do good!"

And Ivan Ivanych uttered all this with a pitiful, imploring smile, as if he were asking for himself personally.

Then all three sat in arm chairs in different corners of the room and were silent. Ivan Ivanych's story satisfied neither Burkin nor Alyokhin. When the generals and ladies, who looked alive in the dusk, were looking out from the gold frames, it was tedious to listen to a story about a poor clerk who ate gooseberries. For some reason they wanted to speak and hear about elegant people, about women. And the fact that they were sitting in a drawing-room where everything—the chandelier in a dust cover and the arm chairs and the carpets under their feet—said that here these same people who were looking out from the frames had once walked, sat, drank tea here, and the fact that now the beautiful Pelageya was walking about noiselessly here—these were better than any stories.

Alyokhin had a strong desire to go to sleep; he had gotten up early to work on the farm, before three o'clock, and now his eyes felt sticky, but he was afraid that his guests would tell something interesting without him, so he had stayed. Whether what Ivan Ivanych had just said was intelligent or correct he did not comprehend; his guests were not talking about groats, or hay, or tar, but something which did not have a direct relation to his life; and he was glad and wanted them to continue.

"But it's time to go to bed," said Burkin, standing up. "Allow me to wish you good night."

Alyokhin took his leave and went down to his room while the guests remained upstairs. They were both led to a large room for the night; two large wooden beds with carved ornamentation stood there, and in the corner there was a crucifix made of ivory. Their wide, cool beds, which beautiful Pelageya had made up, smelled pleasantly of fresh linen.

Ivan Ivanych undressed silently and lay down.

"Lord, forgive us sinners!" he said and pulled the covers over his head.

His pipe, which was lying on the table, smelled strongly of burnt tobacco, and Burkin did not go to sleep for a long time and could not understand where the oppressive odor was coming from.

The rain beat against the windows all night.

ANTON CHEKHOV

Anna on the Neck

I

THERE WAS NOT EVEN A LIGHT SNACK after the ceremony; the newlyweds drank a glass of wine each, changed clothes, and went to the station. Instead of a merry wedding ball and dinner, instead of music and dances, there was a two hundred mile trip to pray at a shrine. Many people approved of this, saying that Modest Alexeich was no longer young and was already of a high rank, and a noisy wedding might perhaps seem not quite proper; besides, it is boring to listen to music when an official who is fifty-two years old marries a girl who has barely passed eighteen. They also said that Modest Alexeich, as a man of principles, had contrived this trip to a monastery specifically to make his young wife understand that in wedlock too he gave the first place to religion and morality.

The newlyweds were seen off. A crowd of colleagues and relatives was standing with glasses, waiting for the train to start up in order to shout "hurrah"; and her father, Peter Leontych, dressed in a top-hat and teacher's frock-coat, already drunk and very pale,

Translated by CARL R. PROFFER.

kept craning toward the window with his glass and saying imploringly, "Anyuta! Anya! Anya, one word!"

Anya bent towards him through the window, and he whispered something to her, enveloping her with the stale smell of wine and blowing in her ear—she could not understand anything—and he crossed her face, breast, and hands; as he did this his breath came in gasps and tears glittered in his eyes. And Anya's brothers Petya and Andryusha, schoolboys, pulled him back by his frock-coat, whispering confusedly, "Papa, enough . . . Papa, don't. . . ."

When the train started Anya saw her father run a little after the car, stumbling and spilling his wine; and what a pitiful, kind, guilty face he had.

"Hurrah-ah-ah!" he shouted.

The newlyweds were left alone. Modest Alexeich looked around the compartment, arranged their things on the shelves, and sat down opposite his wife smiling. He was an official of medium height, rather corpulent, puffy, very well fed, with long side whiskers and without a moustache; and his shaven, round, sharply outlined chin resembled a heel. The most characteristic thing about his face was the absence of a moustache, the freshly shaven bare spot which gradually turned into fatty cheeks that shook like jelly. He carried himself in a dignified way, his movements were slow, his manners suave.

"I cannot help recalling a certain circumstance now," he said smiling. "Five years ago when Kosorotov received the order of St. Anna, second class, and came to express his thanks—his excellency phrased it thus: 'This means you now have three Annas—one in your buttonhole and two on your neck.' I should tell you that at the time Kosorotov's wife had just returned to him—a light-headed and shrewish person whose name was Anna. I hope that when I receive an Anna second degree, his excellency will not have cause to say the same to me."

He smiled with his small eyes. And she smiled too, troubled by the thought that at any minute this man could kiss her with his fat, wet lips, and that she no longer had the right to refuse him this. The soft movements of his puffy body frightened her; she felt both terrified and disgusted. He got up, took his medal off his neck, took off his frock-coat and vest, and put on a dressing gown.

"There now," he said, sitting down beside Anya.

She recalled how tormenting the ceremony had been when, it seemed to her, the priest, and the guests, and everyone in the church was looking at her sadly; why, why should she, such a nice, pretty girl marry this uninteresting middle-aged gentleman? Only that morning she was in rapture because everything had been so well arranged, but during the ceremony and now in the coach she felt guilty, deceived, and ridiculous. She had married a rich man, but she still had no money; the wedding dress was made on credit, and when her father and brothers saw her off today, she saw from their faces that they did not have a kopek. Would they have supper today? And tomorrow? And for some reason it seemed to her that her father and the boys were now sitting hungry without her and experiencing exactly the same anguish they had felt the first evening after their mother's funeral.

"Oh, how unhappy I am," she thought. "Why am I so unhappy?"

With the clumsiness of a dignified man unaccustomed to dealing with women, Modest Alexeich was touching her on the waist and patting her on the shoulder; and she was thinking about money, about her mother, about her death. When her mother died, her father, Peter Leontych, teacher of calligraphy and drawing at the gymnasium, started drinking; they became poor, the boys had no boots or galoshes, her father was dragged to the justice of the peace, the court bailiff came and inventoried the furniture. . . . What shame! Anya had to look after her drunken father, darn her brothers' socks, go to the market, and when her beauty, youth, and refined manners were praised it seemed to her that the whole world could see her cheap hat and the holes in her shoes which had been smeared with ink. And at night—tears and the uneasy, haunting thought that soon now father would be dismissed from the gymnasium for his weakness and that she could not bear this and would also die like her mother. But then ladies she knew got busy and started looking for a good man for Anya. Soon this very Modest Alexeich was found, not young and not handsome, but with money. He had one hundred thousand in the bank and a hereditary estate which he leased. He was a man with principles and in a good standing with his excellency; it would be nothing, Anya was told, for him to get a note from his excellency to the director of the gymnasium and even to the trustee and Peter Leontych would not be dismissed. . . .

While she was recalling these details, she suddenly heard music burst through the window along with the noise of voices. The train had stopped at a small station. On the other side of the platform in a crowd an accordion and cheap squeaky violin were being played briskly; and from beyond the tall birches and poplars, beyond the summer homes which were bathed in moonlight, the sounds of a military orchestra could be heard: there must have been a dance at the summer homes. Summer visitors and townspeople were strolling on the platform; the weather was good and they had come here to take a breath of fresh air. Artynov was there too; he was the owner of this whole summer home area—rich, tall, stout, black-haired, with a face like an Armenian, protruding eyes, and wearing a strange costume. He had on a shirt unbuttoned down his chest and high boots with spurs; hanging from his shoulders was a black cloak which dragged on the ground like a bridal train. Behind him walked two borzois with their sharp muzzles to the ground.

Tears were still glistening in Anya's eyes, but she no longer remembered her mother or money or her marriage; she was shaking hands with students and officers she knew, laughing merrily and saying rapidly:

"Hello! How are you?"

She went out on the platform in the moonlight, and stood so that they could see her in her fine new dress and hat.

"Why are we stopping here?" she asked.

"This is a siding," someone answered, "we're waiting for the mail train to pass."

Noticing that Artynov was looking at her, she screwed up her eyes coquettishly and started speaking loudly in French; and because her own voice sounded so beautiful, and the music was playing, and the moon was reflected in a pond, and because Artynov, the well-known Don Juan and rake, was looking at her greedily and inquisitively, and because everyone was feeling merry, she suddenly felt joy; and when the train started up and the officers she knew saluted her good-bye, she was already humming a polka the strains of which reached her from the military band which was blaring somewhere there beyond the trees; and she returned to her compartment feeling as if she had been convinced at the station that she could certainly be happy, no matter what.

The newlyweds spent two days in the monastery, then returned to town. They lived in a government apartment. When Modest Alexeich went to the office Anya would play the piano or cry from boredom, or lie on the couch and read novels, or look through a fashion magazine. At dinner Modest Alexeich ate very much and talked about politics, about appointments, transfers, and bonuses, about how one has to work, how family life is a duty not a pleasure, how rubles take care of themselves if you are careful with kopeks, and how he put religion and morality above anything else in the world. And, holding a knife in his hand like a sword, he would say: "Every person must have his responsibilities!"

And Anya would listen to him, be frightened and unable to eat, and usually she got up from the table hungry. After dinner her husband took a nap, snoring loudly, and she would go to see her family. Her father and brothers looked at her somehow oddly as if just before her arrival they had been condemning her for having married for money a tedious boring man she did not love; her rustling dress, bracelets, and ladylike air in general embarrassed and offended them; in her presence they were somewhat confused and did not know what to talk about with her; but they still loved her as before and were still not used to dining without her. She sat down with them and ate soup, porridge and potatoes fried in mutton fat that smelled of tallow candles. With a trembling hand Peter Leontych poured a glass from a decanter and quickly drank up, with greed, with disgust; then he drank another glassful, then a third. . . . Petya and Andryusha, skinny, pale boys with big eyes, took the decanter and said with embarrassment, "Don't, papa. . . . Enough, papa. . . ."

And Anya would get upset too and implore him not to drink any more, and he would suddenly flare up and pound his fist on the table.

"I do not allow anyone to be my overseer," he shouted, "Little brats! Wretched girl! I'll kick you all out."

But one could hear weakness and kindness in his voice, and no one was afraid of him. He would usually get dressed up after dinner. Pale, his chin cut from shaving, craning his emaciated neck, he stood in front of the mirror for half an hour preening himself—

fixing his hair, twirling his black moustache, sprinkling himself with cologne, tying his cravat in a bow; then he would put on his gloves and top-hat and go off to private lessons. But if it was a holiday he remained home and painted with oils, or he played a harmonium which hissed and growled; he tried to squeeze graceful, harmonious sounds from it and he hummed along with it, or he would get angry at the boys:

"Scoundrels! Good-for-nothings! You've wrecked the instrument!"

In the evenings Anya's husband played cards with his colleagues, who lived under the same roof in the government house. During cards the officials' wives would get together—ugly, tastelessly dressed, and as coarse as cooks—and in the apartment the gossip began—as ugly and tasteless as the women themselves. On occasion Modest Alexeich took Anya to the theater. Between acts he did not let her a step away from him, but walked through the corridors and foyer holding her arm. Having bowed to someone he would immediately whisper to Anya, "a State Councilor . . . received by his excellency . . ." or "a man of means . . . has his own house. . . ." When they walked past the buffet, Anya wanted some sweets very much; she loved chocolate and apple pie, but she had no money and was embarrassed to ask her husband. He would take a pear, squeeze it in his fingers and ask tentatively:

"How much is it?"

"Twenty-five kopecks."

"Really!" he would say and put the pear back; but since it was awkward to go away from the buffet without buying anything, he ordered soda water and drank the whole bottle himself—and tears would come into her eyes, and at such times Anya hated him.

Or, suddenly turning all red, he would quickly say to her:

"Bow to that old lady!"

"But I don't know her."

"It makes no difference. She is the wife of the director of the treasury office! Bow, I tell you!" he would grumble persistently. "Your head won't drop off."

Anya would bow, and her head really didn't drop off, but it was tormenting. She did everything her husband wanted, but she was furious with herself that he had deceived her like the worst fool.

She had married him only for money, but now she had less money than before her marriage. At least her father would give her twenty-kopek pieces before, but now—not a groat. She could not ask for it or take it secretly; she feared her husband, trembled before him. It seemed to her that she had been carrying fear of this man in her soul for a long time. In her childhood she always imagined the director of the gymnasium as an imposing and terrible power bearing down like a stormcloud or locomotive, ready to crush her; his excellency was another such power about which her family was always talking and which for some reason they feared; and there were a dozen more somewhat smaller powers, among them the gymnasium teachers—stern, implacable, with shaven moustaches— and now Modest Alexeich, a man of principles who resembled the director even in looks. And in Anya's imagination all of these powers merged into one, and in the form of one enormous, terrifying white bear they bore down on the weak and guilty, people like her father; and she was afraid to say anything against this, and she put on a forced smile and feigned pleasure when she was coarsely petted and defiled by embraces which horrified her.

Only once had Peter Leontych dared to ask him for a loan of fifty rubles, to pay some very unpleasant debt; but what suffering that was!

"All right, I'll give it to you," said Modest Alexeich after thinking for a moment, "but I forewarn you that I am not going to help you again until you give up drinking. Such weakness is shameful for a man who works in the government service. I cannot help reminding you of the well-known fact that this passion has ruined many capable men, while if they had abstained, with time they would perhaps have become highly-placed men."

And long periodic sentences stretched out: "inasmuch as . . . on the assumption that . . . in view of the aforesaid," and Peter Leontych suffered from the humiliation and felt a strong desire to have a drink.

And when the boys came to visit Anya, usually in torn boots and threadbare pants, they too had to listen to lectures.

"Every person must have his responsibilities!" Modest Alexeich would tell them.

But he gave no money. Still, he did give Anya rings, bracelets, and brooches, saying that these things were good to have for a rainy day. And he would often unlock her chest of drawers and make an inventory to see if all the things were safe.

II

Meanwhile winter had arrived. Long before Christmas it was announced in the local newspaper that the usual winter ball would be held on the twenty-ninth of December. Every evening after cards Modest Alexeich, worried, would whisper with the officials' wives, anxiously glancing at Anya; and then he would pace from corner to corner for a long time, thinking about something. Finally, late one evening he stopped in front of Anya and said:

"You will have to have a ball dress made. Understand? Only, please, consult Maria Grigorievna and Natalia Kuzminishna."

And he gave her one hundred rubles. She took it, but she ordered the ball dress without consulting anyone, except that she talked to her father and tried to imagine how her mother would have dressed for a ball. Her mother always dressed in the latest fashion, and always fussed with Anya—she had dressed her as elegantly as a doll, taught her to speak French and to dance the mazurka magnificently (before her marriage she had served as a governess for five years). Like her mother, Anya could make a new dress out of an old one, clean her gloves in benzine, rent *bijoux*, and like her mother she knew how to screw up her eyes, pronounce "r" as "l" in the fashionable way, strike pretty poses, to fall into raptures when necessary, to assume a sad and mysterious air. And from her father she inherited dark hair and eyes, nervousness, and this way of always looking her best.

When, a half hour before their departure for the ball, Modest Alexeich entered her room without his dress-coat to put his order around his neck in front of her pier-glass, he was enchanted by her beauty and the splendor of her crisp, ethereal attire; he combed his sideburns with a self-satisfied look and said:

"So that's what a wife I have . . . so that's what . . . Anyuta!" he continued, suddenly falling into a solemn tone, "I have made you happy, but tonight you can make me happy. I beg of you, introduce yourself to his excellency's wife! For the sake of God! I could get the post of senior reporting secretary through her!"

They left for the ball. There was the Hall of Nobility and the entrance with a doorman. The vestibule was full of coat-hangers, fur coats, scurrying lackeys, and ladies in décolleté using their fans to protect themselves from the draft; it smelled of gas lights and soldiers. When Anya, walking up the stairs holding her husband's arm, heard the music and saw herself full-length in an enormous mirror illuminated by a multitude of lights, in her soul there awoke joy and the same premonition of happiness which she had felt that moonlit evening at the station. She walked proudly, self-confidently, feeling for the first time that she was a woman rather than a girl, and involuntarily imitating her late mother in her walk and manners. And for the first time in her life she felt rich and free. Even her husband's presence did not bother her because when crossing the threshold of the Hall she already guessed by instinct that the proximity of an old husband did not lower her in the least, but quite the reverse, placed on her the stamp of piquant mysteriousness which men like so much. In the ballroom the orchestra was already thundering and the dancing had begun. After the government apartment, carried away by impressions of light, color, music and noise, Anya cast a glance around the hall and thought, "Oh, how lovely!" and immediately picked out all of her old acquaintances in the crowd, everyone whom she used to meet at parties or on walks, all the officers, teachers, attorneys, officials, landowners, his excellency, Artynov, and the ladies of high society—who were all dressed up wearing extreme décolleté, pretty ones and ugly ones who were already occupying their positions in the booths and pavilions of the charity bazaar to begin selling things for the poor. A huge officer in epaulets—she had met him on Old Kiev street when she was in school but did not remember his last name now— seemed to grow up out of the ground and invited her to waltz; and she flew away from her husband, and it seemed to her she was floating in a sailboat, in a heavy storm, and her husband had been left far away on shore. . . . She danced with enthusiasm, passionately—the waltz, the polka, the quadrille, passing from one pair of arms to another, getting dizzy from the music and noise, mixing Russian and French, pronouncing "r" for "l," laughing, and not thinking about her husband nor anyone nor anything else. She was successful with the men, that was clear, and it could not have been otherwise; she was breathless with excitement, she squeezed her fan spasmodically in her hands and wanted to drink. Her father, Peter Leontych, came up to her wearing a rumpled frock-coat which smelled of benzine and holding out a saucer with pink ice cream:

"You are enchanting tonight," he said, looking at her in rapture, "and I have never so much regretted that you hurried to marry as now. . . . Why? I know you did it for our sake, but. . . ." With trembling hands he took out a packet of money and said, "I got it for lessons today, and I can pay my debt to your husband."

She pushed the saucer at him and, caught up by someone, she was immediately carried far off; over her shoulder she saw her father slip across the parquet, embrace a lady and whirl around the hall with her.

"How nice he is when he's sober," she thought.

She danced a mazurka with the same huge officer; he moved gravely and heavily, like a carcass in uniform, wriggling his shoulders and chest, hardly stamping his feet at all—he wanted desperately not to dance, but she flitted around him, teasing him with her beauty, her bare neck; her eyes burned with fervor, her movements were passionate, but he became more and more indifferent and stretched out his hands to her graciously, like a king.

"Bravo! Bravo!" the onlookers were saying.

But little by little even the huge officer got carried away; he came to life, got excited, and surrendering to her charm, he let himself go; he moved lightly, youthfully and she just wriggled her shoulders and looked slyly at him as though she were a queen and he her slave—and at that moment it seemed to her that everyone in the hall was watching them, that all these people were spellbound and envied them. Scarcely had the huge officer managed to thank her, when the crowd suddenly parted and the men drew themselves up somehow strangely, lowering their arms. . . . It was his excellency, walking toward her in a dress-coat on which there were two stars. Yes, his excellency was walking right toward her, because he was staring straight at her and smiling mawkishly, and as he was doing this he was chewing his lips, which he always did when he saw pretty women.

"Very pleased, very pleased . . ." he began. "And I'll order your husband put in the guardhouse for hiding such a treasure from us until now. I have a request from my wife," he continued, holding out his arm to her. "You must help us. . . . M-m-yes. . . . You must be given a prize for beauty . . . like in America . . . m-m-yes. Americans. . . . My wife is waiting for you impatiently."

He led her to a booth and a middle-aged lady the lower part of whose face was disproportionately large, so that it seemed as if she were holding a big stone in her mouth.

"Help us," she said through her nose, in a sing-song. "All the pretty women are working at the charity bazaar, and you alone, for some reason, are having fun. Why don't you want to help us?"

She left and Anya took her place near a silver samovar with cups. A brisk trade began immediately. Anya did not take less than a ruble for a cup of tea, and she made the huge officer drink three cups. Artynov, the rich man with protruding eyes who suffered from shortness of breath came up—no longer in the strange costume she had seen him in that summer, but in a dress-coat like everyone else. Without taking his eyes from Anya he drank a glass of champagne and paid one hundred rubles, then he drank some tea and gave her another hundred—all of this silently, suffering from asthma. . . . Anya invited customers and took money from them, already deeply convinced that her smiles and looks caused these people nothing but pleasure. She already understood that she was created exclusively for this noisy, glittering, laughing life with music, dances, and admirers; and her old fear of a power bearing down and threatening to crush her seemed ridiculous to her; she was no longer afraid of anyone, and she was just sorry that her mother was not there now to rejoice with her at her success.

Peter Leontych, already pale but still firmly keeping his feet, walked up to the booth and asked for a glass of cognac. Anya blushed, expecting him to say something inappropriate (she was already ashamed that she had such a poor, such an ordinary father), but he drank up, threw out ten rubles from his packet, and walked away gravely, without saying a word. A little later she saw him dancing in the *grand rond*, and this time he was already staggering and, to the great embarrassment of his partner, shouting something; and Anya recalled how he had staggered and shouted just like that at a ball three years ago, and it ended with a policeman taking him home to bed, and the next day the director threatened to dismiss him from the service. What an unfortunate recollection it was!

When the samovars in the booths went out and the exhausted

charity workers handed in their takings to the middle-aged lady with the stone in her mouth, Artynov led Anya by the arm into the room where dinner was being served to those who participated in the charity bazaar. No more than twenty persons were having dinner, but it was very noisy. His excellency proposed a toast: "This luxurious dining room is an appropriate place to drink to the success of those poor dining rooms for which today's bazaar was held." A Brigadier General proposed drinking "to the power before which even artillery is beaten," and they all reached out to clink glasses with the ladies. It was very, very gay!

When Anya was escorted home it was already getting light and the cooks were going to the market. Joyful, drunk, full of new impressions, exhausted, she undressed, fell into bed, and immediately fell asleep.

It was past one in the afternoon when the maid waked her and informed her that Mr. Artynov had come to visit. She dressed quickly and went into the drawing-room. Soon after Artynov, his excellency came to thank her for participating in the charity bazaar. Staring at her mawkishly and chewing his lips, he kissed her hand, asked permission to visit again, and then left; she was standing in the middle of the drawing-room, amazed, enchanted, not believing the change, the surprising change in her life had taken place so fast, when her husband Modest Alexeich walked in. . . . And he now stood before her with the same ingratiating, sweet, cringingly respectful expression she was accustomed to seeing on him in the presence of the powerful and illustrious; and with ecstasy, with indignation, with contempt, already certain that nothing would happen to her for it, she said, distinctly articulating each word:

"Get out, blockhead!"

After this Anya did not have a single free day, because she took part in picnics, excursions, theatricals. Each day she returned home early in the morning and lay down on the floor in the drawing-room, and afterwards she told everyone touchingly how she slept under flowers. She needed a lot of money, but she no longer feared Modest Alexeich and spent his money as if it were her own; and she did not ask for it or demand it, she just sent him the bills or notes: "pay the bearer 200 rubles," or "immediately pay 100 rubles."

At Easter Modest Alexeich received the order of St. Anna, second class. When he went to thank him, his excellency put his newspaper aside and sat back deeper in his armchair.

"This means you now have three Annas," he said, examining his white hands with their pink nails, "one in your buttonhole and two around your neck."

Modest Alexeich pressed two fingers to his lips to be sure he did not burst out laughing loudly and said: "Now it remains to wait for the appearance in the world of a little Vladimir. May I make so bold as to ask your excellency to be godfather?"

He was hinting at the order of St. Vladimir, fourth class, and already imagining how he would tell everyone about his pun, which was so successfull in its aptness and audacity; and he wanted to say something else just as successful, but his excellency again buried himself in his newspaper and nodded his head. . . .

And Anya kept riding about in troikas, she went hunting with Artynov, acted in one-act plays, went to dinners, and she visited her family more and more rarely. Now they had supper alone. Peter Leontych drank even more than before, there was no money, and the harmonium had long since been sold for debt. The boys did not let him out in the street alone now, and followed him wherever he went to see that he did not fall; and when they met Anya driving down Old Kiev Street in a carriage drawn by two horses abreast and an off-horse cantering stylishly, with Artynov on the box instead of a coachman, Peter Leontych would take off his top-hat and get ready to shout something, but Petya and Andryusha would take him by the arms and say imploringly:

"Don't, papa. . . . Enough, papa. . . ."

ANTON CHEKHOV

The Darling

I

OLENKA PLEMYANNIKOVA, the daughter of a retired collegiate assessor, was sitting on her porch, deep in thought. It was hot, the flies persisted annoyingly and it was so pleasant to think that it would soon be evening. Dark rain clouds were moving in from the east, and from time to time there was a breath of moisture from that direction.

Kukin, an entrepreneur and manager of the Tivoli amusement park, whose quarters were in a small building in the same courtyard, was standing in the middle of the yard looking at the sky.

"Again!" he was saying with despair. "It's going to rain again! Rain every day, rain every day—as if to spite me! Why, it's a noose! It's ruining me! Terrible losses every day!"

He clapped his hands together, and continued, turning to Olenka:

"That's our life for you, Olga Semyonovna. You could cry! You work, strive, torture yourself, don't sleep at night, you keep thinking what you could do to make it better—and what happens? On

Translated by CARL R. PROFFER.

the one hand the public is ignorant, barbarous. I give them the very best operetta, spectacle, excellent vaudeville artists, but do you think they want that? Do they understand any of this? They want slapstick! Give them trash! On the other hand, look at the weather. Rain almost every evening. It started raining on the tenth of May and it's kept on going all during May and June. Simply horrible! The public doesn't come, but don't I have to pay the rent? Don't I have to pay the actors?"

Toward evening the next day, clouds began to move in again, and Kukin said with hysterical laughter:

"Well go ahead and rain! Let it flood the whole park, and me too! I don't have any luck either in this world or the next. Let the actors drag me into court! What's court! I don't care if I'm sent to prison in Siberia! Even to the scaffold! Ha, ha, ha!"

And on the third day it was the same thing over again . . .

Olenka listened to Kukin, silently, seriously, and sometimes tears would appear in her eyes. Finally Kukin's misfortunes moved her; she fell in love with him. He was a short, emaciated man with a sallow face and hair combed back over his temples; he spoke in a thin little tenor, and when he spoke he twisted his mouth; and despair was always written on his face—but nevertheless, he aroused genuine, deep feeling in her. She was constantly in love with someone, and could not live otherwise. First, she loved her papa, who was now ill, sitting in an armchair in a dark room, and breathing with difficulty; she loved her aunt who used to come from Briansk once or twice a year, and even before this, when she went to the gymnasium, she loved her French teacher. She was a quiet, kind, soft-hearted girl with meek, gentle eyes, and she was very healthy. Looking at her full, pink cheeks, at her soft, white neck with a dark birth mark, at the kind, naive smile which was on her face when she listened to anything pleasant, men thought:

"Yes, not bad at all. . . ." —And they smiled too, while the ladies present could not refrain from suddenly seizing her hand in the middle of a conversation and exclaiming in a burst of satisfaction, "You darling!"

The house in which she had lived since the day of her birth, and which was put in her name in her father's will, was located on the outskirts of the city, in the Gypsy Section, not far from the Tivoli Park; in the evening and at night she could hear the music playing in the park and the rockets exploding with a crack, and it seemed to her that Kukin was fighting with his fate and making an assault on his main enemy—the indifferent public; her heart twinged sweetly, she didn't want to sleep at all, and when he returned home toward morning she would tap softly on her bedroom window and, showing him only her face and one shoulder through the curtain, she would smile caressingly . . .

He made a proposal and they were married. And when he had a good look at her neck and plump, healthy shoulders, he clapped his hands together and exclaimed: "Darling!"

He was happy, but since it rained on the day of the wedding, and on that night too, the expression of despair did not leave his face.

They lived well after the marriage. She sat in his box-office, looked after things in the Park, noted down expenditures, paid the salaries, and her pink cheeks, her kind, naive, seemingly radiant smile flashed now in the box-office window, now in the windows of the theater, now at the buffet. And she was already telling her acquaintances that the most remarkable, the most important and necessary thing in the world was the theater, and that only in the theater could one experience true pleasure and become cultivated and humane.

"But does the public understand this? They want slapstick! Yesterday we played 'Faust Inside-Out' and almost all the boxes were empty, but if Vanechka and I had put on some trash, believe me, the theater would have been jammed full. Tomorrow Vanechka and I are putting on 'Orpheus in Hell,' do come."

And what Kukin said about actors and the theater, she would repeat. Like him, she despised the public for its indifference to art and its ignorance; she interfered in the rehearsals, corrected the actors, kept track of the musicians' behavior, and when there was an unfavorable review in the local paper, she wept, and then went to the editor to argue.

The actors loved her and called her "Vanechka-and-I" and "Darling;" she felt sorry for them and gave them small loans, and if they occasionally cheated her, she just cried in private and did not complain to her husband.

They lived well in the winter too. They rented the city theater for the whole winter and for short periods they leased it now to a Ukrainian troupe, now to a magician, now to the local amateurs.

Olenka gained weight and shone and beamed all over from pleasure, but Kukin was getting thinner and more sallow, and was complaining about the terrible losses, even though things didn't go badly all winter. He would cough at night and she would have him drink a mixture of raspberries and linden blossoms, she would rub him with eau de cologne, and wrap him in her soft shawls.

"What a glorious thing you are to me!" she would say quite sincerely, smoothing his hair. "What a fine thing you are to me!"

During Lent he left for Moscow to recruit a troupe and she could not sleep without him; she kept sitting at the window and looking at the stars. And while doing this she would compare herself to the hens—when the rooster is not in the hen-house, they too are disturbed and unable to sleep at night. Kukin was delayed in Moscow, and he wrote that he would return by Easter and in his letter he was already making arrangements for the Tivoli. But late in the evening on Monday of Passion Week an ominous knock on the gate rang out; someone was knocking on it as if it were a barrel—boom! boom! boom! Splashing through the puddles in her bare feet, the sleepy cook ran to open it.

"Open up, please!" someone behind the gate said in a deep bass. "There's a telegram for you."

Olenka had received telegrams from her husband before, too, but for some reason this time her heart sank. With trembling hands she unsealed the telegram and read the following:

"Ivan Petrovich died suddenly today awaiting quchl instructions huneral Tuesday."

That was exactly what was printed in the telegram—"huneral" and some other still incomprehensible word "quchl"; the signature was that of the director of the operetta company.

"My dove!" sobbed Olenka. "My dear Vanechka, my dove! Why did we ever meet? Why did I get to know you and fall in love? Who can your poor Olenka, poor unhappy woman, turn to?"

Kukin was buried on Tuesday in the Vagankovo Cemetery in Moscow; Olenka returned home on Wednesday, and as soon as she entered her room she fell onto the bed and began to sob so loudly that it could be heard on the street and in neighboring yards.

"The darling!" said the neighbors, crossing themselves. "Darling Olga Semyonovna, how the sweet dear is lamenting!"

Three months later Olenka was returning from Mass, sad, in deep mourning. It happened that Vasily Andreich Pustovalov, the manager of the merchant Babakaev's lumberyard, who was also returning from church, was walking beside her. He was wearing a straw hat and a white vest with a gold chain, and he looked more like a land-owner than a businessman.

"Everything has its own order, Olga Semyonovna," he said in a dignified way, with sympathy in his voice, "and if one of those who is close to us dies, it means that it pleases God, and in that case we must remember who we are and bear it with submission."

Seeing Olenka to the gate he said good-bye and walked on. All day long after this she kept hearing his dignified voice, and scarcely would she close her eyes than she envisioned his dark beard. She liked him very much. And, apparently, she made an impression on him too, because not long after a certain middle-aged lady, whom she knew only slightly, came to have coffee with her; and as soon as she sat down at the table she began to talk about Pustovalov— that he was a good, solid man and that any eligible female would marry him with pleasure. Three days later Pustovalov himself came to visit; he did not stay long, about ten minutes, and he did not say much, but Olenka fell in love with him, so much in love that all night long she could not sleep and burned as if in a fever—and in the morning she sent for the middle-aged lady. Soon the match was made; then came the wedding.

Pustovalov and Olenka, having married, lived well. He usually stayed at the lumberyard until dinnertime, then he made business calls, and he was replaced by Olenka, who would stay in the office until evening making out bills and seeing that shipments were made.

"Lumber costs twenty percent more each year now," she would say to buyers and acquaintances. "Goodness, we used to sell local timber, but now Vasechka has to go to Mogilev province every year. And the freight rate!" she would say, covering both of her cheeks with her hands in horror. "What a freight rate!"

It seemed to her that she had been selling lumber for a long, long time, that lumber was the most important and necessary thing in life, and she found something intimate and touching in words like beam, lag, batten, plank, box board, lath, scantling, slab . . . When she went to sleep at night she dreamed of whole mountains of boards and planks, endlessly long columns of wagons hauling somewhere far out of town; she dreamed that a whole regiment of beams, twenty-eight feet by eight inches, standing on end, went to war against the lumberyard, that beams, lags, and slabs knocked against each other with the hollow sound of dry wood; all of them were falling and getting up again, piling on each other. Olenka would scream in her sleep, and Pustovalov would say to her tenderly:

"Olenka, what's wrong, dear? Cross yourself!"

Whatever thoughts her husband had, she had. If he thought it was hot in the room or that business was slow, she thought so too. Her husband did not like any amusements and sat home on holidays, and she did too.

"You're always home or at the office," acquaintances would say. "You should go to the theater, darling, or to the circus."

"Vasechka and I have no time to go to theaters," she would answer in a dignified way. "We are working people; we aren't interested in trifles. What is good about these theaters?"

On Saturdays Pustovalov and she went to vespers, on holidays to early matins; and returning from the church they would walk side by side, faces full of emotion; both smelled good and her silk dress rustled pleasantly; and at home they would drink tea with shortbread and various jams, and afterwards they ate pie. Every day at noon, both in the yard and in the street outside the gates, there was a tasty smell of borsch and roast lamb or duck, and fast days of fish; and it was impossible to pass by the gates without wanting to eat. The samovar in the office was always boiling, and customers were treated to tea and rolls. Once a week the couple went to the bath-house and returned from there side by side, both with red faces.

"Not bad, we live well," Olga would say to acquaintances, "glory to God. May God grant everyone else live like Vasechka and I."

When Pustovalov went away to Mogilev province for timber, she was extremely bored; she cried and could not sleep at night. Sometimes in the evenings the regiment veterinarian Smirdin, a young man who rented a room in her outbuilding, would come to visit her. He would tell her some story or play cards with her, and this distracted her. Especially interesting were the stories from his own family life; he was married and had a son, but separated from his wife because she betrayed him; and now he hated her and sent her forty rubles a month for the support of his son. And hearing about this, Olenka would sigh and shake her head, and she felt sorry for him.

"Well, the Lord keep you," she would say, taking leave of him and accompanying him to the stairs with a candle, "Thanks for sharing my boredom, God grant you health, the Queen of Heaven . . ."

And she expressed herself so gravely, so reasonably, imitating her husband; the veterinarian had already disappeared behind the door downstairs, but she would call out to him and say, "You know, Vladimir Platonych, you should make peace with your wife. You should forgive her at least for the sake of your son! The child probably understands everything."

And when Pustovalov returned, she would tell him in a low voice about the veterinarian and his unhappy family life; and both would sigh and shake their heads and talk about the child who was probably lonesome for his father; then by some strange current of thoughts they would both stand before the ikons, bow down to the ground and pray for God to send them children.

And thus the Pustovalovs lived quietly and peacefully, in love and complete accord for six years. But then once in the winter when Vasily Andreich was at the office, he drank some hot tea and went out without a hat to dispatch timber; he caught cold and fell ill. The best doctors treated him, but his illness had its way and he died after four months of sickness. And Olenka was widowed again.

"Whom can I turn to now, my dove?" she sobbed, having buried her husband. "How can I live without you now? I am bitter and unhappy. Good people, have pity on me, a complete orphan . . ."

She wore a black dress with white mourning bands and she gave up hats and gloves forever; she went out of the house rarely, only to church or her husband's grave, and she lived at home like a nun. And only when six months had passed did she take off the mourning bands and begin to open the shutters on the windows. Then sometimes in the mornings she was seen walking to the market with her cook for groceries, but one could only guess about how she lived alone now or what happened in her house. For example, people guessed when they saw her in her garden drinking tea with the veterinarian and he was reading the newspaper to her aloud, and also by the fact that, when meeting a certain lady acquaintance at the post office, she said:

"Our town has no proper veterinary inspection, and many diseases result from that. You keep hearing how people get sick from milk and infected from horses and cows. In essence, we should take care of the health of domestic animals just as we do the health of humans."

She would repeat the veterinarian's ideas, and now she was of the same opinion about everything as he. It was clear that she could not live without an attachment for even one year and had found her new happiness in her own outbuilding. Anyone else would have been condemned for this, but no one could think badly of Olenka; and everything in her life was so understandable. The veterinarian and she said nothing about the change that had taken place in their relations and tried to hide it, but they did not succeed, because Olenka could not keep secrets. When he had guests, his regimental colleagues, she would begin to talk about cattle plague when pouring the tea or serving dinner—or about the pearl disease, about municipal slaughterhouses—and he would be terribly embarrassed, and when the guests left, he would grab her by the arm and hiss angrily:

"Didn't I tell you not to talk about things you don't understand? When we veterinarians are talking among ourselves, please don't butt in. Really, it's unbearable!"

But she would look at him with amazement and with alarm and ask:

"Volodechka, what am I to talk about?"

And with tears in her eyes she would embrace him, implore him not to be angry, and both were happy.

But, nevertheless, this happiness did not continue long. The veterinarian left with his regiment, left forever, since the regiment was transferred somewhere very far away, almost in Siberia. And Olenka was left alone.

Now she was completely alone. Her father had long ago died and his chair was stuck in the attic, dusty, minus one leg. She grew thin and homely, and people she met on the street no longer looked at her as before, and they did not smile at her; obviously the best years had already passed, were left behind, and now some kind of new life was beginning, an unknown one about which it was better not to think. In the evenings Olechka sat on the porch, and she could hear the music playing and rockets bursting at the Tivoli, but this no longer gave rise to any thoughts. She looked absently at her empty yard, thought about nothing, wished for nothing, and later, when night set in, she went to bed and saw her empty yard in her dreams. She ate and drank as if involuntarily.

But the main thing, what was worst of all, was that she no longer had any opinions. She saw objects around herself and understood everything that was happening, but she could not form an opinion about anything and did not know what to talk about. And how terrible it is not to have any opinion! For example, you see a bottle standing there, or the rain, or a peasant driving a cart; but what the bottle or rain or peasant is for, what the sense of them is, you cannot say; and even for a thousand rubles you would not say anything. With Kukin and Pustovalov, and later with the veterinarian, Olenka could explain everything and express her opinion about anything you want, but now there was as much emptiness in her thoughts and heart as in the yard. And it was as sinister and as bitter as if she had stuffed herself with wormwood.

Little by little the town was expanding in all directions; the Gypsy Section was now called a street, and where the Tivoli garden and lumberyards used to be houses had grown up, and a series of lanes had been formed. How fast time flies! Olenka's house grew dark, the roof rusted, the shed tilted, and the whole yard grew over with burdock and stinging nettles. Olenka herself grew old and homely; in the summer she sits on the porch, and as formerly her soul is empty and dreary and tinged with wormwood; and in the winter she sits at the window and stares at the snow. If it breathes of spring or the wind carries the tolling of the church bells, suddenly memories of the past sweep forth, the heart contracts sweetly, and copious tears gush from the eyes; but this is only for a moment, and then again there is emptiness and you do not know why you live. Shoo, the black kitten, rubs against her and purrs softly, but the feline caresses do not touch Olenka. Is that what she needs? She would like a love which would grasp her whole being, whole soul, and mind, which would give her thoughts, a direction in life, which would warm her aging blood. And she shakes black Shoo off her lap and says with vexation:

"Scat, scat . . . There's nothing here!"

And thus it is day after day, year after year—not a single joy and no opinions. Whatever Mavra the cook said was all right.

One hot July day, at evening when the town cattle were being driven along the street and the whole yard was filled with clouds of dust, someone suddenly knocked at the gate. Olenka went to open it herself, and when she took a glance she fairly melted: the veterinarian Smirdin was standing behind the gates, already gray and in civilian clothes. She suddenly recalled everything; she could not hold back, burst out crying, and put her head on his chest without saying a word; and in her powerful agitation she did not notice how they both then entered the house and sat down to drink tea.

"My dove!" she mumbled, trembling from joy. "Vladimir Platonych! Where has God brought you from?"

"I want to settle here permanently," he told her. "I applied for retirement, and now I've come to try my luck on my own, to live a settled life. And it's already time to send my son to the gymnasium. He's grown up. You know, I've made peace with my wife."

"But where is she?" asked Olenka.

"She's with my son in the hotel, and I'm going around looking for an apartment."

"Lordy, dear Vladimir Platonych, take my house! Isn't it as good as an apartment? Oh, Lordy, and I won't charge you anything." Olga was very agitated and burst out crying again. "Live here, and the outbuilding is enough for me. Such joy, Lordy!"

The next day they were already painting the roof of the house and whitewashing the walls, and Olenka, strutting sideways, walked around the yard and supervised. Her former smile lit up her face, and she came to life, grew fresh, as if she had come to after a long dream. The veterinarian's wife came, a thin, unattractive woman with short hair and a capricious expression; and with her the little boy, Sasha, short for his age (he was already ten), plump, with clear blue eyes and dimples on his cheeks. And scarcely had the boy entered the yard when he ran after the cat, and immediately his gay, joyous laughter rang out.

"Auntie, is that your cat?" he asked Olga. "When it whelps, please give us one kitten. Mama is very afraid of mice."

Olenka chatted with him, fed him some tea, and the heart in her breast suddenly became warm and contracted sweetly, as if this boy were her own son. And in the evening when he sat in the dining room repeating his lessons, she would look at him with tender emotion and pity and whisper:

"My dove, handsome little fellow . . . My little child, and you were born so bright, so white . . ."

"An island," he read, "is a piece of land surrounded on all sides by water."

"An island is a piece of land . . ." she repeated, and this was the first opinion which she had expressed with confidence after so many years of silence and emptiness in her thoughts.

And she soon had her own opinions, and at dinner she talked to Sasha's parents about how it is hard for students to study in the gymnasium now, but that nevertheless a classical education is better than an apprenticeship, because from the gymnasium the road is open in all directions: if you want—become a doctor, if you want—an engineer.

Sasha began to go to the gymnasium. His mother went to visit her sister in Kharkov and did not return; his father drove off somewhere to inspect herds every day, and it happened that he did not live at home for three days or so; and it seemed to Olenka that they had completely abandoned Sasha, that he was superfluous in the house, that he was dying of hunger; and she moved him to her own place in the outbuilding and fixed up a small room for him there.

And now six months has passed with Sasha living in her outbuilding. Every morning Olenka goes into his room; he sleeps soundly with his hand under his cheek, barely breathing. She regrets having to wake him.

"Sashenka," she says sadly, "get up, my dove! It's time for school."

He gets up, dresses, prays to God, then sits down to drink tea; he drinks up three glasses of tea and eats two large bagels and half a French roll with butter. He is not yet fully awake and therefore in a bad mood.

"Sashenka, you didn't memorize the fable well," says Olenka, and she looks at him as if seeing him off on a long journey. "I have such a time with you. Just try, my dove, study . . . Listen to your teachers."

"Oh, leave me alone, please!" says Sasha.

Then he walks along the street to the gymnasium; though he is small, he wears a large cap and has a bookbag on his back. Olenka walks noiselessly behind him.

"Sashenka-a-a!" she cries out.

He looks back, and she shoves a date or a caramel into his hand. When he turns into the lane where the gymnasium stands he feels ashamed that a tall, stout woman is walking behind him; he looks back and says:

"Auntie, go home; now I'll go by myself."

She stops and looks after him without blinking until he disappears in the gymnasium entrance. Oh, how she loves him! None of her former attachments was as deep, never before had her soul surrendered so unreservedly, so unselfishly and with such joy as now when her maternal feeling kept flaring up more and more. For this boy who was not hers, for the dimples on his cheeks, for his cap, she would give her whole life, give it with joy, with tears of tender emotion. Why? But who knows why?

Having accompanied Sasha to the gymnasium she returns home quietly, so satisfied, calm, full of love; her face, grown younger in the last six months, smiles, shines; seeing her, those she meets feel pleasure and say to her:

"Hello, darling Olga Semyonovna! How are you, darling?"

"It's gotten hard to study in the gymnasium now," she tells people at the market. "It's no joke, yesterday the first grade was assigned a fable to learn by heart, and a Latin translation, and a homework problem . . . Well, is this for a small child?"

And she begins to talk about teachers, about lessons, about textbooks—the same things that Sasha says about them.

At three o'clock they have lunch together, in the evening they prepare the lessons and cry together. Tucking him in bed, she crosses him for a long time and whispers a prayer; then, lying down in bed she dreams about the distant and misty future when Sasha, having finished the course, will become a doctor or an engineer, will have his own large house, horses, carriage, will marry and have children . . . She dozes and keeps thinking of the same things, and tears flow down her cheeks from her closed eyes. And the black kitten lies at her side purring.

"Purr . . . purr . . . purr."

Suddenly a heavy knock on the gate. Olenka wakes up and does not breathe from terror; her heart beats loudly. Half a minute passes, and again a knock.

"It's a telegram from Kharkov," she thinks, starting to shake all over, "Sasha's mother is demanding he come to her in Kharkov . . . oh, Lordy!"

She is desperate, her head, hands, and feet go cold, and it seems that there is no more unhappy person on earth. But another minute passes, voices are heard: it's the veterinarian returning home from his club.

"Well, thank God," she thinks.

Little by little the heaviness leaves her heart, again it feels light; she lies down and thinks about Sasha who is sleeping soundly in the next room and occasionally says in his sleep:

"I'll fix you! Get out! Don't fight!"

MAXIM GORKY

Chelkash

T HE BLUE SOUTHERN SKY was so obscured by dust that it had a
murky look. The hot sun stared down at the greenish sea as
through a thin grey veil, and its rays found poor reflection in the
water, churned up as it was by the strokes of oars, the propellers
of steamers and the sharp keels of Turkish feluccas and other craft
which ploughed the crowded harbor in all directions. The waves
of the sea, crushed within their granite encasements by the enormous weights gliding over their surfaces, hurled themselves at the
shore and the sides of the ships—hurled themselves growling and
foaming, their flanks littered with all sorts of rubbish.

The clang of anchor chains, the clash of the buffers of goods
cars, the metallic wail of sheets of iron being unloaded on to paving-
stones, the dull thump of wood against wood, the clatter of carts,
the whistle of steamships rising from a wail to a shriek, the shouts
of stevedores, seamen and customs guards—all this merged to form
the deafening music of the working day which surged rebelliously
in the sky above the harbor, while from the earth below new waves

Translated by MARGARET WETTLIN. *Reprinted from* Stories. *Moscow,*
[*n.d.*].

of sound kept rising to meet it—now a rumble that shook the earth, now a crash that rent the sultry air.

The granite, the steel, the wood, the paving-stones, the ships and the people—everything was impregnated with the mighty sounds of this impassioned hymn to Mercury. But human voices could hardly be detected in the general chorus, so weak and even ridiculous were they. And the people themselves, they whose efforts had given birth to all this sound, were ridiculous and pitiable; their ragged dirty wiry bodies were bent double under the loads on their backs as they rushed hither and thither in the dust and the heat and the noise, and they were as nothing compared with the steel leviathans, the mountains of merchandise, the clanging railway cars, and all the other things which they themselves had created. The things of their own creating had enslaved them and robbed them of personality.

The gigantic ships lying with steam up whistled and hissed and heaved great sighs, and every sound they uttered was filled with mocking contempt for the drab and dusty creatures crawling over their decks to load their deep holds with the products of the servile labor. It made one laugh till the tears ran to see these long files of stevedores carrying thousands of poods of grain on their backs to be deposited in the iron bellies of the ships so that they themselves might earn a few pounds of grain to fill their own bellies. A poem of bitter irony could be read in the contrast between these ragged sweating men, stupefied by the heat, the noise, and the exhausting labor, and the powerful machines these men had made and which stood radiating well-being in the sunlight—machines which, when all is said and done, had been set in motion not by steam, but by the blood and muscles of those who made them.

The noise was oppressive; the dust tickled the nose and got into the eyes; the heat scorched and enervated the body, and everything seemed tense, as if the end of endurance had been reached and catastrophe was imminent, a tremendous explosion that would clear the air so that men might breathe freely and easily. And then silence would descend on the world and there would be no more dust and turmoil to deafen and irritate people and drive them mad; and the air of the town, of the sea, and of the sky would be fresh and clear and beautiful. . . .

Twelve measured strokes of a bell were heard. When the last brassy vibrations had died away the savage music of labor was found to have subsided, and a minute later it turned into a mere rumble of discontent. Now the voices of the people and the plash of the sea were more audible. It was the dinner hour.

I

When the stevedores stopped work and scattered over the docks in noisy groups to buy victuals from the vendors and find shady corners where they could squat on the pavement to take their meal, Grishka Chelkash put in an appearance. He was well known to all the dockers, a confirmed drunkard, a bold and clever thief. He was barefooted and bareheaded, had on a pair of threadbare corduroy trousers and a filthy cotton shirt with a torn collar that exposed a bony chest covered by brown skin. The matted state of his iron-grey hair and the crumpled look of his lean and hawk-like face indicated that he had just waked up. A straw had become caught in his moustache, another in the stubble of his left cheek, while behind his ear he had stuck a sprig of linden. Long and lanky and a bit stooped, he sauntered slowly down the cobbled street, sniffing the air with his hooked nose and casting a glittering grey eye about him as he searched for someone among the dockers. His long dark moustache kept twitching like a cat's; he held his hands behind his back and kept rubbing them together and twisting his crooked grasping fingers. Even here, among hundreds of other roughs, he instantly attracted attention because of the resemblance to a steppe-hawk conveyed by his predatory leanness and aimful walk, which, like the flight of the bird of prey he resembled, concealed a tense alertness under an appearance of poised tranquillity.

As he came up to a group of stevedores sitting in the shadow cast by a pile of coal baskets, a stocky young chap, with a blotched and vapid face and with scratches on his neck suggesting a recent fight, got up to meet him. He fell into step beside Chelkash and said under his breath:

"The seamen have discovered two bales of cloth missing. They're searching."

"So what?" Chelkash asked, calmly running his eyes over him.

"What d'ye mean 'so what'? They're searching, I tell you."

"And you thought I might join in the search?"

"Go to hell!"

The chap turned back.

"Wait! Who gave you those beauty-marks? A pity to mess up your shop front like that! Seen Mishka?"

"Not for a long time," called back the chap as he joined his comrades.

Everybody who met Chelkash greeted him as an old acquaintance, but he, usually so cheery and biting, must have been out of sorts, for his replies were all very terse.

From behind a pile of merchandise suddenly appeared a customs guard—dark-green, dusty, aggressively erect. He planted himself in front of Chelkash in a challenging pose, his left hand on the hilt of his dirk, his right reaching out for Chelkash's collar.

"Halt! Where you bound?"

Chelkash retreated a step, lifted his eyes to the guard's red face and gave a cool smile.

The face, wily but good-natured, tried to assume a dread aspect: the cheeks puffed out and turned purple, the brows drew together, the eyes rolled, and the effect on the whole was extremely comical.

"I told you once to keep away from these docks if you didn't want me to smash your ribs in, and here you are again!" he roared.

"Howdy, Semyonich! Haven't seen you for a long time," said the imperturbable Chelkash, holding out his hand.

"I wouldn't cry if I didn't see you for another fifty years. Move on, move on."

But he shook the extended hand.

"Here's what I wanted to ask," went on Chelkash, holding the guard's hand in steel fingers and shaking it in an intimate sort of way. "Seen Mishka anywhere?"

"What Mishka? I don't know any Mishka. Move on, man, or the packhouse guard may see you and then—"

"The red-headed chap I worked with on the *Kostroma* last time," persisted Chelkash.

"That you *thieved* with, you mean. They've put him in hospital, that Mishka of yours—got his leg crushed by some iron. Get out of here, I tell you, get out before I throw you out by the scruff of the neck."

"Listen to that, now! And you said you didn't know no Mishka. What makes you so nasty, Semyonich?"

"None of your talk! Get out!"

The guard was getting angry; he glanced about him and tried to free his hand, but Chelkash held on to it as he looked at him calmly from under bushy eyebrows and went on talking:

"What's the rush? Don't you want to have a nice little chat with me? How you getting on? How's the wife and kiddies? Well?" His eyes twinkled and his teeth flashed in a mocking grin as he added: "Been wanting to drop in to see you for ever so long, but just can't seem to manage it. It's the drink—"

"Drop it, I tell you! None of your joking, you lanky lubber. I mean what I say. But maybe you're turning to house-breaking, or robbing people in the street?"

"Why should I? There's enough here to keep you and me busy a lifetime. Honest there is, Semyonich. But I hear you've snitched another two bales of cloth. Watch out, or you'll find yourself in trouble yet!"

Semyonich trembled with indignation and the saliva flew as he tried to give voice to it. Chelkash let go of his hand and calmly strode off on his long legs to the dock gates. The guard followed at his heels, cursing him roundly.

Chelkash was in better spirits now; he whistled a tune through his teeth, thrust his hands into his pockets, and retarded his steps, tossing off well-aimed quips to right and left. He was paid in his own coin.

"Just see what good care of you the bosses are taking, Grishka!" called out a stevedore who was stretched out on the ground with his comrades, taking a rest after their meal.

"Semyonich's seeing I don't step on any nails in my bare feet," replied Chelkash.

They got to the gates. Two soldiers ran their hands down Chelkash's clothes and pushed him out into the street.

He crossed the road and sat down on the curb-stone opposite a pub. A line of loaded carts came thundering out of the dock gates, while a line of empty ones moved in the other direction, their drivers bouncing in their seats. The docks belched forth a roar of sound and clouds of dust that stuck to the skin.

Chelkash was in his element amid this mad welter. He was anticipating a good haul that night, a haul that would cost him little effort but require a great deal of skill. He did not doubt but that his skill was sufficient, and he screwed up his eyes with pleasure as he reflected on how he would spend all his banknotes the next morning. He though of his pal Mishka. He needed him badly, and here he had gone and broken his leg. Chelkash cursed under his breath, for he feared he could not handle the job alone. What would the weather be like? He glanced up at the sky, then down the street.

Sitting on the pavement, his back against a hitching post some half a dozen paces away, was a young lad in a blue homespun shirt and trousers, with bast sandals on his feet and a torn brown cap on his head. Beside him lay a small knapsack and a haftless scythe wrapped in straw and neatly tied with string. The lad was sturdy, broad-shouldered, fair-haired, his face was tanned by wind and sun, and he had large blue eyes that stared amiably at Chelkash.

Chelkash bared his teeth, stuck out his tongue, made a frightful face and stared back with popping eyes.

The boy blinked in astonishment at first, then he burst out laughing, calling out between spasms: "Crazy as a loon!" Without getting up, he hitched along the curbstone to where Chelkash was sitting, dragging his knapsack through the dust and allowing the tip of his scythe to clank over the cobbles.

"Been on the booze, eh?" he said to Chelkash, giving a tug at his trousers.

"You're right, baby-face, you're right," confessed Chelkash with a smile. He was instantly drawn to this wholesome good-natured chap with eyes as clear as a baby's. "Been haymaking?"

"Yes. Made hay, but no money. Times are bad. You never saw so many people! They all come drifting down from the famine districts. No point in working for such pay. Sixty kopeks in the Kuban, think of that! They say they used to pay three or four rubles, or even five."

"Used to! They used to pay three rubles just to get a look at a Russian! That's how I earned a living ten years ago. I'd come to a Cossack village: 'Here I am, folks, an honest-to-God Russian!' They'd all crowd round, look me over, poke me, pinch me, oh-and-ah and pay me three rubles. Give me food and drink besides and invite me to stay as long as I liked."

At first the boy opened wide his mouth, an expression of wondering admiration on his round face, but as he realized Chelkash was fabricating, he snapped his mouth shut, then burst out laughing again. Chelkash kept a straight face, hiding his smile in his moustache.

"A queer bird you are, talking talk as if it was God's truth and me swallowing it. But honest to goodness, it used to be—"

"Isn't that just what I was saying? It used to be—"

"Oh, come!" said the boy with a wave of his hand. "What are you, a cobbler, or a tailor, or what?"

"Me?" Chelkash mused awhile and then said: "I'm a fisherman."

"A fisherman? Think of that! So you catch fish, do you?"

"Why fish? The fishermen here don't only catch fish. Mostly dead bodies, old anchors, sunken boats. There's special fish-hooks for such things."

"Lying again. Maybe you're one of those fishermen who sing:

> We cast our nets
> Upon the shores,
> In market stalls, in open doors.

"Ever met fishermen like that?" asked Chelkash, looking hard at the boy and grinning.

"No, but I've heard about them."

"Like the idea?"

"Of people like that? Why not? At least they're free; they can do what they please."

"What's freedom to you? Do you hanker after freedom?"

"Of course. What could be better than to be your own boss, go where you like and do what you like? Only you've got to keep straight and see that no millstones get hung round your neck. Outside of that, go ahead and have a good time without a thought for anything save God and your conscience."

Chelkash spat contemptuously and turned away.

"Here's what I'm up against," went on the boy. "My father died without leaving anything much, my mother's old, the land's sucked dry. What am I supposed to do? I've got to go on living, but how? God knows. I have a chance to marry into a good family. I wouldn't mind if they'd give the daughter her portion. But they won't. Her old man won't give her an inch of land. So I'd have to work for him, and for a long time. For years. There you are. If only I could lay hands on, say, a hundred and fifty rubles I'd be able to stand up to her father and say: 'Do you want me to marry your Marfa? You don't? Just as you say; she's not the only girl in the village, thank God.' I'd be independent, see? and could do what I liked." The boy heaved a sigh. "But it looks as if there was nothing for it but to be his son-in-law. I thought I'd bring back a couple of hundred rubles from the Kuban. That would be the thing! Then I'd be a gentleman! But I didn't earn a damn thing. Nothing for it but to be a farm-hand. I'll never have a farm of my own. So there you are."

The boy squirmed and his face fell at the prospect of being this man's son-in-law.

"Where you bound now?" asked Chelkash.

"Home. Where else?"

"How do I know? Maybe you're bound for Turkey."

"Turkey?" marvelled the boy. "What honest Christian would ever go to Turkey? A fine thing to say!"

"You *are* a blockhead," murmured Chelkash, turning away again. Yet this wholesome village lad had stirred something in him; a vague feeling of dissatisfaction was slowly taking form within him, and this kept him from concentrating his mind on the night's task.

The boy, offended by Chelkash's words, muttered to himself and threw sidelong glances at the older man. His cheeks were puffed up in a droll way, his lips were pouting and his narrowed eyes blinked rapidly. Evidently he had not expected his talk with this bewhiskered ruffian tramp to end so suddenly and so unsatisfactorily.

But the tramp paid no more attention to him. His mind was on something else as he sat there on the curbstone whistling to himself and beating time with a dirty toe.

The boy wanted to get even with him.

"Hey, you fisherman! Do you often go on a bout?" he began, but at that moment the fisherman turned to him impulsively and said:

"Look, baby-face, would you like to help me to do a job to-night? Make up your mind, quick!"

"What sort of job?" asked the boy dubiously.

" 'What sort'! Whatever sort I give you. We're going fishing. You'll row."

"Oh, I wouldn't mind doing that, I'm not afraid of work. Only —what if you get me into trouble? You're a queer bird; there's no understanding you."

Chelkash had a sensation as of heart-burn.

"Don't go spouting on things you don't know anything about," he said with cold animosity. "I'll give you a good crack over the bean, and then you'll understand a thing or two."

He jumped up, his eyes flashing, his left hand pulling at his moustache, his right clenched in a hard and corded fist.

The boy was frightened. He glanced quickly about him and then he, too, jumped up, blinking nervously. The two of them stood there silently measuring each other with their eyes.

"Well?" said Chelkash harshly. He was seething inside, twitch-ing all over from the insult taken from this puppy he had held in such contempt so far, but whom he now hated with all his soul because he had such clear blue eyes, such a healthy tanned face, such short sturdy arms; because he had a native village and a house there, and an offer to be the son-in-law of a well-to-do muzhik; he hated him for the way he had lived in the past and would live in the future, but most of all he hated him because he, a mere child as compared with Chelkash, dared to hanker after a freedom he could neither appreciate nor have need of. It is always unpleasant to discover that a person you consider beneath you loves or hates the same things you do, thereby establishing a certain resemblance to yourself.

As the lad looked at Chelkash he recognized in him a master.

"I don't really—er—mind," he said. "After all, I'm looking for work. What difference does it make whether I work for you or somebody else? I just said that because—well, you don't look much like a workingman. You're so—er—down at heel. But that can happen to anybody, I know. God, haven't I seen drunks before? Plenty of them, some even worse than you."

"All right, all right. So you're willing?" said Chelkash in a milder tone.

"With pleasure. State your price."

"The price depends on the job. How much we catch. Maybe you'll get five rubles."

Now that the talk was of money, the peasant wanted to be exact and demanded the same exactness from the man who was hiring him. Once more he had his doubts and suspicions.

"That won't suit me, brother."

Chelkash played his part.

"Don't let's talk about it now. Come along to the tavern."

And they walked down the street side by side, Chelkash twirling his moustache with the air of a master; the lad fearful and distrusting, but willing to comply.

"What's your name?" asked Chelkash.

"Gavrilla," answered the lad.

On entering the dingy, smoke-blackened tavern, Chelkash went up to the bar and in the off-hand tone of a frequenter ordered a bottle of vodka, cabbage soup, roast beef and tea, he repeated the list and then said nonchalantly: "On tick," to which the barman replied by nodding silently. This instantly inspired Gavrilla with respect for his employer, who, despite his disreputable appearance, was evidently well known and trusted.

"Now we'll have a bite and talk things over. Sit here and wait for me; I'll be right back."

And he went out. Gavrilla looked about him. The tavern was in a basement; it was dark and damp and filled with the stifling smell of vodka, tobacco smoke, pitch, and something else just as pungent. A drunken red-bearded sailor smeared all over with pitch and coal-dust was sprawling at a table opposite him. Between hiccups he gurgled a song made of snatches of words which were all sibilant one minute, all guttural the next. Evidently he was not a Russian.

Behind him were two Moldavian women. Swarthy, dark-haired, ragged, they too were wheezing out a drunken song.

Out of shadows loomed other figures, all of them noisy, restless, dishevelled, drunken. . . .

Gavrilla was gripped by fear. If only his boss would come back! The noises of the tavern merged in a single voice, and it was as if some huge multiple-tongued beast were roaring as it vainly sought a means of escape from this stone pit. Gavrilla felt some intoxication seeping into his body, making his head swim and his eyes grow hazy as they roved the tavern with fearful curiosity.

At last Chelkash came back and the two men began to eat and drink and talk. Gavrilla was drunk after his third glass of vodka. He felt very gay and was anxious to say something nice to this prince of a chap who had treated him to such a fine meal. But somehow the words that surged in his throat would not come off his tongue, suddenly grown thick and unwieldy.

Chelkash looked at him with a condescending smile.

"Stewed? Ekh, you rag! On five swigs. How are you going to work tonight?"

"Ol pal!" lisped Gavrilla. "Don't be 'fraid. I'll show you. Gimme a kiss, c'mon."

"That's all right. Here, take another guzzle."

Gavrilla went on drinking until he reached the point at which everything about him seemed to be moving up and down in rhythmic waves. This was unpleasant and made him sick. His face wore an expression of foolish solemnity. Whenever he tried to say anything, his lips slapped together comically and garbled sounds came through them. Chelkash twisted his moustache and smiled glumly as he gazed at him abstractedly, his mind on something else.

Meanwhile the tavern was roaring as drunkenly as ever. The red-headed sailor had folded his arms on the table and fallen fast asleep.

"Time to go," said Chelkash, getting up.

Gavrilla tried to follow him but could not; he let out an oath and laughed idiotically, as drunks do.

"What a wash-out!" muttered Chelkash, sitting down again.

Gavrilla kept on laughing and looking at his boss with bleary eyes, while Chelkash turned a sharp and thoughtful eye on him. He saw before him a man whose fate he held in his wolfish paw. Chelkash sensed that he could do what he pleased with him. He could crush him in his hand like a playing-card, or he could help him get back to the solid peasant way of life. Conscious of his power over him, he reflected that this lad would never have to drink the cup it had been the fate of him, Chelkash, to drink. He envied and pitied the boy; he despised him, and yet he was sorry to think that he might fall into other hands, no better than his own. In the end, Chelkash's various emotions combined to form a single one that was both fatherly and practical. He pitied the boy and he needed him. And so he took Gavrilla under the arms and lifted him up, giving him little pushes with his knee as he led him out into the tavern yard where he laid him down in the shade of a wood-pile, he himself sitting beside him and smoking his pipe. Gavrilla tossed about awhile, gave a few grunts and fell asleep.

II

"Ready?" whispered Chelkash to Gavrilla, who was fussing with the oars.

"In a minute. The oarlock's loose. Can I give it a bang with the oar?"

"No! Not a sound! Push it down with your hands; it'll slip into place."

Both of them were noiselessly busy with a boat tied to the stern of one of a whole fleet of barges loaded with oaken staves and of Turkish feluccas carrying palm and sandal wood and thick cyprus logs.

The night was dark, heavy banks of tattered clouds floated across the sky, the sea was calm and black and as heavy as oil. It gave off a moist saline odor and made tender little noises as it lapped at the shore and the sides of ships, causing Chelkash's boat to rock gently. At some distance from shore could be seen the dark outlines of ships against the sky, their masts tipped by vari-colored lights. The sea reflected these lights and was strewn with innumerable yellow spots that looked very beautiful quivering upon the background of black velvet. The sea was sleeping as soundly as a workman who has been worn out by the day's labor.

"Let's go," said Gavrilla, dipping an oar into the water.

"Let's." Chelkash pushed off hard with the steering oar, sending the boat into the lanes between the barges. It glided swiftly over the water, which gave off a blue phosphorescent glow wherever the oars struck it and formed a glowing ribbon in the wake of the boat.

"How's your head? Ache?" asked Chelkash solicitously.

"Something fierce. And it's heavy as lead. Here, I'll wet it."

"What for? Wet your insides; that'll bring you round quicker," said Chelkash, holding out a bottle.

"Ah, God be thanked."

There was a gurgling sound.

"Hey! That's enough!" interrupted Chelkash.

Once more the boat darted forward, weaving its way among the other craft swiftly and soundlessly. Suddenly it was beyond them, and the sea—the mighty boundless sea—stretched far away to the dark-blue horizon, from which sprang billowing clouds: grey-and-mauve with fluffy yellow edges; greenish, the color of sea water; leaden-hued, throwing dark and dreary shadows. Slowly moved the clouds across the sky, now overtaking each other, merging in color and form, annihilating each other only to appear again in new aspects, grimly magnificent. There was something fatal in the slow movement of these inanimate forms. It seemed as if there were endless numbers of them at the rim of the sea, and as if they would go on crawling across the sky for ever, impelled by a vicious desire to keep the sky from gazing down upon the slumbering sea with its millions of golden orbs, the many-hued stars, that hung there alive and pensively radiant, inspiring lofty aspirations in the hearts of men to whom their pure shining was a precious thing.

"Nice, the sea, isn't it?" asked Chelkash.

"I suppose so, but it makes me afraid," said Gavrilla as he pulled hard and evenly on the oars. The water let out a faint ring and splash as the oars struck it, and it still gave off that blue phosphorescent glow.

"Afraid! You *are* a boob," grunted Chelkash.

He, a thief, loved the sea. His nervous, restive nature, always thirsting for new impressions, never had enough of contemplating its dark expanses, so free, so powerful, so boundless. And he resented such a tepid response to his question about the beauty of the thing he loved. As he sat there in the stern of the boat letting his steering oat cut through the water while he gazed calmly ahead, he was filled with the one desire to travel as long and as far as he could over that velvety surface.

He always had a warm expansive feeling when he was on the sea. It filled his whole being, purging it of the dross of daily life. He appreciated this and liked to see himself a better man here among the waves and in the open air, where thoughts about life lose their poignancy and life itself loses its value. At night the soft breathing of the slumbering sea is wafted gently over the waters, and this boundless sound fills the heart of man with peace, crams away its evil impulses, and gives birth to great dreams.

"Where's the fishing tackle?" asked Gavrilla suddenly, glancing anxiously about the boat.

Chelkash gave a start.

"The tackle? I've got it here in the stern."

He did not wish to lie to this green youth and he regretted having his thoughts and feelings dispelled in this abrupt way. It made him angry. Again he had that burning sensation in his throat and chest and said to Gavrilla in a hard and impressive voice:

"Listen, sit where you are and mind your own business. I hired you to row, so you row; and if you start wagging your tongue it will go hard with you. Understand?"

The boat gave a little jerk and came to a halt, the oars dragging and stirring up the water. Gavrilla shifted uneasily on his seat.

"Row!"

A fierce oath shook the air. Gavrilla lifted the oars and the boat, as if frightened, leaped ahead in quick nervous spurts that made the water splash.

"Steady!"

Chelkash half rose without letting go of the steering oar and fastened cold eyes on Gavrilla's white face. He was like a cat about to spring as he stood there bent forward. The grinding of his teeth could be heard, as could the chattering of Gavrilla's teeth.

"Who's shouting there?" came a stern cry from out at sea.

"Row, you bastard! Row! Shhh! I'll kill you, damn your hide! Row, I tell you! One, two! Just you dare to make a sound! I'll rip you to pieces!" hissed Chelkash.

"Holy Virgin, Mother of God!" murmured Gavrilla, trembling with fear and exertion.

The boat swung round and went back to the harbour where the ships' lanterns formed clusters of colored lights and their masts stood out distinctly.

"Hi! Who's shouting?" came the cry again.

But it came from a distance now. Chelkash was reassured.

"It's you who's shouting!" he called back, then turned to Gavrilla who was still muttering a prayer.

"Luck's with you this time, lad. If those devils had chased us it would have been all over with you. I'd have fed you to the fishes first thing."

Seeing that Chelkash had calmed down and was in a good humour, the trembling Gavrilla pleaded with him:

"Let me go; for the love of Christ, let me go. Set me down somewheres. Oi, oi, oi, I've been trapped! For God's sake, let me go. What do you want of me? I can't do this. I've never been mixed up in such business. It's the first time. God, I'm lost for sure. Why have you done this to me? It's a sin. You'll pay for it with your soul. Oh, what a business!"

"Business?" asked Chelkash sharply. "What business?"

He was amused by the boy's terror; he took pleasure in contemplating it and in thinking what a ferocious fellow he himself was.

"Bad business, brother. Let me go, for the love of God. What do you need me for? Come, be a good chap—"

"Hold your tongue! If I didn't need you I wouldn't have brought you, understand? So shut up!"

"Dear God," murmured Gavrilla.

"Stop blubbering," Chelkash cut him off sharply.

But Gavrilla could no longer control himself; he whimpered softly, coughed, sniffled, wriggled, but rowed with a strength born of despair. The boat flew ahead like an arrow. Once more they found themselves surrounded by the dark forms of ships. Their boat became lost among them as it turned and twisted through the narrow lanes of water.

"Listen, you! If you get asked any questions, keep your mouth shut if you value your life, understand?"

"God!" breathed Gavrilla, adding bitterly: "It must be my fate."

"Stop blubbering," whispered Chelkash again.

This whisper robbed Gavrilla of his mental power; he was benumbed by a chill premonition of disaster. Like one in a trance he dropped his oars into the water, threw himself backwards as he pulled, lifted them and dropped them again, his eyes fixed steadily on his bast sandals.

The sleepy plash of the waves was dreary and terrifying. But now they were in the docks. From the other side of a stone wall came the sound of human voices, of singing and whistling and a splashing of water.

"Stop," whispered Chelkash. "Put down your oars. Push with your hands against the wall. Shhh, damn you!"

Gavrilla guided the boat along the wall by holding on to the slippery masonry. The boat moved without a sound, the slime on the stones deadening the sound of its bumping.

"Stop. Give me the oars; give them to me, I say. Where's your passport? In your knapsack? Let's have it. Hurry up. That's to keep you from running away, pal. No danger of that now. You might have run away without the oars, but not without your passport. Wait here. And mind, if you blab, I'll find you even if it's at the bottom of the sea!"

And then, pulling himself up by his hands, Chelkash disappeared over the wall.

It happened so quickly that Gavrilla gave a little gasp. And then the heaviness in his heart and the fear inspired by that lean bewhiskered theif fell from him like a garment. Now he would run away! Drawing a free breath, he glanced round. To his left rose a black hull without a mast, a sort of gigantic coffin, empty and abandoned. Every time the waves struck it, it let out a hollow sound that might have been a groan. To the left was the slimy wall of the breakwater, a cold heavy serpent uncoiled upon the sea. Behind him loomed other dark forms, while ahead, in the opening between the wall and the coffin, he got a glimpse of the empty sea with black clouds banked above it. Ponderous, enormous, they moved slowly across the sky, spreading horror in the darkness, threatening to crush human beings with their great weight. Everything was cold, black, sinister. Gavrilla was frightened. And his present fear was greater than that inspired by Chelkash. It clamped him tightly round the chest, squeezing all resistance out of him and pinning him to his seat.

Everything was quiet. Not a sound was to be heard but the sighing of the sea. The clouds moved as slowly and drearily as ever, and so many of them rose out of the sea that the sky was like a sea itself, an agitated sea turned upside down over this smooth, slumbering one. The clouds were like waves whose foamy crests were rushing down upon the earth, rushing back into the chasms out of which they had sprung, rushing upon the new-born billows which had not yet broken into the greenish foam of savage fury.

So oppressed was Gavrilla by the austere silence and beauty about him that he was anxious to have his master come back. What if he should not come? Time dragged slowly—slower than the movement of the clouds across the sky. And the longer he waited, the more menacing grew the silence. But at last a splash, a rustle, and something like a whisper came from the other side of the breakwater. Gavrilla felt that he would die in another minute.

"Hullo! Sleeping? Here, catch this. Careful," came the muffled voice of Chelkash.

Something square and heavy was let down over the wall. Gavrilla put it in the boat. A similar bundle followed. Then the lanky form of Chelkash slid down, the oars appeared, Gavrilla's knapsack fell at his feet, and Chelkash, breathing hard, took his seat in the stern.

Gavrilla gave a diffident smile of joy.

"Tired?" he asked.

"Ra-ther! Well, lay on the oars. Pull with all your might. You've earned a neat little sum. Half the job's over; all you've got to do now is slip past those bastards and then—collect and go back to your Masha. I s'pose you've got a Mashka, haven't you?"

"N-no." Gavrilla was putting forth his best effort, his lungs working like bellows, his arms like steel springs. The water gurgled under the boat and the blue ribbon in its wake was wider than before. Gavrilla became drenched in sweat but he did not let up on the oars. Twice that night he had a great fright; he did not wish to have a third one. The only thing he wanted was to get this accursed job over as quickly as possible, set foot on dry land and escape from that man while he was still alive and out of jail. He resolved not to talk to him, not to oppose him in any way, to do everything he ordered him to, and if he managed to get away safely, to say a prayer to St. Nicholas the Miracle-Worker on the very next day. An impassioned prayer was ready on his tongue, but he held it back, panting like a locomotive and glancing up at Chelkash from under drawn brows.

Chelkash, long and lean, was crouching like a bird about to take wing, his hawk-like eyes piercing the darkness ahead, his hooked nose sniffing the air, one hand clutching the steering oar, the other pulling at his moustache, which twitched as his thin lips spread in a smile. Chelkash was pleased with his haul, with himself, and with this youth whom he had terrorized and converted into his slave. As he watched Gavrilla exerting himself, he felt sorry for him and thought he would offer him a word of encouragement.

"Ekh!" he said softly, with a little laugh, "got a good scare, did you?"

"Not so bad," grunted Gavrilla.

"You can take it easier now. The danger's over. There's just one place more we've got to slip past. Take a rest."

Gavrilla obediently stopped rowing, and dropped his oars into the water again.

"Row softly. Keep the water from talking. There's a gate we've got to get past. Shhh. The men here can't take a joke. Always ready with their guns. You'll have a hole in your head before you know what's struck you."

Now the boat was gliding through the water almost without sound. The only sign of its movement was the blue shine of the water driping off the oars and the blue flare of the sea as the drops struck it. The night grew darker and stiller. The sky no longer resembled an agitated sea—the clouds had spread out to form a heavy blanket that hung low and immobile over the water. The sea was even more calm and black, its warm saline odor was stronger than ever, and it no longer seemed so boundless.

"If only it would rain!" murmured Chelkash. "It would hide us like a curtain."

Great forms rose out of the water to right and left of the boat. They were barges—dark and dreary and motionless. On one of them a light could be seen moving: someone was walking about with a lantern in his hand. The sea made little pleading sounds as it patted the sides of the barges, and they gave chill and hollow answers, as if unwilling to grant the favors asked of them.

"A cordon!" said Chelkash in a scarcely audible voice.

Ever since he had told Gavrilla to row softly, the latter had again been gripped by a feeling of tense expectation. As he strained ahead into the darkness it seemed to him that he was growing—his bones and sinews ached as they stretched and his head ached, too, filled as it was with a single thought. The skin of his back quivered and he had a sensation of pins-and-needles in his feet. His eyes felt as if they would burst from straining so hard into the darkness, out of which he expected someone to rise up any minute and shout at them: "Stop, thieves!"

Gavrilla shuddered on hearing Chelkash say "A cordon." A dreadful thought flashed through his mind and struck upon his taut nerves: he thought of calling out for help. He even opened his mouth, pressed his chest against the side of the boat and took a deep breath, but horror of what he was about to do struck him like a lash; he closed his eyes and fell off the seat.

From out of the black waters rose a flaming blue sword of light; rose and cleaved the darkness of night; cut through the clouds in the sky and came to rest on the bosom of the sea in a broad blue ribbon of light. There it lay, its rays picking the forms of ships, hitherto unseen, out of the darkness—black silent forms, shrouded in the gloom of night. It was as if these ships had lain for long at the bottom of the sea, to which they had been consigned by the forces of the storm, and now, at the will of this flaming sword born of the sea, they had been raised, that they might gaze on the sky and on all things that exist above water. The rigging of their masts was like clinging seaweed that had been brought up from the bottom of the sea along with the gigantic black forms it enmeshed as in a net. Then once again this fearsome blue sword rose, flashing, off the bosom of the sea, and once again it cleaved the night and lay down again, this time in another spot. And again the forms of ships which had not been seen before were illuminated by its light.

Chelkash's boat stopped and rocked on the water as if deliberating what to do. Gavrilla was lying in the bottom of the boat, his hands over his face, while Chelkash poked him with his foot and whispered savagely:

"That's the customs cruiser, you fool! And that's its spotlight. Get up. They'll have it pointed at us in a minute. You'll be the ruin of me and yourself as well, you idiot. Get up!"

A particular effective kick in the back brought Gavrilla to his feet. Still afraid to open his eyes, he sat down, felt for the oars, and began to row.

"Easy! Easy, damn you! God, what a fool I picked up! What you afraid of, snout-face? A lantern—that's all it is. Easy with those oars, God damn you! They're searching for smugglers. But they won't catch us. They're too far out. Oh, no, they won't catch us.

Now we're—" Chelkash looked about triumphantly "—we're out of danger. Phew! Well, you're a lucky devil, even if you are a block-head."

Gavrilla rowed on, saying nothing, breathing heavily, stealing sidelong glances at the flaming sword that kept rising and falling. Chelkash said it was only a lantern, but he could not believe it. There was something uncanny about this cold blue light cleaving the darkness, giving the sea a silver shimmer, and once more Gavrilla was gripped by fear. He rowed mechanically, all his muscles taut as in expectation of a blow from above, and there was nothing he wanted now; he was empty and inanimate. The excitement of that night had drained everything human out of him.

But Chelkash was jubilant. His nerves, used to strain, quickly relaxed. His moustache twitched with gratification and his eyes sparkled. Never had he been in better humor; he whistled through his teeth, drew in deep breaths of the moist sea air, looked about him, smiled good-naturedly when his eyes came to rest on Gavrilla.

A wind sprang up, rousing the sea and covering it with little ripples. The clouds grew thinner and more transparent but the whole sky was still covered with them. The wind rushed lightly back and forth across the sea, but the clouds hung motionless, as if deeply engrossed in drab, uninteresting thoughts.

"Come, snap out of it, brother. You look as if you'd had all the spirit knocked out of you; nothing but a bag of bones left. As if it was the end of the world."

Gavrilla was glad to hear a human voice, even if it was Chelkash's.

"I'm all right," he murmured.

"You look it! Got no stuffings in you. Here, take the steering oar and let me row. You must be tired."

Gavrilla got up mechanically and changed places with him. In passing, Chelkash got a look at the boy's white face and noticed that his knees were trembling so that they could hardly hold him. This made him more sorry than ever for him, and he gave him a pat on the shoulder.

"Come, chin up! You did a good job. I'll reward you well for it. What would you think if I handed you a twenty-five ruble note, eh?"

"I don't want anything. Nothing but to get on shore."

Chelkash gave a wave of his hand, spat, and began to row, swinging the oars far back with his long arms.

The sea was quite awake now. It amused itself by making little waves, ornamenting them with fringes of foam, and running them into each other so that they broke in showers of spray. The foam hissed and sighed as it dissolved, and the air was filled with musical sounds. The darkness seemed to have waked up, too.

"So now," said Chelkash, "you'll go back to your village, get married, start working the land, raise corn, your wife will bear children, there won't be enough to eat, and all your life you'll work yourself to the bone. What fun is there in that?"

"Fun?" echoed Gavrilla faintly and with a little shudder.

Here and there the wind tore rifts in the clouds, revealing patches of blue sky set with one or two stars. The reflection of these stars danced on the water, now disappearing, now gleaming again.

"Bear more to the right," said Chelkash. "We're almost there. Hm, the job's over. A big job. Just think, five hundred rubles in a single night!"

"Five hundred?" repeated Gavrilla incredulously. Frightened by the words, he gave the bundles a little kick and said, "What's in them?"

"Things that are worth a lot of money. They'd bring in a thousand if I got the right price, but I can't be bothered. Slick, eh?"

"Good Lord!" said Gavrilla unbelievingly. "If only I had as much!" He sighed as he thought of his village, his wretched farm, his mother, and all those dear and distant things for whose sake he had set out in search of work; for whose sake he had undergone the tortures of that night. He was caught up in a wave of memories—his little village on the side of a hill running down to the river, and the woods above the river with its birches, willows, rowans, and bird-cherry.

"How I need it!" he sighed mournfully.

"You don't say. I s'pose you'd jump straight on a train and make a dash for home. And wouldn't the girls be mad on you! Why, you could have any one of them you liked. And you'd build yourself a new house although the money's hardly enough for a house."

"No, not a house. Timber's dear up our way."

"At least you'd repair the old one. And what about a horse? Have you got a horse?"

"Yes, but it's a feeble old thing."

"So you'll need to buy a new horse. A first-rate horse. And a cow. . . . And some sheep. And some poultry, eh?"

"Ekh, don't mention it! Couldn't I set myself up fine!"

"You could, brother. And life would be like a song. I know a thing or two about such things myself. I had a nest of my own once. My father was one of the richest men in the village."

Chelkash was scarcely rowing. The boat was tossed by the waves splashing mischievously against its sides, and it made almost no progress through the dark waters, now growing more and more playful. The two men sat there rocking and looking about them, each absorbed in his own dreams. Chelkash had reminded Gavrilla of his village in the hope of quieting the boy's nerves and cheering him up. He had done so with his tongue in his cheek, but as he taunted his companion with reminders of the joys of peasant life, joys which he himself had long since ceased to value and had quite forgotten until this moment, he gradually let himself be carried away, and before he knew it he himself was expounding on the subject instead of questioning the boy about the village and its affairs.

"The best thing about peasant life is that a man's free, he's his own boss. He's got his own house, even if it's a poor one. And he's got his own land—maybe only a little patch, but it's his. He's a king, once he's got his own land. He's a man to be reckoned with. He can demand respect from anybody, can't he?" he ended up with animation.

Gavrilla looked at him curiously, and he, too, became animated. In the course of their talk he had forgotten who this man was; he saw in him only another peasant like himself, glued fast to the land by the sweat of many generations of forefathers, bound to it by memories of childhood; a peasant who of his own free choice had severed connections with the land and with labour on the land, for which he had been duly punished.

"True, brother. How very true! Look at you, now; what are you without any land? The land, brother, is like your mother; there's no forgetting it."

Chelkash came back to his surroundings. Again he felt that

burning sensation in his chest that always troubled him when his pride—the pride of a reckless dare-devil—was injured, especially if injured by someone he considered a nonentity.

"Trying to teach me!" he said fiercely.

"Did you think I meant what I said? Know your place, upstart!"

"You're a funny one," said Gavrilla with his former timidity. "I didn't mean you. There's lots of others like you. God, how many miserable people there are in the world! Homeless tramps."

"Here, take over the oars," snapped Chelkash, holding back the flood of oaths that surged in his throat.

Once more they exchanged places, and as Chelkash climbed over the bundles he had an irresistible desire to give Gavrilla a push that would send him flying into the water.

They did no more talking, but Gavrilla emanated the breath of the village even when he was silent. Chelkash became so engrossed in thoughts of the past that he forgot to steer, and the current turned the boat out to sea. The waves seemed to sense that this boat was without a pilot, and they played with it gleefully, tossing it on their crests and leaping in little blue flames about the oars. In front of Chelkash's eyes passed a kaleidoscope of the past, of the distant past, separated from the present by the gulf of eleven years of vagrancy. He saw himself as a child, saw his native village, saw his mother, a stout red-cheeked woman with kindly grey eyes, and his father, a stern-faced, red-bearded giant. He saw himself as a bridegroom, and he saw his bride, the plump black-eyed Anfisa with a mild, cheerful disposition and a long plait hanging down her back. Again he saw himself, this time as a handsome Guardsman; again his father, now grey-haired and stooped with labour; and his mother, wrinkled and bent to earth. He saw the reception the village gave him when his army service was over, and he recalled how proud his father had been to show off this healthy, handsome, bewhiskered soldier-son to the neighbours. Memory is the bane of those who have come to misfortune; it brings to life the very stones of the past, and adds a drop of honey even to the bitterest portion drunk at some far time.

It was as if a gentle stream of native air were wafted over Chelkash, bringing to his ears his mother's tender words, his father's earnest peasant speech and many other forgotten sounds; bringing to his nostrils the fragrance of mother-earth as it thawed, as it was new-ploughed, as it drew on an emerald coverlet of springing rye. He felt lonely, uprooted, thrown once and for all beyond the pale of that way of life which had produced the blood flowing in his veins.

"Hey, where are we going?" cried Gavrilla.

Chelkash started and glanced about with the alertness of a bird of prey.

"Look where we've drifted, damn it all. Row harder."

"Daydreaming?" smiled Gavrilla.

"Tired."

"No danger of getting caught with them things?" asked Gavrilla, giving the bundles a little kick.

"No, have no fear. I'll turn them in now and get my money."

"Five hundred?"

"At least."

"God, what a pile! If only I had it! Wouldn't I play a pretty tune with it, just!"

"A peasant tune?"

"What else? I'd. . . ."

And Gavrilla soared on the wings of his imagination. Chelkash said nothing. His moustache drooped, his right side had been drenched by a wave, his eyes were sunken and lustreless. All the hawkishness had gone out of him, had been wrung out of him by a humiliating introspection that even glanced out of the folds of his filthy shirt.

He turned the boat sharply about and steered it towards a black form rising out of the water.

Once more the sky was veiled in clouds and a fine warm rain set in, making cheerful little plopping sounds as its drops struck the water.

"Stop! Hold it!" ordered Chelkash.

The nose of the boat ran into the side of a barge.

"Are they asleep or what, the bastards?" growled Chelkash as he slipped a boat-hook into some ropes hanging over the side. "Throw down the ladder! And the rain had to wait till this minute to come down! Hey, you sponges! Hey!"

"Selkash?" purred someone on deck.

"Where's the ladder?"

"Kalimera, Selkash."

"The ladder, God damn you!"

"Oo, what a temper he's in tonight! Eloy!"

"Climb up, Gavrilla," said Chelkash to his companion.

The next minute they were on deck, where three bearded, dark-skinned fellows were talking animatedly in a lisping tongue as they stared over the gunwale into Chelkash's boat. A fourth, wrapped in a long chlamys, went over to Chelkash and shook his hand without a word, then threw Gavrilla a questioning look.

"Have the money ready in the morning," Chelkash said to him briefly. "I'm going to take a snooze now. Come along, Gavrilla. Are you hungry?"

"I'm sleepy," said Gavrilla. Five minutes later he was snoring loudly while Chelkash sat beside him trying on somebody else's boots, spitting off to one side and whistling a sad tune through his teeth. Presently he stretched out beside Gavrilla with his hands behind his head and lay there with his moustache twitching.

The barge rolled on the waves, a board creaked plaintively, the rain beat on the deck and the waves against the sides of the barge. It was all very mournful and reminded one of the cradle-song of a mother who has little hope of seeing her child happy.

Chelkash bared his teeth, raised his head, glanced about him, muttered something to himself and lay down again with his legs spread wide apart, making him look like a pair of giant scissors.

III

He was the first to wake up. He glanced anxiously about him, was instantly reassured, and looked down at Gavrilla, who was snoring happily, a smile spread all over his wholesome, sunburnt, boyish face. Chelkash gave a sigh and climbed up a narrow rope-ladder. A patch of lead-colored sky peered down the hatchway. It was light, but the day was dull and dreary, as is often so in autumn.

Chelkash came back in a couple of hours. His face was red and his whiskers had been given a rakish twist. He was wearing a sturdy pair of high-boots, a leather hunting jacket and breeches as a hunter wears. The outfit was not new, but in good condition and very becoming to him, since it filled out his figure, rounded off the edges and gave him a certain military air.

"Get up, puppy," said he, giving Gavrilla a little kick.

Gavrilla jumped up only half-awake and gazed at Chelkash with frightened eyes, not recognizing him. Chelkash burst out laughing.

"Don't you look grand!" said Gavrilla with a broad grin at last. "Quite the gentleman."

"That don't take us long. But you're a lily-livered fellow if there ever was one. How many times were you about to pass out last night?"

"You can't blame me; I'd never been on a job like that before. I might have lost my soul."

"Would you do it again, eh?"

"Again? Only if—how shall I put it? What would I get for it?"

"If you got, let's say, two smackers?"

"You mean two hundred rubles? Not bad. I might."

"And what about losing your soul?"

"Maybe I wouldn't lose it after all," grinned Gavrilla.

"You wouldn't lose it, and you'd be fixed up for the rest of your life."

Chelkash laughed gaily.

"Well, enough of joking; let's go ashore."

And so they found themselves in the boat again, Chelkash steering, Gavrilla rowing. Above them stretched a solid canopy of grey clouds; the sea was a dull green and it played joyfully with the boat, tossing it up on waves that had not yet grown to any size, and throwing handfuls of pale spray against its sides. Far up ahead could be glimpsed a strip of yellow sand, while behind them stretched the sea, chopped up into coveys of white-caps. Behind them, too, were the ships—a whole forest of masts back there to the left, with the white buildings of the port as a background. A dull rumble came pouring out of the port over the sea, mingling with the roar of the waves to form fine strong music. And over everything hung a thin veil of fog that made all objects seem remote.

"Ekh, it'll be something to see by nightfall!" exclaimed Chelkash, nodding out to sea.

"A storm?" asked Gavrilla as he ploughed powerfully through the waves with his oars. His clothes were soaked with wind-blown spray.

"Uh-huh," said Chelkash.

Gavrilla looked at him inquisitively.

"Well, how much did they give you?" he asked at last, seeing that Chelkash had no intention of broaching the subject.

"Look," and Chelkash pulled something out of his pocket and held it out.

Gavrilla's eyes were dazzled by the sight of so many crisp bright bank-notes.

"And here I was thinking you had lied to me! How much is it?"

"Five hundred and forty."

"Phe-e-w!" gasped Gavrilla, following the course of the notes back to the pocket with greedy eyes. "God! If only I had that much money!" and he gave a doleful sigh.

"You and me'll go on a big spree, mate," cried Chelkash ecstatically. "We'll paint the town red. You'll get your share, never fear. I'll give you forty. That enough, eh? Give it straight away if you want me to."

"All right, I'll take it if you don't mind."

Gavrilla was shaking with anticipation.

"Ekh, you scarecrow, you! 'I'll take it!' Here, go ahead and take it. Take it, damn it all. I don't know what to do with so much money. Do me a favor and take some of it off my hands."

Chelkash held out several notes to Gavrilla, who let go of the oars to clutch them in trembling fingers and thrust them inside his shirt, screwing up his eyes as he did so and taking in great gulps of air as if he had just scalded his throat. Chelkash watched him, a squeamish smile on his lips. Once more Gavrilla picked up the oars and began to row nervously, hurriedly, with his eyes cast down, like a man who has just had a bad fright. His shoulders and ears were twitching.

"You're a greedy bloke. That's no good. But what's to be expected?—you're a peasant," mused Chelkash.

"A man can do anything with money!" exclaimed Gavrilla in a sudden flare of excitement. And then hurriedly, incoherently, chasing his thoughts and catching his words on the fly, he drew the contrast between life in the village with money and without it. Honour, comfort, pleasure!

Chelkash followed him attentively, his face grave, his eyes narrowed thoughtfully. From time to time he would give a pleased smile.

"Here we are!" he interrupted Gavrilla's tirade.

The boat was caught on a wave that drove it into the sand.

"Well, this is the end. But we've got to pull the boat up good and high so that it don't get washed away. Some people will come for it. And now it's good-bye. We're about ten versts from town. You going back to town?"

Chelkash's face was beaming with a sly and good-natured smile, as if he were contemplating something very pleasant for himself and very unexpected for Gavrilla. He thrust his hand into his pocket and rustled the notes there.

"No—I'm not going. I'm—I'm—" Gavrilla stammered as if choking.

Chelkash looked at him.

"What's eating you?" he said.

"Nothing." But Gavrilla's face turned first red, then grey, and he kept shifting on his feet as if he wanted to throw himself at Chelkash or do something else of insuperable difficulty.

Chelkash was nonplussed by the boy's agitation. He waited to see what would come of it.

Gavrilla broke into laughter that sounded more like sobbing. His head was hanging, so that Chelkash could not see the expression of his face, but he could see his ears going from red to white.

"To hell with you," said Chelkash with a disgusted wave of his hand. "Are you in love with me, or what? Squirming like a girl. Or maybe you can't bear to part with me? Speak up, spineless, or I'll just walk off."

"You'll walk off?" shrieked Gavrilla.

The deserted beach trembled at the shriek, and the ripples of yellow sand made up by the washing of the waves seemed to heave. Chelkash himself started. All of a sudden Gavrilla rushed towards Chelkash, threw himself at his feet, seized him round the knees and gave him a tug. Chelkash staggered and sat down heavily in the sand; clenching his teeth, he swung up his long arm with the hand closed in a tight fist. But the blow was intercepted by Gavrilla's pleadings, uttered in a cringing whisper:

"Give me that money, there's a good fellow! For the love of Christ give it to me. What do you need with it? Look, in just one night—in one single night! And it would take me years and years. Give it to me. I'll pray for you. All my life. In three churches. For the salvation of your soul. You'll only throw it to the winds, while

I? I'll put it in the land. Give it to me! What is it to you? It comes so easy. One night, and you're a rich man. Do a good deed once in your life. After all, you're a lost soul; there's nothing ahead of you. And I'd—oh what wouldn't I do with it! Give it to me!"

Chelkash—frightened, dumbfounded, infuriated—sat in the sand leaning back on his elbows; sat without a word, his eyes boring into this boy whose head was pressed against his knees as he gasped out his plea. At last Chelkash jumped to his feet, thrust his hand into his pocket and threw the notes at Gavrilla.

"Here, lick it up!" he cried, trembling with excitement, with pity and loathing for this greedy slave. He felt heroic when he had tossed him the money.

"I was going to give you more anyway. Went soft last night thinking of my own village. Thought to myself: I'll help the lad. But I waited to see if you'd ask for it. And you did, you milksop, you beggar, you. Is it worth tormenting yourself like that for money? Fool. Greedy devils. No pride. They'd sell themselves for five kopeks."

"May Christ watch over you! What's this I've got? Why, I'm a rich man now!" squealed Gavrilla, twitching all over in ecstasy and hiding the money inside his shirt. "Bless you, my friend. I'll never forget you. Never. And I'll have my wife and children say prayers for you, too."

As Chelkash heard his joyful squeals and looked at his beaming face distorted by this paroxysm of greed, he realized that, thief and drunk that he was, he would never stoop so low, would never be so grasping, so lacking in self-pride. Never, never! And this thought and this feeling, filling him with a sense of his own freedom, made him linger there beside Gavrilla on the shore of the sea.

"You've made me a present of happiness," cried Gavrilla, snatching Chelkash's hand and pressing it against his own face.

Chelkash bared his teeth like a wolf but said nothing.

"And just to think what I almost did!" went on Gavrilla. "On the way here I thought—to myself—I'll hit him—you, that is—over the head—with an oar—bang!—take the money—and throw him—you, that is—overboard. Who'd ever miss him? And if they found his body—nobody'd bother to find out who did it and how. He's not worth making a fuss over. Nobody needs him. Nobody'd go to the trouble."

"Hand over that money!" roared Chelkash, seizing Gavrilla by the throat.

Gavrilla wrenched away once, twice, but Chelkash's arm wound about him like a snake. The sound of a shirt ripping, and—there was Gavrilla flat on his back in the sand, his eyes popping out of his head, his fingers clutching the air, his feet kicking helplessly. Chelkash stood over him lean, erect, hawk-like, his teeth bared as he gave a hard dry laugh, his whiskers twitching nervously on his sharp bony face. Never in all his life had he been wounded so cruelly, and never had he been so furious.

"Well, are you happy now?" he laughed, then turned on his heel and set off in the direction of the town. Before he had gone five steps Gavrilla arched himself like a cat, sprang to his feet, swung out with his arm and hurled a big stone at him.

"Take that!"

Chelkash let out a grunt, put his hands to his head, staggered forward, turned round to Gavrilla, and fell on his face in the sand. Gavrilla was frozen with fear. Chelkash moved one leg, tried to lift his head, stretched out, trembling like a harp string. Then Gavrilla ran for all he was worth, ran out into the dark space where a shaggy black cloud was hanging over the fog-enshrouded steppe. The waves rustled as they scurried up the sand, mingled with the sand for a brief moment, scurried back again. The foam hissed and the air was filled with spray.

It began to rain. At first it came down in single drops, but soon turned into a torrent that came pouring out of the sky in thin streams. These streams wove a net of watery threads that enveloped the whole expanse of the steppe, the whole expanse of the sea. Gavrilla was swallowed up in it. For a long time nothing was to be seen but the rain and the long figure of the man laying in the sand at the edge of the sea. Then Gavrilla came swooping like a bird out of the darkness. When he reached Chelkash he fell on his knees beside him and tried to lift him up. His hand came in contact with something warm and red and sticky. He shuddered and started back, with a wild expression on his white face.

"Get up, brother, get up!" he whispered in Chelkash's ear above the noise of the rain.

Chelkash opened his eyes and gave Gavrilla a little push.

"Go away," he whispered hoarsely.

"Brother! Forgive me! It was the devil's doings," whispered Gavrilla trembling as he kissed Chelkash's hand.

"Go away. Leave me."

"Take this sin off my soul. Forgive me, brother."

"Away! Go away! Go to hell!" Chelkash suddenly cried out and sat up in the sand. His face was white and angry, his eyes were hazy and kept closing as if he were sleepy. "What else do you want? You've done what you wanted to do. Go away. Get out!" He tried to give the grief-stricken Gavrilla a kick, but he could not and would have collapsed again had not Gavrilla put an arm round his shoulders. Chelkash's face was on a level with Gavrilla's. Both faces were white and dreadful to see.

"Bah!" And Chelkash spat into the wide-open eyes of his assistant.

Gavrilla humbly wiped his face on his sleeve.

"Do what you want to me," he whispered. "I won't say a word. Forgive me, in the name of Christ."

"Scum. Can't even do your dirty work like a man," cried Chelkash scathingly as he slipped his hand inside his jacket and ripped off a piece of shirt with which he silently bound his head, grinding his teeth from time to time. "Have you taken the money?" he asked through his teeth.

"I haven't, brother. And I won't. I don't want it. Nothing but bad luck comes of it."

Chelkash thrust his hand into a pocket of his jacket, pulled out the pile of notes, peeled off a hundred-ruble one, put it back into his pocket, and threw the rest at Gavrilla.

"Take it and go away."

"I won't, brother. I can't. Forgive me what I've done."

"Take it, I say," roared Chelkash, rolling his eyes fearfully.

"Forgive me. I can't take it if you don't," said Gavrilla humbly, falling at Chelkash's feet in the rain-drenched sand.

"That's a lie. You will take it, you scum," said Chelkash with conviction. Pulling up his companion's head by the hair, he thrust the money under his nose.

"Take it. Take it. You didn't work for nothing. Don't be afraid, take it. And don't be ashamed that you almost killed a man. Nobody would hunt you down for killing a man like me. They'd even say thank you if they found out. Here, take it."

Seeing that Chelkash was laughing, Gavrilla's heart grew lighter. He clutched the money.

"And do you forgive me, brother? Don't you want to do that for me?" he begged tearfully.

"My beloved friend," replied Chelkash in the same vein, as he got up and stood swaying on his feet. "What's there to forgive? Nothing to forgive. Today you get me; tomorrow I get you."

"Ah brother, brother," sighed Gavrilla disconsolately, shaking his head.

Chelkash stood in front of him with an odd smile on his face. The rag on his head, which had gradually been getting redder, resembled a Turkish fez.

The rain had become a downpour. The sea gave a low roar, the waves hurled themselves savagely at the shore.

The two men were silent.

"Well, good-bye," said Chelkash mockingly as he turned to go.

He staggered, his legs were shaking, and he held his head as if afraid of losing it.

"Forgive me, brother," pleaded Gavrilla once more.

"That's all right," said Chelkash coldly, setting off.

He stumbled away, holding his head with his left hand, pulling gently at his dark moustache with his right.

Gavrilla stood watching him until he disappeared in the rain which kept coming down in fine endless streams, enveloping the steppe in impenetrable steel-grey gloom.

Then he took off his wet cap, crossed himself, looked at the money in his hand, heaved a deep sigh of relief, hid the money in his shirt, and strode off firmly down the shore in the opposite direction to that taken by Chelkash.

The sea growled as it hurled its huge waves on the sand, smashing them to foam and spray. The rain lashed at the water and the land. The wind howled. The air was filled with a roar, a howl, a murmur. The rain cut off sight of sea and sky.

Soon the rain and the spray washed away the red spot on the sand where Chelkash had lain, washed away the footsteps of Chelkash, washed away the footsteps of the youth who had walked so bravely down the beach. And not a sign was left on this deserted shore to testify to the little drama enacted here by these two men.

ALEXANDER KUPRIN

The Garnet Bracelet

Ludwig van Beethoven. 2 Son. (op. 2, No. 2)
LARGO APPASSIONATO

I

In mid August, before the new moon, there suddenly came a
spell of bad weather, of the kind peculiar to the north coast of
the Black Sea. Dense, heavy fog lay on land and sea, and the huge
lighthouse siren roared like a mad bull day and night. Then a
drizzle, as fine as water dust, fell steadily from morning to morning
and turned the clayey roads and foot-paths into a thick mass of
mud, in which carts and carriages would be bogged for a long time.
And then a fierce hurricane began to blow from the steppeland
in the north-west; the tree-tops rocked and heaved like waves in a
gale, and at night the iron roofing of houses rattled, as if someone
in heavy boots were running over it; window-frames shook, doors
banged, and there was a wild howling in the chimneys. Several fishing boats lost their bearings at sea, and two of them did not come
back; a week later the fishermen's corpses were washed ashore.

The inhabitants of a suburban seaside resort—mostly Greeks
and Jews, life-loving and over-apprehensive like all Southerners—
were hurrying back to town. On the muddy highway an endless

Translated by Stepan Apresyan. *Reprinted from* The Garnet Bracelet.
Moscow, [n.d.].

succession of drays dragged along, overloaded with all kinds of household things—mattresses, sofas, chests, chairs, wash-stands, samovars. Through the blurred muslin of the drizzle, it was a pitiful and dismal sight—the wretched bag and baggage, which looked so shabby, so dirty and beggarly; the maids and cooks sitting atop of the carts on soaked tarpaulin, holding irons, cans or baskets; the exhausted, sweaty horses which halted every now and again, their knees trembling, their flanks steaming; the draymen who swore huskily, wrapped in matting against the rain. An even sorrier sight were the deserted houses, now bare, empty and spacious, with their ravaged flower-beds, smashed panes, abandoned dogs and all kinds of rubbish—cigarette ends, bits of paper, broken crockery, cartons, and medicine bottles.

But the weather changed abruptly and quite unexpectedly in late August. There came calm, cloudless days that were sunnier and mellower than they had been in July. Autumn gossamer glinted like mica on the bristly yellow stubble in the dried fields. The trees, restored to their quietude, were meekly shedding their leaves.

Princess Vera Nikolayevna Sheyina, wife of the marshal of nobility, had been unable to leave her villa because repairs were not yet finished at the town house. And now she was overjoyed by the lovely days, the calm and solitude and pure air, the swallows twittering on the telegraph wires as they flocked together to fly south, and the caressing salty breeze that drifted gently from the sea.

II

Besides, that day—the seventeenth of September—was her birthday. She had always loved it, associating it with remote, cherished memories of her childhood, and always expected it to bring on something wonderfully happy. In the morning, before leaving for town on urgent business, her husband had put on her night-table a case with magnificent ear-rings of pear-shaped pearls, and the present added to her cheerful mood.

She was all alone in the house. Her unmarried brother Nikolai, assistant public prosecutor, who usually lived with them, had also gone to town for a court hearing. Her husband had promised to bring to dinner none but a few of their closest friends. It was fortunate that her birthday was during the summer season, for in town they would have had to spend a good deal of money on a grand festive dinner, perhaps even a ball, while here in the country the expenses could be cut to a bare minimum. Despite his prominence in society, or possibly because of it, Prince Sheyin could hardly make both ends meet. The huge family estate had been almost ruined by his ancestors, while his position obliged him to live above his means: give receptions, engage in charity, dress well, keep horses, and so on. Princess Vera, with whom the former passionate love for her husband had long ago toned down to a firm, true, faithful friendship, spared no pains to help him ward off complete ruin. Without his suspecting it she went without many things she wanted, and ran the household as thriftily as she could.

She was now walking about the garden, carefully clipping off flowers for the dinner table. The flower-beds, stripped almost bare, looked neglected. The double carnations of various colours were past their best, and so were the stocks—half in bloom, half laden with thin green pods that smelled of cabbage; on the rose-bushes, blooming for the third time that summer, there were still a few undersized buds and flowers. But then the dahlias, peonies and asters flaunted their haughty beauty, filling the hushed air with a grassy, sad autumnal scent. The other flowers, whose season of luxurious love and over-fruitful maternity was over, were quietly dropping innumerable seeds of future life.

A three-toned automobile horn sounded on the nearby highway, announcing that Anna Nikolayevna Friesse, Princess Vera's sister, was coming. She had telephoned that morning to say that she would come and help about the house and to receive the guests.

Vera's keen ear had not betrayed her. She went to meet the arrival. A few minutes later an elegant sedan drew up at the gate; the chauffeur jumped nimbly down and flung the door open.

The two sisters kissed joyfully. A warm affection had bound them together since early childhood. They were strangely unlike each other in appearance. The elder sister, Vera, resembled her mother, a beautiful Englishwoman; she had a tall, lithe figure, a delicate but cold and proud face, well-formed if rather large hands, and charmingly sloping shoulders such as you see in old miniatures. On the other hand, the younger sister, Anna, had inherited the Mongol blood of her father, a Tatar prince, whose grandfather had not been christened until the early nineteenth century and whose forbears were descended from Tamerlane himself, or Timur Lenk, the Tatar name by which her father proudly called the great murderer. Standing half a head shorter than her sister, she was rather broad-shouldered, lively and frivolous, and very fond of teasing people. Her face, of a markedly Mongol cast—with prominent cheek-bones, narrow eyes which she, moreover, often screwed up because she was short-sighted, and a haughty expression about her small, sensuous mouth, especially its full, slightly protruding lower lip—had, nevertheless, an elusive and unaccountable fascination which lay perhaps in her smile, or in the deeply feminine quality of all her features, or in her piquant, coquettish mimicry. Her graceful lack of beauty excited and drew men's attention much more frequently and strongly than her sister's aristocratic beauty.

She was married to a very wealthy and very stupid man, who did absolutely nothing though he was on the board of some sort of charity institution and bore the title of *Kammerjunker*. She loathed her husband, but she had borne him two children—a boy and a girl; she had made up her mind not to have any more children and she did not. As for Vera, she longed to have children, as many as possible, but for some reason she had none, and she morbidly and passionately adored her younger sister's pretty, anaemic children, always well-behaved and obedient, with pallid, mealy faces and curled doll hair of a flaxen color.

Anna was all gay disorder and sweet, sometimes freakish contradictions. She readily gave herself up to the most reckless flirting in all the capitals and health resorts of Europe, but she was never unfaithful to her husband, whom she, however, ridiculed contemptuously both to his face and behind his back. She was extravagant and very fond of gambling, dances, new sensations and exciting spectacles, and when abroad she would frequent cafés of doubtful repute; but she was also generously kind and deeply, sincerely religious—so much so that she had secretly become a Catholic. Her back, bosom and shoulders were of rare beauty. When she went to a grand ball she would bare herself far beyond the limits allowed by decorum or fashion, but it was said that under the low-cut dress she always wore a hair shirt.

Vera, on the other hand, was rigidly plain-mannered, coldly, condescendingly amiable to all, and as aloof and composed as a queen.

III

"Oh, how nice it is here! How very nice!" said Anna as she walked with swift small steps along the path beside her sister. "Let's sit for a while on the bench above the bluff, if you don't mind. I haven't seen the sea for ages. The air is so wonderful here—it cheers your heart to breathe it. Last summer I made an amazing discovery in the Crimea, in Miskhor. Do you know what surf water smells like? Just imagine—it smells like mignonette."

Vera smiled affectionately.

"You always fancy things."

"No, no. Once everybody laughed at me, I remember, when I said moonlight had a kind of pink shade. But a couple of days ago Boritsky—that artist who's doing my portrait—said that I was right and that artists have known about it for a long time."

"Is that artist your latest infatuation?"

"You always get queer ideas!" Anna laughed, then, stepping quickly to the very edge of the bluff, which dropped in a sheer wall deep into the sea, she looked down and suddenly cried out in terror, starting back, her face pale.

"Oh! How high!" Her voice was faint and tremulous. "When I look down from so high up it gives me a sort of sweet, nasty creeps, and my toes ache. And yet I'm drawn to it!"

She was about to look down again, but her sister held her back.

"For heaven's sake, Anna dear! My own head spins when you do that. Sit down, I beg you."

"All right, all right, I will. But see how beautiful it is, how exhilarating—you just can't look enough. If you knew how thankful I am to God for all the wonders he has wrought for us!"

Both fell to thinking for a moment. The sea lay at rest far, far below. The shore could not be seen from the bench, and that enhanced the feeling of the immensity and majesty of the sea. The water was calm and friendly, and cheerfully blue, except for pale blue oblique stripes marking the currents, and on the horizon it changed to an intense blue.

Fishing boats, hardly discernible, were dozing motionless in the smooth water, not far from the shore. And farther away a three-master, draped from top to bottom in white, shapely sails bellied out by the wind, seemed to be suspended in the air, making no headway.

"I see what you mean," said the elder sister thoughtfully, "but somehow I don't feel about it the way you do. When I see the sea for the first time after a long interval, it excites and staggers me. I feel as if I were looking at an enormous, solemn wonder I'd never seen before. But afterwards, when I'm used to it, its flat emptiness begins to crush me. I feel bored as I look at it, and I try not to look any more."

Anna smiled.

"What is it?" asked her sister.

"Last summer," said Anna slyly, "we rode in a big cavalcade from Yalta to Uch Kosh. That's beyond the forester's house, above the falls. At first we wandered into some mist, it was very damp and we couldn't see well, but we climbed higher and higher, up a steep path, between pine-trees. Then the forest ended, and we were out of the mist. Imagine a narrow foothold on a cliff, and a precipice at your feet. The villages seemed no bigger than match-boxes, the forests and gardens were like so much grass. The whole landscape lay below like a map. And farther down was the sea, stretching away for fifty or sixty miles. I fancied I was hanging in mid-air and was going to fly. It was so beautiful, and made me feel so light! I turned and said happily to the guide, 'Well, Seyid Oghlu, isn't it lovely?' But he clicked his tongue and said 'Ah, leddy, you don't know how fed up I am vid all dat. I sees it every day.'"

"Thank you for the comparison," said Vera with a laugh. "But I simply think that we Northerners can never understand the charm of the sea. I love the forest. Do you remember our woods back in Yegorovskoye? How could you ever be bored by them? The pine-trees! And the moss! And the death-cups—looking as if they were made of red satin embroidered with white beads. It's so still, so cool."

"It makes no difference to me—I love everything," answered Anna. "But I love best of all my little sister, my dear sensible Vera. There are only two of us in the world, you know."

She put her arm round her sister and snuggled against her, cheek to cheek. And suddenly she started.

"But how silly of me! We sit here like characters in a novel, talking about Nature, and I quite forgot about my present. Here, look. Only I'm afraid you may not like it."

She took from her handbag a small notebook in an unusual binding: on a background of old blue velvet, worn and grey with time, there wound a dull-golden filigree pattern of exquisite intricacy, delicacy, and beauty, apparently the diligent handiwork of a skilful and patient artist. The notebook was attached to a gold chain, thin as a thread, and the sheets inside it had been replaced by ivory plates.

"What a beautiful thing! It's gorgeous!" said Vera, and kissed her sister. "Thank you. Where did you get such a treasure?"

"In a curiosity shop. You know my weakness for rummaging in old trash. That was how I came upon this prayer-book. See how the ornament here shapes into a cross. I only found the binding, and everything else—the leaves, clasps and pencil—I had to think up myself. Hard as I tried to explain my idea to Mollinet, he simply refused to see what I wanted. The clasps should have been made in the same style as the whole pattern—dull in tone, of old gold, finely engraved—but he's done God knows what. However, the chain is of genuine Venetian workmanship, very old."

Admiringly Vera stroked the magnificent binding.

"What hoary antiquity! I wonder how old this notebook is," she said.

"I am afraid to say exactly. Approximately the end of the seventeenth or mid-eighteenth century."

"How strange," said Vera, with a pensive smile. "Here I am holding an object that may have been touched by the hand of Marquise de Pompadour or Marie Antoinette herself. Oh, Anna, it's so like you, to make a lady's *carnet* out of a prayer-book. But let's go and see what's going on inside."

They went into the house across a large terrace paved with flagstone and enclosed on all sides by trellises of Isabella grape-vine. The black rich clusters smelling faintly of strawberries hung heavily amid the dark green, gilded here and there by the sun. The terrace was submerged in a green half-light, which cast a pale reflection on the faces of the two women.

"Are you going to have dinner served here?" asked Anna.

"I was at first. But the evenings are so chilly now. I prefer the dining-room. The men may come out here to smoke."

"Will you have anybody interesting?"

"I don't know yet. All I know is that our Grandad is coming."

"Ah, dear Grandad! How lovely!" cried Anna, clasping her hands. "I haven't seen him for ages."

"Vasya's sister is coming too, and Professor Speshnikov, I think. I was at my wits' end yesterday. You know they both like good food —Grandad and the professor. But you can't get a thing here or in town, for love or money. Luka came by quail somewhere—ordered them from a hunter—and is now trying his skill on them. The beef isn't bad, comparatively speaking—alas! the inevitable roast beef! Then we have very nice lobsters."

"Well, it doesn't sound so bad, after all. Don't worry. Between you and me, you like good food yourself."

"But we'll also have something special. This morning a fisherman brought us a gurnard. I saw it myself. It's a monster, really. Terrible even to look at."

Anna, who was eagerly inquisitive about everything whether it concerned her or not, wanted to see the gurnard at once.

Luka, a tall man with a clean-shaven sallow face, came in carrying a white oblong basin, which he held with difficulty by the lugs, careful not to spill the water on the parquet floor.

"Twelve and a half pounds, Your Highness," he said, with the peculiar pride of a cook. "We weighed it a while back."

The fish was too big for the basin and lay with its tail curled. Its scales were shot with gold, the fins were a bright red, and two long fan-like wings, of a delicate blue, stood out from the huge rapacious head. It was still alive and vigorously worked its gills.

The younger sister cautiously touched the fish's head with her little finger. But the gurnard lashed out with its tail, and Anna with a scream snatched back her hand.

"Don't worry, Your Highness, we'll arrange everything in the best manner," said the cook, obviously aware of Vera's anxiety. "Just now the Bulgarian brought two honey-rock melons. They're a bit like cantaloups, only they smell much nicer. And may I ask your Highness what gravy you will have with the gurnard: *tartare* or *polonaise*, or simply rusk in butter?"

"Do as you like. You may go," said the princess.

IV

After five o'clock the guests began to arrive. Prince Vasily Lvovich brought his widowed sister, Lyudmila Lvovna Durasova, a stout, good-natured, extremely taciturn woman; Vasyuchok, a wealthy young scapegrace and rake, whom everybody in town called by that familiar name, and who was very good company because he could sing and recite poetry, as well as arrange tableaux, plays and charity bazaars; the famous pianist Jennie Reiter, a friend of Princess Vera's from the Smolny Institute; and also his brother-in-law, Nikolai Nikolayevich. After them came in a motor-car Anna's husband, along with the fat, hulking Professor Speshnikov, and the vice-governor, von Seck. The last to arrive was General Anosov, who came in a fine hired landau, accompanied by two officers: Staff Colonel Ponamaryov, looking older than his age, a lean, bilious man worn out by clerical drudgery, and Guards Lieutenant Bakhtinsky of the Hussars, who was reputed to be the best dancer and master of ceremonies in Petersburg.

General Anosov, a silver-haired old man, tall and obese, stepped heavily down from the footboard, holding on to the rail of the box with one hand and to the back of the landau with the other. In his left hand he carried an ear-trumpet and in his right a rubber-tipped cane. He had a large, coarse, red face with a fleshy nose, and he looked out of narrowed eyes with the dignified, mildly contemptuous good humor typical of courageous and plain men who have often met danger and death face to face.

The two sisters, who recognized him from afar, ran up to the landau just in time to support him half-jokingly under the arms.

"You'd think I was the bishop," said the general in a friendly, husky bass.

"Grandad, dear Grandad!" said Vera, a little reproachfully. "All these days we've been expecting you, and you haven't let us get so much as a glimpse of you."

"Our Grandad's lost all conscience here in the south," said Anna with a laugh. "As if you couldn't have thought of your godchild. You behave like a shameless old fop, and you've forgotten all about us."

The general, who had bared his majestic head, kissed the hands of the sisters, then he kissed both women on the cheeks and again on the hands.

"Wait, girls, don't scold me," he said, pausing for breath after each word, because of his long-standing asthma. "Upon my honour —those wretched doctors—have been treating my rheumatism all summer—with some sort of foul jelly—it smells awful— And they wouldn't let me go— You're the first—I'm calling on— Very glad —to see you— How are you getting along? You're quite the lady, Vera—you look very much like—your late mother— When'll you be inviting me to the christening?"

"I'm afraid never, Grandad."

"Don't give up hope—it'll come yet— Pray to God. And you, Anna, you haven't changed a bit— At sixty you'll be—the same fidget. But wait. Let me introduce these gentlemen to you."

"I had the honor long ago," said Colonel Ponamaryov, bowing.

"I was introduced to the princess in Petersburg," added the Hussar.

"Well, then, Anna, may I introduce to you Lieutenant Bakhtinsky. He's a dancer and brawler, but a good horseman all the same. There, my dear Bakhtinsky, take that thing from the carriage. Come along, girls. What are you going to feed us on, Vera dear? After the starvation diet—those doctors kept me on—I have the appetite of an ensign—on graduation."

General Anosov had been a companon-in-arms and devoted friend of the late Prince Mirza Bulat-Tuganovsky. After the prince's death he had passed on to his daughters all his love and affection. He had known them when they were quite small—indeed, he was Anna's godfather. At that time he had been, as he still was, governor of a big but almost abandoned fortress in the town of K., and had come to Tuganovsky's almost daily. The children literally adored him because he pampered them, gave them presents, and offered them boxes at the circus or the theater, and also because no one could play with them so divertingly as he could. But what enchanted them and they remembered best were his stories of military campaigns, of battles and bivouacs, of victories and retreats, of death and wounds and severe frosts—artless unhurried stories, calm as an epic, told between evening tea and the hated hour when the children were told to go to bed.

This fragment of old times appeared as a colossal and extraordinarily picturesque figure. He combined those simple but deep and touching traits which, even in his day, were more often to be found among the privates than among the officers, those purely Russian, muzhik traits which, taken together, form an exalted character that sometimes makes our soldier not only invincible but a martyr, almost a saint. He has a guileless, naive faith, a clear, cheerfully good-natured view of life, cool and matter-of-fact courage, humility in the face of death, pity for the vanquished, infinite patience, and amazing physical and moral stamina.

Since the Polish War Anosov had taken part in every campaign except the Japanese. He would not have hesitated to go to that war, either, but he was not called upon, and he had a maxim which was great in its modesty: "Never challenge death until you're called." Throughout his service he never struck any of his men, let alone had them flogged. During the Polish uprising he refused to shoot a group of prisoners despite the regimental commander's personal orders. "If it's a spy, I can not only have him shot," he said, "but am ready to kill him with my own hand if you command me to. But these men are prisoners, and I can't do it." And he said that simply and respectfully, without the least hint of challenge or bravado, looking his superior straight in the eyes with his own clear, steady eyes, so that instead of shooting him for disobeying orders they let him alone.

During the war of 1877-1879, he rose very quickly to the rank of colonel, although he lacked proper education or, as he put it himself, had finished only a "bear's academy." He took part in crossing the Danube and the Balkan Mountains, camped at Shipka through the winter, and was among those who launched the last attack on Plevna; he was wounded five times, once seriously, and got severe concussion from a grenade splinter. General Radetsky and Skobelev knew him personally and had a great respect for him. It was about him that Skobelev had said, "I know an officer who is much braver than I am, and that officer is Major Anosov."

He returned from the war almost deaf from the grenade splinter; three toes on one foot had been amputated as a result of frost-bite during the Balkan march, and he had contracted an acute rheumatism at Shipka. After two years of peace-time service it was deemed timely to retire him, but he rebelled. The governor of the territory, who had witnessed his cool courage in crossing the Danube, brought his influence to bear at the critical moment. The Petersburg authorities decided not to hurt the feelings of the distinguished colonel and gave him for life the governorship of K., an office which was honorary rather than indispensable for the defense of the country.

Everyone in town knew him and good-naturedly made fun of

his foibles and habits and the way he dressed. He never carried arms, and he went about in a long, old-fashioned coat and cap with a large top and an enormous straight visor, a cane in his right hand and an ear-trumpet in his left; he was always accompanied by two fat, lazy, hoarse pugs with tongues lolling between their clamped jaws. If in the course of his morning stroll he met an acquaintance, the passers-by several blocks always could hear him shouting and the pugs barking in unison.

Like many people who are hard of hearing, he was passionately fond of opera, and sometimes, during a romantic duet, his commanding boom would suddenly resound throughout the hall, "Why, that was a good C, damn him! Cracked it right through like a nut." Subdued laughter would ripple across the hall, but the general would not even suspect this: in his naiveté he thought that he had whispered a spontaneous comment to his neighbor.

As part of his official duties he often visited, together with his wheezing pugs, the guard-house where officers under arrest relaxed very comfortably from the hardships of military service, telling stories over tea and cards. He would carefully question each of them, "Your name? Who arrested you? For how long? What for?" Sometimes he would quite unexpectedly commend an officer for a courageous if unlawful act, or take him to task so loudly that he could be heard outside. But when he had finished shouting he would inquire almost in the same breath where the officer got his meals and how much they cost him. It sometimes happened that a lieutenant, who had erred and been sent for a prolonged detention from an out-of-the-way corner that had no guard-room of its own, would confess that, being short of funds, he had to eat with the privates. Anosov then would immediately order meals to be supplied to the poor devil from his own home, which was no more than a hundred yards from the guard-house.

It was in K. that he had grown intimate with the Tuganovsky family and established such close ties with the children, so that with him it had become a virtual necessity to see them every evening. If it so happened that the young ladies went away somewhere or he himself was kept away by his official duties, he would feel terribly lonely and melancholy in the large rooms of the governor's . mansion. Every summer he would take his leave and spend a whole month at the Tuganovsky estate, Yegorovskoye, some forty miles from K.

All his repressed tenderness and his longing for love had gone out to the children, especially the girls. Once he had been married, but that had been so long ago that he hardly remembered it. It was before the war that his wife had eloped with a strolling actor, who had fascinated her with his velvet jacket and lace cuffs. Anosov paid her an allowance as long as she lived, but did not permit her to come back to him despite all the scenes of repentance and tearful letters. They had had no children.

v

Unexpectedly, the evening was calm and warm, and the candles on the terrace and in the dining-room burned with a steady flame. At dinner Prince Vasily Lvovich amused the company. He had an extraordinary and very peculiar gift for telling stories. He would take some incident that had happened to one of the company or a common acquaintance, but would embellish it so and use so serious a face and so matter-of-fact a tone that his listeners would split their sides with laughter. That night he was telling the story of Nikolai Nikolayevich's unhappy wooing of a wealthy and beautiful lady. The only authentic detail was the husband's refusal to give her a divorce. But the prince skilfully combined fact and fancy. He made the grave, rather priggish Nikolai run down the street in his stocking-feet at the dead of night, his boots under his arm. At a corner the young man was stopped by the policeman, and it was only after a long and stormy explanation that Nikolai managed to convince him that he was an assistant public prosecutor and not a cat burglar. The wedding all but came off, or so the narrator said, except that at the crucial moment a band of false witnesses, who had a hand in the affair, suddenly went on strike, demanding a raise in pay. Being a stingy man—which he actually was, to some extent—and also being opposed on principle to all forms of strike, Nikolai flatly refused to pay more, referring to a certain clause in the law, which was confirmed by a ruling of the court of appeal. Then, in reply to the customary question, "Does anyone here present know of any impediment to the lawful joining together of these two in matri-

mony?" the enraged perjurers said as one man, "Yes, we do. All
that we have testified under oath in court is a falsehood to which
the prosecutor here forced us by intimidation and coercion. As for
this lady's husband, we can only say from personal knowledge that
he is the most respectable man in the world, chaste as Joseph and
kind as an angel."

Having begun to tell wedding stories, Prince Vasily did not
spare even Gustav Ivanovich Friesse, Anna's husband, who, he said,
had on the day following his wedding called the police to evict the
young bride from her parents' house because she had no passport
of her own and to install her in her lawful husband's home. The
only part of the tale which was true was the fact that, in the very
first days of her married life, Anna had had to be continually with
her sick mother because Vera had gone off south, and poor Gustav
Ivanovich was plunged into gloom and despair.

Everybody laughed. Anna smiled with her narrowed eyes. Gustav Ivanovich roared in delight, and his gaunt face with the tight,
shining skin, the thin, light hair sleeked carefully down and the
deep-set eyes, was like a skull mirthfully baring a set of very bad
teeth. He still adored Anna as on the first day of their married life;
he was always trying to sit beside her, and touch her surreptitiously,
and he danced attendance on her with such smug infatuation that
you often pitied him and felt embarrassed for him.

Before rising from the table Vera Nikolayevna mechanically
counted the guests. There were thirteen of them. She was superstitious and she said to herself, "What a nuisance! Why didn't I think
of counting them before? And Vasya's to blame too—he told me
nothing on the telephone."

When friends gathered at Sheyin's or Friesse's they usually
played poker after dinner, because both sisters were ridiculously fond
of games of chance. In fact, certain rules had been established in
both houses: all the players would be given an equal number of
ivory tokens of a specific value, and the game would go on until all
the tokens passed to one of the players; then it would be stopped
for the evening, no matter how earnestly the others insisted on continuing. It was strictly forbidden to take fresh tokens from the cash-
box. Experience had shown that these rigid rules were indispensable
to check Vera and Anna, who would grow so excited in the course

of the game that there was no stopping them. The total loss seldom exceeded one or two hundred rubles.

This time, too, they sat down to poker. Vera, who was not playing, was about to go out on to the terrace, where the table was being set for tea, when the housemaid, looking rather mysterious, suddenly called her from the drawing-room.

"What is it, Dasha?" asked Princess Vera in annoyance, passing into her little study next to the bedroom. "Why are you staring at me so stupidly? And what are you holding there?"

Dasha put on the table a small square object, neatly wrapped in white paper and tied by a pink ribbon.

"It isn't my fault, Your Highness, honest to God," she stammered, blushing offendedly. "He came in and said—"

"Who is *he*?"

"A messenger boy, Your Highness."

"Well?"

"He came into the kitchen and put this on the table. 'Give it to your mistress,' he said. 'Only,' he says, 'be sure to hand it to her personally.' 'Who's it from?' I asked. 'It's written here,' he said. And then he ran away."

"Go and bring him back."

"Oh, but I couldn't do that, Your Highness. He came when you were in the middle of dinner, so I didn't dare to disturb you. It must have been half an hour ago."

"All right, you may go."

She cut the ribbon with scissors and threw it into the wastebasket along with the paper bearing her address. Under the wrapping she found a small jeweller's box of red plush, apparently fresh from the shop. She raised the lid, which was lined with light-blue silk, and saw, stuck into the black velvet, an oval gold bracelet, and inside it a note carefully folded into a neat octagon. Quickly she unfolded the paper. She thought she knew the handwriting, but, woman that she was, she put aside the note to take a look at the bracelet.

It was of low-standard gold, very thick but hollow and studded on the outside with small, poorly polished old garnets. But in the center there arose, surrounding a strange small green stone, five excellent cabochon garnets, each the size of a pea. As Vera happened to turn the bracelet at a lucky angle under the electric light, beautiful crimson lights flashed suddenly, deep under the smooth egg-shaped surface of the stones.

"It's like blood!" Vera thought with unexpected apprehension.

Then she recalled the letter and opened it. It was written in an elegant calligraphy and ran as follows:

"Your Highness, Princess Vera Nikolayevna,

"Respectfully congratulating you on your bright and happy birthday, I take the liberty of sending to you my humble, faithful offering."

"Oh, so that's who it is," Vera said to herself resentfully. But she read the letter to the end.

"I should never have dared to offer you a present of my own choice, for I have neither the right, nor the refined taste, nor, to be frank, the money to do so. Moreover, I believe there is no treasure on earth worthy of adorning you.

"But this bracelet belonged to my great-grandmother, and my late mother was the last to wear it. In the middle, among the bigger stones, you will see a green one. It is a very rare stone—a green garnet. We have an old family tradition that this stone enables the women who wear it to foresee the future, and keeps off unhappy thoughts, and protects men from violent death.

"All the stones have been carefully transferred from the old, silver bracelet, and you may rest assured that no one has worn this bracelet before you.

"You may at once throw away this absurd trinket, or present it to someone else; I shall be happy to know that your hands have touched it.

I beseech you not to be angry with me. I blush to remember my audacity of seven years ago, when I dared write to you, a young lady, stupid and wild letters, and even had the assurance to expect an answer to them. Today I have nothing for you but awe, everlasting admiration and the humble devotion of a slave. All that I can do now is to wish you perpetual happiness and to rejoice if you are happy. In my mind I bow deeply to the chair on which you sit, the floor you tread, the trees which you touch in passing, the servants to whom you speak. I no longer even presume to envy those people or things.

"Once again I beg your pardon for having bothered you with a long, useless letter.

"Your humble servant till death and after.

"G.S.Z."

"Shall I show it to Vasya or not? If so, when? Now or after the guests have left? No, I'd better do it later—now I'd look as silly as this poor man."

While debating thus with herself Princess Vera could not take her eyes off the five blood-red lights glowing inside the five garnets.

V I

It was only with great difficulty that Colonel Ponamaryov was induced to play poker. He said that he knew nothing about the game, that he did not gamble even for fun and that the only game he cared for and had any skill in was *vint*. But he could not resist their entreaties and in the end he gave in.

At first they had to teach and prompt him, but rather soon he mastered the rules of the game, and within half an hour he had all the chips piled in front of him.

"That isn't fair!" said Anna in mock reproach. "You might have allowed us a little more of the excitement."

Vera did not know how to entertain three of the guests—Speshnikov, the colonel and the vice-governor, a doltish, respectable and dull German. She got up a game of *vint* for them and invited Gustav Ivanovich to make a fourth. Anna thanked her by lowering her eyelids, and her sister at once understood. Everybody knew that unless Gustav Ivanovich was disposed of by suggesting a game of cards he would hang about his wife all evening, baring the rotten teeth in his skull-face and spoiling her mood.

Now things went smoothly, in an easy and lively atmosphere. Vasyuchok, accompanied by Jennie Reiter, sang in an undertone Italian folk canzonets and Oriental songs by Rubinstein. He had a light but pleasant voice, responsive and true. Jennie Reiter, a very exacting musician, was always willing to accompany him; but then it was said that he was courting her.

Sitting on a couch in a corner, Anna was flirting audaciously with the Hussar. Vera walked over and listened with a smile.

"No, please don't laugh," said Anna gaily, narrowing her lovely, mischievous Tatar eyes at the officer. "Of course, you think it's a feat to gallop at the head of a squadron, or to clear hurdles at races. But look at *our* feats. We've just finished a lottery. Do you think that's easy? Fie! The place was so crowded and full of tobacco smoke, there were porters and cabbies and God knows who else, and they all pestered me with complaints and grievances. I didn't have a moment's rest all day. And that isn't all, either, for now there's to be a concert in aid of needy gentlewomen, and then comes a charity ball—"

"At which you will not refuse me a mazurka, I hope?" Bakhtinsky put in and, bending slightly forward, clicked his heels under the arm-chair.

"Thank you. But the saddest case is our children's home. You know what I mean—a home for juvenile delinquents."

"Oh, I quite understand. That must be very amusing."

"Don't, you should be ashamed of laughing at things like that. But do you know what the trouble is? We'd like to give shelter to those unfortunate children, whose souls are corrupted by inherited vice and bad example, we'd like to give them warmth and comfort—"

"Humph!"

"—to improve their morality, and instill in them a sense of duty. Do you see my point? And every day hundreds and thousands of children are brought to us, but there isn't a single delinquent among them! If you ask the parents whether their child is delinquent they take offence—can you imagine that? And so the home has been opened and dedicated, everything is ready and waiting, but it hasn't a single inmate! We're almost at the stage of offering a prize for every delinquent brought in."

"Anna Nikolayevna," the Hussar interrupted her, with insinuating earnestness. "Why offer a prize? Take me free. Upon my honor, you couldn't find a more delinquent child than I am."

"Stop it! It's impossible to talk to you seriously." She burst out laughing, and sat back on the couch, her eyes shining.

Seated at a large round table, Prince Vasily was showing his sister, Anosov and his brother-in-law a family album of drawings done by himself. All four were laughing heartily, and gradually those other guests who were not playing cards gathered round them.

The album was a sort of supplement to Prince Vasily's satirical stories—a collection of illustrations. With imperturbable calm he showed "The Story of the Amorous Adventures of the Brave General Anosov in Turkey, Bulgaria and Elsewhere," "An Adventure of Prince Nicole Boulate-Touganofski the Coxcomb in Monte Carlo," and so on.

"I'll now acquaint you, ladies and gentlemen, with a brief biography of my beloved sister, Lyudmila Lvovna," he said, with a swift teasing glance at his sister. "Part One. Childhood. The child was growing. Her name was Lima."

The album leaf displayed the figure of a little girl, purposely drawn in childish style, her face set in profile and yet showing both eyes; two broken lines sticking out from under her skirt represented her legs, and the fingers of both hands were spread out.

"Nobody ever called me Lima," said Lyudmila Lvovna with a laugh.

"Part Two. First Love. A cavalry cadet, kneeling before the damsel Lima, presents her with a poem of his own production. It contains these lines of truly pearl-like beauty:

> Your gorgeous leg, I do opine,
> Is a thing of love divine!

"And here is an original likeness of the leg.

"Here the cadet induces the innocent Lima to elope from her parents' home. Here you see them in flight. And here is a critical situation: the enraged father has overtaken the fugitives. The faint-hearted cadet leaves the meek Lima in the lurch.

> You powdered your nose in a manner so slack
> That now our pursuers are hot on our track;
> So just do your best to hold them at bay,
> While into the bushes I run away."

The story of "the damsel Lima" was followed by one entitled "Princess Vera and the Infatuated Telegraphist."

"This moving poem is so far only in illustrations in ink and colored pencil," Vasily Lvovich explained with a serious air. "The text is in the making."

"That's something new," said Anosov, "I haven't seen it before."

"It's the latest issue. First edition from the book market."

Vera gently touched his shoulder.

"Don't, please," she said.

But Vasily Lvovich did not hear, or perhaps he did not take it seriously.

"It dates from prehistoric times. One fine day in May a damsel by the name of Vera received a letter with kissing doves on the first page. Here's the letter, and here are the doves.

"The letter contains an ardent confession of love, written against all rules of spelling. It begins: 'O Beutiful Blonde who art—a raging sea of flames seathing in my chest. Thy gaze clings to my tormented soal like a venomus serpent,' and so on. It ends in this humble way: 'I am only a poor telegrafist, but my feelings are worthy of Milord George. I dare not reveel my full name—it is too indecent. I only sign my inicials: P.P.Z. Please send your anser to the post-office, posté restanté.' Here, ladies and gentlemen, you can see the portrait of the telegraphist himself, very skilfully executed in crayon.

"Vera's heart was pierced (here's her heart and here's the arrow). But, as beseemed a well-behaved and good-mannered damsel, she showed the letter to her honorable parents, and also to her childhood friend and fiancé, Vasya Sheyin, a handsome young man. Here's the illustration. Given time the drawings will be supplied with explanations in verse.

"Vasya Sheyin, sobbing, returned the engagement ring to Vera. 'I will not stand in the way of your happiness,' he said, 'but, I implore you, do not be hasty. Think it over before you take the final step—test his feelings and your own. Child, you know nothing about life, and you are flying like a moth to a glowing flame. But I—alas! I know the cold, hypocritical world. You should know that telegraphists are attractive but perfidious. It gives them an indescribable pleasure to deceive an innocent victim by their proud beauty and false feelings and cruelly abandon her afterwards.'

"Six months rolled by. In the whirl of life's waltz Vera forgot her admirer and married young handsome Vasya, but the telegraphist did not forget her. One day he disguised himself as a chimney-sweep and, smearing himself with soot, made his way into Princess Vera's boudoir. You can see that he left the traces of his five fingers and two lips everywhere: on the rugs and pillows and wallpaper, and even on the floor.

"Here, dressed as a countrywoman, he takes up the duties of dish-washer in our kitchen. But the excessive favor which Luka the cook bestows upon him puts him to flight.

"Here he is in a mad-house. And here you see him as a monk. But every day he unfailingly sent a passionate letter to Vera. And where his tears fell on the paper the ink ran in splotches.

"At last he died, but before his death he willed to Vera two telegraph-office buttons and a perfume bottle, filled with his tears."

"How about some tea, ladies and gentlemen?" asked Vera Nikolayevna.

VII

The long autumn sunset was dying. The narrow crimson slit glowing on the edge of the horizon, between a bluish cloud and the earth, faded out. Now earth and trees and sky could no longer be seen. Overhead big stars shimmered with their eyelashes in the blackness of night, and the blue beam of the lighthouse shot upwards in a thin column that seemed to splash into a liquid, blurred circle of light as it struck the firmament. Moths fluttered against the glass hoods over the candles. In the front garden the star-shaped flowers of the tobacco-plant gave off a stronger scent in the cool darkness.

Speshnikov, the vice-governor and Colonel Ponamaryov had left long ago, promising to send the horses back from the tramway terminus to pick up the general. The remaining guests sat on the terrace. Despite his protests General Anosov was made to put on his greatcoat, and his feet were wrapped in a warm rug. He sat between the two sisters, with a bottle of his favorite Pommard claret in front of him. They waited on him eagerly, filling his thin glass with the heavy, thick wine, passing the matches, cutting cheese for him, and so on. The old general all but purred with bliss.

"Yes, autumn, autumn, autumn," said the old man, gazing at the candle-light and thouhtfully shaking his head. "Autumn. And I must start packing up. What a pity! It would have been so nice to stay here at the seaside, in ease and quiet, now that the weather's so fine!"

"And you could live with us, Grandad?" said Vera.

"I can't, my dear, I can't. Duty calls. My leave is over. But I certainly wish I could. How the roses smell! I can feel it from here. And in summer the flowers somehow had no scent, except the white acacias—and they smelled like candy."

Vera took two little roses—pink and carmine—out of a small jug and stuck them in the buttonhole of the general's greatcoat.

"Thanks, Vera dear." He bent his head to smell the flowers, and smiled the friendly smile of a kind old man.

"I remember when we took up our quarters in Bucharest. One day as I was walking down the street there came a strong smell of roses. I stopped and saw two soldiers, with a fine cut-glass bottle of attar standing between them. They had already oiled their boots and rifle-locks with it. "What's that you've got?" I asked. 'It's some sort of oil, sir. We put some of it in our gruel but it's no good—rasps the tongue—but it smells all right.' I gave them a ruble and they gladly let me have it. The bottle was no more than half-full, but considering the high price of the stuff it would fetch at least two hundred rubles. The soldiers were quite content, and they said, 'Here's another thing, sir. Peas of some kind. We tried hard to boil them, but the accursed stuff won't get soft.' It was coffee-beans, so I told them, 'That's only good for the Turks—it's of no use to soldiers.' Fortunately they hadn't eaten any opium. In some places I had seen opium tablets trampled into the mud."

"Tell us frankly, Grandad," said Anna, "did you ever know fear in battle? Were you afraid?"

"How strangely you talk, Anna. Of course I was afraid. Please don't believe those who say they weren't afraid and think the whizzing of bullets the sweetest music on earth. Only cranks or braggarts can talk like that. Everybody's afraid, only some shake in their boots with fear, while others keep themselves in hand. And though fear always remains the same, the ability to keep cool improves with practice; hence all the heroes and brave men. That's how it is. But once I was frightened almost to death."

"Tell us about it, Grandad," both sisters begged in unison.

They still listened to Anosov's stories with the same rapture as in their early childhood. Anna had spread out her elbows on the table quite like a child, propping her chin on her cupped hands. There was a sort of cosy charm about his unhurried, simple narrative. The somewhat bookish words and figures of speech which he used in telling his war memories sounded strange and clumsy. You would have thought he was imitating some nice ancient story-teller.

"It's a very short story," he responded. "It happened at Shipka in winter, after I was shell-shocked. There were four of us in our dug-out. That was when something terrible befell me. One morning when I rose from bed, I fancied I was Nikolai and not Yakov, and I couldn't undeceive myself, much as I tried. Sensing that my mind was becoming deranged, I shouted for some water to be brought to me, wet my head with it, and recovered my reason."

"I can imagine how many victories you won over women there, Yakov Mikhailovich," said Jennie Reiter, the pianist. "You must have been very handsome in your youth."

"Oh, but our Grandad is handsome even now!" cried Anna.

"I wasn't handsome," said Anosov, with a calm smile. "But I wasn't shunned, either. There was a moving incident in Bucharest. When we marched into the city, the people welcomed us in the main square with gunfire, which damaged many windows; but where water had been placed in glasses the windows were unharmed. This is how I learned that. Coming to the lodgings assigned to me, I saw on the window-sill a low cage and on the cage a large cut-glass bottle of clear water that had goldfish swimming in it, and a canary perched among them. A canary in water! I was greatly surprised, but inspecting it I saw that the bottle had a broad bottom with a deep hollow in it, so that the canary could easily fly in and perch there.

"I walked into the house and saw a very pretty Bulgarian girl. I showed her my admission slip and took the opportunity to ask her why the panes in the house were undamaged after the gunfire, and she told me it was because of the water. She also told me about the canary; how dull-witted I had been! While we were talking, our eyes met, a spark flew between us like electricity, and I felt that I had fallen headlong in love—passionately and irrevocably."

The old man paused and slowly sipped the black wine.

"But you confessed it to her afterwards, didn't you?" asked the pianist.

"Well, yes, of course. But I did it without words. This is how it came about—"

"I hope you won't make us blush, Grandad?" Anna remarked, smiling slyly.

"Not at all, the affair was perfectly respectable. You see, the townspeople didn't give us the same welcome everywhere, but in Bucharest the people were so easy-going with us that one day when I started playing a violin the girls at once came in their Sunday dresses and began to dance, and then it became a daily habit.

"One evening during the dances, when the moon was shining, I went into the passage where my Bulgarian girl had disappeared. On seeing me she pretended to be picking dry rose petals, which, incidentally, are gathered there by the sackful. But I put my arms round her, held her close to my heart and kissed her several times.

"From then on, when the moon and stars came out in the sky, I would hurry to my beloved and forget the day's worries while I was with her. And when the time came for us to march on we swore eternal love, and parted for ever."

"Is that all?" asked Lyudmila Lvovna, disappointed.

"What else did you expect?" replied the general.

"You will pardon me for saying so, Yakov Mikhailovich, but that isn't love—it's just an army officer's camp adventure."

"I don't know, really, whether it was love or some other sentiment."

"What I mean is, have you never known genuine love? A love that—well, in short, the kind of love that is holy and pure and eternal—and divine— Have you never experienced love like that?"

"I can't tell, honestly," faltered the old man, rising from his arm-chair. "I suppose not. At first, when I was young, I had no time, what with merry-making and cards and war. It seemed as if life and youth and good health would last for ever. Then I looked back and saw that I was already an old wreck. And now, Vera dear, please don't keep me any longer. I'll say goodbye to you all. Hussar," he said to Bakhtinsky, "the night is warm, let's go and meet our carriage."

"I'll go with you, Grandad," said Vera.

"So will I," added Anna.

Before leaving Vera stepped up to her husband.

"There's a red case in my drawer," she said to him softly. "In it you'll find a letter. Read it."

VIII

Anna and Bakhtinsky led the way, followed at some twenty paces by the general, arm-in-arm with Vera. The night was so black that during the first few minutes, before their eyes got used to the darkness, they had to grope for the way with their feet. Anosov, who despite his age still boasted surprisingly keen eyesight, had to help his companion. From time to time his big cold hand fondly stroked Vera's hand, which lay lightly on the bend of his sleeve.

"She's a funny woman, that Lyudmila Lvovna," he said suddenly, as if continuing aloud the thoughts that had been going through his head. "I've seen it so often in my life: as soon as a lady gets past fifty, especially if she's a widow or a spinster, she longs to hang about somebody else's love. She either spies, gloats and gossips, or offers to take care of your happiness, or works up a lot of treacly talk about exalted love. But I would say that nowadays people no longer know how to love. I see no real love. Nor did I see any in my time!"

"How can that be, Grandad?" Vera objected as she squeezed his arm slightly. "What slander! You were married yourself, weren't you? Then you must have loved."

"It doesn't mean a thing, Vera. Do you know how I got married? She was a peach of a girl, young and fresh, and she would sit by my side, her bosom heaving under her blouse. She'd lower her beautiful long eyelashes, and blush suddenly. The skin of her cheeks was so delicate, her neck so white and innocent, and her hands so soft and warm. God! Her papa and mamma slunk about us, eavesdropped at the door, and looked wistfully at me—with the gaze of faithful dogs. And I'd get little swift pecks when I was leaving. At tea her foot would touch mine as if by chance. Well, they got me before I knew where I was. 'Dear Nikita Antonovich, I have come to ask you for the hand of your daughter. Believe me, this angel—' Before I had finished the papa's eyes were moist, and he started to kiss me. "My dear boy! I guessed it long ago. May God keep you. Only take good care of our treasure!' Three months later the angelic treasure was going about the house in a shabby dressing-gown and slippers on her bare feet, her thin hair unkempt and hung with curl-papers. She wrangled with orderlies like a fish-wife and made a fool of herself with young officers, lisping, giggling, rolling her eyes. In the presence of others she for some reason called me Jacques, pronouncing it with a languid, long-drawn nasal twang, 'Oh, Ja-a-acques.' A spendthrift and a hypocrite, slovenly and greedy. And her eyes were always so insincere. It's all over now, finished and done with. I'm even grateful to that wretched actor. It was lucky we had no children."

"Did you forgive them, Grandad?"

" 'Forgive' isn't the word, Vera dear. At first I was like a madman. If I'd seen them then I'd certainly have killed them. Then the whole thing gradually wore off, and nothing was left but contempt. So much the better. God warded off useless bloodshed. Besides, I was spared the lot of most husbands. Indeed, what would have become of me if it hadn't been for that disgusting incident? A pack-camel, a despicable abettor and protector, a milk cow, a screen, some sort of household utensil. No! It's all for the best, Vera."

"No, no, Grandad, the old grievance still rankles in your heart, if you'll allow me to say so. And you extend your own unhappy experience to all mankind. Take Vasya and me. You couldn't call our marriage an unhappy one, could you?"

Anosov did not speak for a rather long time.

"All right, let's say your case is an exception," he said at length reluctantly. "But why do people generally get married? Let's take the woman. She's ashamed of remaining single, especially after all her friends have married. It's unbearable to be a burden on the family. She wants to be mistress of the house, mother of a family, enjoy independence. Then there's the need—the outright physical need—for motherhood, and for making a nest of her own. Men's motives are different. First of all they get sick of their bachelor life, the disorder in their rooms, restaurant meals, dirt, cigarette ends, torn or unmatching linen, debts, unceremonious friends, and so on, and so forth. Secondly, they feel that it's healthier and more economical to live in a family. In the third place, they think that after they've died, a part of them will be left in their children—an illusion of immortality. In the fourth place, there's the temptation of innocence, as in my case. And sometimes there is the consideration of a nice dowry. But where does love come in? Disinterested, self-sacrificing love that expects no reward? The love said to be 'stronger than death'? I mean that kind of love for which it's not an effort but sheer joy to perform any feat, give your life, accept martyrdom. Wait, Vera, are you going to talk to me about your Vasya again? Believe me, I like him. He's all right. Who knows if the future may not show his love in a light of great beauty. But try to understand what kind of love I am talking about. Love must be a tragedy. The greatest mystery in the world! No comforts, calculations or compromises must affect it."

"Have you ever seen such love, Grandad?" Vera asked softly.

"No," the old man replied firmly. "I know of two instances that come close to it. But one of them was prompted by stupidity, and the other—it was—a kind of sour stuff—utterly pitiful. I can tell you about them if you like. It won't take long."

"Please do, Grandad."

"All right. A regimental commander in our division—but not in our regiment—had a wife. She was a regular scarecrow. I must tell you. She was bony, red-haired, long-legged, scraggy, big-mouthed. Her make-up used to peel off her face like plaster off an old Moscow house. But, for all that, she was a kind of regimental Messalina, with a lot of spirit, arrogance, contempt for people, a passion for variety, and she was a morphine addict in the bargain.

"One day in autumn a new ensign was sent to our regiment, a greenhorn fresh from military school. A month later that old jade had him under her thumb. He was her page, her slave, her eternal dance partner. He used to carry her fan and handkerchief and rush out in snow and frost to get her horses, with nothing on but his flimsy coat. It's awful when an innocent lad lays his first love at the feet of an old, experienced, ambitious debauchee. Even if he manages to get away unscathed, you must give him up for lost just the same. He's marked for life.

"By Christmas she was fed up with him. She fell back on one of her previous, tried and tested passions. But he couldn't do without her. He trailed after her like a shadow. He was worn out; he lost weight and turned black. In high-flown language, 'death had marked his brow.' He was terribly jealous of her. They said that he used to stand under her window all night long.

"One day in spring they got up a kind of picnic in the regiment. I knew the two personally, but I was not there when it happened. As usual on such occasions, a lot was drunk. They started back after nightfall, along the railway. Suddenly they saw a freight train coming. It was creeping up a rather steep incline. They heard whistles. And the moment the headlights of the engine came alongside she suddenly whispered in the ensign's ear, 'You keep telling me you love me. But if I tell you to throw yourself under this train I'm sure you won't do it.' He didn't say a word in reply, but just rushed under the train. They say he had worked it out well, and meant to drop between the front and back wheels, where he would have been neatly cut in two. But some idiot tried to keep him back and push him away. Only he wasn't strong enough. The ensign clung to the rail with both his hands and they were chopped off.''

"How dreadful!" Vera exclaimed.

"He had to resign from military service. His comrades collected a little money for his journey. He couldn't very well stay in a town where he was a living reproach both to her and to the entire regiment. And that was the end of the poor chap—he became a beggar, and then froze to death somewhere on a Petersburg pier.

"The second case was quite a pitiful one. The woman was just like the other, except that she was young and pretty. Her behavior was most reprehensible. Light as we made of domestic affairs like that, we were shocked. But her husband didn't mind. He knew and saw everything but did nothing to stop it. His friends gave him hints, but he waved them away. 'Cut it out. It's no business of mine. All I want is for Lena to be happy.' Such a fool!

"In the end she got herself seriously involved with Lieutenant Vishnyakov, a subaltern from their company. And the three of them lived in two-husband wedlock, as if it were the most lawful kind of matrimony. Then our regiment was ordered to the front. Our ladies saw us off, and so did she, but, really, it was sickening: she didn't so much as glance at her husband, at least to keep up appearances if for no other reason. Instead she hung on her lieutenant like ivy on a rotten wall, and wouldn't leave him for a second. By way of farewell, when we were settled in the train and the train started, the hussy shouted after her husband, 'See that you take good care of Volodya! If anything happens to him I'll leave the house and never come back. And I'll take the children with me.'

"Perhaps you imagine the captain was a ninny? A jelly-fish? A sissy? Not at all. He was a brave soldier. At Zeloniye Gori he led his company against a Turkish redoubt six times, and of his two hundred men only fourteen were left. He was wounded twice, but refused to go to the medical station. That's what he was like. The soldiers worshipped him.

"But *she* had told him what to do. His Lena had!

"And so, like a nurse or a mother, he took care of that coward and idler Vishnyakov, that lazy drone. At night in camp, in rain and mud, he'd wrap him in his own greatcoat. He would supervise a sapper's job for him, while he lounged in a dug-out or played faro. At night he'd inspect the outposts for Vishnyakov. And that was at a time, mark you, when the Turks used to cut down our pickets as easily as a Yaroslavl countrywoman cuts down her cabbages. It's a sin to say so, but, upon my honor, everybody was happy to learn that Vishnyakov had died of typhus in hospital."

"How about women, Grandad? Have you never met loving women?"

"Of course I have, Vera. I'll say more: I'm sure that almost every woman in love is capable of sublime heroism. Don't you see, from the moment she kisses, embraces, gives herself, she is a *mother*. Love to her, if she does love, is the whole meaning of life—the whole universe! But it is no fault of hers that love has assumed such vulgar forms and degenerated into a sort of everyday convenience, a little diversion. The ones to blame are the men, who are surfeited at twenty, who have a chicken's body and a rabbit's heart, and are incapable of strong desires, heroic deeds, the tenderness and worship of love. They say real love did exist at one time. If not, then isn't it what the best minds and souls of the world—poets, novelists, musicians, artists—have dreamt of and longed for? The other day I read the story of Manon Lescaut and Cavalier des Grieux. It brought tears to my eyes—it really did. Tell me in all honesty, doesn't every woman dream, deep in her heart, of such a love—a single-minded, all-forgiving love ready to bear anything, modest and self-sacrificing?"

"Of course she does, Grandad, of course."

"And since it isn't there women take their revenge. In another thirty years or so from now—I won't live to see it, Vera dear, but you may; remember what I'm telling you—some thirty years from now women will wield unprecedented power in the world. They will dress like Indian idols. They'll trample us men underfoot as contemptible, grovelling slaves. Their extravagant wishes and whims will become painful laws for us. And all because throughout the generations we've been unable to worship and revere love. It will be a vengeance. You know the law: action and reaction are equal and opposite."

He paused a while, then asked suddenly, "Tell me, Vera, if only you don't find it embarrassing, what was that story about a telegrapher which Prince Vasily told us tonight? How much of it is fact and how much his usual invention?"

"Do you really wish to know, Grandad?"

"Only if you care to tell me, Vera. If for some reason you'd rather not—"

"Not at all. I'll tell you with pleasure."

And she told the general in detail about a crazy man who had begun to pursue her with his love two years before her marriage.

She had never seen him, and did not know his name. He had only written to her, signing G.S.Z. Once he had mentioned that he was a clerk in some office—he had not said a word about the telegraph office. He was apparently watching her movements closely, because in his letters he always mentioned very accurately where she had spent this or that evening and in what company, and how she had been dressed. At first his letters sounded vulgar and ludicrously ardent, although they were quite proper. But once she wrote to ask him—"by the way, Grandad, don't let that out to our people: nobody knows it"—not to annoy her any more with his protestations of love. From then on he wrote no more about love and sent her only an occasional letter—at Easter, on New Year's Eve, and on her birthday. Princess Vera also told the general about that day's parcel and gave him almost word for word the strange letter from her mysterious admirer.

"Y-es," the general drawled at last. "Perhaps he's just an addle-head, a maniac, or—who knows?—perhaps the path of your life has been crossed by the very kind of love that women dream about and men are no longer capable of. Just a moment. Do you see lights moving ahead? That must be my carriage."

At the same time they heard behind them the blare of a motor-car and the road, rutted by wheels, shone in a white acetylene light. Gustav Ivanovich drove up.

"I've taken your things with me, Anna. Get in," he said. "May I give you a lift, Your Excellency?"

"No, thank you, my friend," answered the general. "I don't like that engine. All it does is shake and stink—there's no pleasure in it. Well, good night, Vera dear. I'll be coming often now," he said, kissing Vera's forehead and hands.

There were goodbyes all round. Friesse drove Vera Nikolayevna to the gate of her villa and, swiftly describing a circle, shot off into the darkness in his roaring puffing motor-car.

IX

With a disagreeable feeling Princess Vera stepped on to the terrace and walked into the house. From a distance she heard the loud voice of her brother Nikolai and saw his gaunt figure darting back and forth across the room. Vasily Lvovich sat at the card table, his large head with the cropped tow hair bent low as he traced lines on the green cloth with a piece of chalk.

"It should have been done long ago!" said Nikolai irritably, making a gesture with his right hand as if he were throwing down some invisible burden. "I was convinced long ago that an end should have been put to those foolish letters. Vera wasn't yet your wife when I told you that you and she ought not to make fun of them like children, seeing only what was laughable in them. Here's Vera herself, by the way. Vasily Lvovich and I were talking about that madman of yours, P.P.Z. I consider the correspondence insolent and vulgar."

"There was no correspondence," Sheyin interrupted him coldly. "He was the only one who wrote."

Vera blushed at that, and sat down on the sofa, in the shade of a large fan-palm.

"I'm sorry," said Nikolai Nikolayevich, and threw down the invisible heavy object, as if he had torn it from his chest.

"I wonder why you call him mine," Vera put in, heartened by her husband's support. "He's mine as much as he's yours."

"All right, I'm sorry again. In short, what I mean is that we must put an end to his foolishness. I think this matter is getting beyond the stage where we may just laugh and draw funny pictures. Believe me that what I'm concerned about is Vera's reputation and yours, Vasily Lvovich."

"I think you're exaggerating, Koyla," replied Sheyin.

"Perhaps I am. But you risk finding yourself quite easily in a ridiculous position."

"I don't see how," said the prince.

"Suppose this idiotic bracelet"—Nikolai lifted the red case from the table and at once threw it down again with disgust—"this monstrous thing remains in our house, or we throw it out or present it to Dasha. Then, first of all, P.P.Z. will be able to brag to his acquaintances or friends that Princess Vera Nikolayevna Sheyina accepts his gifts, and, secondly, the first opportunity will encourage him to further exploits. Tomorrow, he may send her a diamond ring, the day after a pearl necklace, and then, for all we know, he may land in the dock for embezzlement or fraud and Prince and Princess Sheyin will be summonded to testify as witnesses. A nice prospect, eh?"

"The bracelet must certainly be sent back!" cried Vasily Lvovich.

"I think so too," Vera assented, "and the sooner the better. But how are we to do it? We don't know the name or address."

"Oh, that's child's play," Nikolai Nikolayevich replied carelessly. "We know the initials of this P.P.Z. Is that what they are, Vera?"

"G.S.Z."

"Very good. Besides, we know that he's employed somewhere. That's quite enough. Tomorrow I'll take the town directory and look up an official or clerk with those initials. If I don't find him for some reason, I'll simply call a detective and get him to trace the man for me. In case of difficulty I'll have this paper here with his handwriting. In short, by two o'clock tomorrow I'll know the exact name and address of the fellow and even the hours when he's in. And then we'll not only give him back his treasure tomorrow but will also see that he never reminds us of his existence again."

"What are you going to do?" asked Prince Vasily.

"What? I'm going to call on the governor."

"Not the governor—please! You know what terms we're on with him. We'd only make ourselves ridiculous."

"All right. I'll go to the chief of police. He's a clubmate of mine. Let him summon that Romeo and shake his finger under the man's nose. Do you know how he does it? He brings his finger close to your nose but doesn't move his hand—he just wags his finger and bawls, 'I won't stand for this, sir!' "

"Fie! Fancy dealing with the police!" said Vera, pulling a wry face.

"You're right, Vera," the prince agreed. "We'd better not drag any outsiders into this. There'd be rumors and gossip. We all know what our town is like. One might as well live in a glass jar. I think I had better go to that—er—young man myself; God knows he may be sixty. I'll hand him the bracelet and give him a talking to."

"Then I'll go with you," Nikolai Nikolayevich cut in. "You're too soft. Leave it to me to talk with him. And now, my friends"—he pulled out his watch and glanced at it—"you'll excuse me if I go to my room. I can hardly stand on my feet, and I have two files to look through."

"Somehow I feel sorry for that unfortunate man," said Vera hesitantly.

"No reason to feel sorry for him!" Nikolai retorted, turning in the doorway. "If anyone of our own class had played that trick with the bracelet and letter Prince Vasily would have sent him a challenge. Or if he hadn't, I would. In the old days I'd simply have had him flogged in the stable. You'll wait for me in your office tomorrow, Vasily Lvovich. I'll telephone you."

x

The filthy staircase smelled of mice, cats, paraffin-oil, and washing. Before they had reached the fifth floor Prince Vasily Lvovich halted.

"Wait a bit," he said to his brother-in-law. "Let me catch my breath. Oh, Kolya, we shouldn't have come here."

They climbed another two flights. It was so dark on the stairs that Nikolai Nikolayevich had to strike two matches before he made out the number of the flat.

He rang and was answered by a stout, white-haired, grey-eyed woman wearing spectacles, and slightly bent forward, apparently as a result of some disease.

"Is Mr. Zheltkov in?" asked Nikolai Nikolayevich.

The woman's eyes looked in alarm from one to the other and back. The two men's respectable appearance seemed to reassure her.

"Yes, won't you come in?" she said, stepping back. "First door on your left."

Bulat-Tuganovsky knocked three times, briefly and firmly. A rustling noise could be heard inside. He knocked again.

"Come in," a faint voice responded.

The room had a very low ceiling, but it was very wide—almost square in shape. Its two round windows, which looked very much like port-holes, let in little light. In fact, it was rather like the mess-room of a cargo ship. Against one of the walls stood a narrow bedstead, against another was a broad sofa with an excellent but worn Tekke rug, and in the middle stood a table spread with a colored Ukrainian cloth.

At first the visitors could not see the occupant's face, for he stood with his back to the light, rubbing his hands in perplexity. He was tall and thin, with long, silky hair.

"Mr. Zheltkov, if I'm not mistaken?" Nikolai Nikolayevich asked haughtily.

"Yes, that's my name. Very glad to meet you."

Holding out his hand, he took two paces towards Tuganovsky. But Nikolai Nikolayevich turned to Sheyin as if he had not noticed the gesture of welcome.

"I told you we weren't mistaken."

Zheltkov's slim, nervous fingers ran up and down the front of his short brown jacket, buttoning and unbuttoning it. At last he said with an effort, pointing to the sofa and bowing awkwardly, "Pray be seated."

He had now come into full view, a man with a very pallid, delicate girl's face, blue eyes and a firm, child-like, dimpled chin; he looked somewhere between thirty and thirty-five.

"Thank you," said Prince Sheyin, who had been scanning him with keen interest.

"*Merci*," Nikolai Nikolayevich answered briefly. And both remained standing. "It'll only take us a few minutes. This is Prince Vasily Lvovich Sheyin, the marshal of nobility in this province. My name is Mirza Bulat-Tuganovsky. I'm assistant public prosecutor. The business which we shall have the honor to discuss with you concerns in equal measure the prince and myself, or, to be exact, concerns the prince's wife, who is my sister."

Completely dazed, Zheltkov sank down on the sofa and stammered through blanched lips, "Please, sit down, gentlemen." But, apparently recalling that he had already suggested that, he jumped up, rushed to the window, tousling his hair, and came back again. And once more his trembling hands ran up and down, tugging at his buttons, plucking his light-colored, redding moustache, and touching his face.

"I am at your service, Your Highness," he said in a hollow voice, with an entreating gaze at Vasily Lvovich.

But Sheyin made no reply. It was Nikolai Nikolayevich who spoke.

"First of all, may I return something that belongs to you," he said, and, taking the red case from his pocket, he carefully put it down on the table. "To be sure, it does credit to your taste, but we earnestly request that no further surprises of this kind shall be sprung on us."

"Please forgive me. I know I'm very much at fault," whispered Zheltkov, flushing, his eyes on the floor. "Wouldn't you like a glass of tea?"

"You see, Mr. Zheltkov," Nikolai Nikolayevich went on, as if he had not heard Zheltkov's last words. "I'm very glad to see you are a gentleman, who can take a hint. I believe we shall reach agreement promptly. If I'm not mistaken, you have been pursuing Princess Vera Nikolayevna for the last seven or eight years?"

"Yes," answered Zheltkov softly, and lowered his eyelashes in awe.

"But so far we haven't taken any action against you, although you'll concede that we could and, indeed, *should* have done so. Don't you agree?"

"Yes."

"Yes. But by your last act, namely, by sending this garnet bracelet, you overstepped the limit of our forbearance. Do you understand? the limit. I shall not conceal from you that our first thought was to refer the matter to the authorities, but we didn't do so, and I'm glad we didn't, because—I'll say it again—I saw at once that you are an honorable man."

"I beg your pardon. What was that you said?" Zheltkov asked suddenly, and laughed. "You were about to refer the matter to the authorities? Did I understand you rightly?"

He put his hands in his pockets, made himself comfortable in a corner of the sofa, took out his cigarette-case and matches, and lighted a cigarette.

"So you said you were about to refer the matter to the authorities? You will pardon my sitting, Prince?" he said to Sheyin. "Well, go on."

The prince pulled a chair up to the table and sat down. Mystified and eager, he gazed at the face of the strange man with serious curiosity.

"It's open to us to take that step at any time, my good man," Nikolai Nikolayevich continued, with some insolence. "Butting into a stranger's family—"

"I beg to interrupt you—"

"No, I beg to interrupt *you*," all but shouted the assistant prosecutor.

"As you wish. Go on. I'm listening. But I want a word with Prince Vasily Lvovich."

And paying no more attention to Tuganovsky, he said, "This is the most difficult moment of my life. And I must speak without any regard for convention. Will you listen to me?"

"I'm listening," said Sheyin. "Be quiet, Kolya, please!" he said impatiently as he saw Tuganovsky make an angry gesture. "Yes?"

For a few seconds Zheltkov's breathing came in choking gasps, and suddenly he burst out in a torrent of words. He spoke with only his jaws; his lips were a ghastly white and rigid like a dead man's.

"It's hard to utter those words—to say that I love your wife. But seven years of hopeless and unassuming love give me some right to it. I'll own that at first, while Vera Nikolayevna was still unmarried, I wrote her foolish letters and even expected her to answer them. I agree that my last step, namely, sending the bracelet, was an even more foolish thing to do. But—I look you straight in the eyes and I feel that you'll understand me. I know it's beyond my power ever to stop loving her. Tell me, Prince—supposing you resent the whole thing—tell me what you would do to break off that feeling? Would you have me transported to some other town, as Nikolai Nikolayevich suggested? But there I would go on loving Vera Nikolayevna as much as I do here. Put me in jail? But there, too, I'd find means to remind her of my existence. So the only solution is death. If you so desire I'll accept death in any form."

"Instead of talking business, here we are up to our necks in melodrama," said Nikolai Nikolayevich, putting on his hat. "The point is quite clear: either you cease completely persecuting Princess

Vera Nikolayevna or, if you don't, we shall take such measures as are available to men of our standing, our influence, and so on."

But Zheltkov did not so much as glance at him, although he had heard him. Instead he asked Prince Vasily Lvovich, "Would you mind my leaving you for ten minutes? I'll admit that I'm going to speak to Princess Vera Nikolayevna on the telephone. I assure you I will report to you as much of the conversation as I can."

"All right," said Sheyin.

Left alone with his brother-in-law, Nikolai Nikolayevich set upon him at once.

"This won't do," he shouted, his right hand as usual throwing down some invisible object from his chest. "This just won't do. I warned you I would take care of the matter. But you turned sloppy and gave him a chance to expatiate on his feelings. I'd have put everything in two words."

"Wait," said Prince Vasily Lvovich, "everything will be cleared up in a moment. The important thing is, I think he has the face of a man who is unable to deceive or lie deliberately. But is it his fault that he's in love? And how can you control a feeling like love, which people still can't account for?" He paused thoughtfully, and added, "I feel sorry for the man. Moreover, I feel as if I'm looking at a tremendous tragedy of the soul, and I can't behave like a clown."

"That's decadence," said Nikolai Nikolayevich.

Ten minutes later Zheltkov came back. His eyes were shining and deep, as if they were filled with unshed tears. And it was obvious that he had quite forgotten about his good manners, about who should sit where, and had stopped behaving like a gentleman. And once again Prince Sheyin understood the reason with great sensitivity.

"I'm ready," he said. "From tomorrow you'll hear nothing more of me. For you, I'm as good as dead. But there's one condition—I say this to *you*, Prince Vasily Lvovich—I've embezzled money and must fly from this town anyway. Will you permit me to write a last letter to Princess Vera Nikolayevna?"

"No. If it's finished, it's finished. No letters!" shouted Nikolai Nikolayevich.

"All right, you may," said Sheyin.

"That's all," said Zheltkov, smiling haughtily. "You'll hear no more of me, let alone see me. Princess Vera Nikolayevna didn't want to speak to me at all. When I asked her if I might remain in town so as to see her at least occasionally—without being seen by her, of course—she said, 'If only you knew how tired I am of the whole business! Please stop it as soon as you can.' And so I'm stopping the whole business. I think I've done all I could, haven't I?"

Coming back to the villa that evening, Vasily Lvovich told his wife in detail about his interview with Zheltkov. He seemed to feel it was his duty to do that.

Vera was worried, but not surprised or bewildered. Later that night, when her husband came into her bed, she suddenly turned away to the wall and said, "Leave me alone—I know that man is going to kill himself."

XI

Princess Vera Nikolayevna never read the newspapers because, firstly, they dirtied her hands, and, secondly, she could never make head or tail of the language which they use nowadays.

But fate willed it that she should open the page and come upon the column which carried this news:

"A Mysterious Death. G. S. Zheltkov, an employee of the Board of Control, committed suicide about seven o'clock last night. According to evidence given at the inquest, his death was prompted by an embezzlement. He left a note to that effect. Since testimony furnished by witnesses has established that he died by his own hand, it has been decided not to order a post-mortem."

Vera thought, "Why did I feel it was coming? Precisely this tragic finale? And what was it: love or madness?"

All day long she wandered about the flower-garden and the orchard. The anxiety growing in her from minute to minute made her restless. And all her thoughts were riveted on the unknown man whom she had never seen, and would hardly ever see—that ridiculous "P.P.Z."

"Who knows? Perhaps a real, self-sacrificing, true love has crossed the path of your life." She recalled what Anosov had said.

At six o'clock the postman came. This time Vera Nikolayevna recognized Zheltkov's handwriting, and she unfolded the letter with greater tenderness than she would have expected of herself.

This was what Zheltkov wrote:

"It is not my fault, Vera Nikolayevna, that God willed to send to me, as an enormous happiness, love for you. I happen not to be interested in anything like politics, science, philosophy, or man's future happiness; to me life is centered in you alone. Now I realize that I have thrust myself into your life like an embarrassing wedge. Please forgive me for that if you can. I am leaving today and shall never come back, and there will be nothing to remind you of me.

"I am immensely grateful to you just because you exist. I have examined myself, and I know it is not a disease, not the obsession of a maniac—it is love with which God has chosen to reward me for some reason.

"I may have appeared ridiculous to you and your brother, Nikolai Nikolayevich. As I depart I say in ecstasy, '*Hallowed be thy name.*'

"Eight years ago I saw you in a circus box, and from the very first second I said to myself: I love her because there is nothing on earth like her, nothing better, no animal, no plant, no star, because no human being is more beautiful than she, or more delicate. The whole beauty of the earth seemed to be embodied in you.

"What was I to do? Fly to some other town? But my heart was always beside you, at your feet, at every moment it was filled with you, with thoughts of you, with dreams of you, with a sweet madness. I am very much ashamed of, and blush in my mind for, that foolish bracelet—well, it cannot be helped; it was a mistake. I can imagine the impression it made on your guests.

"I shall be gone ten minutes from now. I shall just have time to stick a postage stamp on this letter and drop it into a box, so as not to ask anyone else to do it. Please burn this letter. I have just heated the stove and am burning all that was precious to me in life: your handkerchief which, I confess, I stole. You left it on a chair at a ball in the Noblemen's Assembly. Your note—oh, how I kissed it!—in which you forbade me to write to you. A program of an art exhibition, which you once held in your hand and left forgotten on a chair by the entrance. It is finished. I have cut off everything, but still I believe, and even feel confident, that you will think of me. If you do—I know you are very musical, for I saw you mostly at performances of the Beethoven quartets—if you do think of me, please play, or get someone else to play, the Sonata in D-Major No. 2, op. 2.

"I wonder how I shall close my letter. I thank you from the

bottom of my heart because you have been my only joy in life, my only comfort, my sole thought. May God give you happiness, and may nothing transient or commonplace disturb your wonderful soul. I kiss your hands.

"G.S.Z."

She went to her husband, her eyes red with crying and her lips swollen, and, showing him the letter, she said, "I don't want to conceal anything from you, but I have a feeling that something terrible has come into our life. You and Nikolai Nikolayevich probably didn't handle the matter properly."

Prince Sheyin read the letter with deep attention, folded it carefully, and said after a long pause, "I don't doubt this man's sincerity, and what's more, I don't think I have a right to analyze his feelings towards you."

"Is he dead?" asked Vera.

"Yes, he's dead. I think he loved you and wasn't mad at all. I watched him all the time and saw his every movement, every change in his face. There was no life for him without you. I felt as if I were witnessing a tremendous agony, and I almost realized that I was dealing with a dead man. You see, Vera, I didn't know how to behave or what to do."

"Look here, Vasya," she interrupted him. "Would it pain you if I went to town to take a look at him?"

"No, no, Vera, please go. I'd like to go myself, but Nikolai's bungled the whole thing. I'm afraid I should feel awkward."

XII

Vera Nikolayevna left her carriage two blocks off Luteranskaya Street. She found Zheltkov's flat without much difficulty. She was met by the same grey-eyed old woman, very stout and wearing silver-rimmed spectacles, who asked as she had done the day before, "Who do you wish to see?"

"Mr. Zheltkov," said the princess.

Her costume—her hat and gloves—and her rather peremptory tone apparently impressed the landlady. She began to talk.

"Please step in, it's the first door on your left, and there—he is—

He left us so soon. Well, suppose he did embezzle money. He should have told me about it. You know we don't make much by letting rooms to bachelors. But if it was a matter of six or seven hundred rubles I could have scraped it together to pay for him. If only you knew, madam, what a wonderful man he was. He had been my lodger for eight years, but he was more like a son to me."

There was a chair in the passage, and Vera sank down upon it.

"I'm a friend of your late lodger," she said, carefully choosing her words. "Please tell me something about his last minutes, about what he said and did."

"Two gentlemen came to see him, madam, and had a very long talk with him. Then he told me they'd offered him the position of bailiff on an estate. Then Georgy ran out to telephone and came back so happy. And then the two gentlemen left, but he sat down and began writing a letter. Then he went out to mail the letter, and then we heard something like a shot from a toy pistol. We paid no attention to it. He always had tea at seven o'clock. Lukerya, the maid, went to knock at his door, but he didn't answer, and she knocked again and again. We had to force the door, and there he lay dead."

"Tell me something about the bracelet," Vera Nikolayevna commanded.

"Ah, the bracelet—I quite forgot. How do you know about it? Before writing the letter he came to me and said, 'Are you a Catholic?' 'Yes,' I said. Then he says, 'You have a nice custom'—that was what he said—'a nice custom of hanging rings, necklaces, and gifts on the image of the Holy Virgin. So won't you please hang this bracelet on your icon?' I promised."

"Will you let me see him?" asked Vera.

"Of course, madam. There's his door, the first on the left. They were going to take him to the dissecting-room today, but he has a brother who asked permission to give him a Christian burial. Please come."

Vera braced herself and opened the door. The room smelled of incense, and three wax candles were burning in it. Zheltkov was lying on the table, placed diagonally. His head rested on a very low support—a small soft cushion that someone seemed to have pushed under it purposely, because that did not make any difference to a corpse. His closed eyes suggested deep gravity, and his lips were set in a blissful, serene smile, as if before parting with life he had learned some deep, sweet mystery that had solved the whole riddle of his life. She remembered having seen the same peaceful expression on the death-masks of two great martyrs, Pushkin and Napoleon.

"Would you like me to leave you alone, madam?" asked the old woman, a very intimate note in her voice.

"Yes, I'll call you later," said Vera, and she at once took a big red rose from the side pocket of her jacket, slightly raised the head of the corpse with her left hand, and with her right hand put the flower under his neck. At that moment she realized that that love of which every woman dreams had gone past her. She recalled what General Anosov had said, almost prophetically, about everlasting, exclusive love. And, pushing aside the hair on the dead man's forehead, she clutched his temples with her hands and put her lips to his cold, moist forehead in a long, affectionate kiss.

When she was leaving the landlady spoke to her in her ingratiating Polish accent.

"I can see, Panny, that you're not like others, who come out of mere curiosity. Before his death, Pan Zheltkov said to me, 'If I happen to die and a lady comes to look at me tell her that Beethoven's best work is—' He wrote it down for me. Here, look."

"Let me see it," said Vera Nikolayevna, and suddenly she broke into tears. "Please excuse me—this death shocked me so I couldn't help myself."

She read the words, written in the familiar hand: "*L. Van Beethoven. Son. No. 2, op. 2. Largo Appassionato.*"

XIII

Vera Nikolayevna came home late in the evening and was glad not to find either her husband or her brother in.

However, Jennie Reiter was waiting for her; troubled by what she had seen or heard. Vera rushed to her and cried as she kissed her large beautiful hands, "Please play something for me, Jennie dear, I beg of you." And at once she went out of the room and sat on a bench in the flower-garden.

She scarcely doubted for a moment that Jennie would play the passage from the sonata asked for by that dead man with the odd name of Zheltkov.*

And so it happened. From the very first chords Vera recognized that extraordinary work, unique in depth. And her soul seemed to split in two. She thought that a great love, of the kind which comes but once in a thousand years, had passed her by. She recalled General Anosov's words, wondering why Zheltkov had made her listen, of all Beethoven, to this particular work. Words strung themselves together in her mind. They fell in with the music to such an extent that they were like the verses of a hymn, each ending with the words: "*Hallowed be thy name.*"

"I shall now show you in tender sounds a life that meekly and joyfully doomed itself to torture, suffering, and death. I knew nothing like complaint, reproach, or the pain of love scorned. To you I pray: '*Hallowed be thy name.*'

"Yes, I foresee suffering, blood, and death. And I think that it is hard for the body to part with the soul, but I give you praise, beautiful one, passionate praise, and a gentle love. '*Hallowed be thy name.*'

"I recall your every step, every smile, every look, the sound of your footsteps. My last memories are enwrapped in sweet sadness— in gentle, beautiful sadness. But I shall cause you no sorrow. I shall go alone, silently, for such is the will of God and fate. '*Hallowed be they name.*'

"In my sorrowful dying hour I pray to you alone. Life might have been beautiful for me too. Do not murmur, my poor heart, do not. In my soul I call death, but my heart is full of praise for you: '*Hallowed be thy name.*'

"You do not know—neither you nor those around you—how beautiful you are. The clock is striking. It is time. And, dying, in the mournful hour of parting with life I still sing—glory to you.

"Here it comes, all-subduing death, but I say—glory to you!"

With her arms round the slender trunk of an acacia and her body pressed to it, Princess Vera was weeping. The tree shook gently. A wind came on a light wing to rustle in the leaves, as if in sympathy. The smell of the tobacco-plant was more pungent. Meanwhile the marvellous music continued, responding to her grief:

* Derived from *zheltok*, yolk.—*Translator.*

"Be at peace, my dearest, be at peace. Do you remember me? Do you? Your are my last, my only love. Be at peace, I am with you. Think of me, and I shall be with you, because you and I loved each other only an instant, but for ever. Do you remember me? Do you? Here, I can feel your tears. Be at peace. Sleep is so sweet, so sweet to me."

Having finished the piece, Jennie Reiter came out of the room and saw Princess Vera, bathed in tears, sitting on the bench.

"What's the matter?" asked the pianist.

Her eyes glistening, Vera, restless and agitated, kissed Jennie's face and lips and eyes as she said, "It's all right, he has forgiven me now. All is well."

IVAN BUNIN

The Gentleman
from San Francisco

Alas, alas, Babylon, that mighty city!
APOCALYPSE

THE GENTLEMAN FROM SAN FRANCISCO—nobody in either Naples or Capri could remember his name—was on his way to the Old World with his wife and daughter, there to spend two whole years devoted entirely to pleasure.

He was firmly convinced that he was entitled to a rest, to enjoyment, to a long and comfortable voyage, and to any number of other things. He had his own reasons for being so firmly convinced; firstly, he was a wealthy man, and secondly, he was only beginning to live, although he was already fifty-eight. Until then he had not lived, he had merely existed, not badly at all it must be said, but nevertheless it was nothing but existence, for he had centered all his hopes on the days to come. He had worked without a breathing spell—the Chinese, whom he imported in thousands to work for him, well knew what that meant! And at last he saw that he had achieved a great deal, that he had almost come up to the level of those he had once set up as an example to himself; and then he decided to take a

Translated by OLGA SHARTSE. *Reprinted from* The Gentleman from San Francisco. *Moscow,* [*n.d.*].

holiday. It was a custom with the class of men to which he belonged to start off with a trip to Europe, India and Egypt when they were ready to enjoy life. He decided to do the same. Naturally, his chief concern was to reward himself for his years of toil; however, he was glad for the sake of his wife and daughter, too. His wife was never known to be particularly impressionable, but then all middle-aged American women are passionate travellers. And as for his daughter, a girl no longer young and rather sickly, the trip was an outright necessity for her. To say nothing of the good it would do her health, what of those happy friendships known to have been made on board ship? You sometimes actually find yourself sitting next to a multi-millionaire at dinner or studying frescoes together in the lounge.

The route planned by the gentleman from San Francisco was an extensive one. During the months of December and January he was hoping to bask in the sun of southern Italy, to enjoy the ancient sights, the tarantella, the serenades of the wandering singers, and something that men of his age appreciate with a peculiar poignancy —the love of young Neapolitan girls, even if it isn't entirely disinterested; he proposed to spend Carnival week in Nice and Monte Carlo, where the most select society gathers at that time, the society which rules and dispenses all the blessings of our civilized world—such as the latest cut of dinner-jackets, the stability of thrones, the declaration of wars and the welfare of the hotels— where some of the guests plunge excitedly into automobile and yacht races or into roulette, others into what is customarily known as "light flirtation," and still others into shooting pigeons which, released from their cotes, soar beautifully over the emerald-green lawns, against the background of the forget-me-not sea, and then instantly flop on the ground like little white balls; the first part of March he wanted to devote to Florence and arrive in Rome for Passion Week in order to hear the *Miserere* sung there; his plans included Venice and Paris, bullfighting in Seville, bathing in the British Isles, then Athens, Constantinople, Palestine, Egypt, and even Japan—on the way back of course. . . . And everything began splendidly.

It was the end of November. Icy fogs and slushy snowstorms accompanied them all the way to Gibraltar, but they sailed on quite safely. There were many passengers on board. The famous *Atlantic* was like a huge hotel with so many facilities—an all-night bar, Turkish baths, a newspaper of its own, and life on board ran a scheduled course: they got up early, roused by the bugles blaring shrilly in the corridors in that dusky hour of the morning when day was just breaking so slowly and glumly over the grey-green expanse of the sea, rolling heavily in the fog; they put on their flannel pyjamas and had coffee, chocolate or cocoa; after that they bathed in marble bath-tubs, did their exercises to work up a good appetite and a feeling of fitness, dressed and had their breakfast; until eleven they were supposed to walk briskly up and down the deck, breathing in the cool freshness of the ocean, or to play shuffle-board and other games in order to work up their appetites anew, and at eleven they fortified themselves with sandwiches and beef tea; thus fortified, they read the ship's newspaper with relish and calmly awaited lunch, which was even more nourishing with a greater variety of dishes than breakfast; the next two hours were devoted to rest: deck chairs were then ranged along all the decks, and the passengers lay back in them, wrapped in rugs, gazing at the cloudy sky and the frothy waves through the railing, or falling into a sweet doze; between the hours of four and five, refreshed and cheered, they had strong, fragrant tea and biscuits served to them; at seven, the bugles signalled the approach of the moment that formed the main purpose of this existence, its crowning glory. . . . And, roused by the bugles, the gentleman from San Francisco, rubbing his hands in an access of life and vigour, hurried to his sumptuous cabin *de luxe* to dress for dinner.

At night the *Atlantic* seemed to gape into the darkness with countless blazing eyes, while a great number of servants worked busily in the kitchens, sculleries and wine cellars below. The ocean, moving beyond the walls, was awesome, but no one thought about it, firmly believing it to be in the hands of the Captain, a red-haired man of monstrous size and corpulence, who always looked sleepy and resembled an enormous idol in his black coat with gold-braid bands, and who very seldom emerged from his secret abode to be among the passengers. In the forecastle the siren kept wailing with infernal gloom or squealing in frantic fury, but not many of the diners heard the siren, for it was drowned by a splendid string orchestra, playing exquisitely and indefatigably in the two-storeyed marble dining-room, which had deep pile carpets on the floor, was festively flooded with lights, thronged with ladies in low-cut evening-gowns and gentlemen in tail-coats or dinner-jackets, with slender waiters, deferential *maîtres d'hôtel*, and a wine waiter who actually wore a chain around his neck like a lord mayor. The dinner-coat and starched shirt made the gentleman from San Francisco look very much younger than he was. Lean and not tall, ungainly in build but well-knit, polished to a sheen and reasonably gay, he sat in the pearly-golden halo of this room with a bottle of amber-colored Johannesburg in front of him, an array of glasses of the finest crystal, and a vase of curly hyacinths. His yellowish face with the neatly trimmed silver moustache had something Mongolian in it, gold fillings gleamed in his teeth, and his strong skull shone like old ivory. His wife, a large, broad and serene woman, wore clothes that were expensive but suitable to her age; while the daughter—tall and slim, with beautiful hair charmingly dressed, her breath sweetened with violet cachous, and with the faintest of little pink pimples, slightly dusted over with powder, around her lips and be-tween her shoulder-blades—wore a gown that was elaborate but light and transparent, innocently frank. . . . The dinner went on for over an hour, and after that there was dancing in the ballroom, during which the men—the gentleman from San Francisco among them of course—sprawled in arm-chairs with their feet up and de-cided the fate of whole nations on the basis of the latest stock exchange news, smoking themselves red in the face with Havana cigars and getting drunk on liqueurs in the bar attended by red-coated Negroes with eyeballs that looked like shelled hard-boiled eggs. The ocean roared and heaved in black mountains on the other side of the wall, the storm whistled through the sodden, heavy rigging, the ship shuddered and shook as it struggled through the storm and the black mountains, cutting like a plough through their rippling mass which kept swirling into a froth and flinging high its foamy tails. The siren, suffocating in the fog, wailed in mortal agony; the watch up in the crow's-nest froze in the cold, their minds reeling from the unbearable strain on their attention, and the ship's belly below the water-line was like the abyss of hell at its most sinister and sultry, its ninth circle—the belly in which the giant furnaces rumbled with laughter as, with their blazing maws, they devoured ton after ton of coal, flung down them with a clatter by men drenched in pungent sweat, dirty, half-naked and purple in the glow of the flames; while up here in the bar, legs were flung carelessly over the arms of chairs, brandy and liqueurs were sipped at leisure, clouds of aromatic smoke hung in the air, and in the ballroom all was brilliance, radiating light, warmth and joy; couples whirled in a waltz or swayed in a tango, and the music, insistently and with a sadness that was voluptuous and shameless, sang its plea, always that one plea. . . . Among this brilliant crowd of people there was a certain well-known millionaire, a lanky, clean-shaven man in an old-fashioned dress-coat, who resembled a prelate; there was a famous Spanish author, a world-celebrated beauty, and an elegant pair of lovers watched by all with curiosity, who made no secret of their happiness, for he danced with no one but her. And all this was so exquisitely and charmingly performed that no one but the Captain knew that the couple was hired by Lloyds to play at love for a good wage, and had been sailing on the company's ships for a long time.

Everyone was glad of the sun in Gibraltar, it seemed like early spring. A new passenger appeared on board the *Atlantic*, instantly drawing everyone's attention to himself. He was the crown prince of a certain kingdom in Asia, travelling incognito; a small man, perfectly wooden, broad-faced and narrow-eyed, wearing gold-rimmed spectacles, slightly unpleasant because the coarse black hairs of his moustache were stringy like a corpse's, but a nice, simple and unpresumptuous man on the whole. In the Mediterranean there was once again a breath of winter; the sea billowed in high varicoloured waves like a peacock's tail, blown by the tramontane which came rushing towards the ship madly and merrily in the brilliant light of a perfectly clear day. And then, on the second day, the sky began to pale, the horizon was wrapped in mist: land was nearing, now there was a glimpse of Ischia and Capri, now if you looked through your binoculars you could see the lumps of sugar strewn at the foot of something dusky-blue, Naples. Many of the ladies and gentlemen had already put on their light fur coats; the meek Chinese "boys," who never spoke above a whisper, bow-legged youngsters with pitch-black plaits hanging down to their heels, with thick maidenly eyelashes, were quietly carrying rugs, canes, suit-cases and dressing-cases towards the companion-way. The daughter of the gentleman from San Francisco stood on deck next to the prince, to whom she had been introduced the night before by a happy chance, and pretended she was following his pointed finger into the distance as he explained something to her hastily and softly; he was so short he looked like a little boy beside the others, seeming quite unprepossessing and odd—his spectacles, bowler hat and English overcoat, the horsehair coarseness of his stringy moustache, the thin olive skin stretched tight across his flat face which might have been thinly coated with varnish—but the girl stood listening to him and she was so excited she could not understand a word he was saying; her heart was beating fast, strangely enraptured; everything, every single thing about him was different from everyone else—his slim hands, his clear skin, beneath which coursed the blood of ancient kings, his very clothes—European and quite plain, but somehow exceptionally neat—held an extraordinary fascination for her. And meanwhile, the gentleman from San Francisco himself, wearing grey spats over his patent-leather shoes, kept glancing at the famous beauty who stood beside him, a tall blonde with a marvellous figure and eyes painted in the latest Parisian fashion, who was talking to a tiny, humpbacked hairless dog which she held on a thin silver chain. And the daughter, feeling vaguely discomfited, tried to take no notice of the father.

He was rather generous when travelling, and therefore he quite believed in the solicitude of all those who fed and waited on him from morning to night forestalling his slightest wish, who safeguarded his peace and kept him immaculate, who summoned porters for him and delivered his trunks to hotels. It had been like this everywhere, it had been so on board ship, it should be so in Naples, too. The city grew larger and nearer; the ship's band, with brass instruments flashing in the sun, was already crowded on deck and suddenly burst into a deafening and triumphant march; the gigantic Captain appeared on the bridge in his dress uniform and, like a merciful pagan god, waved to the passengers with an affable gesture. And, like everyone else, the gentleman from San Francisco fancied that the thundering strains of proud America's march were being played for him alone, and that the Captain was wishing him personally a happy landing. When at last the *Atlantic* entered harbour and its many-storied bulk, with people clustering at the rails, tied up to the pier and the chains of the gang-planks clattered—countless hotel porters and their assistants in gold-braided caps, all sorts of commissionaires, whistling urchins and hefty beggars with stacks of colored postcards in their hands, rushed forward offering their services. And he smiled at these beggars as he walked to the car of the hotel where the prince might also be putting up, and calmly spoke through his teeth first in English then in Italian:

"Go away! Via!"

Life in Naples instantly took on a clock-work regularity: in the morning there was breakfast in the gloomy dining-room, an overcast sky that held little promise, and a crowd of guides at the lobby doors; then came the first smiles of the warm rosy sun, a view of Vesuvius from the high hanging balcony, the mountain cloaked entirely in the shimmering vapours of dawn, of the pearly-silver ripples on the bay and the pale silhouette of Capri on the horizon, of tiny donkeys harnessed into dogcarts, tripping along the muddy quay below, and detachments of toy soldiers marching somewhere to the sounds of vigorous and challenging music; after that came the waiting car and a slow drive through the thronged, narrow grey corridors of streets, between tall, many-windowed houses, visits to the funereally stark and clean museums, lighted evenly and pleasantly but with a snow-like dullness, or to the churches, cold and smelling of wax, where the same thing was repeated over and over again: a stately entrance hung with a heavy leather curtain, and inside a vast emptiness and silence, the soft lights of the seven-branched candelabrum flickering redly in the depths upon the altar draped in lace, a solitary old woman among the dark wooden pews, slippery gravestones underfoot, and on the wall someone's *Descent from the Cross*—invariably famous; at one, there was lunch on the San Martin Hill, where quite a number of the very first-class people gathered towards noon, and where on one occasion the daughter of the gentleman from San Francisco had nearly fainted: she thought she saw the prince sitting in the room, whereas the newspapers said he was in Rome; at five, tea was served at the hotel in the beautiful drawing-room which was so warm with its thick carpeting and blazing fires; and after that, dressing for dinner, once again the gong booming sonorously and masterfully through the whole building, once again the string of ladies in low-cut gowns, rustling down the stairs in their silks, reflected in the mirrored walls, once again the doors of the dining-room flung open, wide and hospitably, and the red jackets of the musicians on their platform, the black crowd of waiters round the *maître d'hôtel* while he deftly ladled out the creamy pink soup into the plates. . . . The dinners were again so rich in food, wine and mineral waters, in sweets and fruit, that by eleven o'clock the maids were required to bring hot-water bottles to all the rooms for the guests to warm their stomachs with.

December, however, was not a very good month that year; when one talked to the porters about the weather they merely raised their shoulders guiltily and muttered that as far as they could remember, there had never been a winter like it, although it wasn't the first year they were obliged to mutter this and blame it on the fact that "something awful was happening all over the world." On the Riviera it stormed and rained as never before, in Athens there was snow, Etna, too, was covered with snow and cast a glow at night; and as for Palermo, the tourists were simply running away from the cold, helter-skelter. . . . The early-morning sun deceived them every day. At noon, the sky invariably turned grey and fine rain began to fall, becoming colder and harder as the day wore on; and then the palm-trees at the hotel entrance would shine with a metallic sheen, the town appeared particularly dirty and cramped, the museums too monotonous, the cigar ends, thrown by the fat cabmen whose rubber capes flapped in the wind like wings, unbearably foul, the vigorous cracks of their whip over the heads of their skinny-necked hacks too obvious a sham, the boots of the men sweeping the tramway lines dreadful, and the women, splashing through the mud in the rain with their black heads uncovered, disgustingly short-legged; but as for the dampness and the stench of rotting fish coming from the frothing water's edge, the least said about it the better. The gentleman and the lady from San Francisco began to quarrel in the mornings now; their daughter either had a headache and went about looking wan and pale, or all at once she brightened up, was enthusiastic and keen on everything, and then she was both sweet and beautiful; beautiful were the tender and complex feelings awakened in her by the ugly man with the unusual blood coursing through his veins, for after all, what awakens a girl's heart—whether it is wealth, fame, or an illustrious name—is not really of great consequence. Everyone assured them that it was quite different in Sorrento and Capri—there it was warmer and sunnier, lemon-trees were in bloom, the people more virtuous and the wine better. And so the family from San Francisco decided to proceed to Capri, taking all their trunks along, with the intention of settling down in Sorrento after they had gone all over Capri, had trod the stones where once the palaces of Tiberius stood, visited the fabulous caves of the Azure Grotto, and listened to the Abruzzian bagpipers who, during the month before Christmas, roamed the island singing praises to the Virgin Mary.

On the day of departure—a very memorable day for the family from San Francisco—even the usual early morning sun was missing. A heavy fog completely hid Vesuvius, hanging in a low grey cloud over the leaden surface of the sea. There was no sight of Capri—as if it had never existed in the world at all. And the small ship making towards it lurched so heavily from side to side that the family from San Francisco had to lie prone on their sofas in the wretched saloon of this poor ship, their feet wrapped in rugs and their eyes closed from nausea. The lady thought she suffered more than the others; nausea gripped her again and again and she believed she was dying, while the maid who came running to her with a basin, and who had for many years been sailing this sea day in, day out, in all weathers, hot or cold, but was indefatigable nevertheless, merely laughed. The daughter was dreadfully pale and she held a slice of lemon between her teeth. The father, who lay on his back dressed in a loose overcoat and a large cap, never unclenched his jaws once during the voyage; his face had grown dark, his moustache seemed whiter, and his head was racked with pain: what with the miserable weather, he had been drinking too heavily and enjoying too many "living tableaux" in certain haunts during the last nights on shore. And meanwhile the rain lashed at the rattling port-holes, water dribbled down on to the sofas, the wind tore through the masts with a howl, and now and again came together with the onslaught of the swell to lay the little ship on its side, and then something could be heard rolling and rumbling below. It was a little quieter at the stops in Castellammare and Sorrento, but even there the swell was dreadful and the shores with all their precipes, gardens, pineries, pink and white hotels and dusky curly-green hills, flew up and down as though on swings; boats kept knocking against the side of the ship, the third-class passengers were shouting heatedly, a child was choking with screams somewhere as if it had been crushed, a damp wind blew in at the door with never a moment's pause, from a boat tossing on the waves, flaunting a flag of the Royal Hotel came the sound of a boy's shrill lisping voice shouting incessantly as he tried to entice the passengers with his *"Kgoyal! Hôtel Kgoyal!"* And the gentleman from San Francisco, feeling very old—which was what he should have felt—now thought with boredom and anger of all these "Royals," "Splendids" and "Excelsiors," and of those greedy, garlic-stinking little wretches called Italians. Once, during a stop, he opened his eyes and, sitting up on the sofa, saw a pile of such miserable little stone hovels, mouldy through and through, stuck one on top of the other at the foot of a sheer rock close to the water's edge beside some boats, heaps of rags, empty tins and brown fishing nets, that a feeling of despair seized him as he remembered that this was the real Italy which he had come to enjoy. . . . At last, when it was already dusk, the black mass of the island, shot through with the little red lights at its foot, began to bear down on them; the wind abated, becoming warmer and more fragrant, and golden snakes, gliding away from the lamp-posts on the quay, came floating on the subdued waves which gleamed like black oil. Then, suddenly, the anchor began to rumble and with a clatter of chains flopped into the water with a splash, the furious cries of boatmen, vying with one another, came from all sides; and instantly one felt one's spirits lifting, the cabin lights shone more brightly, one wanted to eat, drink, smoke and move about. Then minutes later the family from San Francisco boarded a roomy barge; in a quarter of an hour they disembarked on the quay, and then they were sitting in a bright little car and were going up a sheer mountainside with a buzz, past vine poles, crumbling stone walls and wet, gnarled orange-trees protected here and there with matting, their bright-coloured fruit and thick shiny leaves flashing past the open windows of the car and gliding downhill. In Italy the earth smells sweetly after rain, and every one of the islands has its own peculiar smell.

The Island of Capri was damp and dark that night. But now it came to life for a moment and put on lights here and there. A crowd of those whose duty it was to give the gentleman from San Francisco a fitting welcome, were already waiting at the top of the hill on the funicular platform. There were other arrivals, too, but they deserved no attention—a few Russians who had settled down in Capri, absent-minded and untidy men wearing spectacles and beards, the collars of their threadbare overcoats turned up; and a party of long-legged, round-skulled young Germans in Tyrolese suits with canvas rucksacks slung on their shoulders, who were in need of no services from anyone and felt at home wherever they happened to be and were not at all generous with their money. As for the gentleman from San Francisco, who calmly shunned both the Russians and Germans, he was instantly marked down. He and his ladies were hurriedly helped out of the car; men started running ahead of him to show him the way; he was again surrounded by urchins and those stalwart Capri peasant women who carry on their heads the suitcases and trunks of decent tourists. Their wooden sandals cluttered down the small square which was like an opera set with its globe of light swinging above in the damp breeze, and its crowd of urchins breaking into bird-like whistling and turning somersaults. And the gentleman from San Francisco strode in their midst as though he were making a stage entrance, through a kind of mediaeval archway formed by the houses, merging together overhead, beyond which lay the noisy little street, climbing up towards the brilliantly lighted hotel entrance, with a tuft of palm leaves showing above the flat roofs on the left and a black sky studded with blue stars above and ahead. And once again it seemed that it was in honor of the guests from San Francisco that this damp little stone town on the rocky island in the Mediterranean had come to life, that it was they who had made the owner of the hotel so happy and hospitable, that for them the Chinese gong was waiting to boom all through the building, summoning everyone to dinner the minute they entered the lobby.

The owner who welcomed them with a polite and courtly bow, an exceedingly elegant young man, gave the gentleman from San Francisco a momentary start, for when he saw him he suddenly remembered that among all the other muddled dreams which had thronged his sleep the previous night he had seen the replica of this gentleman, wearing the same roundly cut away morning coat, his hair plastered down to the same mirror-like gloss. Amazed, he all but stopped in his tracks. But since his soul had been cleansed of any so-called mystical feelings years ago, to the last mustard seed, his amazement instantly faded away; he jokingly mentioned this strange coincidence between dream and reality to his wife and daughter as they walked down the hotel corridor. His daughter, however, looked up at him in alarm when she heard it; her heart suddenly cringed with a feeling of sadness, of frightening loneliness on this strange, dark island. . . .

A person of exalted rank—Rais XVII—who had been visiting Capri, had just left. And the guests from San Francisco were allotted the suite he had occupied. They had the prettiest and smartest maid appointed to them, a Belgian girl whose waist was drawn hard and thin by her corsets, and whose starched cap perched on her head like a small toothed crown; they were given the most imposing of valets, a black-haired fiery-eyed Sicilian, and the nimblest of "boots," a small, plump man called Luigi, who had held many such jobs in his time. And a minute later, the gentleman from San Francisco heard a light knock on his door, followed by the appearance of the French *maître d'hôtel* coming in to inquire if the new guests would be dining, and to inform them, should their answer be in the affirmative (of which, however, there was no doubt), that there was lobster, roast beef, asparagus, pheasants, and so on, on the menu. The gentleman from San Francisco still felt the floor rising and falling under him—that's how sea-sick that rotten little Italian ship had made him—but he calmly went and rather clumsily closed the window which had burst open at the *maître d'hôtel*'s entrance, and through which came the smells of a kitchen far away and wet flowers in the garden below. He replied with unhurried precision that they would be dining, that their table was to be placed well back in the room, a good distance away from the doors, that they would be drinking a local wine, and every word he uttered was echoed by the *maître d'hôtel* in tones of the most varied pitch, all of which, however, had but one meaning: that the rightness of the gentleman's wishes could not be doubted, and that everything would be carried out to the letter. Finally he inclined his head and asked tactfully:

"Will that be all, sir?"

And, hearing a thoughtful "y-yes" in reply, he volunteered the information that after dinner that night a tarantella would be danced in the lounge by Carmella and Giuseppe, well-known all over Italy and to all the "tourist world."

"I've seen her on postcards," said the gentleman from San Francisco in a voice that expressed nothing. "And that Giuseppe fellow—is he her husband?"

"Her cousin, sir," the maître d'hôtel replied.

And after a moment of hesitation, thinking of something but saying nothing, the gentleman from San Francisco dismissed the man with a nod.

After that he started dressing for dinner with as much care as if he were preparing for his wedding. He switched on all the lights, flooding all the mirrors in the room with brilliance, glitter and the reflection of furniture and open trunks. He began to shave and to wash, ringing the bell incessantly, while other impatient rings, coming from the rooms of his wife and daughter, clashed with his and assailed the corridor with peals. And Luigi, in his red apron, distorting his face with a grimace of horror which reduced the maids, who were running past with jugs of water, to tears of laughter, bounded along to answer the gentleman's bell with the lightness inherent in so many fat men. Rapping on the door with his knuckles, he asked with feigned humility, exaggerated to inanity:

"Ha sonato, signore?"

And from the other side of the door came a drawling, rasping and pointedly polite voice:

"Yes, come in. . . ."

What did the gentleman from San Francisco feel, what did he think about on that night that was to be so momentous for him? Like anyone else who had just had a rough crossing, he wanted nothing but his dinner and dreamed with relish of his first spoonful of soup, his first sip of wine; he was actually somewhat flurried as he performed his customary ritual of dressing for dinner, so he had no time for thought or feeling.

When he had shaved and washed and neatly fitted his false teeth back into place, he stood before the looking-glass and wielding a pair of silver brushes vigorously put the strands of sparse pearly-white hair into place on his dark yellow skull; then he pulled his cream-coloured underwear on his strong, senile body, its waistline thickened from over-nourishment, put his black silk socks and pumps on his lean flat feet; then bending his knees he adjusted the silk braces that held up his black trousers, tucked in his snow-white shirt with its bulging starched front, fixed a pair of shining links into his cuffs, and began the struggle to force the collar stud into the stiff collar. He still felt the floor was heaving, the tips of his fingers hurt dreadfully, the stud pinched the sagging skin under his Adam's apple, but he was adamant and at last he got the better of the job; his eyes shining from exertion, his face livid because the tight collar was strangling him, he sank down exhausted on the stool in front of the dressing-table and faced his full-size reflection which was repeated in all the other mirrors in the room.

"Oh, it's dreadful!" he muttered, dropping his strong bald head, without trying to understand, without thinking what it was he found so dreadful. Then, from habit, he keenly inspected his short fingers with their gout-hardened joints, his large almond-shaped, almond-coloured fingernails, and repeated with conviction, "It's dreadful. . . ."

But just then the dinner gong boomed for the second time, sonorously as in a pagan temple. And, getting up hurriedly, the gentleman from San Francisco tightened his collar still more with a tie, drew in his stomach with a waistcoat, put on his coat, straightened his cuffs, and looked himself over in the glass once more. "That Carmella girl, olive-skinned with artifice in her eyes, like a mulatto, in her flowery orange dress, must be an exceptionally good dancer," he mused. And briskly walking out of the room, he followed the carpeted corridor to his wife's room next door and asked in a loud voice if they would be ready soon.

"In five minutes!" his daughter's voice, lilting and already gay, called back.

"Fine," said the gentleman from San Francisco.

And with leisurely steps he started down the corridors and red-carpeted stairs in quest of the reading-room. The servants he met flattened themselves against the wall when they saw him, while he strode by, apparently unaware of them. There was an old lady, who was late for dinner, hurrying along the corridor in front of him as quickly as she could—an old lady with milky-white hair and a back that was already stooped, but who wore, despite this, a low-cut gown of pale-grey silk. Her gait was funny, like an old hen's, and he had no difficulty in catching up with her and leaving her behind. At the glass doors leading into the dining-room, where everybody was already seated and had begun to eat, he stopped in front of a table loaded with boxes of cigars and Egyptian cigarettes and, choosing a large Manila, he threw three lire down on the table. As he passed through the winter garden he glanced casually out of the open window. A gentle breeze wafted from the darkness, he fancied he saw the top of the old palm-tree spreading its gigantic-looking branches from star to star, he heard the steady wash of the sea in the distance. In the quiet, cosy reading-room, unlighted but for the lamps shining over the tables, was an old grey-haired German who stood reading some rustling newspapers, a man who looked like Ibsen, with crazy, bewildered eyes behind round silver-rimmed spectacles. Eyeing him coldly up and down, the gentleman from San Francisco settled himself in a deep leather arm-chair in a corner, beside a green-shaded lamp, put on his pince-nez and, twitching his head because the collar was choking him, he disappeared entirely behind his newspaper. He quickly ran through some of the head-lines, read a few lines about the never-ending war in the Balkans, turned the page over with a customary gesture—and suddenly the lines blazed up before him with a glassy brilliance, his neck strained forward, his eyes bulged, and the pince-nez slipped down his nose. He jerked forward, he tried to take a breath—and gave a bestial wheese; his lower jaw sagged open, gold fillings gleamed in his mouth, his head fell back on his shoulder and lolled helplessly, the hard front of his shirt jutted out, and his whole body began to slip down to the floor, while he kept struggling with someone and kicking up the carpet with his heels.

If it had not been for the presence of the German in the reading-room, they would have managed to hush up this horrible occurrence quickly and neatly, instantly whisking away the gentleman from San Francisco by his head and his feet down the back alleys, as far away as possible, and never a soul from among the hotel guests would have known what he had been up to. But the German rushed screaming out of the reading-room, raised a commotion in the dining-room, and roused the whole place. Many of the guests jumped up from their dinner, overturning chairs, many went pale and ran to the reading-room, crying, "What's happened, what's it all about?" in different languages, and no one gave them an answer, no one could make out what had happened because to this day people find death the most amazing thing in the world, and they flatly refuse to believe in it. The hotel-owner dashed from one guest to the other in an effort to hold back the rout and to calm them with hurried assurances that it was nothing, a mere trifle, a little fainting fit that had seized a certain gentleman from San Francisco. But no one was listening to him, for many had seen the waiters and valets tearing off the gentleman's tie, waistcoat and crumpled dinner-jacket, and even, for some unknown reason, dragging the pumps off his black, silk-clad flat feet. But he was still writhing. He doggedly struggled with death, he refused to give in to the thing that had borne down on him so unexpectedly and rudely. He jerked his head from side to side, he wheezed as though his throat had been cut, he rolled his eyes drunkenly. When they had hastily carried him in and laid him on the bed of room No. 43—the smallest, poorest, dampest and coldest room at the end of the ground floor corridor—his daughter came running in with her hair streaming, her dressing-gown gaping open to reveal the bare bosom lifted high by her corsets, and after that came his wife, big and heavy, quite dressed for dinner, her mouth round with horror. But by that time he had even stopped jerking his head.

Within a quarter of an hour everything more or less settled down to normal at the hotel. But the night was irreparably ruined. Some of the guests came back into the dining-room and finished their dinner, but in silence and with injured expressions, while the owner went from table to table, shrugging in helpless and seemly annoyance, feeling that he was blamelessly guilty, assuring everyone that he understood perfectly "how unpleasant it all was" and promising to do "everything in his power" to remove this unpleasantness. But the tarantella had to be cancelled, nevertheless; extra lights were put out, most of the guests left for the beer hall, and everything grew so quiet that you could hear the clock ticking in the lobby which was deserted except for the parrot who muttered woodenly, fussing in its cage before settling down to sleep and finally doing so with one claw flung ridiculously over the top perch. The gentleman from San Francisco lay on a cheap iron bed, covered with coarse woollen blankets, in the dim light of a single bulb close to the ceiling. A rubber ice bag hung down on his cold, wet forehead. His livid and already dead face was cooling gradually, the horse rattle, breaking through his open mouth with its glitter of gold, was growing weaker. It was no longer the gentleman from San Francisco who was wheezing—he was no more—it was someone else. His wife, his daughter, the doctor and the servants stood and looked at him. Suddenly, the thing they had been waiting for, the thing they dreaded, happened—the wheezing ceased. And slowly, very slowly, before the eyes of all of them, a pallor spread over the face of the deceased, his features grew finer and lighter, with a beauty that would have befitted him long ago.

The owner came in. "*Già é morto*," the doctor told him in a whisper. The owner shrugged, his face impassive. The lady came up to him with tears trickling down her cheeks, and timidly suggested that the deceased should now be taken up to his room.

"*Mais non, madame*," the owner objected hastily and politely but with no gallantry whatsoever now, and he spoke to her in French and not in English, for he had no further interest at all in those trifles which the visitors from San Francisco might now leave behind in his cash-box. "It's quite impossible, madame," he said and added, in explanation, that he valued the suite most highly and that if he agreed to her request, the whole of Capri would come to know of it and tourists would refuse to stay in the rooms.

The daughter, who had been looking strangely at him all this time, dropped into a chair and, smothering her mouth with her handkerchief, burst into sobs. The mother's tears dried instantly and her face flushed red. She raised her voice, she became insistent, stating her demands in her own language and still unable to believe that all respect for them had been irrevocably lost. The owner rebuked her in politely dignified tones: if madame disapproved of the hotel's rules, he dared not hold her there; and he declared firmly that the body was to be removed by morning, that the police had been notified and a representative was due immediately to carry out the necessary formalities. Was it possible to get a coffin, even if it was only a plain ready-made one on Capri, madame asked? No, he was sorry, it was quite impossible and the time was too short to have one made. Some other way would have to be found. His English soda-water, for instance, was shipped out to him in large, long packing cases . . . the partitions from one of the cases could be taken out. . . .

The hotel was plunged in sleep. They opened the window in room No. 43—which faced a corner of the garden where a sickly banana-tree grew in the shadow of the tall stone wall with broken glass stuck on top. They switched off the light, left the room and locked the door. The dead man remained in the darkness. Blue stars gazed down on him from the sky. A cricket in the wall began to chirp its melancholy, carefree song.

Two maids were sitting on the window-sill in the dimly lit corridor, darning. Luigi came in with a pile of clothes in his arms and shoes on his feet.

"*Pronto?*" (Ready?), he asked anxiously in a loud whisper, rolling his eyes at the frightening door at the end of the corridor. And, waving his free hand lightly in that direction, he hissed loudly, "*Partenza!*" which is the usual shout in Italy when a train steams out of a station, and the maids clung closely together, choking down their soundless laughter.

And then he ran up to the door with soft leaps, rapped upon the panel lightly and with his head inclined asked in an undertone, in a most deferential manner:

"*Ha sonato, signore?*"

Now, constricting his throat, jutting his lower jaw forward, in a voice that was rasping, sad and drawling, he spoke the answer, as if it was coming from the other side of the door:

"Yes, come in."

At daybreak, when the sky grew light beyond the window of room No. 43 and the damp breeze rustled in the ragged leaves of the banana-tree, when the blue sky of morning awakened and spread its cloak over the Island of Capri, and the pure, clear-cut top of Monte Soliaro turned golden in the reflection of the sun, rising beyond the distant blue mountains of Italy, when the road-menders started out on their way to work, repairing the island's paths for tourists to tread, then a long soda-water packing-case was brought to room No. 43. Shortly afterwards it became very heavy and pressed painfully against the knees of the junior porter who was taking it in a one-horse cab at a brisk pace along the white highroad that wound down the mountain-side. The driver, a flabby man with bloodshot eyes, in a shabby old coat, short in the sleeves, and down-at-heel boots, had a hangover, for he had been playing dice all night long at the inn. He kept whipping his sturdy young horse, which was decked out in the Sicilian fashion with briskly jingling, clamouring bells of different shapes on the bridle, adorned with red wool pompons, and on the tips of the high copper ridge of the pommel, and with a quivering, yard-long feather sticking up from its trimmed forelock. The cabman was silent, crushed by his own dissoluteness and his vices, and the fact that the night before he had lost all those coppers with which his pockets had been crammed. But the morning was crisp and with air as fresh as this, the nearness of the sea and the blue skies above, a head is soon cleared of its drunken haze, and light-heartedness is quickly recovered; and then the cabman also found consolation in the unexpected fee he had earned from some gentleman from San Francisco, who was rolling his dead head about in the packing-case behind his back. The small ship, lying like a beetle on the bright and delicate blue that filled the Bay of Naples so generously, was already sounding the last hoots and these were eagerly echoed over the whole of the island whose every bend, every mountain ridge and every stone was so clearly visible, as if there were no atmosphere at all. At the quay the cab was overtaken by the car in which the senior porter was bringing the mother and daughter, both of them pale, with eyes sunken from tears and a sleepless night. And ten minutes later, the little ship was again chugging away in a swish of water to Sorrento and Castellammare, taking the family from San Francisco away from Capri for ever. And once again peace and quiet was restored to the island.

On that island, two thousand years ago, there lived a man who got hopelessly entangled in his foul and cruel deeds, who for some reason rose to power over millions of people and who, losing his head from the senselessness of this power and from his fear that someone might thrust a knife into his back, committed atrocities beyond all measure. And mankind remembered him for ever, and those who with combined effort are now ruling the world with as little reason and, on the whole, with as much cruelty as he did, come here from all over the world to take a look at the remains of the stone house on one of the sheerest sides of the island, where he used to live. That beautiful morning, all those who had arrived in Capri for this particular reason were still asleep in their hotels, although a string of little mouse-grey donkeys with crimson saddles were already being led up to the hotel entrances, for the Americans and Germans—men and women, young and old—to clamber onto when they got out of bed and had stuffed themselves with food, to be followed at a run along the rocky paths, all the way to the very top of Monte Tiberio, by old Capri beggarwomen with staffs in their gnarled hands. The travellers slept in peace, comforted by the thought that the dead man from San Francisco, who had been planning to go with them but had instead just frightened them with a reminder of death, had already been shipped to Naples. And the island was still wrapped in silence, the shops were still shut.

The fish and vegetable market in the small square was the only place open to business, and there was no one there but the common people. Among them, idling his time away as usual, stood the tall boatman Lorenzo, a carefree old rake so unusually handsome that he was known all over Italy, where he had often sat for painters; he had brought along a couple of lobsters he had caught in the night and had already sold them for next to nothing, and now they were rustling in the apron of the cook from the same hotel where the family from San Francisco had spent the night. Lorenzo was now free to stand there till evening if he so wished, glancing about him in a regal air and cutting a figure with his tatters, his clay pipe and his red flannel beret, worn over one ear. Two Abruzzian mountaineers came down the steep Monte Soliaro from Anacapri, down the ancient Phoenician path, with steps hewn out of the rock. One of them had a bagpipe under his leather cloak—a large goatskin bag with two pipes—while the other carried something that looked like a wooden flute. They were coming downhill, and the whole country lay below, joyous, beautiful and fulgent: the rocky humps of the island, almost all of which lay at their feet, the fabulous azure in which it floated, the vapours of morning rising from the sea towards the East, shimmering in the blinding sun which was already hot as it rose higher and higher in the sky, the dimly-blue bulk of Italy with its mountains near and far still vague in the morning haze, the beauty of which man has no words to express. Halfway down the mountain they slowed their pace. There, above the path, in a niche in the rocky wall of Monte Soliaro, stood the Mother of God, bathed in sunlight, warmth and brilliance, clad in snow-white plaster robes, wearing the crown of a queen, rustily-golden from the rains, meek and merciful, with eyes raised heavenward to the eternal and blissful abode of Her thrice blessed Son. They bared their heads and raised their flutes to their lips—and praises poured forth, naïve and humbly joyous, to the sun, to the morning, and to Her, the Immaculate Intercessor for all the suffering in this wicked and beautiful world, and to the One who had been born of Her womb in a cave at Bethlehem, in the poor shepherds' shelter, in the far land of Judea.

And in the meantime, the body of the old man from San Francisco was returning home to its grave on the shores of the New World. After suffering much humiliation, much carelessness at the hands of men, travelling from one harbour warehouse to another for about a week, it found itself at last on board the same famous ship which had only such a short while ago brought it to the Old World in so stately a manner. But now they were hiding him from the living—they lowered him in his tarred coffin into the blackness of the hold. And once again the ship sailed off on its long voyage. That night it passed the Island of Capri and its lights, slowly vanishing in the dark sea, seemed sad to those who were watching it from the island. But there, on board, its halls flooded with light and gleaming with marble, a great ball was being held that night, true to custom.

A ball was held on the second and the third night out too—once again a furious storm was raging over the ocean, making it drone like a dirge and roll in mountains that were sombre and black like a funeral pall, edged with a silvery fringe. To the Devil watching from the rock of Gibraltar, the stony gateway between the two worlds, the countless, blazing eyes of the ship were hardly visible behind the curtain of snow, as the ship sailed away into the night and the storm. The Devil was as vast as a rock, but the ship was even vaster than he was, many-tiered and many-funnelled, created by the arrogance of a New Man with an old heart. The storm tore at its rigging and its wide-mouthed funnels, white with snow, but it was firm, stalwart, majestic and—frightening. On the very top deck, lonely amid the whirling snow, rose the cosy, dimly lighted apartments, where the corpulent Master, so like a pagan god, presided over the whole ship, sleeping lightly and fitfully. He heard the deep howls and the furious squeals of the siren choking in the storm, but he sought reassurance in the proximity of something in the next room that was, in reality, the thing he could understand least of all: that large cabin, armour-clad it seemed, which every now and again was filled with a mysterious roar, a flickering and a dry sputtering of blue lights, which flared up and burst around the pale-faced radio-operator with a half circle of metal round his head. At the very bottom, in the underwater depths of the *Atlantic* where the twenty-ton steel bulks of the boilers and other machinery shone dimly, hissed out steam and dripped boiling oil and water, in that kitchen where the motion of the ship was being cooked over infernal fires heated from below, power was churning, power frightening in its concentration, transmitted to the very keel, to the endlessly long vault, into the rounded and dimly lighted tunnel, where a colossal shaft rotated slowly in its oily bed with a dauntlessness that was crushing to a man's soul, as if it were a live monster stretched out in the muzzle-like tunnel. But the middle part of the *Atlantic*, its dining-rooms and ballrooms, radiated light and joy; they hummed with the voices of a well-dressed crowd, sang with string orchestras and emanated the fragrance of flowers. And again there was the slender and graceful couple of hired lovers, swaying sinuously or clinging together convulsively, among the crowd, amid the brilliance of lights, silks, diamonds and women's naked shoulders: the pretty girl with downcast eyes that were depraved and modest, with innocence in her coiffure, and the tall young man with black hair that seemed glued down, his face pale with powder, dressed in a narrow long-tailed dress-coat and graceful patent-leather pumps, a beautiful man who looked like a huge leech. And no one knew that it had long been nothing but drudgery for this couple to writhe in their sham bliss to the strains of the lewdly sad music, nor did anyone know that a coffin stood on the floor of the dark hold, far, far below them, close to the gloomy, sultry depths of the ship fighting against the darkness, the ocean and the storm. . . .